JACK MALLOCH

LEGEND OF THE AFRICAN SKIES

EX MONTIBUS MEDIA

26 Caledon Street, Darling, 7345

Cataloguing-in-publication data is available from the South African National Library.

Typesetting and layout: New Voices Publishing Services

Cover design: Kristen Barrett and Thinus du Plessis

Proofreader: Jerry Buirski

First edition, first impression October 2020

First edition, second impression December 2020

For a complete list of EX MONTIBUS MEDIA titles, please contact:

Email: admin@exmontibusmedia.co.za

Telephone (27) 73 777 2745

www.exmontibusmedia.co.za

JACK MALLOCH

LEGEND OF THE AFRICAN SKIES

ALAN BROUGH

Contents

Acknowledgements

Over the years literally hundreds of people have contributed to this book and they have all been vital in piecing this story back together. They all have my deepest thanks and appreciation.

There are several who need to be mentioned by name. Firstly Jack's wife Zoe Malloch, who, right at the very beginning, gave me permission to write this book. Jack's entire family who were all very supportive and trusting of the vision I had for this biography, specifically Jack's children Alyson Dawson Ross and Greg Malloch and his sister Blythe Kruger. I am also very grateful for the contribution of Jack's old World War II comrades from 237 Squadron who are no longer with us: Bill Musgrave, Paul Pearson and the Honourable Ian Douglas Smith.

Most importantly there are Jack's colleagues and ex-employees, many of whom willingly shared their logbooks, observations and adrenalin-charged recollections. Of these, specifically I would like to thank Cacho Cabral and Ian Hunt who were instrumental in getting this book published, along with Mike Gibson, Henry Kinnear and Ronnie Small who provided both in-depth information and endless encouragement.

My thanks also go to Judy Chapman, Alan Clements, Ian Dixon, Chris Halse, Nigel Hart, Nori Mann, Gustavo Marón, Stefano Merli, Kevin Milligan, Peter Petter-Bowyer, Jerry Puren, Paul Sheppard and of course Bill Sykes, along with scores of others, some of whom have asked not to be identified. They have all generously provided very important pieces of this puzzle for which I am extremely grateful.

Thank you.

Alan Brough

Dedication

This book is dedicated to my father Mike Brough. He was a remarkable man who had a great admiration for Jack Malloch. Bound by his own code of silence he wouldn't divulge much, though encouraged me to write this book so that Jack's story would be preserved as part of the history of Rhodesia, Africa and of aviation on the continent as a whole.

About the author

Alan was born in Rhodesia, growing up through the drama of UDI and the ensuing war. Those experiences influenced both his love of Africa and his interest in politics and history. Almost all of his career has been in writing and research, much of it in advertising and marketing. His first book was a travel guide to Botswana, and since then he has written numerous articles and commentaries covering a range of topics from tourism and international trade, through to politics, aviation and military history. He was also a regular columnist for *Africa Review* magazine covering business, investment opportunities and politics.

He is exceptionally well-travelled, having lived in eight different countries including Canada, where he is now based. There he works as a senior brand manager, although he spends as much time as he can exploring the vastness of the unspoiled Canadian wilderness.

Introduction

Alan Brough is a writer and historian who grew up in Rhodesia. During those turbulent years he heard the whispered stories of Jack Malloch, an amazing flyer who many credited with the very survival of the breakaway country. Yet on the surface Jack seemed to be nothing more than a hard-working entrepreneur who owned a nondescript little cargo operation serviced by a few battered old aircraft. After Jack's untimely death in 1982 many lamented the fact that the truth about his extraordinary exploits would never be known.

So began Alan's long and painstaking period of meticulous research, as he slowly but surely gathered and collated all the scattered documents, classified intelligence reports and fractured memories that he could find. Now, after more than two decades of investigation, the true story of Jack Malloch and his wildly eventful life can at last be told.

While this is a biography, it is also an action packed historical record that, in a sense, starts and ends in the cockpit of the iconic Spitfire with fast-paced accounts of tumultuous times in dangerous places; from sanctions-busting in the battle to save Rhodesia; to the brutal Biafran war and the coups in the Comoros with Bob Denard; to the killing fields of Katanga with Mike Hoare and his buccaneering band of mercenaries.

But when the dust settled Jack Malloch was a dedicated family-man who was motivated by patriotism, compassion and strong Christian values. His honesty, reliability, dedication and courage, along with his detailed knowledge of Africa and the 'Big Men' who counted, uniquely qualified him for the many covert operations he undertook for the Secret Services of France, Portugal, the United States and Rhodesia.

Jack Malloch inspecting the cockpit of his Mk.XXII Spitfire
in the Air Trans Africa hanger.

Picture provided by Ian Hunt © RhAF Photographic Section, New Sarum.

CHAPTER 1

Friday 26th March 1982

The Spitfire dipped its starboard wing and turned to the right, dodging away from its pursuer. The late afternoon sun glinted off the Perspex canopy as the camouflaged port wing, with its long black cannon-barrels, arched around towards the ominous storm clouds up ahead.

The sleek aircraft was newly painted in the greens and greys of the late World War Two 'temperate climate' camouflage. On its fuselage and wings were the large blue and red roundels of the British Royal Air Force.

In the dark green fighter aircraft streaking after the Spitfire, the pilot was caught unawares by the unexpected manoeuvre. Frowning, he released his grip on the

Jack Malloch skirting the edge of the deadly tropical storm in the restored Spitfire Mk XXII that bore his initials. Within minutes of this image being taken Jack had been killed. *Screen-grab from the film 'Pursuit of a Dream' produced by Bill Sykes. © Bill Sykes.*

gun trigger that his gloved hand had been working so feverishly for the last twenty minutes. He peered at the receding Spitfire through the gun-sight as he pulled the control column hard to the right, glancing nervously up at the huge cumulonimbus thundercloud looming up ahead. And then he glanced down at the deep black shadow that was devouring the landscape below.

The Spitfire made another turn, tracing the edge of the huge storm-cloud that loomed up well over ten kilometres from its sodden base, dwarfing the two aircraft that were now separated by little more than one hundred metres. The Spitfire was back in the centre of the De Havilland Vampire's gun-sights when suddenly the renovated fighter banked forty-five degrees to port and dropped its nose down into a fifteen degree dive – straight towards the middle of the storm. The Vampire copied the bank and dive, trying to catch up.

The cockpit view immediately changed from blue to white, as they sliced through the curtain-edges that cloaked the monster storm within. Seconds later the white turned to steel-grey and then to a strange, deadly blue-green. Instantly the light went out, throwing the pilots into the dim glow of the instruments. Then a crash as the rain burst across the Perspex followed seconds later by heavy stoning hail.

Both aircraft were violently tossed up and down and the Spitfire was lost from sight through the swirling pillars of knotted rain and hail. As the planes buckled under the pounding both pilots increased power, fighting to stay level as the thunderous downpour blasted them with tons of heavy rain and more hail.

Several seconds later they were together again. The roaring sound and turbulence was gone, and visibility was back. Both aircraft lunged forward as the pilots stabilised their wings and throttled back in the unexpected momentary calm. Looking around they knew they were now in extremely grave danger. They were in a vast cavern of deep blues, greens and greys. It was the heart of a huge and violent tropical storm. The green-glowing walls of this churning aerial lake, stretched kilometres up above the aircraft, where, on the edge of the atmosphere itself, the water had turned to ice and was already plummeting back down towards the scurrying victims below, like a mighty descending Thor-hammer.

All around them thousands of tons of water and ice in surreal aquatic colours churned up and down the storm-cell. The vintage aircraft had been caught in a giant cocktail-shaker the likes of which neither had been built to withstand. All they could hope to do was to punch their way out the other side.

A second later, at a speed of three hundred knots, the Spitfire disappeared into the rapidly approaching wall of hail. One hundred metres behind and slightly to the left, Group Captain Bill Sykes caught a last glimpse of the old aircraft and its Squadron initials 'JMM' emblazoned on its side, as it ploughed headlong into the turbulence. They were not squadron letters. They were the initials of the Spitfire pilot: Captain John McVicar Malloch. John – or Jack, as he was universally known was a highly capable and experienced pilot. He had flown through many difficult situations before, many of them in Spitfires. But now, at sixty-one years of age Jack Malloch knew he was facing his greatest challenge ever.

Visibility was down to zero and the noise of the cannonball-size lumps of hard pack-ice pummelling the aircraft was deafening. The Vampire throttled back. There was a real danger of collision as both planes were uncontrollably tossed about in the blackness, each completely unaware of the other's position.

Fighting the turbulence Group Captain Sykes turned ten degrees to port, away from where he thought the Spitfire might be, and climbed five hundred feet. The action was instant and effortless as the storm sucked the plane up at a rate of over four thousand feet per minute.

In the vibrating cockpit Bill Sykes caught sight of the needle on the vertical speed indicator spinning crazily upwards. He extended the airbrakes and throttled right back, but to no avail.

At the centre of the storm wall, as suddenly as they were being swept helplessly upwards, the storm's violent downdraft grabbed them and hurled them earthwards. Instantly they were descending at over four thousand feet per minute. The pilots slammed full power on and tucked their airbrakes in, battling to maintain their altitude.

In the Vampire Bill and his co-pilot Flight Lieutenant Neville Weir were expecting the engines to fail at any second as the jet intakes were choking on tons of high-velocity ice being forced into the turbines. Grimly they struggled to keep their wings level as they were caught in another updraft. Once more it was airbrakes out and power off, as the vertical speed indicator wound back up the ascent. All in zero visibility, uncontrollable vibration and increasing disorientation.

As quickly as it had started, it then all happened in reverse. The hail and rain stopped and the battered Vampire shot out the other side of the storm into a calm blue sky.

Glancing around they searched for the Spitfire. It was not ahead of them where it should have been.

They were alone in the sky.

Reducing power, Bill dipped the aircraft's wing and turned back towards the raging black storm cloud. He and Flight Lieutenant Weir scanned the ground in silence. They knew what had happened. Jack was on the ground somewhere. The question was whether or not he was alive.

"Spitfire from Vampire..." the Group Captain called into the radio. There was no response.

"Spitfire from Vampire..." he called again. Nothing. After a few long seconds he called Air Traffic Control.

"Tower from Vampire..."

"Vampire, this is Tower. Go ahead." came the instant reply.

"Tower, this is Vampire. I think there has been an accident. Can you get a helicopter airborne as soon as possible for the Goromonzi area?"

Group Captain Sykes turned the ageing Vampire back towards New Sarum air force.

It was just after 4.30 p.m. on Friday, 26th March 1982.[1]

---

1 Written notes, correspondence and various interviews with Bill Sykes in Harare in 2002, 2003, 2006 and 2007.

CHAPTER 2

The Beginning: 1920 to 1939

Jack Malloch was born in South Africa on October 8th 1920 to an immigrant family who could trace their lineage back to the famous Scottish astronomer Thomas Dick. Having survived the Industrial Revolution in the textile factories of Almondbank, and the Boer War in the Siege of Ladysmith, the family had eventually settled in Durban.

Like his father and grandfather, Jack was christened John McVicar Malloch (pronounced Mal-'loch', as in 'Loch' Ness), a name which reflected the family's strong Scottish heritage. His father, who was known as 'Vic' for 'McVicar,' was a World War One Navy veteran. Although he was a highly qualified accountant work was hard to find during the Great Depression. He heard that Southern Rhodesia was a land of opportunity so decided to move. Unfortunately there weren't any jobs there either.

Eventually, having a heavy vehicle licence from the Navy, he took a job with the Rhodesian Railways as a truck driver. They transferred him to the town of Umtali in the country's Eastern Highlands. From there he made deliveries to all the small farming communities in the mountain ranges along the Mozambique border.

Whenever he could, Vic would take young Jack along with him on these trips. The boy loved the excitement of driving with his father into the remote wilds of Africa and they spent many hours of quality time together, many of which included working under the bonnet making numerous repairs to their 'train-on-wheels'. It was during these repair sessions that Jack picked up a remarkable mechanical aptitude. He loved taking things apart, finding out how they worked and fixing them. But his real dream was to fly.

Granny Malloch with Jack, Beth and baby Ruth in approximately 1926
soon after the family moved to Umtali.

Picture from Jack Malloch's private collection. © Greg Malloch.

Jack had three sisters, Beth, Ruth and Blythe. Beth was two years younger than him, while Ruth and Blythe were eight and ten years younger. They were all brought up in a Seventh Day Adventist home and although he was not overtly religious, the church's teachings had a considerable influence on Jack. These included treating everyone as equals, the importance of honesty and the avoidance of tobacco and alcohol.

The Church also had a very strong stand against 'bearing arms' or participating in any form of military activity. That was a major problem for Jack as his only way of getting to fly was through the military. In the end he was destined to spend much of his life in war zones, and, if not actually using arms, he certainly was involved in 'bearing' them.

The Mallochs were not rich, but they knew that a good education was vital for the success of their children and the Seventh Day Adventist Helderberg College near Cape Town was highly recommended. By the beginning of 1932 they could afford to send one of their children to Helderberg, but it was a boarding school and almost two and a half thousand kilometres away. So, at the age of twelve, Jack, their first-born, climbed onto the train and set off on his four-day journey into the unknown.

Helderberg, was a farm school, so all the cooking, cleaning and laundry was done by the girls. While all the harvesting of the fruit and vegetables, ploughing and milking was done by the boys. This in addition to their classes and homework.[1]

Jack hated 'Hellsburg', as he called it, and half-way through his first year he decided he had had enough. Sneaking away one Friday afternoon of a long weekend he worked his way back, hitch-hiking lifts on trucks and trains until several days later, having negotiated his way across the border with his clutched travel letter, he arrived home, much to his parents' horror. Relieved that he had survived the ordeal, Vic was still unsympathetic about the complaints. He explained that education was just something you had to go through, and that Jack would have to go back and make the best of it. After a few good meals and with a new pack of provisions he was sent back to Somerset West and the inevitable meeting with a cane.[2]

Jack wasn't good at academics, but he loved mechanical work and quickly became invaluable driving and servicing the farm tractor. In time, in preference to his studies, he spend more and more time working on the farm and fixing the machinery. By the end of his first year his grades were not good, and his parents began to wonder if they were wasting the education on him. After yet another worrying report at the end of the first term in 1933 they warned Jack that if things did not improve he would lose his place at school. At the end of the second term they discovered that the school had been allowing Jack to focus on the farm instead of his lessons. Yet the headmaster was quite happy to put all the blame on the boy, telling Vic and Rita that "I can see no point in wasting further money on your son's education." He then dismissed Jack saying, "You'll never get anywhere in this world."[3]

1 Interview with Blythe Kruger, January 1998.

2 Personal correspondence with Bill Musgrave, March 17, 1998.

3 'Adventurous pilot gets top award' article in the Rhodesian Herald, November 3, 1978.

Vic and Rita discussed the situation and made the decision to pull Jack out of school and sent Beth in his place. They hoped that a year off would teach Jack his lesson and that he would ask to go back. That did not happen and at the beginning of 1934 at the age of just fourteen Jack was looking for a job in the little pioneer town of Fort Victoria where his father had been transferred. Becoming a pilot with little education and no money was out of the question. Instead he started working as a mechanic at one of the local garages where he was able to apply his mechanical aptitude.

For the Mallochs life was good. They had settled into the local community and were even able to save a little bit of extra money. A couple of years went by, but at the end of 1937 tragedy struck.

It was a Tuesday evening one week after Blythe's seventh birthday. The family had a guest in the house who had been in town doing some Christmas shopping. As the afternoon drew to a close Vic offered to drive her back home. Ruth and Blythe had been practicing on the piano, but when there was talk of a drive the two young children wanted to go along as well. As it was quite a long way on a slow dirt road in the gathering dusk Vic didn't want the girls to go. The girls begged, and eventually Vic conceded, and so, off they all went. Vic, Jack and their guest sat together on the front bench seat of the big family car and the three girls, Beth, Blythe and Ruth played together on the back seat.

In the growing darkness Jack took the Umtali road out of town. It was a narrow strip road that weaved through the woodlands and kopjes and there were plenty of antelope that would wander across the road. After travelling for about twenty minutes they saw another car parked up ahead. It was on the opposite side of the road facing them and the bonnet was up with the driver peering inside. Without question they stopped and offered to help. The road was narrow, so Jack parked some distance away and as it was dark Vic instructed the two young girls to stay in the car and not get out.

There seemed to be some problem with the carburetor and the broken-down car would not start. The men decided to pour fuel directly into the carb to try and get it going. From the back of their car Ruth and Blythe watched what was going on. Beth was standing on the running-board holding the torch, while Jack tried to start the car – to no avail. It was dark in the Mallochs car and with the sounds of the African night around them the young children started to get scared. They decided it would be safer to be closer to the adults. Quietly they opened the car door and slipped out.

Knowing what their father had said, they were a little cautious so waited in the darkness, unseen, five or six metres away on the edge of the torch light. At that very moment the car engine spluttered to life, but the fuel was still being poured and in a bright flash it ignited in a balloon of orange flame, engulfing the petrol can that the driver was holding. Without thinking the man quickly stepped backwards, turned and flung the tin of blazing fuel as far away as he could – right onto the two children who were standing in the dark behind of him.

The flaming petrol engulfed both of the girls and the blazing container knocked Ruth to the ground. There was fire everywhere. Screaming in panic and pain, both children went up like torches. Their long hair and silk dresses were instantly ablaze. Little Blythe ran screaming and thrashing at the flames, while Ruth rolled in the dirt between the two tar strips trying to put out the fire, which had already consumed her mop of beautiful curls.

Jack raced after Blythe while Vic and Beth leapt to Ruth trying to smother the huge orange flames with handfuls of dirt. As Blythe ran she ignited the tall yellow bush grass around her and Jack was burnt before he even reached his screaming sister. Pulling her down he stamped out the flames with his bare hands.

Blythe had some protection from her coat but Ruth, who took the brunt of the fuel, took longer to put out. When the flames were finally smothered most of her tiny body had been badly burnt. Vic carefully wrapped her in a blanket and held her in the back seat of the car, with Blythe lying crying next to him. Without so much as a word to the stranded driver they accelerated away, leaving the horrified man standing in smoky shock.

Jack raced down the road as fast as he dared. His burnt hands leaving charred skin and blood on the steering wheel. But he did not feel the pain. He just heard Ruth quietly saying “Dad, will you pray for me Dad, pray for me Dad...” She wasn’t screaming anymore. She was calm, just wanting to be prayed for.

Ruth died in Fort Victoria hospital the next day. She was just nine years old. It was three days before Christmas.

Vic, Jack, Beth and Blythe were all to carry the physical and emotional scars of that terrible night for the rest of their lives.[4]

By the beginning of 1938 war clouds were gathering in Europe. The world knew a showdown was coming and across the British Empire the colonies, including Southern Rhodesia, started to prepare. The Mallochs didn't notice and were still devastated by Ruth's tragic death. With the 'superpower arms race' in full swing and war seeming inevitable, 1938 gave way to 1939.

In this tense pre-War year Mr. Trycos was to be a god-send for Jack. Trycos was a very successful Greek trader who, over the years had become close friends of the Mallochs. So, when Trycos offered to sponsor flying lessons for two young men 'with potential,' the young Malloch, with his exceptional interest in aircraft was an obvious choice.[5] It was a fairly informal arrangement, but the answer to Jack's prayers.[6]

After a few ground lessons in flying theory from the instructor, on Thursday 6th July 1939, Jack took to the air for the first time ever. The aircraft was a Tiger Moth. By modern standards it was a flimsy 'string and canvas' biplane. But in the late 1930s it was the pinnacle of aviation technology. On that first flight Jack was a passenger carefully watching the instructor explain how the controls worked. On the second trip, trembling with excitement, he finally took the controls and, at last, actual flew.

Almost every evening for the rest of the month Jack would do short half-hour training flights around the Fort Victoria area. After just nine hours of instructional flight, on Wednesday 26th it was time to go solo. After taxiing up and down a few times, Jack lined up at the top end of the dirt air strip. He revved the engine a few times and released the brakes allowing the little plane to bounce forward over the rough ground. Reaching take-off speed he pulled the joystick back and the aircraft effortlessly leapt into the air. In the open cockpit with the warming tropical air vibrating the strings and struts around him, Jack watched in wonder as the world fell away beneath his wings. He could hardly contain his excitement. As instructed, he did a quick circuit around the runway and after just

4 Interview with Blythe Kruger, Plettenberg Bay, January 1998 and personal correspondence with Blythe Kruger, February 25, 2008.

5 Interview with Blythe Kruger, January 1998.

6 Personal correspondence with Beth Lawson, July 20, 2004.

five minutes did a perfect landing, stopping right next to his smiling instructor.

At the end of the first week of August 1939, after Jack had clocked up fourteen more dual and solo flights, the Southern Rhodesian Air Unit's (SRAU) 'Flying Circus' arrived at Fort Victoria where they were based until mid-September.[7] The young man spent as much time as possible at the airfield, watching the flying, chatting to the pilots, and getting to know their commanding officer, Charles Prince, who was impressed with Jack's passion for flying.

On his solo practice flights Jack had a habit of 'beating up' his parents homestead, coming in very low and roaring up over the house, skimming just inches over the roof. Every time, Rita would get very flustered and run outside frantically waving a white tablecloth in the air shouting "Go away! Go away!" – much to Jack's delight.[8]

But war was coming. On Friday 25th August 1939, while Jack was doing a forty-minute training flight[9] the Governor of Southern Rhodesia received a desperate message from the Ministry of Defence in England. It read, "Request SRAU move to Kenya earliest possible moment…" Within forty-eight hours Number 1 Squadron of the Southern Rhodesia Air Unit left Salisbury for Nairobi. Many of them would not survive the war.

By the end of August everyone knew war was inevitable. Jack also knew that the military would be desperate for pilots, though with his limited education and a religion that refused to allow any military participation his chances were thin at best. But he had no choice. Jack had to find a way of making a career of flying – even if it was going to kill him.

7 'A Pride of Eagles' by Beryl Salt, published by Covos Day Books. ISBN: 0-620-23759-7.
8 Personal correspondence with Beth Lawson, July 20, 2004.
9 Jack Malloch's personal flying logbook.

CHAPTER 3

The Second World War: 1939 to 1945

On the morning of the first of September 1939, the BBC World Service broadcast the grave news that Germany had launched a massive attack against Poland. It had not been unexpected. The Southern Rhodesian Air Unit was already in the air patrolling the Somaliland border. This earned them the motto, '*Primum Agmen in Caelo*,' which meant 'First into the air'.[1]

On the afternoon of Friday 1st September, Jack had his last lesson in Trycos's Tiger Moth. He had accumulated fourteen hours of dual instruction and two hours of solo flying[2] but his instructor had signed up and was going to war.

Seeing the sudden demand for pilots Jack knew that with this world crisis, if he played his cards right, he would be able to build a career as a pilot. Sure enough on Thursday 14th September the Air Force ran a front page recruitment ad in the Rhodesia Herald.[3] He knew he was a perfect candidate and met all the criteria. But he was a Seventh-day Adventist. As Jack was still living with his parents he carefully broached the subject with them. They were not sympathetic.

Jack had the greatest respect for his parents, but he was not one to give up either. Hoping that the war would be over quickly, his parents decided that the best approach was to try and stall their son for as long as possible. Through his contacts at the Railways Vic discovered that they were desperate for truck drivers as all the able-bodied men were heading off to war. He organised a job for Jack, who, being ready for a change, took it.[4] It was familiar work and the job reminded him of his happy youth travelling with his Dad.

1 'A Pride of Eagles' by Beryl Salt, published by Covos Day Books. ISBN: 0-620-23759-7.
2 Jack Malloch's personal flying logbook.
3 'A Pride of Eagles' by Beryl Salt, published by Covos Day Books. ISBN: 0-620-23759-7.
4 Interview with Blythe Kruger, January 1998.

Jack quickly earned the respect of everyone he worked with, although not all his challenges were physical or mechanical. One day he was driving along in the middle of the bush somewhere in the remote Tribal Trust Lands. His truck was a heavy flatbed designed for cargo, but being empty, he had a load of African passengers bouncing along in the back. Suddenly they all started shouting and banging on the roof. Jack stopped to see what was going on. "Quick, quick, you must help this woman; she is having a baby!" the hitchhikers shouted.

Sure-enough the woman was in the advanced stages of labour with almost continual contractions. They were hundreds of miles from the nearest hospital and the woman obviously only had minutes to go. He then noticed they were alone. All the other passengers had melted away into bush. Now there wasn't even any hope of help or advice. Fortunately, by just using common sense and empathy Jack managed to successfully deliver the baby.[5]

At the end of May 1940 Rhodesia's first flying school opened and a large intake of recruits was taken in. When Jack saw the article in the newspaper he felt left out. He then read about Claire Chennault's recruitment drive for the famous 'Flying Tigers' in China. It got him thinking. He longed for adventure and he knew he was a good pilot. He also hoped that defending innocent foreigners might be acceptable in the eyes of the Church. Jack wrote to Chennault's recruiting address and enquired about opportunities in his new 'American Volunteer Group.' He knew that there was little chance his inquiry would even be acknowledged, but he felt he needed to try.

Just six months later the fifth flying school was opened. This time it was at Thornhill in Gwelo. Sensing a weakening in his parents resolve Jack went to see the recruiters, but when he said he wanted to be a pilot they said that the RAF already had too many pilots. What they were looking for were capable engineers, and Jack's mechanical experience was ideal. The young man refused, insisting that he needed to be a pilot. For the rest of 1941 it was always the same story – too many pilots, not enough engineers.

Jack could not accept that by the beginning of 1942 with a total of eight RATG flying training schools in the country[6] that they didn't want recruits for these

5 Interview with Blythe Kruger, January 1998.

6 'A Pride of Eagles' by Beryl Salt. Published by Covos Day Books. ISBN: 0-620-23759-7.

facilities. In was a good argument and after a while the senior officer explained that it was not just because of too many pilots. The truth of the matter was that Jack's formal school results and qualifications were not good enough. They did not think he would be able to get through the academically demanding course.

Jack wouldn't accept that either and spent the first half of 1942 continually harassing the Air Force recruitment office in Salisbury. He was very worried that he had missed his chance for pilot training. Meanwhile his parents were worried that he was going to be arrested as a draft-dodger.[7]

Finally, his perseverance wore down the recruiters and in July 1942 they finally cracked. Although the senior officer said that he would certainly fail and that they were only giving him a place on the course to make him go away. It was good enough for Jack and he was ecstatic at finally having got the chance he had been dreaming of all his life. His acceptance papers to I.T.C. (Initial Training School) arrived in August and he was due to report to the RAF Flying Training School in Belvedere in September.

The day Jack left for Salisbury to report for his pilot training course, Blythe was diagnosed with chicken pox and she was immediately confined to bed. When it came time to leave, he stood at his little sister's bedroom door, not venturing any nearer. "I can't kiss you goodbye because I don't want to catch your chicken pox." Jack explained, tossing a half-crown across to the eleven-year-old.[8] They were very close, and for all his flippancy, it was an emotional farewell.

Jack Malloch joined the Air Force on 7th September 1942, but within two weeks he was in the isolation ward with severe chicken pox. He was dropped off the course and sent back home. A month later he was back on his feet grateful to be allowed to join the next intake at the beginning of 1943.

After ten grueling weeks Jack graduated from Ground Training School. But it had been extremely tough. Jack was not an academic and it was only through visualising the flying application of the mathematics that he managed to scrape through. He was bottom of the class, but at least he was still there.

Knowing that the flying was about to start Jack felt he was through the worst and he was right. He was a natural pilot and what he lacked in the classroom

7 Interview with Blythe Kruger, Plettenberg Bay, January 1998.
8 Ibid.

he more than made up for with his remarkable flying abilities. His first military flying lesson was on Monday 29th March 1943. It was in a Southern Rhodesian Air Force Tiger Moth. Although it had been nearly three and a half years since his last flight, Jack was very familiar with the aircraft. This made the lesson a much-needed success. His superiors closely monitored him, continually debating whether they should throw him off the course or not. The next day he was cleared for his first 'military' solo flight. It was a short ten-minute test flight and, as expected, he did well.[9]

With the move to flight training school Jack's confidence rose, and once he had passed the first few training flights and had got to know the training flight areas, he wrote a letter to Blythe at her boarding school in Umtali. He said, "...I'm going to come and see you. But you won't see me..." Blythe knew what he meant, and it was not long before Jack arrived at the school.

Umtali High School was a small community school with the classrooms in a big square around a large quadrangle. One day, as Blythe was just getting to the end of her lessons, she heard the distinctive sound of an approaching aircraft. Seconds later the aircraft appeared, skimming the school roof, and barreling down the length of the quad. Children and teachers poured out of the classrooms to see the spectacle. Waggling its wings, the aircraft soared and looped over the tall palm tree, as Blythe ran out waving frantically. She knew it was her brother. Tears streamed down her face as she stared up at him with a mix of pride and fear.[10]

April and May were intensive months of flying for Jack, sometimes with three or four flights a day. The training also evolved to include night flying, cross country navigation, forced landings and aerobatics.

At the end May 1943 he had his final Elementary Flight Training assessments. He scored 70.2% and was rated as being an 'average' pilot. But contrary to his initial hopes, there were also tough written exams. Exams which, as predicted, Jack failed. The pass mark was high and had been pushed up to force more trainees to become navigators and flight engineers.[11]

---

9 Jack Malloch's personal flying logbook.

10 Interview with Blythe Kruger, Plettenberg Bay, January 1998.

11 Interview with Ted Kruger, Plettenberg Bay, January 1998.

Jack should have been dropped from the course along with the other failures, but he had only failed by a few percent. After much consideration he was allowed to drop to the next course and sit his exams again.[12] It was a life changing decision for Jack that enabled him to keep pursuing his dream.

After an intensive run of 'refreshers' Jack was able to pass both his flying assessment and his written exams on August 5th. He then moved on to the Advanced Training Squadron, where they started flying the new Harvards. The move to the monoplane was dramatic and Jack marveled at the improved performance and speed of the aircraft.

The pressure of Advanced Training steadily increased and in early November 1943 it peaked with seven flights a day, with a combination of solo and instructional day and night flights. Jack was now learning about the military applications of flying, practicing things like live firing on the range and high and low-level dive bombing.[13]

Finally, in mid-December he did his final assessment. This time he scored 78.2% and was rated as an above average pilot. The next day, Jack, along with the other 35 successful graduates were awarded their Wings. The ceremony was attended by his parents, who, for all of their religious concerns, were extremely proud of him.

But there was little time to celebrate. The very next day the new pilots were deployed to 'Service Flying Training' in Egypt. With just a day to get their affairs in order, Jack spent the afternoon with his parents. By the time he needed to go his parents were distraught with his mother fussing around his kit bag and his father putting on a brave face. The journey began that Saturday evening at Salisbury's central railway station. Having found his compartment and loaded his kit-bag Jack handed over the keys to his car. Vic accepted them with a nod. No-one said what would happen to the car if Jack didn't come back. Vic then took off his watch and handed it to his son. "I want you to have it." Vic began, trying to find his words, "...for good luck..." Jack accepted it and carefully strapped it onto his own wrist, unable to say anything.[14]

---

12 Interview with Paul Pearson, Nairobi, March 2003.

13 Jack Malloch's personal flying logbook.

14 Interview with Paul Pearson, Nairobi, March 2003.

Paul Pearson at the controls of a Spitfire Mk. V flying over the Nile Delta. Two days after this photograph was taken Paul clipped another aircraft and crash landed. He was unscathed, but JL-242 never flew again.
© Crown Copyright, 1944, licensed under the Open Government Licence v3.0.

The whistle blew and after a quick teary farewell he boarded the train, waving from the compartment window as the noisy steam engine pulled out of the station.

The long journey halfway up Africa on a variety of trains and trucks took a full two weeks, eventually getting them to the port town of Mwanza on the banks of Lake Victoria in the Great East African Rift Valley. From there they travelled a couple of hundred miles by boat from Mwanza up to the Kenyan fishing village of Kisumu. There a massive Sunderland flying boat was waiting for them. Three days later, following the northerly course of the Nile the men finally arrived in Cairo where they were transferred to their training squadrons.[15]

After seemingly endless ground familiarisation and theoretical lectures, at the end of January 1944, flight training started. For the first three weeks they flew in Harvards. Then, on Tuesday 22nd February, they finally graduated onto the iconic Spitfire.

The Spitfire that Jack had his first flight in was a Mark V armed with a

15 Interview with Paul Pearson, Nairobi, March 2003.

Jack (in RAF cap), Peter Sutton (in sunglasses) and Paul Pearson (right) sailing to Corsica, 1944. *Picture from Jack Malloch's private collection.© Greg Malloch.*

combination of 20 mm cannons and machine-guns. Once strapped in, he found that the cockpit was very compact. It gave him a tight feeling which matched that same excited knot in his stomach. After several flights he had practiced flapless and crosswind landings, forced landing and cloud flying, as well as low flying and formations.[16] For the next four weeks they flew every day in either the Spitfire Mark I or the Mark IV with a combination of guns and cannons. During this intensive combat conversion, they honed their skills in aerial combat, ground attack and live-firing exercises.

Two weeks later, on 15th March 1944, having reached their required forty hours of flying time, the combat training at Abu Suer ended with final tests and appraisals. As anticipated Jack Malloch and all the other Rhodesians who had got their wings in December were transferred to 237 (Rhodesia) Squadron. 237 had eighteen aircraft divided into two flights, 'A' Flight and 'B' Flight. Jack and his friend Paul Pearson were both assigned to 'B' Flight.[17]

When they arrived at 237 the Squadron was in the middle of one of their regular transfers. But this move was much bigger than usual. They were moving out of Africa heading for the island of Corsica to start taking part in the main European war.

It was a complicated move and took a full ten days from start to finish. The senior pilots were allocated aircraft to fly to the island while the junior pilots

16 Notes from Paul Pearson's flying logbook.
17 Interview with Paul Pearson, Nairobi, March 2003.

Jack Malloch's assigned Spitfire, DV-M parked on the Corsican dune-grass.
Picture from Jack Malloch's private collection. © Greg Malloch.

were transported on a troop ship called the Vil D'Oran that took them to the Corsican port of Ajaccio.[18] From there they were trucked to Poretta Aerodrome on the eastern side of the island.

On April 1st, 1944, the day after their arrival, the juniors were allowed their first flight in the Squadron's brand new Mark IX Spitfires. By then Jack was beginning to seriously wonder if he would ever get to participate in the war. The Squadron letters were 'DV', Delta Victor, and Jack was allocated the Spitfire 'M,' appropriate for 'Malloch'.

In addition to bomber escort duties, 237's main task from Poretta was to attack road and rail links in northern Italy which was less than a hundred miles away across the Ligurian Sea. Although on the numerous occasions that the pilots suffered from flak damage this short strip of water seemed impossibly long, consequently they all flew wearing their bulky 'Mae West' life jackets.

After all the Spitfires had been serviced Jack's first operational sortie with 'B' Flight was on 23rd April 1944. His first mission was to bomb a bridge over the River Arno near Florence. The Spitfires were started and revved, and as the triangular wooden wheel-blocks were pulled out from under DV-M and Jack got the 'chocks away' thumbs up, he had butterflies in his stomach. Fortunately, his first combat sortie was a success and all the aircraft returned safely to base. Although both Jack and Paul were shocked at the ferocity of German anti-aircraft fire. Several of the aircraft, including DV-M, came home with

18 Interview with Paul Pearson, Nairobi, March 2003.

bullet holes in them. It was their 'baptism of fire' and the new pilots realised that war was real.

At 11 a.m. the next morning a flight of twelve Spitfires from 237 Squadron took off in a massed formation for a fighter sweep into northern Italy. On the 25th there were another two large formation raids, both of which Jack was involved in. The morning sortie was his first bomber escort mission. He was part of a flight of twelve Spitfires and they were escorting twenty-four American B-26 Marauder bombers. The Spitfires flew slightly behind and above the bombers, protecting their backs from German fighter aircraft. Jack was a bit nervous with the full collection of forty-eight rear and roof gun turrets pointing up at him.

Over the target the formation of Marauders and Spitfires flew into a solid curtain of heavy anti- aircraft fire.[19] Jack suddenly noticed black puffs of smoke silently blossoming in lines around the bombers. With painful slowness they tried to spread out a bit as the high explosive shells tore chunks off the lumbering aircraft. The Spitfires broke formation, twisting and darting away. Flying through the patches of dissipating smoke Jack could smell the explosive cordite and could hear the nearer explosions. Although the flak was very heavy the Marauders resolutely stuck to their formation. Within seconds a couple were smoking and losing altitude while another took a direct hit in the belly and started breaking up in mid-air. Suddenly an 88mm anti-aircraft shell exploded right next to Jack. There was a deafening crack and he felt the whole aircraft shudder as it was hit by the explosive shockwave and a showering of shrapnel.[20]

Once back at base there was just enough time for lunch and a quick mission-briefing. Then the pilots were back in their cockpits and heading off to new targets. The afternoon raid involved twelve aircraft in six fighting pairs. The mission was an armed recce along the Piombina road. A three-ton truck was caught and flamed, plus some hits were scored on several railway flat-beds and a signal box.[21]

237 Squadron was part of the American 251 Desert Air Force which consisted of three fighter squadrons, all equipped with Spitfire's. They were 451 Australian

19 'A Pride of Eagles', by Beryl Salt. Published by Covos Day Books. ISBN: 0-620-23759-7.
20 Personal correspondence with Bill Musgrave. 17, March 1998.
21 'A Pride of Eagles', by Beryl Salt. Published by Covos Day Books. ISBN: 0-620-23759-7.

Squadron, 237 Rhodesian Squadron and 238 Squadron which was a hybrid with Rhodesians, Australians, English and some Canadians in their ranks. 251 Desert Air Force fell under the overall command of the US 12th Air Force. For the Rhodesians this association with the American forces was wonderful. Not only did they receive American rations, but on returning from missions they were welcomed back by American girls who served them coffee and doughnuts.[22]

The three Spitfire squadrons had their Squadron Headquarters at Poretta airfield, but their tents were spread out in the nearby woods. Jack shared a tent that was set under the trees on the bank of a little clear stream. The nearby squadron mess was a marquee, and the ablutions were a traditional 'long-drop' dug a short distance from the camp. The men bathed in either the stream or in a nearby irrigation furrow. Most of the nearby villages also had public Roman-style baths where Jack and the others would have their 'weekly scrub'.

Every evening the men dressed formally for dinner. Formal dress consisted of mosquito boots, long khaki trousers, khaki shirt and a black standard issue RAF tie. As the drinking often continued long into the night a favourite trick was to creep up behind someone and cut off his tie. Fortunately, there was a plentiful supply of ties in the Squadron stores.[23] There was also a plentiful supply of bully-beef. It was served, thinly sliced and fried with an egg for breakfast, cold for lunch with salad and at night hashed up in pie or dumplings. Although 237 was luckier than most of the other squadrons as one of their mess cooks had been a pastry chef with the Savoy Hotel in London before the war and could produce an amazing assortment of bully-beef disguises.

In addition to bully-beef the men of 237 Squadron received weekly rations of cigarettes, beer and chocolate. Jack swapped both his cigarettes and beer for more chocolate. There was also a supply of spirits that went behind the mess bar. Being true to his upbringing, at most Jack would have the occasional shandy, though usually he would stick to plain lemonade or fruit juice. Even so, he was still a popular participant in the bar and mess sessions.[24]

With his mechanical aptitude Jack was made Officer-In-Charge of all transport

---

22 Personal correspondence with Bill Musgrave. 17, March 1998.
23 Personal correspondence with Rodney Simmonds, February 10, 2000.
24 Personal correspondence with Bill Musgrave, March 17, 1998.

The American B-24 Liberator that visited 237 Squadron at Poretta in May 1944. It was destroyed that night in a Ju-87 Stuka bombing attack.

Picture from Jack Malloch's private collection. © Greg Malloch.

for the Squadron. This gave him responsibility for a range of heavy trucks, petrol bowsers, and an assortment of light vehicles.[25] All of these he had to keep running reliably. With this fleet he would organise transport to the social venues that the men frequented most nights. As he did not drink much Jack was the perfect 'designated driver' to ensure that the men found their way back to base.

By the beginning of May the pace of daily bombing and strafing sorties was ramped up as the Squadron had to stop the German reinforcements that were being poured into the battlefields of central Italy. With the intensive combat flying the new pilots gained valuable experience, especially in strafing ground targets. The most difficult of these were tanks. Jack found that with the right angle of approach and enough tarmac in front of the target it was possible to ricochet his 20mm shells off the ground and up into the thin underside of the tank. With luck, this would result in a balloon of flame bursting out of the turret.

But the one thing the new pilots of 237 Squadron had no experience of was aerial combat. On Friday 5th May 1944 that was to change. Jack was part of a flight of ten Spitfires that were ambushed by a pair of Focke-Wulf 190s. The Germans sprayed machine-gun fire into the Spitfire formation, sending it scattering. Wildly spinning and dodging, some of the Spitfires tried to curl back behind the enemy while hot tracers lined the sky all around them. From then on, they no longer took the absence of fighters for granted.

25 Personal correspondence with Bill Musgrave, June 1, 1998.

The pilots of 237 Squadron in mid-1944. Jack is in the back row second from the right.

Jack (centre with RAF cap) and his ground-crew friends posing with his 'M', otherwise known as 'Mad Malloch's Milling Machine.'

Picture from Jack Malloch's private collection.

In mid-May, a B-24 Liberator visited the Squadron. That night, the men hosted their American guests to dinner. By about eleven o'clock the party was loud and raucous when suddenly they heard the sound of approaching aircraft. "I bet that's Jerry!" someone said. Then the anti-aircraft artillery along the coast opened up. Parachute flares were dropped first. Then came the bombs. The first few landed some distance away. Then suddenly they were exploding right on top of the men. Everyone instinctively threw themselves to the floor as burning hot earth, debris and shrapnel rained down on them. The scream of the Stuka Ju-87 dive-bombers was almost continual – as was the burr of their machine-guns and the loud blasting of the anti-aircraft artillery.

After about twenty minutes the raid was over. The Germans had been using sticks of small shrapnel bombs which had damaged every single aircraft that had been parked out on the airfield. Several were ablaze, and their burning ammunition continued to explode into the early hours of the morning. The burning planes, which included the visiting Liberator, all ended up as little more than blackened piles of twisted smouldering metal.

The Ju-87s had struck most of the fighter airfields in north-eastern Corsica, destroying hundreds of aircraft. Out of a total strength of twenty-four aircraft, 237 could only find three – including Jack's DV-M, that were at all airworthy. All the others were written off for spare parts. According to one of the Squadron air controllers, fifty percent of the aircraft stationed in the area were destroyed on the ground that night.[26]

Within just ten days of the raid, 237 was back up to full strength with more new Spitfires Mk IXs. They were armed with two Oerlikon 20 mm cannons and four Vickers .303 machine guns. Although with a rate of a thousand rounds per minute, even fully loaded they could only fire for twenty seconds. After the tangle with the 190s the 237 pilots always kept a few spare rounds in reserve just in case they were ambushed again on the way home. Consequently, the pilots learnt to carefully count each-and-every second of firing.

The rest of May was a blur of intensive flying, with each pilot putting in several sorties every day. With the loss of Monte Cassino the Germans had begun a

26 'The War History of Southern Rhodesia, Vol. 2.' by J.F. MacDonald. Published by Books of Rhodesia Publishing Co. ISBN 0-86920-140-9.

full-scale retreat and the Squadron's mission was changed to target and cripple the armoured columns as they began to pull back.

At the end of May Ian Smith and Jack Malloch were part of an eight-plane escort for the B-26s. This time they were attacking bridges at Incisa. As they flew over the target the flak was heavy, punching into the vulnerable bombers. While ducking and diving Jack watched as the Marauder beneath him buckled under a couple of direct hits, shedding large chunks of steel and spar in billowing black smoke. The aircraft began to yaw and started breaking up with the shattered tail-plane twisting and snapping off as more anti-aircraft rounds exploded into it. The starboard wing bent upwards as the plane started its death spiral. Out of the gaping hole at the back of the fuselage, Jack saw a single figure leap out of the stricken aircraft. As the airman fell away his parachute opened. Jack made a mental note for the debriefing – one survivor.[27]

The next day, 28th May 1944, Jack was coming back from a long bomber escort mission. There had been little flak and he was feeling confident as he crossed the Italian coast, heading back for Corsica. As he crossed over the ocean, his engine started coughing inexplicably. It was suddenly a very long stretch of open water that he had to get over, with the engine threatening to cut out any second. Jack had to admit that 'M', as he affectionately called his aircraft, was temperamental at the best of times. In-fact most of the other pilots did not like flying her at all. He limped along, praying hard the whole way until the Corsican coast came up and the Squadron airfield was in sight. Jack lined up for the landing, keeping the revs as high as possible.

With the engine still coughing, and with just twenty feet of clearance left, Jack pushed the throttle forward to compensate for the rough engine, which seemed to correct the swing, but his alignment was wrong and he was heading for the edge of the strip. Fifteen feet of clearance. He shifted the rudder a bit harder than he should have. Ten feet. In a split second he decided to try and overshoot and approach again. He jammed the throttle forward and pulled back the flaps to try and get lift – to no avail.

There was a bone-jarring thud as the main wheels crashed into the ground.

27 Interview with the Hon. Ian Douglas Smith, Harare, December 1998, and written reference from Jack Malloch's personal flying logbook.

The front of the plane bounced up slamming the tail-plane into the ground and bending the tailwheel. The heavy front of the plane crashed down again collapsing the front wheels. The propeller blades dug into the steel plates of the runway and bent back around the engine in a shower of bright sparks. After a few very rough seconds, the Spitfire slid to a smokey halt. Jack was okay but 'M' needed a great deal of urgent repairs.[28]

Yet there was no let-up in the pace. On June 5th Jack flew several sorties clocking up a good score, as he noted in his logbook, "We had very good hunting, getting 20 flamers and 30 motor transport damaged not to mention a train damaged. I had several goes at a convoy of 25 large Army trucks... when we left 7 were burning merrily."[29]

A week later Jack scored his first aircraft 'kill'. On the way back from a two-hour sweep he stumbled across a German Ju 52 transport plane lining up for take-off on a small hidden aerodrome. Swooping down he sprayed it with cannon shells, leaving it in flames.

With the ever-increasing demand for heavy bombing raids the fighter squadrons found themselves doing more and more bomber escort duties. At the beginning of July a large bombing raid was assembled for an attack on the Po Valley. It was escorted by the Spitfires of both 237 Squadron who did top cover and 238 Squadron who were close support. Just before they reached their target one of the B-25s developed engine trouble and Jack was ordered to escort the bomber back home.

As he turned Jack saw a pack of twenty German Me 109 fighters sneaking up on them. The formations of opposing aircraft swarmed into each other and in the ensuing dogfight one of Jack's friends was awarded the Distinguished Flying Cross. Almost thirty years later while on one of his many trips to Europe Jack met a German Air Force officer and after reminiscing for a while, they realised that they had fought each other in this very melee over the Po Valley. Jack was amazed by the coincidence and immediately sat down with his old adversary and shared a couple of beers and a lot of memories.

---

28 Interview with Paul Pearson, Nairobi, March 2003 and written reference in Jack Malloch's flying logbook.

29 Notes from Jack Malloch's flying logbook.

The 'Fearless' P-51 that Jack refused to fly. Within an hour of this photograph being taken the aircraft had crashed killing its pilot.

Picture from Jack Malloch's private collection. © Greg Malloch.

A few days after their big aerial battle the Squadron was transferred to the seaside town of Calvi on the north-western side of Corsica in preparation for the planned invasion of Southern France. But the pressure didn't let up and with intensive daily flying Jack was building his reputation as a skilled fighter pilot. Since his first brush with the Focke-Wulfs Jack had been working on how to get better control of the aircraft in a high-speed dive. Consequently, according to Bill Musgrave, he had become a 'master' pilot; "A common measure of a good pilot was the number of vertical rolls that could be completed after coming out of a high-speed dive. Jack could manage five – which I think was some sort of record. In terms of ethics, character and flying ability I would compare him to Chuck Yeager, arguably the finest test pilot of all time…"[30] As a result of Jack's fearless flying exploits, the senior pilots in 237 referred to him as 'Mad Malloch'.

It was about this time that Jack had one of his 'aeroplane premonitions'. A couple of the new P-51 Mustangs were deployed to Calvi and the Rhodesian pilots were very interested in the new aircraft. After getting to know each other in the Mess, one of the American pilots, who was equally fascinated by the famous Spitfire suggested to Jack that they "take a spin" in each other's aircraft. Jack was keen and after getting the necessary clearance and a bit of familiarisation they suited up for their flights.

30 Personal correspondence with Bill Musgrave, March 17, 1998.

The American took off in Jack's DV-M first, spending an exhilarating half hour doing aerobatics over the mountain tops of northern Corsica. Then Jack taxied the Mustang out for his turn. But suddenly he was overcome with a strong feeling that he should not fly the plane. He revved the engine several times listening intently. He checked the flaps and the rudder. They were all fine. Holding the brakes, Jack pushed the throttle forward again. The pitch and tone of the engine changed and the aeroplane shook in anticipation. There was nothing wrong at all. He just had an ominous feeling about it. He tried to find a reason to turn back as he felt he would need some sort of excuse as to why he didn't want to fly the Mustang. There was no reason. In the end he simply taxied back and parked the Mustang on the hardstand. He apologised and said that he just had a bad feeling about the aircraft and was not comfortable flying it. The American assured him that the aircraft was almost brand new and that there was nothing wrong, but Jack couldn't be persuaded.

Soon afterwards the Mustangs were assigned to a bomber escort mission, but Jack's premonition was getting stronger and seemed to be forming a tight knot of dreadful anticipation in the pit of his stomach. Flustered, but unsure of what to do about it, he went up into the control tower to get a better view of the Mustangs forming up and taking off in pairs. Suddenly at the far end of the runway, just as another pair took off, one had an engine failure and veered to the side, crashing back down. It smacked into the ground, bounced and cartwheeled. Leaping into one of his trucks Jack raced off towards the strewn debris. He found the mortally wounded pilot lying in the wreckage. Gasping for his last breath the American looked up at Jack, blinking through his mask of blood. The young man gripped Jack's arm and through clenched teeth stammered out, "Thank goodness you did not take it." He died a few minutes later.[31] Jack never forgot the lesson that sometimes his life would depend on listening to his instincts.

In early August 1944 Jack had 'M' trouble again. The aircraft had been repaired after his crash-landing at the end of May, but she hadn't lost her grouchy personality. The now battered Spitfire still seemed to have an aversion to long stretches of water – and anything else for that matter. After a few nasty flights in DV-M, 'Dinks' Mowbray, christened the plane 'Mad Malloch's Milling

31 Interview with Greg Malloch and Alyson Dawson, Fishhoek, May 2008.

Jack with his new DV-M just before losing its tail on 8th September 1944.
Picture from Jack Malloch's private collection. © Greg Malloch.

Machine', and refused to fly it again for fear of his life.

At the end of August, the Squadron was on the move again. This time they were transferred to Cuers Airfield in mainland France, a short distance north of St. Tropez and within earshot of the artillery duels that were still raging nearby. From Cuers they were tasked with providing close air support for the advancing troops, although the consistent rain was more often than not keeping the Spitfires grounded.

On Friday 8th September 1944 a new Spitfire was delivered. It was Jack's replacement for his old 'Milling Machine' which had become so unreliable that it had to been scrapped. The next day was eventful. This time the mission was to fly across the French border into Italy and attack road and rail transports in the area north of Cuneo. With the wet weather the Germans had become bolder and there were many trucks and trains on the move. Jack managed to destroy several of them.

As he was pulling up from his last strafing run there was suddenly a loud bang and the plane jolted hard. White hot lines of tracers shot up around him as plumes of black smoke exploded on either side of the Spitfire. The German anti-aircraft guns had zeroed in on him. Jack instinctively tumbled the plane, moving the stick hard to the right and jamming full rudder, throwing the aircraft into an erratic dive. The controls felt a bit thick and unresponsive, which wasn't a good sign. He had definitely been hit but could not see any damage to the front of the aircraft. Swooping down low and accelerating hard, Jack managed to get out of range of the guns. Out of ammunition he turned west and headed for home. When he landed he found a ragged hole punched right through the aircraft's tail. The ground crew we amazed that he had managed to get back to base at all. So much for his first flight in the brand new aeroplane. Later that night, Jack wrote a single-line entry in his logbook; 'Turin – got hit by flak – new tail had to be fitted.'[32]

At the end of September 1944, after just a month at Cuers, 237 Squadron was redeployed again. Although with the difficulty of the wet autumn weather it was early October by the time they arrived at their new base at Falconara on Italy's Adriatic Coast. From there the squadron's missions were armed reconnaissance along the Yugoslavian coastline. But their flights were few and far between with torrential rain and heavy overcast. In the end the whole of October was sodden, and the fighters of 237 Squadron were grounded for a full three weeks.

The few times that the Spitfires did actually fly, they made up for it with excessive adrenalin and danger. The mission they were given was to attack the heavily fortified and strongly defended German radar stations along the north-west coast of Yugoslavia. On these carefully coordinated attacks 237 Squadron worked in conjunction with a squadron of rocket-firing Bristol Beaufighters. The tactic for attacking the radar installations was both daring and dangerous.

The plan was for the Rhodesian Spitfires to go in at high speed, a short distance ahead of the Beaufighters and attack the German installations with cannon fire distracting the anti-aircraft batteries. The Beaufighters would then swoop down on the targets while the German gunners were busy shooting at the Spitfires. It sounded fine in theory, but the reality of being 'bait' only really sank in as the Spitfires of 237 Squadron approached the island-studded enemy coastline for the first time. Accelerating straight into the radar stations they sprayed everything with their 20 mm cannons. As Jack streaked passed, he could see the muzzle-flashes of numerous anti-aircraft machine guns firing

---

32 Jack Malloch's personal flying logbook.

wildly at him. They had been briefed to keep in range of the guns, and it was a nerve-wracking experience. Jack knew how to hide, but instead had to force himself not to, gently turning to give a better profile to the gunners who were intent on killing him.

The plan worked perfectly and the Beaufighters were able to pump rails of high-explosive rockets straight into the heart of the radar stations, completely knocking them out of action. Miraculously, all the Spitfires managed to escape undamaged. The planners were pleased – and wanted to do it again, just as soon as the weather allowed. In total they carried out three or four similar raids, and each was as successful as the first. Remarkably the Spitfires sustained no losses.[33]

Germany had recently introduced their revolutionary new jet fighter, the Me-262. They were using it to carry out reconnaissance flights over northern Italy which was a great worry to the Allied central command. They decided to transfer 237 Squadron's 'B' Flight to Pisa to try and catch these aircraft. For the entire time that they were in Pisa the Flight was ready for immediate scramble in anticipation of the Luftwaffe's new jet aircraft appearing overhead.[34] There were numerous scrambles, but 'B' Flight were never able to intercept the enemy. The entries in Jack's logbook during this time reflected his growing frustration; 'Never saw a thing.', 'Scrambled, but returned after 15 minutes.', 'Got off in

Jack and the 'B' Flight ground crew in Pisa during the Squadron's flood evacuation in November '44. The famous Leaning Tower is in the distance.
Picture from Jack Malloch's private collection. © Greg Malloch.

33 Personal correspondence with Bill Musgrave, March 17, 1998.
34 Interview with Paul Pearson, Nairobi, March 2003.

good time but nothing to report…'[35]

The weather, with its continuous cold, driving rain was equally frustrating. It turned the entire airfield into a quagmire of sticky mud. The pilots built 'duck-boards' to try and keep it out of their tents and installed home-made stoves to try and keep the interiors dry, all to no avail. The rain just fell harder, eventually flooding the tents completely. The congestion at the airfield was also becoming a challenge. When he was scrambled against an overflying Me-262 at the beginning of November, Jack nearly ran into several American DC-3s that were parked on the runway.

On Thursday 2nd November news arrived that the Arno River was about to burst its banks. This caused a ripple of panic at the airfield, which was now in imminent danger of being submerged. The American and Rhodesian pilots urgently scrambled the aircraft, but Jack volunteered to stay behind with the ground crew to look after his vulnerable vehicles. They sandbagged the buildings and tried to move as much vital equipment as they could to higher ground. Then, as the town flooded, they shifted their focus to rescuing people in a commandeered rowing-boat.

A few days later on 10th November, crippled by the mud and rain in Pisa, it was decided to move 'B' Flight to Rosignano, about 80 kilometres south of Pisa where it was felt conditions might be better. Four Spitfires and a Hurricane

Jack and his 'B' Flight ground crew rescuing civilians trapped by the floodwaters after the Arno River swamped the city of Pisa.

Picture from Jack Malloch's private collection. © Greg Malloch.

35 Jack Malloch's personal flying logbook.

Jack Malloch and the men of 'B' Flight, 237 Squadron during their muddy, sodden stay at Rosignano. *Picture from Jack Malloch's private collection. © Greg Malloch.*

were able to make the flight to Rosignano. The rest were unserviceable and left with the ground crew at Pisa.

'B' Flight was billeted in an ex-Italian Army barracks in the little fishing village of Cecina-Marina right on the beach, where Jack shared a room with his friends Paul Pearson and Peter Sutton. It was pure luxury after the trauma of camping in the rain and cold for the whole of October. But even in Rosignano the weather quickly became more dangerous than the Germans themselves. In the rain, Flying Officer Ewart Seagrief flew straight into one of Jack's lorries that was parked on the side of the runway. In the poor visibility he just did not see it. The Spitfire was written off and there was a lot of repairs to do on the lorry. Shortly afterwards Flight Sergeant Hummer hit a mud patch on landing, rolled his aircraft and broke his arm.

In mid-December 237's flying duties were extended to including shipping recces, fighter sweeps and armed recces. But the lack of visibility, misty conditions and low cloud were a constant threat. These were the most likely factors in the disappearance of Flying Officer Little who, less than a week before Christmas was seen flying into cloud chasing after an enemy aircraft – and was never seen again. Then on the 22nd another Spitfire was written off on landing,

A 237 Squadron Spitfire taxiing out for its next mission in February 1945.
Picture from Jack Malloch's private collection. © Greg Malloch.

sliding in the mud and crashing.

On Boxing Day, after the Squadron's traditional Christmas dinner, a new Spitfire was delivered. It was assigned to Bill Musgrave as his 'old kite' had taken quite a bit of damage and was becoming dangerous to fly. It was registered as 'DV-T' and Bill christened it 'Tagati,' the Ndebele word for an evil spell usually cast by a witch doctor.

By early January the weather started to dry out. It was cold, but at least the rain stopped. And that wasn't all. On January 9th the new steel runway at Rosignano was also completed. This meant that the number of sorties they could carry out was significantly increased. While the ground forces were at stalemate, the Spitfires were able to pile up the pressure with armed recces and missions in support of the US Navy.[36] For these bombing missions they used one-thousand-pound bombs fitted beneath the fuselage.

For the next two weeks the weather improved and the squadron flew numerous sorties every day. But the increased flying meant increased chances that their luck would run out.

By now they were in mid-winter and the weather was very cold, the rain having given way to snow, which the Rhodesians, from the warm tropics were not used to. But the men were becoming ever more optimistic as the Nazis where now retreating on all fronts. They quietly hoped the German collapse would come before their 'numbers were up,' which, in war is often just a matter of time.

36 Jack Malloch's personal flying logbook.

But it was bad luck to tempt fate, and Jack was to be the Squadron's first loss of the New Year. His day of reckoning was February 22nd, 1945.

Despite the freezing conditions, the action started early that day with a bombing strike against a German headquarters building and a radar station southwest of Parma. The raid was successful and all of the aircraft returned safely. Mid-afternoon a formation of Spitfires was sent out to recce the area around Genoa and Parma. Jack wasn't part of that flight, but soon afterwards he was scrambled for a bombing mission against a small arms factory in the town of Alexandria. The flight to the target was 250 kilometres and took about forty minutes over the mountains. Reaching the target, they dive-bombed out of the sun, dropping bombs and strafing the building, leaving it in flames.

With such a high concentration of bottlenecked enemy, the Spitfires were given licence to attack any juicy target they happened to stumble across and on the way back Jack saw just such a target. It was a loaded truck trundling down the road about twenty miles north of Genoa.

Jack swooped down, lining up the truck into his gun sights. He squeezed an initial burst of 20 mm rounds at the vehicle. The brace of shells exploded just behind it, ricocheting up into the canopy. The truck swerved wildly, spilling several panicked soldiers out from under the torn canopy. Jack tapped the control column, readjusting his aim, and pressed the firing-button again. This time the vehicle was caught and disappeared in a cloud of flame, smoke and debris.

Anti-aircraft guns erupted from both sides of the road. Jack accelerated hard, spiraling his wings to dodge the hail of bullets as he barreled away as quickly as he could. Suddenly he felt the plane take a hard hit. The control stick was almost kicked out of his hand as the whole aircraft yawed to the left as a cannon-hole was punched through his starboard wing, shattering the gun-well and peeling back the wing's metal skin, leaving a jagged, gaping hole.

A second later the plane was hit again. This time on the port side of the engine, kicking the whole airframe to the right. A large strip of the engine cowling was ripped clean off, and black oil from cut lines sprayed across the aircraft as smoke and debris billowed over the cockpit.

It was a direct hit. Jack was not prone to swear, but this seemed an appropriate time. He fled away as quickly as he could, streaming a thin golden-brown trail.

Jack quickly regained height and turned back towards base. Within seconds the oil pressure began to drop while both the oil and glycol temperatures started rising.

Glycol was the engine's coolant. Without it, it was just a matter of time before the engine was going to burst into flames. But just how much time did he have? The rule was that if you lost your coolant you had less than four minutes before you had to crash-land or bail out. Jack still had some glycol left, so maybe the clock hadn't started ticking yet. He just didn't know. Every second would count.

Peering forward he was shocked by the damage. The whole left side of the engine was exposed. He could see broken bits of metal and piping jutting out. Black oil was streaming out across the sides and belly of the wounded aircraft. He could also smell petrol and from under the instrument panel, fuel was pouring into the cockpit onto his legs and feet.[37] The fuel tank, which was still half full, had been ruptured.

He managed to climb to eight thousand feet. It was high enough to jump. He grasped the lever near his shoulder and pushed it forward jettisoning the canopy. As the glass casing blew off, an unexpected blast of cold air struck him hard. He unlocked the side door on the left of the cockpit and flapped it down. Jack leaned out of the open side-door as far as he could. But something was holding him back. Looking down he saw that his parachute had got caught on the Very pistol cartridge clamp and about a foot of silk had been torn and pulled out of the pack. Quickly Jack reconsidered the idea of baling out. He wriggled back into his Sutton harness, but found the locking pin had been broken. He would have to jump after all. But he had lost a lot of height.

Jack could smell burning metal. He was leaving a smoke trail and there was a heavy knocking coming from the engine. He glanced at his watch. It was half past four. Suddenly there was a burst of bright light in front of the cockpit and Jack felt the searing heat of flame. His time was up. He needed to get out immediately. There was a loud bang and in less than a single turn the propeller came to an immediate stop. The force of the jam twisted the engine mounts,

37 Interview with Paul Pearson, Nairobi, March 2003.

ripping bolts, pipes and cables deep in the heart of the stricken aircraft.[38]

The flames were beginning to cook the left side of the open cockpit blistering the paint and threatening to ignite the fuel sloshing around in the cockpit. Jack grasped the canopy rail and hauled himself up, lunging towards the small open hatch as the aircraft tilted over in its smoky death spiral. Two and a half thousand feet below Jack saw the squiggly blue line of a river and the squared Romanic grid of a large town beneath him. As he tumbled through the air he ducked as DV-M's tail-plane flashed past his head.

It was not just Jack's parachute that had got stuck, something had caught his watch as well. It was the one his father had given him. The watch strap had broken and as he plummeted to earth, the watch was falling through the air with him. Jack was hypnotised by the tumbling timepiece, glinting silver in the yellowing afternoon sunlight. As he fell Jack tried to catch it. It had been for 'good luck.' He could not afford to lose it now.[39]

Suddenly Jack realised he should have pulled his parachute ripcord instead of trying to retrieve the watch. Time had run out. And so too, it seemed, had his luck. Jack wrenched the cord and felt the parachute pack unfolding with a loud flap behind him. He expected the earth to smash into him at any second. Glancing down, the snowy ground was close – and coming up fast. Then he felt the reassuring pull as the silk canopy began to arrest his descent. He looked up. But instead of a nice round disc it was only half-round and spinning. At least four of the silk panels had been torn. Jack raised his arms and tried to pull the two cords of strings apart to open the chute a bit better.

Before he could look down again, with splayed kicking legs, he hit the ground. He heard a loud snap and felt a stabbing pain shooting up through his body, cutting his breath short.

Everything went black.

Sometime later Jack felt he was floating in darkness. He was numb. Floating in nothing. No pain, no cold, no wind. Nothing.

---

38 Jack's official report on being shot down addressed to the 237 Squadron Commanding Officer dated 16 May 1945.

39 Interview with Paul Pearson, Nairobi, March 2003 and Henry Kinnear, Johannesburg, November 2003.

He opened his eyes, blinking hard. There was a bright whiteness all around him. As his eyes began to focus Jack became aware of an angel standing over him. She was marble-white with hands clasped together looking down at him. He was pleased that he was in Heaven and that the angel was so much like the classic angels he had been taught about.

It was strange, though, that she just stood there like marble, looking down at him with her odd, sad expression.[40] Strange too that there was a growing pain in his leg. He could also smell his petrol-soaked boots. He gasped and struggled up as if his soul had suddenly been plugged back into reality.

There were parachute strings all over him – and the angel was marble! Jack was lying in a bank of snow looking up at the headstone he had slammed into. He looked around. There were other ornate headstones and crosses all around him. He realised he had landed in a graveyard. In the distance he could hear people shouting.

It was time to go. Jack quickly unclipped the parachute straps and wriggled out of the harness. He pulled his legs up and tried to run. With a sharp stab of blinding pain he fell face forward into the snow again, groaning where he lay. He knew he was injured. Probably badly.

Seconds later people pulled him up. The pain was intense, and their foreign jabbering confused him. Jack was half carried, half frog-marched out of the cemetery, leaving a streak of red blood in the snow behind him. He seemed to be floating in a sea of grasping hands. He closed his eyes and slumped forward drifting in and out of consciousness as they bundled him away.[41]

Later he woke, swimming up through a sea of pain. He was lying on a hard bed in the orange of candlelight. There was someone peering down at him. It was a young woman. Silhouetted against the candlelight he could not make out her features, but could see that she had long fair, almost reddish hair. There were two other people in the room. Another younger girl and an older man. After a while the village doctor arrived. Jack's ankle had been shattered. The physician did his best to re-set it and carefully wrapped it in bandages. Although he had

---

40 Interview with Paul Pearson, Nairobi, March 2003.

41 Interview with Blythe Kruger, Plettenberg Bay, January 1998 and 'A Pride of Eagles' by Beryl Salt. Published by Covos Day Books. ISBN: 0-620-23759-7.

landed in deep soft snow, which had certainly saved his life, the resetting of his ankle was an agonising process and there was no medication to stifle the pain.

Maria (left) and her elder sister Rosa while hiding in Baccapaglia.
Picture from Jack Malloch's private collection. © Greg Malloch.

In the house where he was being hidden there were three generations; The ageing grandparents who lived on the ground floor, the head of the household, his wife and their four children, Rosa, who was twenty-one years old, Maria who was eighteen and two younger children. They all lived together in a large double-storey house overlooking the ancient cobbled town of Piacenza. Both Rosa and Maria were very attractive. Rosa was slim and elegant with a very attractive figure, striking blue eyes, and a pale complexion.[42]

As the house they lived in was so big the family were hiding not just Jack, but another downed airman as well. In his wounded state Jack didn't get to know the other fugitive very well and he was only there in transit waiting for the partisans to smuggle him out. But the Germans knew someone was hiding the fallen airmen and it wasn't long before they honed-in on the big red-brick house.

One evening, with just seconds of frantic warning, vehicles screeched up and there was a heavy banging on the door, the two pilots dived into their recess under the floorboards and a big bed was hurriedly pushed over the trap door. A squad of Germans in their heavy jackboots stormed into the house and began ransacking every room.

For the two men lying in the darkness there seemed to be utter confusion with everyone shouting at once – a blur of German demands, Italian pleas and

42 Interview with Paul Pearson, Nairobi, March 2003 and as detailed in 'The Attractions of Rosie' by Wing Commander P. D. Cooke.

screaming children. Then he heard a gunshot.

For a second there was a stunned silence. Then a bellowed instruction in German, followed by more shouting as the interrogation began. After a few minutes the questioning became more stern. Then it got physical with loud shouting, punching and kicking. One of the girls was screaming, and her mother was pleading with the soldiers. The young children were hysterically. Jack whispered to the other airman, saying that he felt it would be better to give himself up to save the family.

"That will be the worst thing you could do," was the hissed reply.

"Why?" Jack asked.

"It will be far worse for them if you do."

But just how much more could they take, Jack wondered, wracked with guilt at what they were having to go through because of him.

Eventually the German commander lost his patience, screaming out his question. The young girl and her mother were now sobbing. Jack strained to hear what was going on. The old man was also trying to plead with the Germans, his heavily accented voice sounding high-pitched and frail.

The stand-off lasted for almost a full minute, every second of which felt like a lifetime. Jack was not breathing. The throbbing in his leg was overwhelming. Then it happened.

The question was bellowed out one more time. Before an answer could be given another shot ran out. Jack jumped at the loud bang. Something heavy crashed to the floor and there were screams and sobs.

The question was screamed again.

Another shot. Another body fell.

The children were hysterical. It seemed that the entire family were going to be slaughtered, one by one.

Jack wondered who had been killed, and pressing his hands against the side of his head, he prayed for the nightmare to stop.

Eventually the stormtroopers began filing out of the house, though not before kicking over some of the chairs and driving a rifle butt through a family picture that was hanging on the wall. The devastated family were left with the dead bodies of the children's murdered grandparents. The sound of the hysterical children and the wailing of their mother became a whirlpool of sound and swirling colours as Jack slipped into unconsciousness.

The next day the elderly couple were buried. The funeral was held in the church where Jack had landed and it was a small and sorrowful affair with most people being too frightened to attend. The long-coated Gestapo kept a careful watch on the church ceremony and the procession to the grave side. The priest was careful not to mention how his parishioners had met their untimely deaths, and everyone was careful to avoid eye-contact with their watchers.

Jack never knew whose parents the old couple were. He was too sorry and guilty to ask. In-fact he hardly even spoke of the horrific incident. Yet it always gnawed away at him, and on one of the few occasions that Jack did relate the story, some thirty years later, it still reduced him to tears.[43]

Yet this was not the last time the Nazis would visit the family in search of Jack. Over the next few weeks they raided the town nine times looking for the airmen, and each time they brought with them more terror and violence.[44]

The question was who had betrayed the family, and so a witch-hunt began. Eventually the villagers found a suspect, and amid great excitement, the mob prepared to lynch him. Rosa's father went to see what all the shouting was about. He returned about ten minutes later and told Jack what had happened. "Not everyone trusts the poor fellow, and now they think he is collaborating with the Germans. You see, after this long war we don't have much, not even enough food, let alone luxury goods, so when someone gets something new, everyone wants to know how they got it." He explained. "Now suddenly our friend here has a fancy new watch."

Jack insisted that he be taken to the accused. Sure enough the watch was the one Jack's father had given him, still with its broken strap. The terrified young man said that he had been walking along one evening, minding his own business when a hole appeared in the snow in front of him. He peered in and found the watch. Of course, the lynch mob did not believable the story and even after

43 Personal correspondence with Donald Mackie, March 30, 2010.
44 Interview with Blythe Kruger, Plettenberg Bay, January 1998.

Jack verified it they were still skeptical.[45]

The Germans got to hear about the story and their searches of the town intensified. It was now just a matter of time before Jack was going to be discovered, and with little choice Mario decided that he had to be moved. But Jack's leg was not healing. In-fact it seemed to be getting worse. He could now hardly walk at all and was in constant pain. Clearly, he wouldn't be able to make the dangerous journey into the mountains. Another solution needed to be found.

Between Rosa's father, the doctor and the local priest they negotiated for Jack to be taken into the orphanage in the Convent of Sant'Anna which was part of the Church of San Stefano.[46] There they hoped he would be able to get better treatment. Very late one night, creeping from one dark doorway to the next the townsmen carried Jack to the convent door where he was quickly bustled inside and hidden deep within the cloisters.

Although medication was scarce Jack's leg was cleaned, redressed and bound into a firm splint. After a few days of sparing lotions, rationed painkillers and plenty of prayers Jack started to feel better. Although he was by no means Catholic, considering the sincerity of the bedside prayers, he was deeply appreciative of the nuns' care, not to mention the risk they were taking for him.[47]

After four or five days it was agreed that Jack was well enough to travel so late one night the partisans came to collect him. As he was passed over to the Resistance guides in the darkness someone came up to assist him. It was a woman, "Ciao Jack." she whispered. Jack was stunned. It was Rosa. With the growing attention from the Germans, her parents felt that the two elder girls would be safer away in the remote mountains with the Resistance so had sent them along as well.

As Jack still could not walk, he was perched on the back of a donkey while the girls walked on either side of him, keeping his balance. They only moved at night, firstly south into the foothills along the west bank of the Nure River, then after carefully crossing it, they picked their way south-east past the town of Salsomeggiore Terme and up into the snow-capped Apennino Tosco mountains

45 Personal correspondence with Henry Kinnear, December 6, 1999.
46 Jack's written debrief to the C.O. 237 Squadron dated May 16, 1945.
47 Interview with Nori Mann, Thakeham, West Sussex. May 8, 2019.

(now part of the Tuscan-Emilian National Park). Heading west over the mountain trails they finally arrived at a tiny farming settlement just to the east of the Cisa Pass, as far away from the Germans as possible.[48]

On the back of this photograph scribbled in Italian is a note that says, 'To Lieutenant Jack, to remember the Partisans.'

Picture from Jack Malloch's private collection. © Greg Malloch.

A couple of days later Paul Pearson flying in a brand-new Spitfire that had been sent to replace Jack's old DV-M was shot down following a raid on some Piacenza bridges. He survived the crash and managed to get away, stumbled across the 31st Garibaldi Brigade of partisans. They quickly put him on the pillion of a stolen German motorcycle and whisked him away. After hiding in a farmhouse for the night, Paul and his accomplice spent the whole of the next day climbing into the heart of the mountains. They were heading for the remote mountain hamlet of Baccapaglia[49] where, according to his rescuer, another English airman 'with a broken leg' was being hidden.

By mid-afternoon on the third day, they arrived at the tiny village. It was tucked away in a small valley hemmed in by tall snowy mountain peaks. It was merely a collection of eight or ten farm buildings and houses clustered together. Paul was taken to his room on the third floor of one of the farmhouses. It was stone-floored with a large double bed, which he was to share with the other Allied pilot. The farmer's cows, goats, chickens and pigs were corralled on the ground floor at night, which made the place very smelly, although the livestock did help to

48 Personal correspondence with Michele Becchi dated May 8, and 11, 2009.

49 This seems to have been a highly localised name which likely was not translated well into English but refers to a countryside area between the Cisa Pass and the tiny hamlet of Cirone in Palma.

Barry's airstrip-building crew. Bert and Barry at the back, with Maria (on the left), two local women from the village, Rosa and Paul in the front.
Picture from Jack Malloch's private collection. © Greg Malloch.

keep the place a bit warmer at night. The attic above had been converted into a small draughty bedroom, where a man named Barry stayed.

Barry was a South African Special Forces sergeant who was coordinating both the route for escaped airmen and the resistance operations in the area. This operational area east of the Cisa Pass was known as 'Blundell Violet' and was run by a Major Holland of the British SOE (Special Operations Executive) who worked mainly with the 32nd Italian Partisan Brigade.[50] The 'airman with the broken leg' turned out to be Jack Malloch himself.

Jack was very pleased to be reunited with his good friend. But Paul was worried about how badly wounded his friend was. Jack could hardly walk and certainly wouldn't be able to make the dangerous mountain crossing to Allied lines. Barry had reported the problem back to special forces command. They said that if they could land a small aircraft nearby, they would consider trying to fly Jack out. The problem was that the landing strip needed to be close to the village as they could give very little notice of the plane's arrival. With the village nestled in a gorge between steep mountains it seemed like an impossible task.

50 Personal correspondence with Michele Becchi, dated May 8, 2009.

For days Paul, Barry and an American pilot by the name of Bert searched for landing options. Eventually they found a place where a stream ran straight for almost six hundred yards and had built up a bank of small boulders and pebbles along one side. They reckoned that if it could be levelled, it might be possible for an agile aircraft such as a Lysander to make the landing. It was a long shot, but they all knew they needed to get Jack to proper medical attention soon. They recruited a labour force of old men, women and children, who for several days filled in hollows, moved boulders and flattened ridges, until they literally ran out of space and energy.

Once done, Paul, Bert and Barry inspected their 'runway'. Bert felt it would be impossible to land a plane on the short pile of rubble they had fashioned, but with no other option Barry radioed the position, dimension and directions of approach and take-off. He was told to stand by for a landing attempt.

While the building was going on Jack stayed behind in the village with Rosa who he was becoming ever more dependent on. For hours they would sit together chatting as she 'taught him Italian'. It was obvious to everyone that they were slowly but surely falling in love, and Barry began to worry that Jack might not want to leave when the rescue plane eventually arrived for him.'[51]

A grainy picture of the captured German Storch that was used to rescue Jack Malloch at the end of March 1945.

Picture provided by Stefano Merli. © Stefano Merli.

51 Interview with Paul Pearson, Nairobi, March 2003.

A few days later there was a burst of excitement when a curt radio message said that the rescue plane was about to land. Shouting for the others, Barry raced down from his attic as the small village exploded in a frenzy of activity. By the time Barry burst out of the front door, people and chickens were running everywhere. Jack and Rosa emerged looking panicked. Jack was thrown onto the back of a donkey and the whole village started jogging down the hill towards 'their' little landing strip. Once they arrived Jack dismounted and straightened himself up, and the others stood around in the warming sun, scanning the sky expectantly. Rosa moved closer to Jack, resting her head against him sadly. Three hours later they all slowly climbed back up to the village.

Over the next few days there were two other false starts, so by the time the fourth call came hardly anyone bothered to make the journey. The small group of airmen stood at the end of the strip and waited – yet again. Just as they were about to give-up, they heard an approaching aircraft. A little plane swooped over a ridge and turned up into the valley towards them. But it was not a Lysander. It was German. The aircraft was a distinctive high-winged Fieseler Storch. Then came more aircraft; two, three, four of them, all American Mustangs.[52] The Storch dipped down, lining up with the short runway, while the Mustangs zoomed low overhead. The tiny German spotter plane touched down, bouncing over the rough ground, braking as hard as it dared, before reaching the bewildered group of spectators.

The Italian pilot quickly turned the aircraft, shouting out of the open cockpit window for the passenger to climb in. Jack was hurriedly squeezed in next to the pilot, with just enough time to give Rosa a quick kiss goodbye. A badly wounded soldier who had just been collected from some other clandestine airstrip, was slumped groaning in the back seat.[53] In less than two minutes, Jack had been loaded and the aircraft bounced its way back down the track, leaping into the air before the tree-line. The pilot, First Lieutenant Furio Lauri gave a slight waggle of his wings as he soared away. Paul, Barry, Bert, Rosa, Maria and the donkey all stood in stunned silence. Jack was suddenly gone. Contrary

52 Interview with Paul Pearson, Nairobi, March 2003.

53 Unbeknown to Jack the casualty in the back of the aircraft was none other than the famous partisan leader Glauco Monducci. He had been seriously wounded while leading an attack on the German 51st Corps Head Quarters at Albinea on March 27, 1945.

to all expectations their landing strip had actually worked.[54]

Once they had crossed over to the Allied side with the Mustangs keeping a close escort, they landed at a small military airstrip, from where the two wounded passengers were quickly transferred to a military hospital just outside Florence. The state of Jack's leg horrified the doctors. As they cut off the makeshift plaster a mass of wriggling fleas and lice spilled out.[55] The leg was badly swollen and although the bones were knitting together again, they were not straight. They had to be re-broken, straightened and re-set. Although excruciatingly painful, at least this time Jack was in a real hospital and had the medication he needed. Within a few days, with a proper cast and glorious painkillers, Jack was feeling much better.

Lt. Furio Lauri who flew Jack out of his mountain hide-out in the above Storch.

Picture provided by Michelle Becchi © Michelle Becchi.

On Sunday 15th April 1945 Jack was discharged from hospital. Bill Musgrave, who had completed his tour of operations the day before, brought him back to the squadron. It was a very happy reunion – until they got back to the airfield at Rosignano. The Spitfires were just getting back from a bombing raid on a factory in the Po Valley. All the aircraft made it back safely, but Sergeant Patrick Adsero's plane had been badly hit. As Bill and Jack arrived at the base, medical staff were trying to extract Patrick from the shattered and bloody cockpit. He was still alive, though was badly injured. Clearly the war was not over yet.

On Tuesday 17th April, two days after Jack's return, four Spitfires attacked a convoy of German trucks. During the melee Flying Office Michael Ward called out over his radio, "They've got me." Neither he nor his aircraft were seen again. The next day, a group of 237's Spitfires were on the way back from a

54 Interview with Paul Pearson, Nairobi, March 2003.
55 Interview with Blythe Kruger, Plettenberg Bay January 1998.

strike against some marshalling yards when Flight Lieutenant John Carlisle, the Commanding Officer of 237's 'B' Flight flew straight into the side of a mountain, killing himself instantly.[56]

On the 24th the Squadron were attacking ships along the northern coastline. As they regrouped, they noticed that Sergeant James Allen was no longer with them. Like Carlisle, Ward and Bennie before him, neither James nor his aircraft were ever seen again. The very next day a flight of Spitfires attacked a railway bridge, and while pulling out of his dive-bombing run, Flying Officer Neville Mansell clipped the roof of a house. The wing snapped straight off and he somersaulted into the ground. His body was never recovered.

It was just ten days before the end of the War in Europe and Neville's death brought to an end the two most bloody and costly months of the entire six-year war for 237 Squadron.[57]

Of Jack's friends the attrition had been severe; Peter Sutton and Frank Barbour were both dead. Paul Pearson, Wilfred Ford, Ian Smith and Jack himself had all been injured. Only Bill Musgrave had got through unscathed.

Although it would take Jack a long time to get back into the pilot's seat, he had actually survived the Second World War, and would eventually be going home. Although it wasn't an immediate transfer back as Jack specifically wanted to stay 'in theatre'.

He was in love with Rosa who he had left deep behind enemy lines.

He needed to find her…

---

56 Personal correspondence with Bill Musgrave, May 19, 2003.

57 'A Pride of Eagles' by Beryl Salt. Published by Covos Day Books. ISBN: 0-620-23759-7.

CHAPTER 4

Prospecting, Trucking and the Spitfire Ferry: 1945 to 1951

On May 8th, 1945 Winton Churchill broadcast his 'VE Day' speech to the world. Jack and the rest of the survivors from 237 Squadron clustered around the big mess 'wireless' radio and listened intently. In Fort Victoria his family also listened to the broadcast, although being away from the war zone it was much more of a celebration. Later that afternoon Vic, Rita, fifteen year-old Blythe and Vic's elderly mother all joined the VE Day Parade in Jack's Morris Minor adorned with life-rings and a huge 'HMS VICTORY' sign.[1]

Meanwhile Jack was devoting all his strength and resources to tracking down Rosa and her family. He was desperate to know whether they had survived. In Mid-May he finally got a letter back from Rosa who confirmed that she and her sister were safely back home. The very next weekend Jack and Paul took a few days off and hitched a ride to Piacenza.

When they knocked on the door Rosa opened it. With a squeal of excitement she threw her arms around Jack, almost knocking him off his crutches. Later that night as the family was sitting down to dinner Rosa asked Jack to help her select an appropriate wine from the cellar. Some twenty minutes later they returned looking innocent and brandishing an arbitrary bottle. Paul couldn't help but notice that Jack had distinct traces of lipstick all over him. After a very pleasant couple of days it was time for the two pilots to return to base, although this time the farewell was a lot more emotional.[2]

While Jack was thinking about how he could organise a permanent deployment in Italy, the rest of 237 Squadron headed home. Jack volunteered as an instructor

1 Personal correspondence with Blythe Kruger, April 28, 2008.
2 Interview with Paul Pearson, Nairobi, March 2003.

and was accepted into 23 Training Squadron. But his mind wasn't on the training. It was always on his next trip to see Rosa. Vic and Rita wondered why their son hadn't returned with the rest of the Squadron. Then they got to hear about the romance which caused great consternation. While Jack was always one to make up his own mind, the pressure did get to him and he was also missing his family. Eventually he decided that he had to go back home. After two months of instructing Jack resigned, giving notice for the end of July. He then sent a long letter to Rosa explaining his decision.

Jack took the same route home as the rest of the Squadron. He flew on a military transport from Italy to Egypt, and then down the Nile, over the Great Lakes, across Kenya, Nyasaland and Northern Rhodesia, eventually landing in Salisbury. He was one of the last out of the aircraft, hobbling down the steps with a cane. Vic, Rita and Blythe knew it was Jack and amid hugs and tears they were reunited at long last.

Jack took his accumulated leave and spent the rest of August at his parents' home in the picturesque granite hills just outside Fort Victoria. The time off enabled him to start to recover, but he desperately missed Rosa and there was little distraction to get her off his mind. At the beginning of September 1945 Jack moved to Salisbury and took up his Air Force duties again. But there was nothing for him to do there either. Mostly the pilots did paperwork with the barest minimum of flying simply to keep their licences valid.

Just before Christmas, Jack decided to send Rosa a telegram. As he limped up to the Post Office counter an attractive young girl looked up from behind the glass. For a second she looked at his blue battle-dress and his RAF cap. It was slanting over his right eye – a position which had come to be known within the ranks of the Southern Rhodesian Air Force as 'the Malloch angle'.[3] Then she looked into his eyes, and suddenly smiled broadly. Jack was stunned – it was Zoe Coventry. Beth's school-friend from Fort Victoria.

Zoe had matured into a beautiful young woman, ending her final year at Chaplin as Head Girl. They chatted for almost half an hour by which time Jack was embarrassed to hand Zoe his intimate telegram. She carefully typed it, surprised by Jack's romantic side. This intrigued her. Once the telegraph had been sent

3 Personal correspondence with Peter Petter-Bowyer, January 17, 2008.

Jack thanked Zoe and left, wishing her a Merry Christmas. As he drove back to the airfield he felt strangely light-headed. Over the next month he found reason to send Rosa four more telegraphs.

But by the end of January 1946 the Southern Rhodesian Air Force, decided to demobilise more staff. This time Jack was given notice. It was the last straw. He was far from Rosa, the war had left deep scars, and now he had lost his flying career as well. He knew that he needed to get away and work out what he was going to do with his life.

He decided to give prospecting a go. Apparently there was a lot of mineral wealth in Bechuanaland. De Beers were predicting huge diamond finds in the Protectorate and alluvial diamonds had already been found in the Kalahari riverbeds. Jack knew that their source had to be somewhere in the 'thirstland' of the vast unexplored interior. He bought an old second-hand motorcycle and gathered the necessary kit which he packed into the bike's big leather panniers. Then, with his childhood friend Gideon perched on the metal box at the back, they set off. They rode west, towards the great unknown.

A week later they were on the shoreline of Sowa pan on a rough deserted track some one hundred miles north-west of Francistown. The pan stretched as far as the eye could see, shimmering bright pink from the millions of flamingoes scavenging shrimp in the shallow salty waters. The men made camp overlooking the pan, marveling at the orange setting sun, the lines of pelicans flying back to their roosts and the grazing herds of springbok and zebra.

Although the nature was rich and unspoiled there didn't seem to be any mineral riches at all. As alluvial diamonds were found in riverbeds Jack decided to explore the Nata River at the north-eastern edge of Sowa Pan. After a frustrating week finding nothing Jack decided to move their search east to the Moutloutse River near the confluence of the Shashe and Limpopo. There they did start to find some interesting crystals.

It was hard going though. During the day the temperature was consistently above one hundred degrees Fahrenheit, and at night the lions were always close to the campfire. Gideon, who was from the Manica tribe seemed relaxed and spent the nights telling Jack the African legends about the animals. These fables explained why the *dassies* (rock hyrax) stare up into the heavens, why the rhino didn't fit into his skin and how the python lost his legs. Jack was fascinated, but always listened with his loaded rifle on his lap, mindful of the prowling carnivores.

A few weeks later at the end of a particularly long day Jack was looking for a place to camp. On the far side of the dry riverbed he saw a thick grove of shady fever trees. It seemed like the perfect spot. But to get there they had to cross the sandy expanse. They loaded up the motorbike and after carefully plotting his course Jack accelerated as fast as he could onto the soft white sand. The bike swerved and growled. Its back wheel kicked up sand, but somehow it kept going.

Suddenly, three-quarters of the way across, Jack saw a deep gully open up right in front of them. Before he could avoid it the motorbike fell straight into the dark hole. The front wheel nose-dived and there was a loud smack from the engine block. Dusting themselves off Jack and Gideon pulled the heavy old bike out of the hole. As they dragged it back, it left a streak of thick black oil on the sand. Jack knew there was serious damage and crouched down to have a look. There was a hairline crack in the engine case that was oozing oil.

They unpacked the crippled bike and pitched their tent in the trees. Both men knew their prospecting days were over. The next morning Jack took one more look at the motorbike, lying on its side where it had bled to death. Without a word they picked up their belongings and started the long walk back to Francistown. The bike was left there – where, no doubt, it still remains.[4]

Once back home Jack had some of his more promising samples tested, but none of it was worth pursuing. Fortunately, while he had been away Vic had come up with a plan. His idea was to set up a garage in the town of Marandellas, one hundred kilometres east of Salisbury, where they could service the country's booming transport industry. He envisioned it as a family-run garage with Rita doing the admin and Jack running the workshop.

During his time prospecting in the Kalahari Jack had thought carefully about Rosa. Although Jack loved her it just seemed impossible to make the relationship work over such a distance. Although he didn't want to admit it, he also couldn't get Zoe out of his mind. Facing the inevitable he wrote to Rosa and broke off their relationship as gently as he could.

Within a few months the family had packed up and moved to their new home

---

4 Interview with Henry Kinnear, Johannesburg, December 1999.

The Malloch family business which prospered in Marandellas in 1946 and 1947. It is telling that their telephone number was just '44.'
Picture from Jack Malloch's private collection. © Greg Malloch.

in Marandellas. The business there did well. Jack was a very capable and experienced mechanic and soon they had a very viable business. Towards the end of 1946 Jack's friend Paul Pearson got married and Jack was Best Man. Zoe accompanied him to the wedding as they were now officially a couple and spent most weekends together either in Salisbury or in Marandellas.[5]

A year later in November 1947, it was announced that the Southern Rhodesian Air Force would be re-established. Jack immediately volunteered for the Auxiliary Squadron and was accepted, being given the rank of Lieutenant. At last he was able to get back into the cockpit. And that wasn't all that was going well for him. After an eighteen-month romance, on Saturday January 17th, 1948 Jack and Zoe got married. The ceremony was held at the Anglican Church in Fort Victoria, and in true story-book tradition they really did 'live happily ever after.' When Bill Musgrave heard that Jack had married Zoe he wrote, "I was very pleasantly surprised that Jack had landed the top prize."[6]

But things were not going well for Jack's parents. In the middle of 1947 they had suffered a bad car accident which had left Vic, Rita and Blythe all seriously injured. This resulted in the collapse of the business and by mid-1948 Vic was compelled to go back to the Railways as a truck driver. After several months

5 Interview with Paul Pearson, Nairobi, March 2003.
6 Personal correspondence with Bill Musgrave, March 17, 1998.

Jack and Zoe's wedding, 17th January 1948.

driving for the Railways he realised just how much money could be made in the trucking business, so bought his first truck and started working on winning his own transport contracts.

Jack meanwhile went into partnership with a mechanic called Shorty Berrat who ran a garage in Marandellas. Quickly they were able to build up a very successful business.[7] Having seen the success of his parent's business, with their encouragement Jack also bought a couple of second hand Foden trucks. As he

One of Jack's old Foden trucks, once again stuck in the mud somewhere in Rhodesia's Eastern Highlands during the rainy season of 1949.

Picture provided by Greg Malloch.
© Greg Malloch.

7 Personal correspondence with Pete Nilson, June 6, 2000 and Hugh Bisset, March 13, 2008.

No. 1 Squadron Southern Rhodesian Auxiliary Air Force 1950. Lt. Malloch is seen sitting on the far right with his cap at the distinctive 'Malloch angle'.
© C.G.S. Macpherson.

was able to maintain and service the heavy vehicles himself, and he already had first-hand experience in trucking, over the next year this transport service grew into a substantial business. A business which began to threaten some of the other established transporters.

In addition to all this Jack also found time for his Air Force flying which he loved. In April 1949 he had qualified on the Auster Autocrat, in October he re-qualified on the Harvard and by the middle of 1950 Jack had qualified on the big twin-engined Rapide biplane. Most of his flights were aerobatic and formation flying, along with some long-distance cross-country flights.

With the Air Force doing a growing number of displays Jack was also steadily building up his flying hours. In August he did a Harvard display to celebrate the opening of the new airport in Livingstone, just north of the Victoria Falls. After the display the pilots took the opportunity to swoop through the spray of the massive mile-wide chasm of the falls. Although the invasion of South Korea overshadowed this celebration and it was no coincidence that on the day that Seoul fell to the communists Jack and his fellow pilots were assigned their first 'battle formation' training flight.

With the Cold War hotting up the Southern Rhodesian Government committed two low-level ground attack squadrons to NATO. No 1 Squadron SRAAF, which had been formed in March 1950 and in which Jack flew, was the first of these two envisaged squadrons. For the rest of 1950 Jack and the other pilots spent every spare moment they had practicing battle formations, and air to air combat. But as they were all unpaid part-time volunteers the flying was done over the weekends, pre-dawn or in the evenings.

At the end of 1950 Vic and Rita decided it was time to retire and Vic handed his transport business over to Jack. The holiday season was a busy time for Jack at the garage, and now he had a significant trucking business on his hands as well.

But there was still a lot of Air Force flying to be done and by the beginning of January they were doing training flights every second day. One of those flights was with his friend Dicky Bradshaw.[8] During the forty-minute flight Dicky asked Jack if he would be interested in helping to fly in a squadron of Spitfires out from the U.K. in mid-February. Apparently the government had just bought twenty two brand new Mark XXII Spitfires, but the catch was that delivery was not included. Although he was busy Jack was very tempted and said he would get back to Dicky by the end of the weekend.[9] He needed to ask Zoe first, although she was always very supportive of his flying career and gave her consent without a second thought.

So, at the beginning of February 1951 the team of sixteen pilots and eight ground-crewmen boarded the Southern Rhodesian Air Force's only Dakota and set off on their long journey to England. The flight from Salisbury to London took a full ten days to complete with frequent re-fueling and over-night stops along the way.

From London they flew up to Derby for their technical ground training. As usual Jack did not enjoy the theoretical class-room sessions. On the first day of their training the Rhodesians were being lectured by a retired RAF Group Captain. During his presentation with a touch of arrogance he stated that they would be

8 Jack Malloch's personal flying logbook.

9 Interview with Dicky Bradshaw, Harare, December 1999, and entry in Dicky Bradshaw's flying logbook.

The Rhodesians at Brize Norton at the start of the longest, most ambitious aircraft ferry ever attempted. Jack is fourth from the left at the back.
Picture from Jack Malloch's private collection. © Greg Malloch.

lucky to get fifty percent of the aircraft back to Southern Africa within thirty days. The pilots all vowed to prove him wrong.[10]

At the end of their technical training at the Rolls Royce facility the men moved to the US Air Force base at Brize Norton, where an RAF maintenance unit had prepared the Spitfires. There the men tried to learn as much as they could about the mechanics of the aircraft. According to Dave Barbour "…the aircrew were allowed to help but only on very mundane tasks, with the exception of Jack Malloch who was very much more practical and mechanically orientated than the rest of us."[11]

After a week of intensive flight training and familiarisation Ted Jacklin held a briefing session during which he went through the details of the long flight home. The briefing sent a ripple of excitement and anticipation through the team. As maintenance of the aircraft would be critical on the long flight the pilots were given basic servicing instructions. According to Dicky Bradshaw, "We were taught to unbutton the cowlings and use a screwdriver – a hell of a job requiring patience and skill; Jack proved to be the master amongst the

10 'Spit Epic' article written by Group Captain J. P. Moss.

11 D. M. Barbour's 'Personal Recollections of the History of the Southern Rhodesian Auxiliary Air Force.' May 1995.

amateurs. He certainly did prove his worth on the trip and must have been a great help to the ground crew…"[12]

The day the ferry began was Monday 12th March 1951. The eleven aircraft were arranged in three sections, 'Bundu Red', which was led by Lieutenant Colonel Jacklin, 'Bundu Yellow' and lastly 'Bundu Blue' which was made up of a V-formation of the remaining three Spitfires. Jack was allocated Spitfire PK 355, which was given the call-sign 'MOZZ-C'. He brought up the rear in the tail-end of 'Blue' formation. The aircraft departed just after eleven o'clock that morning doing a short hop over to Chivenor where the aircraft were prepared for, what was at the time the most ambitious aircraft ferry ever attempted. The ammunition bays along the length of the Spitfire wings were stuffed with extra gear, emergency rations and spare starter cartridges.

In addition to the skeptics at Rolls Royce, the RAF had also stated that if the Rhodesians managed to get seven aircraft to Salisbury within thirty days it would be good; eight very good; nine excellent and if ten aircraft made it they would consider it a miracle. But it was a full eleven Spitfires that were standing at the starting blocks on the Chivenor runway on the morning of Wednesday 14th March. Ted Jacklin, his second-in-command Johnny Deall and each of the twenty-two other men involved were determined that they would all make it home – six and a half thousand miles away.

But the weather on that cold, wet and blustery morning was terrible.

The ground crew assembled at 4.30 a.m. for breakfast, with the howling wind and rain buffeting the base. This, combined with a dull grey breakfast, worked on the men's tension. Eventually the Dakota, or 'Mother Hen' as it had been christened, took off at quarter to nine, disappearing into the soggy, grey cloud. Then, one by one the Spitfires were started and took off in their sections.

After a very eventful first day battling through the challenging winter weather, at quarter past four that afternoon the last of the Spitfires eventually arrived at the town of Istres just outside Marseilles. Fortunately, everyone had made it to Istres, but in at least a few instances it was just by luck.

The next day was even worse. At 5.30 a.m. when the men got up there was a nasty cold wind blowing and solid grey cloud overhead. Their orders clearly

12 Correspondence, documents and personal notes provided by Dicky Bradshaw, Harare, December 1999.

stated that 'generally conditions of 3/8 cloud (or better) must be obtained over a route, before a decision to depart is made.'[13] But no-one was keen on further delay, so Ted played the 'generally' card. Take-off was difficult, but about fifteen minutes after crossing the Mediterranean coastline, the clouds began breaking up, to the relief of the pilots. The sea beneath them was a cold steel grey. It reminded Jack how his old DV-M always used to get 'auto-rough' whenever he flew over the sea.

Suddenly Jack was snapped out of his nostalgia with a real change in the engine-tone of his Spitfire. He listened intently. The engine seemed rougher with a worrying, spluttering undertone. It was all too familiar. Just before reaching the western tip of Sardinia Johnny Deall's radio stopped working, so Jack took over the lead of Blue Section. But his engine was running seriously rough punctuated with loud backfires and spluttering coughs. Numerous times it cut out altogether forcing Jack, with his two following aircraft through an endless oscillation of terrifying ascents and descents.

Commenting on Jack's experience over the Mediterranean John Moss, who was co-piloting the 'Mother Hen' Dakota at the time, said later, "Although Jack Malloch must since have notched up many close shaves, he is unlikely to forget the many thousands of feet lost in coaxing his engine back to life over the Mediterranean whilst beyond gliding range to Sardinia."[14]

Blue Section arrived at El Aouina on Tunisia's northern coast late and the rest of the crew had begun to worry. Jack reported his problem and the engineers discovered dirty petrol was the cause. Although his aircraft was the most contaminated many of the others were also bad. By mid-afternoon most of the aircraft had been cleaned and were being put back together so they decided to try and make their 4 p.m. take-off. By quarter to four the Spitfires were being frantically refueled and 'Bundu Red' was strapping in for a hasty departure. But a couple of the aircraft had trouble starting. Within twenty minutes Red and Yellow Sections were airborne, except for Charles Paxton who was busy eating his way through his stock of starter cartridges.

Eventually it was almost twenty minutes past four by the time the three Spitfires

13 'Special Orders for Ferry Pilots' appendix 'D' to Southern Rhodesian Air Force Commanding Officer No. 2/51.

14 'Spit Epic' article written by Group Captain J. P. Moss.

of 'Bundu Blue' took off, orbiting the airfield as a large crowd tried to get Charles and his Spitfire started. Eventually Johnny ordered Dave Barbour back down to help, or at least to stay with Charles, whilst Johnny and Jack sped off. As Dave shut-down his aircraft Charles burst into life. They too made a hasty take off and tried to catch up with Johnny and Jack. They had more than three hundred nautical miles to cover and less than eighty minutes to do it in. In the end it was deep twilight by the time Jack nursed his temperamental aircraft down onto the darkened airfield at Castel Benito just a few miles inland from the city of Tripoli.

Although everyone landed safely, it had not been a good day. After a quick supper the Dakota ground crew got to work on the aircraft. Jack's aircraft needed to have its plugs changed and more dirt taken out of the filters. It was almost three o'clock in the morning by the time the ground engineers were finished, and of course Jack worked with them all the way through.

Due to his lack of sleep the next day didn't get off to a good start. According to Dicky Bradshaw, "Jack who had earned much praise for fearlessly launching himself into the innards of his engine the previous evening, promptly dirtied his slate by taxiing off with bags of confidence – and his pitot cover still on."[15] It was a dangerous mistake and Jack vowed to never skip his pre-flight checks again.

The plan was to fly from Castel Benito to El Adem for lunch and on to Fayid in the Canal Zone east of Cairo for the night. Flying time to El Adem was just under two and a half hours and that went well. But the desert base was extremely hot and taking off again proved to be almost impossible. Several of the stubborn aircraft refused to start ending up hazed in billowing smoke from the numerous starter cartridges that were piling up next to them. Jack was amazed at the scene and knew that there had to be a better technique for these 'hot starts'. By the time it was 'Bundu Blue's' turn the air was a chocking orange, heavily laced with desert dust, cordite and confusion. The disastrous hot afternoon start at El Adem, which consumed literally hundreds of valuable starter cartridges, became known as 'the duck shooting expedition'.[16]

After several attempts Jack was able to start and get into the air, but his two

15 Documents and notes provided by Dicky Bradshaw, Harare, December 1999.
16 Interview with Dicky Bradshaw, Harare, December 1999.

colleagues in Blue section had no luck at all and eventually had to abort. Jack, now with just his individual call-sign of 'Mozz-C' was instructed to head-off alone. By the time he landed at Fayid on the edge of the 'Great Bitter Lake' it was pitch dark. Sitting on his dinghy pack with his seat fully lowered it was difficult enough to see the dimly-lit flight instruments never mind the hastily assembled flare-path. Luckily Jack was a better pilot than most.

Next morning the two delayed Spitfires took off very early while it was relatively cool and caught up with the rest of the squadron for a late breakfast. They were just under halfway and as there were good RAF facilities at the base the decision was made to spend the day at Fayid so the aircraft could be properly serviced. Jack worked on the aircraft while the rest of the pilots tried to catch up on sleep.

As their next take off was scheduled for 6 a.m. it was decided that the flight briefing should be held the evening before. Jack addressed the assembled crew explaining why he thought they had had trouble in El Adem. His recommendation for 'hot starts' was to put the cut-out in the full back position, the booster pump on and have the engine fully primed, no matter how hot it was. This was in contrast to the way the men had been instructed, but it worked. This certainly boosted the men's respect of Jack's technical capabilities.[17]

The next morning, with the cool air and Jack's new starting technique all the Spitfires started perfectly. Flying time to Wadi Halfa was two hours and twenty-five minutes and it was just after twenty minutes to nine when Jack's 'Bundu Blue' section landed.[18] After refueling, their hot start went well and by ten-thirty all the aircraft were back in the air. Although nothing was said the men realised that Jack obviously knew more about the nuances of aircraft engines than both the RAF instructors and the technicians.[19]

The day ended in Khartoum where they arrived in time for a late lunch. Then Jack and the ground crew fussed over the fighters again. They were worried about the next leg which was the longest of the entire ferry and would take the Spitfires dangerously close to their limit. As there was no suitable halfway stop all eleven Spitfires would have to make the six hundred and fifty nautical mile

17 Interview with Dicky Bradshaw, Harare, December 1999.
18 Jack Malloch's personal flying logbook.
19 Interview with Dicky Bradshaw, Harare, December 1999.

hop to Juba in southern Sudan in one go.

After a few minor challenges by six-thirty the next morning all the aircraft were airborne and on their way. Contrary to expectations, and with just a bit of navigation drama, everyone made it to Juba.

The next leg was due south to Entebbe in Uganda. Again, starting went better than expected, but Ozzie Penten had a serious glycol leak just as he took off. He managed to do a tight turn but before completing his circuit his engine died. With no power and hardly any altitude he hit the end of the runway hard, bouncing a few times before veering off the runway.[20]

It was decided that Yellow section should press on to Entebbe, but that Blue Section and the ground crew should remain in Juba to attempt the necessary repairs. Within an hour the technicians determined that the engine was completely cooked. At seven thirty on Tuesday morning, the three remaining aircraft of Blue Section, followed by 'Mother Hen' took off from Juba, leaving Ozzie's aircraft behind awaiting a new engine. Once they arrived in Entebbe the technicians, who had determined that a perished pipe had caused Ozzie's problem wanted to check the rubber pipes on all the aircraft. This delayed the ferry by another day.

On the morning of Wednesday 21st March it was raining at Entebbe. It was warm tropical rain that everyone appreciated after the sweltering heat of the Sahara. The plan was to fly to Tabora in Tanganyika and then after lunch, continue on to N'Dola in Northern Rhodesia's copperbelt. After a bit more drama involving another hasty emergency landing, all of the Spitfires were able to get airborne. As Jack climbed away from the airport, the sun broke the horizon and painted the rain, clouds and the lake glorious shades of pink and orange. He felt good. They were getting close to home.

The flight took Jack a mere ninety minutes and when he landed he found the entire population of Tabora at the airfield to welcome them. Tables of tea and cake were laid out in preparation for the pilots and everyone was very interested in how the ferry had gone. After lunch it was a 'hot start'. But Jack's technique worked and it wasn't long before they were all in the air again. It was just before 4 p.m. when Jack came into land at N'Dola. Although the runway was very narrow and edged

20 'Spit Epic' article written by Group Captain J. P. Moss.

with six-foot tall elephant grass, everyone managed to land safely.

It was a short overnight stay and the pilots were all back at the airport before dawn, excited to get home. This was to be the only leg of the entire trip where all the Spitfires were to fly together as a squadron with only a few hundred yards separating the three formations. When the Spitfires crossed the wide Zambezi River there was a ripple of congratulations over the radio. Over Inkomo the Spitfires formed section 'vees' for the final approach. By then the men knew there were going to be a lot of people to welcome them, including the Prime Minister himself. Cranborne was not the easiest aerodrome to land at, which added to the pilots' tension. The last thing any of them wanted to do was to crash one of the PM's new aircraft right in front of him.[21]

The Spitfires arrived just before ten o'clock in the morning. In close formation they roared over the aerodrome at a full three hundred miles per hour.[22] They had made it. The most ambitious aircraft ferry ever undertaken had been done with no casualties and just one aircraft short. In time that aircraft was repaired and delivered as well, making it a one hundred percent success, in a third of the estimated time.

In his speech the Prime Minister said, "I must thank you for putting up such a fine show. The R.A.F. said you would be lucky if you managed to bring six Spitfires. You have brought ten. This result has been due to the skill of both pilots and engineering staff."[23] Then there were some official photographs for the press, after which Jack was reunited with Zoe and his parents who were all there waiting for him.

On the day the Spitfire Ferry arrived in Salisbury the Americans bombed bridges north of the Korean city of Chunchon, the last major communist base south of the 38th parallel. Now that the Southern Rhodesian Air Force had their new fighters, it was likely that they too would be heading off to war to fulfil their U.N. obligations.

But the greatest danger Jack was to face over the next few months was not combat, but aerobatics...

21 Documents and notes provided by Dicky Bradshaw, Harare, December 1999.
22 Jack Malloch's personal flying logbook.
23 The Rhodesian Herald, Friday March 23, 1951.

CHAPTER 5

Fish Air and Hunting Clan – Discovering Paradise: 1951 to 1960

Having got back from his six-week Spitfire ferry trip Jack spent the whole of April 1951 concentrating on his garage and trucking business, clearing the backlog and signing up a couple of new contracts. But he wasn't the only transport operator in Marandellas. His main competitor was Jamie Marshall. Jamie was also an ex-Royal Air Force pilot, so although they competed over transport contracts, Jack and Jamie had a lot in common and over time became good friends. In addition to his trucks, Jamie also had his own aircraft. It was a small two-seater Ercoupe and, much to Jack's envy, Jamie would fly it out of his own back garden.

By the beginning of May Jack decided to take up his Air Force duties again. Within a few days of Jack rejoining, the Auxiliary Air Force was invited to

Spitfire SR64 (formerly MK350) parked with a collection of Rhodesian Harvards. This was the Spitfire that Jack Malloch would eventually restore.
© *SRAF Photographic Section.*

participate in an air display at Thornhill. It was decided that two of the new Spitfires would be sent down, and Jack Malloch and Dave Barbour were asked to pilot them. Jack loved aerobatics but with the demands of his business he knew he wouldn't be able to get in any proper practice. Consequently Dave agreed to do a solo display, while Jack would just lead the formation flypast before and after the show.

About two-thirds of the way down to Gwelo Dave's cockpit suddenly filled with blinding acrid smoke. Strangely, it cleared almost as quickly as it appeared. Apart from being seriously shaken, there was no sign of fire so they continued, getting the ground crew to carefully check the aircraft before the afternoon display. No fault was found.

With a fair degree of consternation, it was decided that they would proceed as planned. Their first fly-by was perfect. They then turned to their holding point where Dave quickly positioned himself for his display. But suddenly Dave noticed that his cockpit lights were fading. He clicked on his radio to warn Jack, but his radio was dead too. Dave continued his orbiting circuit while he checked his control and engine responses. Everything else seemed fine, so he decided to proceed with the show.[1]

But Jack was worried. Dave was taking far too long to set off on his display run. Jack tried to raise Dave on the radio. There was no reply which confirmed his worst fears. At that moment Air Traffic Control crackled in Jack's headphones;

"We are waiting for your display but can't raise Spitfire Two. Program is running late. Spitfire One you must take over the show and must start immediately!"

"Roger" Jack confirmed and immediately pulled to starboard accelerating away. Behind him Dave also sped off.

As Jack hadn't practiced any routine he was annoyed that Dave had dropped out. With nothing prepared he decided to do a series of fast low level 'beat-ups' which he knew wouldn't require much precision but would give the crowd a good blast of adrenalin. After four or five extremely low dives over the audience he reckoned his eight minutes was up. He tried to raise Dave on the radio again to organise their final formation fly-past but there was no reply. It seemed that Dave had disappeared altogether. He returned for a low pass, flying low and

1 David Barbour's written notes and recollections.

slow down the length of Thornhill's runway for the crowd to get a good view of the aircraft.

Dave didn't know where Jack was either. In the middle of his display while he was doing a low inverted run, he saw Jack flash past at right angles – right underneath him. He was angry and presumed that Jack had thought his display was so bad that he had joined in to try and save it. Eventually the two Spitfires found each other and landed together parking in front of the crowd.

Simultaneously Dave and Jack both pushed open their cockpit canopies. Jack shouted across at Dave demanding why he had chickened-out. Dave was livid and shouted back, "...And what the hell do you think you were doing?" Fortunately, with the noise of the other aircraft the audience didn't hear the exchange.

During the lowering of the flag ceremony with tense whispers between their clenched teeth Jack and Dave realised to their horror that they had both done independent displays completely oblivious of each other. The Officer Commanding and the entire audience kept congratulating them on such a daring display that involved numerous near misses. Everyone presumed that it had been a carefully rehearsed dare-devil routine that had thoroughly thrilled the audience. Realising what had happened, the two bewildered pilots just smiled and accepted the compliments, grateful to be alive.[2]

In early July 1951 Jack and Zoe invited Jamie and Dorothy Marshall over for dinner. After dinner, being mid-winter, they settled down to chat in front of the crackling fire. They always avoided talking about their respective transport businesses. Instead the conversation somehow got onto the topic of fish. Dorothy lamented the sorry state of what little fish they could get in Marandellas. The husbands joined in the conversation and being 'air minded' suggested that fresh fish could be flown into the country.

Jack was enthralled by the idea. It was the perfect business just waiting to be exploited. He suggested that they fly fish in from Luanda. Jamie took out an atlas. Looking at the distances, he suggested Beira in Portuguese East Africa instead. For the rest of the evening they discussed the logistics, costs and possible profit of such a venture. Zoe and Dorothy didn't take it too seriously, but the

2 'Recollections of the Southern Rhodesian Auxiliary Air Force' by David Barbour.

two men were consumed by the opportunity. A day or two later Jack and Jamie met again, broadening the idea into a general air freight and charter business.[3] After another week of careful consideration Jack took Zoe aside and asked her if she would consider allowing him to go into a flying business with Jamie. Zoe told Jack that she would always support him in whatever he did and that if he wanted to fly, no matter what the risks might be, she wanted him to be happy and would never stand in his way. True to her word, Zoe always supported Jack in whatever he did.[4]

And so Jack and Jamie's air charter business was born. On August 1st, 1951 Jack had his first paying flight. It was to take a passenger from Marandellas to Fort Victoria and back.[5] Jack felt on top of the world. But his euphoria was short-lived. The Southern Rhodesian Auxiliary Air Force Squadron was put on stand-by to go to Korea. With his own flying business at last looking like a reality, this news, which would have excited him two months earlier, was now the last thing that he needed.

As the small two-seater Ercoupe couldn't carry much more than one passenger and two fish it was clear that they needed to get a bigger aircraft. At the end of August the two entrepreneurs purchase a four-seater Fairchild Argus. Although it was a 1944 model the aircraft was a brand new 'crated kit.' After six weeks of careful assembly it was ready and became the second aircraft in their 'fleet.' By the end of October 1951, thanks to the Air Force, Jack qualified on the twin-engined Rapide and had accumulated over forty hours of chartered flying-time. Though the spectre of war was hanging heavily over him, the business was off to a good start.

While Jack was spending a growing amount of time doing air charters, he was also picking up more trucking contracts. All he had to do was make his deliveries on time and the money was guaranteed. It seemed so easy. But there were plotters scheming against him and one morning in February 1952 soon after starting up and leaving their depot both of Jack's trucks mysteriously broke down. After a quick inspection it was clear that they had been sabotaged. Someone had put grinding paste into the fuel tanks and the engines had seized. It was a major

3 'The Inception of Fish Air', recollections by Jamie Marshall.
4 Interview with Alyson Dawson, Fish Hoek, May 2008.
5 Jack Malloch's personal flying logbook.

disaster. Yet Jack had contracts to fulfil and the penalty clauses meant that he had to hire in lorries which cost him dearly. Within just six weeks he was financially ruined and forced to liquidate his transport business completely.[6]

Faced with significant debts Jack's only hope was in the air charter business. Unfortunately though, apart from paying for his flying hours and conversions, the domestic charters were not enough to bring any real money in. If flying was going to be a viable alternative Jack felt that they needed to develop the business, and they needed to do it quickly. The immediate opportunity was their original idea of importing fresh fish.

A week later they loaded up the Fairchild and set off to the port city of Beira on the central Mozambican coast to see if they could actually find any fish. While the obligatory forms were being filled in they asked the Portuguese Customs officials if fish were caught in the area. The officials shook their heads, saying that all the fish sold in the city were flown in by a pilot by the name of Lionel da Silva.

As Lionel was due back with his next consignment Jack and Jamie decided to wait for him and about half an hour later a little plane landed. Walking over, Jack and Jamie introduced themselves and were pleasantly surprised to find that Lionel could speak fluent English. Lionel owned a small property with his own fishing nets at a place called Inhassoro, some one hundred and twenty miles south of Beira and said he would be happy to sell fish to the two Rhodesians. They discussed a price, then, having got directions, agreed to fly down to Lionel's fishing spot to collect their first consignment on their next trip. But first they needed to check what, if any, import and export permits would be required. After a long negotiation with the Portuguese customs officials it was decided that as long as the fish were classified as 'produce of the soil' there would be no need for any export licences.

The next morning they flew back to cool, comfortable Marandellas, taking a four gallon 'sample' tin of Lionel's fish back with them. That evening over a dinner of real fresh fish fried in batter, they discussed the opportunity. But first they need a name for the business. Someone suggested 'JM Air', using Jack and Jamie's common initials, but before the pile of fried fish had been finished

6 Interview with Blythe Kruger, Plettenberg Bay, January 1998.

the name was agreed, it was to be called 'Fish Air.'[7]

Towards the end of March 1952 the Fairchild was granted its Certificate of Airworthiness, and the very next day, after a few more charters in the Ercoupe, Jack and Jamie were back in Beira. They met with Lionel and over platters of piri-piri spiced prawns, discussed their planned trip down to Inhassoro the next morning. Jack had never had prawns before and a few hours later he realised that he was allergic to shellfish. He was violently ill for the rest of the night. Next morning, although still weak, he insisted that they stick to the schedule, although he curled up against the Perspex, groaning with every bit of turbulence.

Jamie flew a course out over a huge gently arched bay, noting, "...the route took us well out to sea, much to Jack's discomfort. He had a great objection to flying over the sea and was always convinced that he was going to have imminent engine failure over the water. I have no idea why. After about fifty minutes we suddenly saw the most beautiful coloured water that I have ever seen. It was every colour imaginable, and as the water was so clean and clear the sand underneath it appeared to be exposed."[8]

From that peninsula, which was known as Bartolomeu Diaz, they flew down the coast for another twenty-five miles before passing some high red cliffs and a little store near the beach.

Just beyond the store they saw a solitary windsock standing in an open patch of dried-out sand-vlei. That was Inhassoro. They made a couple of low passes to check the surface before making a careful landing. As they opened the cabin door a cool sea-breeze washed into the hot aircraft and the two men emerged, revitalised by the fresh air.

There was no sign of anyone as they walked down to the beach. Looking straight out over the calm blue sea they could see the long low outline of an island which was called Bazuruto. To the south, between Bazuruto and the mainland was another little island, which was called Santa Carolina. With the remarkable scenery and fresh air Jack had almost fully recovered.

About half an hour later they heard the sound of a battered old half-ton truck

7 Interview with Chris Marshall, Cape Town, 2000 and Jamie Marshall's personal documents and papers provided by Chris Marshall.

8 'The Inception of Fish Air', recollections by Jamie Marshall.

coming down the beach. It squealed to a halt and a burly figure climbed out. Jack and Jamie greeted the tanned European in their best Portuguese, but to their surprise he spoke English and was, in fact, German. He introduced himself as Irvin von Elling. Irvin, who seemed to be in his late thirties, knew everything about the area, and certainly seemed to have been there for a long time.

How would a German ever get to discover such a remote place as this, Jack thought to himself. Apart from the idyllic beaches which were only used for a bit of fishing, there didn't seem to be any commercial activity at all. With his curiosity getting the better of him Jack asked what Irvin was doing in Inhassoro. Irvin considered the question for a moment. He said that he was researching the potential for commercial fishing in the area. Before the conversation could go any further, a couple of African tribesmen appeared out of the line of coconut palms and approached the vehicle. Irvin quickly changed the subject announcing that Lionel would be landing soon so they needed to prepare the fish that where in the back of his truck.

Once the fish had been gutted and packed Irvin suggested that Jack and Jamie go with him to the store to meet the owner John Portella. The three men piled into the front of the truck and Ivrin accelerated away down the beach. The sand was firm and flat making it a perfect speedway. With a smile on his face Irvin flattened the accelerator exhilarating his awed passengers. With the azure sea to their right, blue sky overhead and the line of green palms flashing past on their left, it was an experience Jack and Jamie would often repeat.

After a while Lionel arrived and convinced their two new friends to stay the night and take their first consignment back the next day. The idea was to see how the cargo, which would be caught fresh in the morning, would travel. The test was going to be a large fish-feast for all their friends to determine the viability of the business. Just as Jack had anticipated, there was a lot of interest, so in mid-April he set off to Inhassoro to collect their first commercial consignment, mostly ordered by their friends who had attended the 'research' dinner.

The next morning after the fish had been prepared John and Lionel helped load as many as they could into the little aircraft. Jack paid for them and headed home. To explore the quickest route Jack flew directly from Inhassoro to Grand Reef. It was a long flight taking almost three hours and Jack was already on his

Jack and Jamie's Rapide on its way to the coast.
Picture from Jack Malloch's private collection. © Greg Malloch.

fuel reserve by the time he landed. He cleared customs, refueled and just an hour later touched down in Marandellas. By the end of the afternoon they had delivered all the fish to their various customers. It was a good feeling having made their first delivery. But they had learnt a few lessons. The main one was that even the Fairchild was too slow and small to be viable for cargo work. Again, Fish Air needed a bigger aircraft.

Jack and Jamie were interested in getting a De Havilland Rapide. Although it was a biplane it was twice as big as the Fairchild, and better still, Jack had recently qualified on the aircraft so there would be no cost of conversion and training. At the end of April they bought an old DH89 Rapide from Central African Airways. It was registered as VP-YDF which they christened 'Dog Fox'. Less than a month later Jack took it on its first flight to Inhassoro. The Rapide did the trip in half the time. Jack was a bit worried about how the bigger plane would handle the rough landing strip but it had no trouble at all. In-fact seeing how sturdy the aircraft was Jack suggested to Jamie that it would probably be able to land on the beach itself. It was a temptation and wasn't long before they tried it out.

After two nights camping on the beach waiting for the full consignment, Jack and Jamie made their deliveries, and the customers were pleased. The fish was good, fresh and affordable. Quickly the commercial orders started picking up. In June Jack did three more flights, the last of which he managed to do, including the delivery of the fish in Salisbury, all in just one day.[9] It was more than seven hours flying, but it showed that it was possible and it made a big difference to the profitability of the flights. There was a degree of physical discomfort to these flights though. As the aircraft did not have any refrigeration capability to keep the fish chilled they had to fly at the highest possible altitude. This meant that Jack and Jamie had to don their thickest winter jackets before they took off from the sweltering humid coast.[10]

In addition to the Inhassoro shuttle Jack continued to fly charters, and even started catching up on his Air Force flying. But his main focus was on the fish and the orders were rolling in from the restaurants and hotels across Salisbury. It was a hectic, demanding schedule that meant many days, nights and week-ends away from home. To make up for it on a couple of the overnight trips Jack and Jamie took their wives along and soon the stories of their adventures in paradise spread. Everyone they knew wanted to come along to see the place as well. With the extra space in the Rapide they could take passengers, but accommodation was a challenge as there was nothing at Inhassoro. So, they decided to build some.

There was a grove of shady coconut palms just beyond the sand dunes south of John's store which was an ideal setting for some rustic palm-thatched chalets. They also flew on to Vilanculos about twenty miles south and found some possible accommodation options there as well. The best was 'Alves Hotel', which was a big square whitewashed building in the middle of the village. It was owned by a flamboyant Portuguese, Joaquim Alves. Joaquim, who could speak English very well, and seemed to know Irvin von Elling even better, was more than happy to help Jack and Jamie with accommodation in Vilanculos. He was also prepared to build chalets for them at Inhassoro.

Jack was surprised to learn that, amongst other things, Joaquim was the local Shell Oil agent.

Considering that there were just a few rusty old vehicles in the area Jack asked what market there was for Shell products. Joachim admitted that there wasn't much business for him now, unlike back in the Second World War.

9 Jack Malloch's personal flying logbook entries.

10 Personal correspondence with Geoff Cartwright dated December 7, 2009.

The long low strip of Santa Carolina island, basking just a couple of kilometres off the Inhassoro beach.

Picture from Jack Malloch's private collection. © Greg Malloch.

Apparently with the German U-boats sinking so many cargo ships off the coast Joachim began to find scores of sealed fuel drums washing up on the beach. He contacted the Shell office in the capital city Lourenco Marques to see if they would be prepared to buy the fuel back from him. With the vast distance and lack of roads Shell were uninterested. But they did agree to appoint Alves as a dealer which would enable him to sell off his findings. During the course of the War, from his remote, inaccessible beach store, Alves sold all of the fuel he had salvaged, and he regularly ordered more from the Shell depot in Lourenco Marques. It was a very profitable business.[11]

Jack couldn't imagine who Alves would have been selling to, considering his immediate clientele lived in grass huts and fished out of dug-out canoes with no currency trade except fresh fish and seashells. Jack also knew that the nearest resupply of fuel for the U-boat wolfpack would have been Europe or Japan…

With regards to their accommodation needs Jamie felt that either Vilanculos or Inhassoro would work, yet Jack was fascinated by the islands, particularly Santa Carolina which he had visited on a couple of his fishing trips. Covered with coconut palms and mangrove forest it had wide golden beaches and a little lagoon surrounded by rich coral reefs. The island was about two miles in length and on its eastern tip a rocky outcrop rose several metres above sea level looking out across the sparkling Indian Ocean. On the huge weather-worn granite boulders Jack found ancient Portuguese inscriptions carved deeply into the rock. The engravings were arranged around a large medieval cross and the

11 Interview with Chris Marshall, Cape Town, January 1999.

Margaret Geddes and her two boys setting off on their 'castaway' island holiday in 1952. They were Fish Air's first holiday-making passengers.

Picture provided by Guy Geddes. © Guy Geddes.

points of the compass. It was a perfect story-book tropical paradise, with all the 'Treasure Island' charm and mystery that you could hope for. Best of all it was just a short boat-ride away and was completely deserted.

Before building the chalets, Jack and Jamie had only taken their friends and family to Mozambique, concentrating instead on importing fish to cover their costs. But it wasn't long before one of the ground hostesses at Salisbury airport Margaret Geddes got to hear the stories of the unspoilt beaches that they had discovered. She asked Jack what the options would be for her and her two young boys to spend a few weeks camping there. Jack recommended Santa Carolina and worked out a good price for the trip. The 'holiday' business was beginning to look viable as well.

A 560 pound Rock Cod that Joachim Alves had Jack deliver to the Nuns at St. Anne's Hospital in Salisbury in appreciation of the treatment they had given him.

Picture provided by Geoff Cartwright. © The Rhodesian Herald.

Margaret's son Guy, who was just a young boy at the time, described their stay on the island; "The temperature averaged thirty degrees Celsius

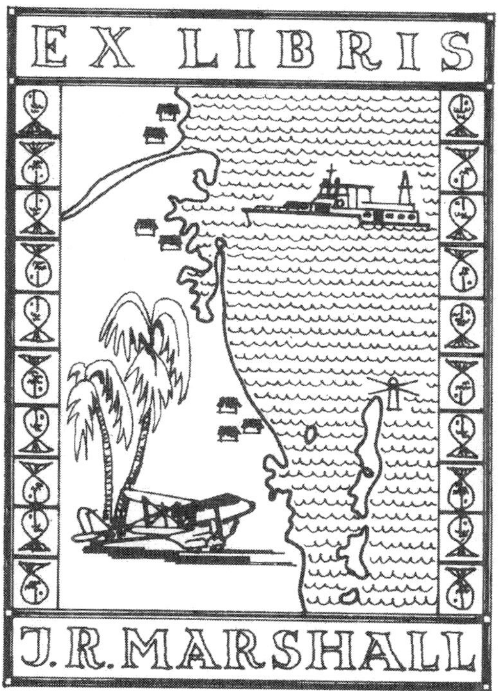

A bookplate illustrated by Jamie Marshall showing the Rapide at Inhassoro and the islands of Bazaruto and Santa Carolina.

Provided by Chris Marshall.
© Chris Marshall.

every day and we spent our days swimming, fishing and collecting coconuts. I supplied all the fish. The abundance was amazing. I sat on the coral reef and watched them investigate the hook. Our main diet was the beautiful turquoise coloured Parrot Fish. They were fantastic eating."

A few weeks later the Rhodesian Herald ran an article about Margaret and her adventures on Santa Carolina, describing her as 'Mrs. Robinson Crusoe'.[12] The article mentioned Jack's Fish Air service and suddenly they were inundated with people wanting exotic beach holidays. Almost overnight Jack and Jamie had enough potential business to fill the chalets they were planning to build. Jack quickly gave Alves the go-ahead to building the first of the chalets in a grassy grove overlooking the Inhassoro beach.

On December 13th, 1952, a day before her twenty second birthday, Jack's sister Blythe gave birth to her first child. The baby boy was Vic and Rita's first grandchild and made Jack an uncle. The whole family was overjoyed. He was christened John Edward Kruger. Although this was a positive ending to 1952, it had been a tough year for Jack. He had lost his transport business and was still in debt. Although on the positive side he had re-established himself as a well-respected Air Force pilot and had managed to set up an air charter business. All in all he was happy, loved his job and was optimistic about the future.

12 Personal correspondence with Guy Geddes, January 27, 2009.

For the Christmas holidays Jamie took the Fairchild with his family for a few weeks to Inhassoro, while Jack took the Ercoupe to Fort Victoria for his week off. Just after New Year Jack got a phone call from Lionel. It was the first time Lionel had ever called so Jack knew it was serious. Apparently, Jamie had landed on a tiny sandbank to buy prawns from the local fishermen, but he had got stuck and damaged the propeller. The spring tide was now coming in and was likely to sweep the aeroplane away. It needed urgent rescuing.

There was no way that Jack could find an aeroplane propeller in Marandellas so Blythe had to go hunting for it in Salisbury. As the Fairchild needed a variable pitch propeller it wasn't an easy task. But, by the end of the day Jack's sister had in her possession the huge polished wooden blade. Early the next morning, this time in the Rapide, Jack, Ted, Blythe and the baby, along with the vital spare part, all headed off to Inhassoro as quickly as they could. As soon as they arrived Jamie swopped places with Blythe and within minutes the men took off again, heading for the distant sandbank.[13]

It was almost fully low tide when Jack found the sandbar with the forlorn Fairchild perched on it. Jack made several low passes to gauge whether he could land or not. The Rapide was heavier than the Fairchild and the last thing they needed was to lose both aircraft. Jack came in slow, touching down as close to the far edge of the sandbank as possible, giving himself as much take-off space as he could.

Apart from the broken propeller and the crippling smell of rotten prawns, the Fairchild seemed fine. The new propeller fitted, but for some reason the retaining bolts that held it in place were short and where only able to grip with a couple of turns. It would be dangerous to fly. But the tide had turned and they needed to go.

Jamie started the Fairchild and the engine kicked into life first time. Starting from the firm sand, Jamie was able to make a perfect take-off. The tide was coming in quickly, and with each wave, the foam-edged waterline was getting closer and closer to the Rapide. Holding down the brakes Jack build up the revs before letting the big biplane surge forward. With just metres to spare he was able to pull it up off the dwindling sandbar.

---

13 Interview with Ted and Blythe Kruger, Plettenberg Bay, January 1998.

Once they were all safely back home the propeller was properly secured by the aviation engineers at Salisbury airport ready for the next fish run.[14] After the drama of rescuing the Fairchild Jack and Jamie had a little less appetite for tempting their luck with any more recklessness – at least for a while.

The first three months of 1953 were busy for Fish Air with holiday and fish flights along with local charters around the country. By April the memory of the 'sandbar incident' had faded and the recklessness started creeping back.

As the numbers of passengers to Inhassoro, Vilanculos and Santa Carolina increased, so Jack's flying instincts sharpened. According to one of his regular passengers, "Jack had phenomenal eyesight and from the height of thousands of feet could identify wind direction by watching the waving grass far below."[15]

Jack and Jamie also worked on improving the experience for their guests. Over the Pungwe flats they would swoop down low over the vast herds of animals that roamed the rich grasslands, as one of their impressionable passengers recalled; "The flight was fun because at times the two Rapides joined up in formation. After crossing the mountains at Umtali Jack stuck his head around the panel behind him and yelled 'Hey... wanna see the game?' We all beamed as the aircraft buzzed buffalo, wildebeest and other animals in their thousands."[16]

South of Beira they would then fly high to show off the amazing colours of the water. On the pristine sand north of Inhassoro the local fishermen would pull their nets up onto the beach. Jamie got into the habit of coming in low over the heads of the tribesmen, who would inevitably dive down onto the sand. It seemed like harmless fun until one day one of the fishermen fought back…

That particular day Jamie was flying in a honeymoon couple who were going to spend a couple of weeks in the new chalets at Vilanculos. They were flying in the Rapide and following his usual routine, Jamie accelerated down upon the fishermen who flung themselves down onto the sand. All except one. That man stood up facing Jamie. He detached his pole from the end of the rope and hurled it up as the Rapide flashed overhead. To Jamie's horror there was a loud thump as the pole skewered into the belly of the aircraft.

---

14 Personal correspondence with Blythe Kruger, May 7, 2008.
15 Personal correspondence with Eddie Blackwell, July 6, 2020.
16 Personal correspondence with Nigel Rittey, March 25 2003.

Immediately Jamie realised that the controls had jammed. Fortunately he was flying straight and level, and although his passengers didn't realise that the aircraft had been critically damaged, Jamie certainly did. Once again, he chastised himself for his irresponsibility and cut back on the power to gently glide into the sandy airstrip at Inhassoro. Miraculously they were lined up perfectly for the slow gentle decent.

Within minutes Irvin von Elling arrived in his battered truck to see what had happened. After a quick inspection they discovered that the makeshift harpoon had hit a point of the mainplane where the aileron wires passed under the floorboards. This had jammed the vital controls. Once they had removed the intrusive pole the aileron seemed to work perfectly again. After closing up the puncture wound with some flattened corrugated iron sheeting the tough old Rapide was back in service.[17]

It was a good lesson though. Jamie never 'buzzed' the fishermen again and both Jamie and Jack realised that their good fortune wouldn't last with any more recklessness. While Jack always liked to fly beyond the envelope, from that incident onwards he no longer risked sheer foolishness.

With the increasing numbers of tourists arriving in the area Joaquim Alves expanded his hotel business into boat hire, camping trips and deep-sea fishing, all of which did well. In-fact to help keep up with the demand Jack and Jamie also decided to buy their own boat. It was large with a comfortable inner deck and a broad open back which was ideal for fishing. Best of all it could be paid off by their clients. Although Jack wasn't a fanatical fisherman he enjoyed catching and eating fresh fish, and the seas off the central Mozambique coast were very rich and unexploited. Jack's best catch off the back of their boat was a four hundred pound grouper. Although impressive, a fish of that size in the 1950s was by no means unique.

In early May 1953 Jack and Jamie bought a second Rapide and to keep it busy decided it was time to get some media promotion. They couldn't afford advertising, but they remembered how much business the 'Mrs. Robinson Crusoe' article had generated, so they decided to go the editorial route. They

---

17 Interview with Chris Marshall, Cape Town, 2000 and Jamie Marshall's personal documents and papers provided by Chris Marshall.

Jack (in his captain's cap) with the Marshall's and other guests christening their new boat. To the right are Irvin von Elling and his wife, Joaquim Alves, Lionel da Silva and John Portella.

Picture from Jack Malloch's private collection. © Greg Malloch.

went to Salisbury to see the editor of the Sunday Mail and proposed that the newspaper send a reporter to Santa Carolina to "write the island up." Less than a week later, journalist Flash Seaton and his photographer were in Jack's Rapide heading to Inhassoro.

They took the cabin cruiser out to Santa Carolina, fishing along the way. According to Flash, "...we landed on the silvery shore, beneath the waving palms, and immediately put up the tent which was to be our home as we braved the mysteries of the island. They were lovely days, in which we walked and ate and slept, then walked again, then slept again, then opened the bottle for an evening chat around the camp fire, with the endless expanse of the Indian Ocean, stretching away for literally thousands of miles beneath the fabulous African night sky."

Back in Salisbury he recalled the mysterious old ruins, the shimmering ocean and the pink flamingoes of the Bazaruto spit. His final article started with the words, "This is Paradise Island..." and it enthralled the Rhodesian public. Business boomed and everyone wanted to fly to paradise. Fish Air quickly

The Fish Air chalets that Jack and Joachim built on the Inhassoro beach.
Jack's first palm frond hut that he built on Paradise Island is inset.
Inhassoro picture © Greg Malloch. Paradise Island picture © Blythe Kruger.

evolved into a passenger charter airline, eventually dropping the fish altogether. For Alves it was a boon and he was able to invest in more boats and equipment. The tourism market had been established and the name 'Paradise Island' stuck.[18]

Several years later Flash Seaton paid another visit to Paradise Island. By then a smart new hotel and a scattering of beautifully appointed chalets had been built among the palm trees. But as he wrote, "It was still the Paradise Island I had known and loved when I first saw it – an ocean refuge with no roads, no cars, no telephones, no shops... nothing but the sea and the wind and the palms."

"But people had started to take an interest in Paradise Island and some of the old stories were coming to light – stories of the convicts who lived in the old settlement; of those who tried to swim to the mainland and were snatched by sharks; of the governor's daughter who fell in love with a prisoner and made away with him in an improvised boat… Then there were the strange stories of the World War Two epic of a U-boat which lurked in the offing between Santa Carolina and the island of Bazaruto, waiting for signals from the neutral Portuguese who (they have since denied it) were standing by to supply her…"

18 'How I named Paradise Island' by Flash Seaton, published by the Sunday Mail.

The large deep-sea fishing vessel 'Santa Carolina' owned by Joaquim Alves.
Picture from Jack Malloch's private collection. © Greg Malloch.

Jack had also heard the stories of the German U-boat and had drawn his own conclusions about his friends Irvin and Joachim. But for Jack the past was the past and there was nothing to be gained in digging up secrets. He never spoke of how Irvin and Joachim had met, who Joachim was selling all his fuel to during the War, or why Irvin knew so much about the remote waterways around the Mozambican islands. Or why there were old German navy lifejackets hidden deep in the back of Joachim's storeroom.[19] They were his friends, and Jack strongly believed that secrets were sacrosanct.

To try and keep up with the increased passenger demands Jack and Jamie found themselves having to fly a hectic schedule of shuttles in and out of Inhassoro and Vilanculos in their two Rapides. With each passenger paying the princely sum of twenty pounds per return trip[20], it was good, fun business. But Jack still had his Air Force flying to do.

It had become the practice of the Auxiliary Squadron to meet every Friday evening for training lectures. In was in one of these sessions at the beginning of August 1953 that it was announced that the Auxiliary Squadron was to be disbanded. Jack and the rest of the men were stunned by the news. So much for going to Korea.

Jack did enjoy military flying though and he appreciated being able to train and

19 Personal correspondence with Geoff Cartwright, February 1, 2010.
20 Personal correspondence with Geoff Cartwright, December 7, 2009.

convert to new aircraft at the government's expense. But mostly he felt it was his patriotic duty to fly in the defence of his country. After a few months Jack spoke to his friends at Headquarters and in mid-November 1953 he received a commissioned rank in the Southern Rhodesian Air Force.

Although for the remainder of the year Jack didn't do any official flying at all. It was just as well, as Fish Air was now a full-time job. They had built up a fleet of light aircraft and were busy with holiday flights to the coast and a growing number of charters within the Federation of Rhodesia and Nyasaland. But cash-flow remained a constant problem. Jack was not a financial person and it was becoming obvious.

As to be expected there were also constant technical challenges. Ian Dixon, who was the aviation manager of Shell and who managed Jack's fuel account used Fish Air for all his business trips. But they didn't always go as planned. One day they were flying to the northwest of the country and about half an hour into the flight they had engine trouble. One of the cowlings had come loose and started flapping hard against the engine. Jack immediately shut it down. But the slapping of the metal was threatening to beat the whole engine apart. Calmly Jack spotted an open area of grassy 'vlei' between a couple of groves of trees down in the bush below. Slowing down as much as he could he came in low to check the dry marsh for any wildlife, tree stumps or anthills that could get in the way. Calculating their chances, he bounced the aircraft down onto the ground, stopping as quickly as he could.

Grabbing his toolkit Jack hopped out of the biplane, leaving Ian white and breathless in the dusty co-pilot seat. It appeared that the nuts that held the cowling in place had not been tightened properly and had come off. Jack removed every fourth one from the other engine panels to secure the loose one. Then, with a confident smile he restarted the engines and accelerated away, taking off without as much as a bump.[21] Jack's only comment was that it was a lot easier than trying to take off from a soggy sandbar.

As stories like this started to circulate so Jack and his flying exploits began to gain legendary status.

This experience confirmed that the tough Rapides were definitely the most

21 Interview with Ian Dixon, Hillcrest, Durban, March 2004.

suitable aircraft in the Fish Air fleet so, in mid-June 1954, they bought another one. It was registered as VP-YLF, which they christened 'Love Fox'. Fish Air now had a fleet of six aircraft, but only two pilots. Jack and Jamie were becoming collectors and were losing sight of the cost of having unused aircraft sitting on the ground.

Reluctantly they decided it was time to start employing more pilots and to take their business beyond the little grass strip 'at the bottom of the garden'. Their first employee was a young pilot by the name of Gordon Brown. As the 'admin' pressure was building up, they also employed a young man by the name of Bob Nesbitt who ran the office and acted as loadmaster. With more pilots and planes, Fish Air established itself as a recognised domestic airline and its Mozambique routes became regular scheduled services.

Unfortunately though, with the success of the business, so too came personal tragedy. Blythe's twenty-fourth birthday was on Tuesday 14th December and in an extraordinarily cruel twist her son Edward, who had just turned two years old fell into a swimming pool and drowned. It was a devastating blow to the family and Ted and Blythe never really recovered from the terrible trauma. Once again, Christmas in the Malloch household was very sombre.

The end of 1954 also saw the end of the Rhodesian Mk. XXII Spitfires. The best seven were sold to Syria for two hundred Pounds each, while the remaining thirteen were scrapped. PK355, the Spitfire that Jack flew from the UK to Salisbury in the famous 1951 ferry was donated to the Military Museum, while PK350 was mounted on a plinth as a gate-guard at New Sarum Air Force base in Salisbury.

As Jack continued to grow his business in the opening months of 1955 Rhodesia's Central African Airways began to regard the operation as competitive. They worried about how quickly the little 'two-man' start-up had become an international service. Yet Jack wasn't content with just Mozambique. He was wanting to open up a route from Southern Africa all the way to the Far East. A lack of money or resources certainly never stopped the remarkable entrepreneur from thinking big, and it was this ability that often enabled him to achieve big things.

For this passenger service Jack considered hopping along the string of tropical islands that linked Southern Africa with the Far East. It would be an extremely

Spitfire PK350, registered in Rhodesia as SR64 mounted on a plinth at the entrance to New Sarum Air Force Base in Salisbury in the early 1970's.
© RhAF Photographic Section, New Sarum.

ambitious route, but as no-one else was going that way he knew he would have a monopoly. But he needed someone on the other side. He contacted, who he believed was the greatest aviation strategist in the Far East – the Famous leader of the Flying Tigers General Claire Lee Chennault himself. Although he was getting old, Chennault was interested enough in Jack's proposal to take a trip out to Rhodesia to discuss the idea with him in person. Chennault was impressed by how Jack had opened up Mozambique. But was worried about whether the much longer route to the Far East – halfway around the world – would be viable. In the end they parted company as friends and committed to keep in contact. Claire then took a commercial flight to the Comoros stopping over on the islands on his way home.[22] Ironically that would have been the first leg in Jack's proposed route.

As always, Jack's constraint was cash-flow. To solve this, he felt that if he could open up bigger routes he could make more money. The challenge was having

22 Personal correspondence between Alan Clements and Chris Whitehead, August 10, 2008.

the money to open up new routes in the first place. This problem was compounded by the amount of money they already owed, the biggest of which was their fuel account with Shell. Ian Dixon had been trying to keep the company off Jack's back for as long as possible, but their patience was running out. Fish Air also needed bigger aircraft. But the largest they could fly was the Rapide. Jack couldn't even fly a Dakota, and that was the absolute minimum for any long-distance service. It was clear that Jack would have to qualify on bigger commercial aircraft – and buy them.

As Jack was becoming more ambitious his partner was becoming less. Jamie Marshall had always enjoyed flying but already had his own well-established business which he did not want to compromise. Jack had lost his other business and wasn't content to just work the Mozambique route, especially with the growing debt hanging over their heads. In August 1955 the two partners started discussing the problem. Jamie was prepared to sell the business to Jack, but he didn't have the money to buy it. There was no immediate solution and Jack was becoming frustrated.

Then an interesting opportunity arose. The UK-based airline Hunting Clan wanted to increase their routes within Southern Africa. To get the local route licences that they needed they approached Jack and Jamie and offered to buy Fish Air along with all their licences, their aircraft and their established business.

Hunting Clan were also more than happy to keep Jack on. He was a well-known and reputable person and they wanted him to look after his old Fish Air routes. As they planned to service these routes with DC-3s Jack saw the opportunity to get the aircraft conversions that he was needing. It was a win-win for everyone, and in October 1955 the sale agreement was signed. It was a 'lock, stock and barrel' sale of all Fish Air's assets – and all its debt. As soon as the deal was signed Jack contacted Ian at Shell, along with all their other debtors and within a few weeks Fish Air's accounts were all paid in full.[23]

At the beginning of November the aircraft were transferred to Hunting Clan and Jack and the rest of his Fish Air staff started working for their new employers. Initially little changed, except for the addition of Kariba to their flying roster. It was the first time that Jack had been a salaried employee since he had left the

23 Interview with Ian Dixon, Hillcrest, Durban, March 2004.

Royal Air Force almost ten years earlier. He had less autonomy but was excited by the prospect of learning from a bigger established airline.

With the need for very early take-offs Jack and Zoe decided to move to Salisbury. They found a comfortable house on Alexander Drive. It wasn't big, but it suited their needs and most importantly it was close to Jack's work. Once they had moved in it didn't take long for Jack and Zoe to become friends with an English couple by the name of Alastair and Nan Wicks who lived next door. With his Harrow accent, impressive physique and short cropped hair, Jack was not surprised to learn that Alastair was a decorated career soldier. Although he was surprised to learn that Alastair was also a close friend of Hunting Clan's Managing Director.

Just before Christmas Jack and Zoe got the unexpected news that Zoe was pregnant. They could hardly contain themselves and although Jack was already thirty-five years old, the timing was good as now he had a salaried job that would guarantee their financial stability. They started to plan their new lives like a couple of excited newly-weds.

In early January 1956 Jack did his first Hunting Clan flight to Vilanculos. Joaquim Alves was pleased to see him again and had been worried about the lack of visitors over the Christmas holidays. Although it was a fast turn-around Jack was able to have a quick chat about how Hunting Clan planned to open up the tourism route with the much bigger Dakotas. Joaquim felt reassured and Jack was pleased to see his old friend again.

Over the next six weeks Jack racked up his flying hours on the Dakota and Hunting Clan was impressed with his flying ability and work ethic. By the end of February he had passed his Instrument Rating Flight Test, received his Flight Radio-Telephony Operator's Licence and his Rhodesia and Nyasaland 'Crew Members Certificate' as an airline pilot. Although Jack was flying a busy schedule, he was very pleased that he was getting the qualifications and experience that he needed to achieve his long-term ambitions.

With the growth of Hunting Clan and the demands on the pilots Jack averaged four hours of flying every single day in April, including weekends. This trend continued into May and June. The vast majority of these hours was in the Dakota, which was exactly what Jack wanted. But he still had his challenges.

In his June 'Captain's Confidential Report' Clive Halse noted, "Malloch is impressive... but not as an airline pilot. He is a 'bush' pilot in the best sense. He has a great deal to learn about dress, passenger handling, paperwork, navigation etc. However, he is loyal, hardworking and can be relied upon for almost anything." In the seven different fields that he was scored on, Jack was rated 'above average' on five of them.[24]

By late May, as Zoe was getting towards the end of her pregnancy Jack requested less flying duties, especially overnight trips. It was their first child and neither Jack nor Zoe really knew what to expect. Jack's sister Blythe had been christened 'Alison Blythe', and although she had never been called 'Alison', Jack had always liked the name and decided that if they were to have a girl they would name her Alison after his sister.

In mid-June the Doctor predicted that Zoe would give birth 'any minute', and sure enough by the end of Saturday 16th, she had given birth to a healthy baby girl. Although Zoe was to remain in hospital for almost a week there was much celebrating. Jack was overwhelmed and on Monday morning, with all the pride of a new father he registered the birth. Only later it was realised that in his excitement he had spelt the baby's name wrong, registering it as 'Alyson' instead of 'Alison' which was the spelling of Blythe's name.[25] So 'Alyson' she was, and right from the day she was born there was always an extremely close bond between her and her Father.

In mid-July Hunting Clan sent Jack and his old colleague John Aldridge to the U.K. to bring back another C-47 Dakota for their Rhodesian fleet. A fleet which had, so far, been led by a single DC-3. Their route back was familiar for Jack, going via Malta, Wadi Halfa and Khartoum, down to Entebbe and Ndola before finally landing back in Salisbury. But even with the second aircraft the workload continued to pile up. For the rest of 1956 Jack had almost daily flights to various destinations all over the Federation, as well as Beira, Vilanculos and Johannesburg. The hectic schedule continued right up until Christmas and Hunting Clan's year-end staff party. All the staff and their families were invited, including Zoe and baby Alyson. But there was no sign of Jack. Then

24 Personal papers and documents belonging to Clive Halse, provided by his son Chris Halse.
25 Interview with Blythe Kruger, Plettenberg Bay, South Africa. 1998.

A Hunting Clan Dakota being unloaded at Kariba before the runway was inundated by the rising flood waters.
Picture provided by Ian Dixon. © Ian Dixon.

shortly after the party started Jack's old Rapide 'Love Fox' landed and taxied up to the hanger. The aircraft's door swung open and to the excitement of the children Father Christmas himself stepped out in his bright red coat, long white beard and a huge sack of presents. Jack, being a stocky six-footer was a perfect Santa Claus.

Two days after Christmas Jack flew as First Officer with Captain Halse from Salisbury to Nairobi. In Clive's 'Confidential Report' he said that Jack was "... obviously a very competent light aircraft captain, and will be just the same on heavier types." He rated Jack's operational competence as 'average,' but noted that he would end up being above average.

Meanwhile, some two hundred miles north of Salisbury, construction of what was to become the world's largest hydro-electric dam continued at Kariba. Consequently there was a growing demand for flights to the work-site. But there were hardly any facilities there. The nearest landing-strip was a short grassy patch that had been designed for little single-seaters used for tsetse fly spraying. But once the dam project was started the strip was hastily extended. Hunting Clan got the contract to fly a planeload of engineers to Salisbury and back every weekend. It was a good contract with a guaranteed full flight.

Jack thoroughly enjoy this route and was able to watch the world's biggest dam wall taking shape. In addition to passengers he also carried supplies into the rapidly growing settlement including provisions and equipment for the construction project. But flying into Kariba was not for the faint-hearted. The temperatures would regularly soar above forty degrees Celsius and the winds coming off the escarpment could cause serious turbulence. Wildlife was also a problem and on many occasions Jack would have to 'buzz' the airfield to chase off the herds of grazing impala, kudu and elephant that blocked his landing.[26]

While Jack was still not qualified to captain the DC-3 he had done a couple of test flights as captain to rate his competency. The last was at the end of December 1956, and he was disappointed that he was still not granted captaincy. He was frustrated that things like 'dress' were holding him back. Surely, he rationalised, any passenger would prefer a competent pilot who maybe didn't tuck his shirt in, to a snazzy dresser who maybe didn't tuck his landing gear in!

Jack felt that Hunting Clan just had too many DC-3 captains. He felt that this was delaying his promotion as they didn't have a need for anymore. To get around this roadblock at the end of January 1957 Jack requested, and got, a posting to Head Office where he could become much more involved with the flight planning, organisation and management of the airline. These were aspects of the business that he definitely wanted to know more about to run his own airline.

During his time at Head Office Jack got to know Hunting Clan's Managing Director Tom Lawler very well. During the War Tom had served in the Royal Navy on HMS Magpie with Prince Philip. Consequently Tom was very well connected. Jack realised that these connections had a huge influence on Tom's business success, so he started building up his own network of connections. As Jack thought about who could be in his 'circle of influence' he kept coming back to his neighbour, Alistair Wicks. Alistair was clearly from the same privileged class, yet never spoke about his connections. In fact, everything about Alistair seemed shrouded in secrecy.

In July, after six months at Head Office Jack relinquishing his management job and happily took to the African skies again. After a few more months of intensive flying he had got most of the cobwebs out of his system and towards the end of August in his 'Captain's Confidential Report' Gordon Brown wrote, "I regard Jack Malloch very highly as an individual and as a pilot."[27]

While Jack had been at Head Office, Kariba airport had been upgraded. It had

26 Personal correspondence with John and Lyn Aldridge, November 6, 2008.
27 Personal papers and documents belonging to Clive Halse, provided by his son Chris Halse.

been given a reception building and a small air traffic control tower. With the improved runway it could now easily take the larger DC-3s which were needed to handle the passenger and freight demands. Along with every other Hunting Clan pilot, Jack was deployed onto this busy route. With the increased traffic Hunting Clan decided that they needed a full-time station manager at Kariba and Jack knew just the right person, his old friend Ian Dixon from Shell, who jumped at the opportunity.

With the rapid development of the Federation, Hunting Clan was opening up many new routes across Central Africa. Soon, in addition to Lusaka, they had secured regular flights to Ndola and Kitwe in the Copperbelt, Mongu in the west of the Federation and Fort Roseberry and Abercorn on the Tanganyika border. These destinations were all brought together with Hunting Clan's sweeping 'hop-on, hop-off' round-trip flights. With these further destinations by the beginning of September Jack had accumulated over four thousand hours on eleven different aircraft. More than half of these hours were on the Dakota, which he had been flying for less than two years.

By the end of 1957 Jack's flying schedule had become even more intense. In December he flew a total of almost ninety hours, being away from home every single Saturday and Sunday. He was lucky to be able to negotiate a mere three days off over Christmas.[28] But Jack was enjoying the flying and appreciated building up his hours. In-fact he was becoming a little over-confident – and his friend Reg picked it up in his six-monthly evaluation report, noting that Jack was "...a sound level-headed officer who should make a good captain." But then he noted that Jack tended "...to be slap-dash about detail and impatient of incompetence and experience."

There was huge agricultural potential in Rhodesia but managing and regulating the available water was a challenge. Dams were being built to sustain commercial irrigation projects, but the rain itself was unpredictable. It usually fell in violent afternoon thunderstorm which caused erosion, and the rainy season was short and prone to periods of drought. What the country really needed was a way to get the rain to fall where and when it was needed most. To achieve this, local scientists were exploring 'cloud seeding' in an attempt to artificially

28 Jack Malloch's personal flying logbook.

The modified cloud-seeding atomiser attached to the underside of Jack's old ex-Fish Air Rapide.

Picture from Jack Malloch's private collection. © Greg Malloch.

trigger rain from saturated clouds. Silver iodine seemed to be the most effective option, but the challenge was how to get it into the tops of the clouds as a fine aerosol to test whether it would work or not.

For this the Ministry of Agriculture needed a robust, easily modifiable aircraft and a courageous pilot to fly directly into storm clouds. Jack Malloch was the obvious man for the job. Jack was fascinated by the idea and without a second thought agreed to help. With Hunting Clan's permission, the scientists started modifying one of the old Rapides.

Over the weekend of 18th and 19th January 1958 Jack flew almost constantly from one cloud-top to the next as he tested the equipment. By the end all of his passengers were suffering from extreme air sickness. Jack, as always, was fine and they had gathered good data, learnt some lessons and knew what modifications needed to be made. By early afternoon on Tuesday 21st the new modifications were ready. This time the scientists brought along their motion-sickness pills – not that they helped in the turbulent, high altitude thunder-heads – much to Jack's amusement.

Jack Malloch making a low level pass to demonstrate the aerosol effect of the cloud-seeding equipment fitted to his Rapide as part of the cloudseeding experiments in January 1958.

Picture from Jack Malloch's private collection. © Greg Malloch.

The flight lasted just under three and a half hours, and again required considerable instrument flying as they darted in and out of the massive columned clouds. The equipment worked well, and by the time they landed the first clouds that they had seeded were raining hard. The next afternoon, after a few more modifications, Jack did another test flight for what had become known as the 'Rain Experiment'. He started with a low-level pass to demonstrate the equipment's 'misting' effect and then he successfully seeded a few more 'candidate' clouds. The equipment worked exactly as designed – and more rain fell.[29]

The University College scientists and ministry officials were very impressed with the results and unanimously agreed that 'cloud seeding' was indeed feasible. Jack returned to his Hunting Clan roster and was thanked for his remarkable piloting skills which certainly contributed to the success. The main thing that Jack learnt from the project was how to fly on instruments through storms and how to read turbulence in volatile, high level clouds, skills that would serve him well in the future.

In early 1958 Ian Dixon was transferred from Kariba to the Hunting Clan Head Office. Soon after arriving back in the capital he was inspecting the old Fish Air hanger with Hunting Clan's Managing Director. It was crammed with Jack's three Rapides, the couple of old Ansons and piles of rusting spare

29 Jack Malloch's personal flying logbook and 'Rain Experiment' records and photographs provided by Greg Malloch.

parts. Shaking his head Tom said, "Ian, there's no room in our hanger because it's full of all this crap. I think you should go down to Joburg and find a buyer for it all…" Ian didn't have the heart to tell Jack what Tom had said about his aircraft. But he was soon in the South African heartland trying to peddle the planes. Eventually he was able to sell all of them to Air Brousse, a subsidiary of Air Congo, for an incredible amount of twenty-five thousand Pounds. Ian felt so guilty at the price that he threw in free delivery.[30] So, in mid-June Jack was in the Congo making the delivery flight. It was to be Jack's last flight in 'Love Fox' and although he understood why the old planes had been sold-off he was sad to see them go.

By August 1958 Jack had qualified on the DC-3 and had gained his full licences, yet he seldom had command of the aircraft. All the Dakota pilots were now qualified captains, so command was usually given to the most senior crewman. This, and the fact that there had been no progress on his formal promotion to the position of captain gnawed on Jack's patience.

By the end of 1958 Jack had accumulated more than five thousand flying hours and was at last beginning to captain more flights. He was confident in his flying abilities and felt that at last he was achieving his own goals at Hunting Clan – getting real airline experience and qualifying on larger commercial aircraft. In his 'Captain's Confidential Report' at the end of December Gordon Brown rated Jack above average in six of the seven appraisal fields – with 'personal appearance' being the only one left that was still just average. At the end of January 1959 Hunting Clan's Chief Pilot also noted that Jack was "...a very steady and careful pilot."[31] Jack's reputation was strengthening.

Since establishing themselves at the end of 1955, Hunting Clan was also strengthening. According to Ian Dixon, "they were a very innovative and 'go-ahead' bunch. But we had a terrible feud with Central African Airways…" British Overseas Airways, who were also losing business to Hunting Clan, saw the opportunity to align with CAA and put a political stranglehold on Hunting Clan. Ultimately their strategy was to find a way of getting Hunting Clan's

30 Interview with Ian Dixon, Hillcrest, Durban, March 2004.
31 Personal papers and documents belonging to Clive Halse, provided by Chris Halse.

licences cancelled.[32]

Hunting Clan responded with a proposal to buy-out Central African Airways, pay off the debts and bring the national airline back to profitability. It was a sound business proposal, but one venomously opposed by the CAA management who feared for their jobs. Shortly after these negotiations started Hunting Clan's Managing Director was transferred to London and was replaced by Charles Meredith. Meredith, who had commanded the RAF Training Group during the Second World War, had retired as an Air Vice-Marshall. Sir Charles was also a close friend of Jack Malloch, and along with Alistair Wicks became part of Jack's growing 'circle of influence.'

As 1958 gave way to 1959 Jack was immersed in flying to every corner of the sprawling Federation. He loved the country, but the political situation was getting worse. In Nyasaland the level of unrest had forced the Federal government to declare a state of emergency. Rumours of rebellion and armed uprising spread across the country like wildfire. Yet the Federation wasn't the only place in Africa were trouble was brewing. In the Belgian Congo riots erupted leaving scores of people dead and several hundred injured. The volatile situation quickly became tribal and spread across the country as resentful communities took up arms against each other. There were street-battles in the towns and massacres in the rural areas. White settlers were caught in the middle and began evacuating as quickly as they could.

Fortunately, in the middle of this growing tension Jack and his friend Clive Halse were given a pleasant distraction. They were asked to fly a Dakota-load of London models with their manager and an extensive wardrobe to Victoria Falls for an exotic location fashion show and photo-shoot.

A few days later, on Wednesday 25th February, Jack flew into Blantyre, the capital of Nyasaland. Zoe was concerned about Jack's safety and told him to be careful. But the trouble hadn't just been contained to the northern territories of the Federation. On Thursday 26th a state of emergency was declared in Southern Rhodesia and the police and army quickly rounded up all known agitators across the country pre-empting any further organised unrest. In Nyasaland by the time

32 Interview with Ian Dixon, Hillcrest, Durban, March 2004 and personal correspondence, January 23, 2008.

Jack Malloch (on far left) with Clive Halse (centre) and a planeload of beauty queens in the regal grounds of the Victoria Falls Hotel in February 1959.
Picture provided by Chris Halse © Chris Halse.

the Emergency had been declared, a mob had taken over the border post with Tanganyika and had occupied the airport, blocking the runway to prevent reinforcements from being flown in. Insurrections were breaking out everywhere.

The police asked families living in isolated areas to move into Blantyre for protection, and women and children started to evacuate. On Sunday 1st March Jack flew two shuttles into Nyasaland, the first was into Lilongwe and the second into Blantyre. On each trip he was taking government officials and journalists in and refugees out. In the past Jack's passengers had always been happy, usually going off on a holiday of a lifetime. But these passengers were different. They mostly just sat staring ahead. The women were particularly afraid and huddled their children. Fear and anxiety hung heavy in the aircraft as many of them wondered if they would ever return to their homes again.

Pushed to the limit on the third of March 1959 the Federal Prime Minister sent in the army. The clamp-down quickly restored order and by the last week of March the soldiers were stood down and Jack was flying his troop shuttles again. On Tuesday 24th Jack did three trips to Nyasaland bringing back loads of fully equipped soldiers with each run. When he got back that night he had two letters on his desk waiting for him. The first was from Clive Halse officially confirming his promotion to Junior Captain and the second was a letter of congratulations from Hunting Clan's U.K. Head Office. It was with this promotion that the 'legend of Captain Jack Malloch' started. Jack was pleased, not just with the promotion, but also with the salary increase that came with it. He was now earning two and a half thousand pounds a year, which was considerable. On his new salary Jack estimated he needed about three years to buy his first aircraft.

In July, August and September 1959, while Jack flew an intense schedule of flights around the country, the British and Federal politicians re-grouped for another wrangle over the future of the Federation. Things had settled down in Nyasaland and it seemed as if Operation Sunrise had saved the country from anarchy. But Jack felt uneasy.

October slipped into November and the political pressure on the Federation started to pick up again. For Jack, of much greater concern was a rumour that Hunting Clan was going to be closing down soon. It was true and in mid-November the Hunting Clan management team were called to a meeting with the Federal Prime Minister. The PM, who was personal friends with several of the men in the room got straight to the point; "Gentlemen, I have some bad news for you. Your licences have been withdrawn owing to pressure from the British and South African governments..."

The men were stunned. They had to close down a very good operation because of petty politics and jealousy. None of them believed the story about the British and South African governments, and instead squarely blamed CAA. But either way it had been a political decision.[33] Jack and the rest of the staff were informed that they would continue to be employed until the end of December, but that all employment contracts would end on the last day of the month when final salaries would be paid.

It wasn't going to be a happy Christmas but with his busy flight schedule Jack had little time to think about it. On Boxing Day Jack was in the air for almost twelve hours. He took off from Salisbury with Captain Halse soon after six in the morning. Matching the depressed mood of the Hunting Clan staff, the

33 Interview with Ian Dixon, Hillcrest, Durban, March 2004.

weather was foul, with low clouds sending squalls of wind-lashed rain scuttling across the length of the airfield.

Behind Jack a French UTA airliner with sixty-four passengers on board lined up for take-off. They didn't make it and crashed at the end of the runway. Three people were killed and fifty were injured.

As Jack came into land that evening, he saw the blackened remains of the airliner smudged across the end of the tarmac. He knew people had died there and couldn't help but feel it was an omen of things to come. Bad things. As it was, he had lost his job and his country seemed to be falling apart.

On Thursday 31st December 1959 Jack and Clive flew Hunting Clan's very last Lusaka-Mongu- Livingstone shuttle. That evening once they had got back and signed over the aircraft Jack filled in his logbook, soberly noting 'Last HCAA flight'.[34] It was, in fact, to be Jack's last day ever as an employee. He would never work for anyone else again.

As he prepared for the New Year's party that they were going to that night, Jack tried to be positive. It was difficult.

1960 was the year of the Rat, and it was going to bring war and bloodshed.

34 Jack Malloch's personal flying logbook entry.

CHAPTER 6

Rhodesian Air Services and the three battles of Katanga: 1960 to 1963

Jack was now unemployed, and he did not like it. But he was not one to sit around feeling sorry for himself. He had always planned to run his own airline and now he realised that his time had come. He knew the routes and he had the qualifications and the experience he needed. He just didn't have an aircraft.

But instead of getting one, he was asked to take one back. Hunting Clan needed to get one of their Dakotas to Europe and asked Jack if he would be prepared to fly it there for them. It was a paying freelance job so Jack readily agreed. This time his final destination was Hamburg and the trip took just thirty-six hours.[1] It was his quickest aircraft ferry ever.

From West Germany Jack caught a commercial flight across to London. He planned to spend a few days finding out what affordable old Dakotas where on the market. But first, as promised, he called in to the Hunting Clan Head Office to say hello to Tom and Sir Charles. They were pleased to see him and had a long chat about his plans for the future. This extended into dinner at an expensive London restaurant. Over dessert and coffee, the Air Vice-Marshal suggested that Hunting Clan might have a spare Dakota that would meet Jack's requirements.

The very next day Jack went to the Hunting Clan hangars at Heathrow to have a look at the aircraft. It was a Douglas C-47A. Although it appeared to be in good shape the aircraft had seen a lot of action. It was a World War Two model, having first flown in 1943. But before the end of that year the aircraft had been

1 Jack Malloch's personal flying logbook entry.

shot down and was lost in the Burmese jungle. By coincidence, it had crashed into one of the Hunting brothers' rubber plantations where the badly damaged wreck was rediscovered several years after the war. Hunting Clan send it back to England to be refurbished. A year or so later the aircraft joined the Hunting Clan fleet and proudly took to the air again.[2]

Knowing that the Dakota had landed in trees Jack was impressed with the quality of the rebuild. Sitting in the cockpit the aircraft felt good too. He took it for a short test flight and was convinced. The only problem was the price. Jack simply did not have the money to buy the aircraft. He broached the subject with Sir Charles, who brushed the question aside. Meredith liked Jack and by the end of the weekend offered him a price that was significantly lower than the aircraft's market value, plus it came with a long-term payment plan. It was more than Jack could have ever hoped for. For the sale agreement and pro-forma invoices, he was asked what airline he represented. Without hesitation he replied, "Rhodesian Air Services."

As soon as he got back home Jack immersed himself in registering his new business and making sure that he would have the cash-flow before his offer period expired. The problem was no-one wanted to invest in a business that didn't have any route licences or any aircraft to fly them. After numerous long meetings with the Department of Civil Aviation they eventually agreed to give Jack back his Vilanculos licence as it had been his in the first place. Then with every penny of his life savings, his house fully remortgaged and any spare money that his parents could add he approached the banks.

Eventually, at the end of February, right on his deadline, Jack managed to secure an overdraft and with just hours to spare he confirmed the sale agreement. He then made the arrangements to collect the aircraft, which Hunting Clan had agreed to re-register and repaint. The problem was that Jack didn't have a logo or livery for Rhodesian Air Services. After a bit of thought he decided on a bright red tail with a huge white stylised 'R' in the middle of it. He then added a small seahorse below the nose. It represented the airline's 'Paradise Island' heritage.

Within days of the deal being signed, Zoe discovered that she was pregnant again. The timing was not so good this time, but Jack did not have a lot of time

2 Interview with Ian Dixon, Hillcrest, Durban, March 2004.

to dwell on it. He needed to collect his new aeroplane and get it into service as fast as possible to start paying off their massive debt.

At the end of the first week of March Jack was back in the UK filing his flight plan for the return journey. After the Suez Crisis no overflying rights were being granted to British aircraft so Jack had to avoid Egyptian airspace. But now that it was his own fuel and he felt the cost of every penny. Soon after passing the last Libyan oasis while still north of the Tropic of Cancer, Jack turned south-east taking a short-cut over enemy territory. He was confident that no one would ever know, and the saving would pay for his accommodation on the way home. Although he still kept an eye out for any Egyptian fighter aircraft defending their airspace. Fortunately none came, and no-one questioned why he arrived ahead of schedule in Wadi Halfa.

Once back in Salisbury Jack met with his old flying buddies to see who would be available on a part-time basis to help crew his flights. With the ex-Hunting crews all looking for work staffing was easier than he expected, and many were more than happy to fly for Jack who they had come to like and trust.

Rhodesian Air Services' first commercial flight was on Monday 28th March 1960, just ten days after the aircraft had arrived in Rhodesia. It was a seven-hour charter flight from Salisbury to Johannesburg and back. Two days later, Jack returned to Vilanculos. He did not have many passengers, but there were enough to pay for the trip and Jack wanted to see Alves to get the same deal for accommodation and meals that Hunting Clan had negotiated with him. Alves was very pleased to see Jack again and offered him all the support he needed. It was a good trip and by the time he got back home Jack felt much more confident about the future.

In early April he did another trip to Vilanculos, this time with more passengers. He flew down in the morning, giving himself time for a trip out to Paradise Island with Alves that afternoon. There they spent the night talking about the development opportunities. The next afternoon, Jack flew back to Salisbury with his first load of returning holidaymakers. They were all abuzz with their holiday experiences, while Jack was all abuzz with his thoughts of 'building Paradise'.

He felt that same excitement as he had on his first trips into Mozambique with Jamie Marshall almost eight years earlier. The April-May school holidays were about to start, and the travel agents had already booked Jack for four more flights to Vilanculos before the end of the month. But first he had a charter all the way up to Nigeria.

After his Vilanculos holiday flights Jack also did a charter to Nairobi and back. April 1960 had been the first month of operation for Rhodesian Air Services and Jack had managed to log over sixty hours of paid flying and had restarted his Vilanculos route. In May he did six more trips to Vilanculos, four to Johannesburg and another to Lagos. By the end of June his attention was almost exclusively on Vilanculos and Johannesburg, which seemed to be emerging as his 'cash-cows'.[3]

On Thursday 30th June 1960, the Belgian Congo was granted independence and became the Republic of the Congo. Within days there was a mutiny amongst the Congolese soldiers who went on the rampage. Quickly the country imploded, with any form of Western influence becoming a target for revenge and destruction.[4]

However, out of this chaos emerged one man who was trying to create order and stability. It was Moïse Tshombe. He was President of Katanga, Congo's southern copper-rich province. According to the United Nations this province was "one of the richest mining regions in Africa." While much of the country beyond Katanga burned, Tshombe tried to court the West with his anti-communist stance and his message of positive racial integration. He also tried to convince everyone that a federal system was the best option for the Congo. This infuriated the national leaders who did not want to see the richest province of their newly won 'empire' carved out from under them.

Fearing an invasion from the Central Government on 11th July 1960 Tshombe decided to break away and proclaimed the independence of Katanga. But with thousands of civilian refugees flooding through Katanga and into the Federation of Rhodesia and Nyasaland, Belgium sent in troops to try and restore order. Enraged Patrice Lumumba, the new Congolese Prime Minister accused Belgium of trying to re-annex the Congo and appealed to the United Nations for military assistance. The UN was very sympathetic to Lumumba's

---

3 Jack Malloch's personal flying logbook entry.

4 'War Dog – Fighting Other People's Wars' by Al J. Venter. Published by Casemate Philadelphia. ISBN 1-932033-09-2.

Pan-Africanism so a force was quickly sent to restore their own order to the Congo. Their agenda was to get Belgium out of the country, and Katanga back in. Within just forty-eight hours the UN Security Council established the UN operation in the Congo which came to be known as 'ONUC' (Operation des Nations Unies au Congo).[5]

Meanwhile Jack was focused on building his new charter business. Vilanculos was doing well, but when he read about the number of refugees who needed to be repatriated back to Belgium, Jack saw a business opportunity. He contacted the Belgian Embassy and offered his aircraft. Jack's price worked out cheaper than a scheduled commercial flight, so he got the charter, along with an up-front deposit. Being a three-day flight each way, with complex hotel accommodation and meals Jack had a lot of organising to do.

His first refugee charter was on Wednesday 20th July 1960. By the end of it Jack had got to know many of the traumatised passengers. Their common stories of terror and loss made a very deep impression on him. Over the next six weeks he did several more refugee flights, along with twelve trips to Vilanculos. The mood of the passengers on each route couldn't have been more different.

On Tuesday 9th August Tshombe gave his military 'agent' approval to start recruiting white mercenaries. After a trip to the south-eastern sugar estates Jack got home late that evening. His neighbour Alastair Wicks was waiting for him, which was a surprise. It was an even bigger surprise when Alastair said he was wanting to book Jack for a long, complicated charter.

Before going through the details Alastair first explained who he really was. He did not call himself a mercenary, rather a freelance professional soldier who was in fact the 'agent' of Moïse Tshombe, the new President of Katanga. Alastair went on to explain why he felt it was so important to support Tshombe, "This man is the shining light for Africa and if we can help him, maybe he will be able to lead by example as a positive role model for other African countries as they gain their independence and take over the reins of power..."

The charter that Alastair was looking for was firstly to Katanga and then onto the central diamond-rich province of South Kasai which had declared its

5 'Banana Sunday – Datelines from Africa' by Christopher Munnion, published by William Waterman Publications. ISBN 1-874959-22-6.

independence from Leopoldville that very morning.[6] It was to be Jack's first trip into the Congo since it had gained independence and both Jack and Zoe were very aware of what was happening in the strife-ridden country. Zoe was eight months pregnant which made the decision all the more difficult. But Alastair was prepared to pay significantly more than normal charter rates and Jack certainly needed the cash.

The trip took them three days one of which was in Luluabourg in South Kasai, just west of the Baluba capital Bakwanga. It was a surreal experience. The town was frantically preparing their defences in anticipation of a mass attack by the Congolese National Army (called the 'Armée Nationale Congolaise', or 'ANC' for short). Things were chaotic. Drunken soldiers where setting up barricades while panicking civilians were fleeing as fast as they possibly could. By the time they left Jack could hear gunfire in the distance. He was disturbed that the ill-prepared town was about to be pillaged, yet no one in the rest of the world seemed to know, or care.

The day Jack and Alastair got back to Salisbury Lumumba, appealed to the Russians for help. Having always been interested in the Congo's vast mineral wealth, they were more than willing. Suddenly the Congo was at the center of the superpowers' tug-of-war. With the country erratically swinging to the extreme left, it was clear that something had to be done. The CIA started working on a series of elaborate assassination plots to remove and replace Lumumba.[7]

For the next two weeks Jack focused on his holiday route, making six trips into Vilanculos before the end of August. Every time he landed there and saw the idyllic beaches, the content fishermen and the happy tourists, he remembered the shattered Congolese refugees. It seemed irreconcilable that both places were on the same continent and were happening at the same time. Jack felt uneasy.

At the beginning of September Alastair booked another charter into a few remote military bases in Katanga. This time the mood was noticeably more tense and everyone was bracing themselves for invasion. Although the Congolese Army were not brave fighters, they were resentful and savage, and now had the help of thousands of Russian and Czech military advisors. Re-equipped with the

---

6 'Mercenary' by Mike Hoare, published by Corgi Books. ISBN: 552-07935-9.

7 Legacy of Ashes. The History of the CIA by Tim Weiner. Published by Anchor Books. ISBN: 978-0-307-38900-8.

latest Soviet military hardware Lumumba had dispatched the army to retake Kasai and Katanga. Kasai was overwhelmed and ravaged. But Tshombe's forces with their Belgian advisors were able to repel the attack on their northern border.

In the middle of all this, Zoe gave birth to her second baby. Late in the evening of Tuesday 13th Zoe went into labour and on Wednesday 14th she gave birth to a baby boy. Jack was there long enough to fleetingly see Zoe and their new son. But he also had a planeload of passengers to take to Mozambique and within an hour of leaving the hospital he was strapping himself into the cockpit for the holiday flight. He resented leaving as he knew Zoe needed him, but he also had to keep the business going. Jack only got back the following afternoon. By then he had made the decision to employ another Dakota captain so he could spend a bit more time with Zoe, Alyson and the new baby, who they named John Duncan Ross. Although in true Malloch tradition he was only ever known as Ross.

Meanwhile there was chaos in the Congo. With the CIA's encouragement President Kasavubu sacked Lumumba, who, after less than three months in power, seemed to be verging on lunacy. Lumumba didn't accept this and declared that he had in fact sacked Kasavubu. Confusion reigned supreme and eventually Lumumba and his deputy, Antoine Gizenga fled.

Gizenga made it to the far-off city of Stanleyville where, with the support of his Russian allies, he established a Lumumbist government, in defiance of Kasavubu. Meanwhile Lumumba managed to spark an anti-Tshombe uprising along the border area between southern Kasai and northern Katanga which was spearheaded by a terrifying new anti-Tshombe 'Youth League' who called themselves the Jeunesse. Under the influence of demonic witchdoctors they were barbaric and savage to the extreme. The Jeunesse's weapon of choice was a bicycle chain with its links honed to razor sharpness. A few blows could tear all the flesh from a leg in just a matter of seconds. The frenzied hordes also attacked with clubs, spears and sharpened sticks.[8] Sweeping all before them, the Jeunesse took over the blood-soaked streets of Manono, declaring it the capital of the 'Baubakat Republic of North Katanga.'

By now no one was sure who was in control of the Congo outside the main

---

8 'Banana Sunday – Datelines from Africa' by Christopher Munnion, published by William Waterman Publications. ISBN 1-874959-22-6.

cities of Leopoldville, Stanleyville and Elisabethville.

Alastair Wicks was keen on another trip into the province of Kasai to find out. There were several reasons he wanted to go. Firstly, Tshombe wanted him to try and negotiate with the provincial leaders in Luluabourg – whoever they might now be – to help crush the Jeunesse. Secondly Alastair wanted to see if he could renegotiate his contract for 'security consultancy' in the diamond-rich region. It was certainly going to be dangerous and Alastair was not even sure who would be there to receive them. He was prepared to put a great deal of money on the table though. The truth was that Jack had underestimated the expenses of running the business. His Shell fuel account was high and he was running a month behind on the Dakota's insurance. This 'in and out' trip into the central Congo could solve all that. But it was too dangerous and Jack decided it wasn't fair to Zoe, Alyson and Ross.

Then Shell suspended the airline's fuel account. Jack, who seldom got angry, was enraged. His only solution was to take the charter and pay the overdue fuel account with the up-front deposit. This time his passengers were a group of armed soldiers. After a few hours flying over the endless green jungle they reached their destination. The airstrip was edged with thick bush which seemed to be deserted and after a few low passes Jack turned into the wind and came in to land.

The passengers had taken their seats as close to the front of the aircraft as they could and as they touched down Jack heard the crackle of machine-gun fire and the ping of bullets striking the fuselage. Instinctively Jack pushed the throttles forward to try and take off again, but Alastair immediately told him to pull back and taxi in nice and slowly. He explained that if they tried to escape it would only look like they were really the enemy after all, and the entire perimeter would open up at them. Holding his nerve, Jack slowed down and taxied up to the low terminal building as instructed, leaving the trigger-happy gunners behind them.

The terminal was a mess. Most of the windows had been shattered and there were lines of bullet-holes crisscrossing the walls. A group of soldiers emerged from the front of the building. Although they were not shooting, their rifles were levelled at the aircraft. Sizing up the situation, Alastair unbuckled his safety-belt and prepared to disembark. "You can't really blame the 'welcoming committee'", he said, nodding towards the battle-hardened soldiers on the tarmac, "The last time any planes landed here it was the Russians with a belly-load of blood-crazed ANC."

After a bit of excited shouting and then waiting a bit longer for steps to be brought to the plane, Alastair and his colleagues disembarked. Jack was left with three red-eyed soldiers who he was convinced were drunk. The fact that they had fixed bayonets did not make him feel any better. With the permission of his guards Jack got out of the aircraft and slowly and carefully took time to inspect every inch of the aeroplane. He found several bullet-holes in the fuselage. They seemed to be from small-arms fire and fortunately hadn't done any done any major damage.

After a couple of hours in the blistering equatorial heat Jack began to worry. It was well after lunchtime and the Baluba were known cannibals, so it was not entirely out of the question that Alastair and his contingent had been taken out for lunch. As the hot afternoon wore on, he also began to wonder about the wisdom of the name 'Rhodesian Air Services'. Like it or not, 'Rhodesians' where beginning to be labelled as white neo-colonialists and although Jack was fiercely patriotic, he realised that in Africa it might be safer to have an anonymous company name.

Eventually there was the sound of approaching vehicles and to Jack's relief the young soldiers climbed out of the back of the aircraft to go and see what was happening. Jack started his pre-flight checks in the hope that they would be taking off soon. Within a few minutes Alastair and his entourage emerged. They stood speaking French with their hosts for a while, then, after shaking hands all round, they climbed into the plane.

Jack immediately started the engines and as soon as the rear door was closed and secured, he taxied off. Without slowing he turned onto the runway and took off, relieved to have survived another trip into Luluabourg. They set a course straight back to Salisbury where they landed just after ten o'clock that night. As soon as he could Jack phoned Zoe to tell her that he was back. She was very relieved. He did not tell her that they had been shot at.

The next day Jack put the Dakota in for servicing. He pointed out the small round holes that needed to be sealed. He didn't say what had caused them, but it obviously was not ordinary 'wear and tear,' especially when some of the copper-coated bullet-heads were found in the passenger compartment. Two days later Jack was off on another overnight trip to Johannesburg and Vilanculos. None of the passengers had the slightest notion that the aircraft they were travelling in had been shot up just a few days earlier.

Alastair had been impressed with Jack's cool-headedness and his ability to stay focused throughout the trip. He quickly offered his neighbor another charter. This time it was to Durban, and although there was not the same amount of danger-money it was still more than the usual civilian charter. Jack agreed and Alastair immediately deposited 50% of the quoted price into Jack's bank account.

At the end of October they flew to Durban where they met another British military consultant by the name of Mike Hoare. Alastair and Mike were working together to recruit the mercenary army for Tshombe. Jack got on well with Mike and with their common mistrust of the communist agenda in Africa they became good friends.

During the closing weeks of 1960 Tshombe realised that he was not going to get the support he needed from the British and decided to look elsewhere. France was the obvious choice and General de Gaulle summoned Colonel Trinquier, briefing him on the opportunity in Katanga. Trinquier, who was a specialist in revolutionary warfare, quickly put a team of military advisors together to take control of the Katangese gendarmerie. Colonel Roger Faulques, an ex-French Foreign Legionnaire was appointed as their Commanding Officer.[9] Unfortunately the French had their own agenda in Katanga and did not want to support or work with Alastair and Mike's mercenary army. However, over time, Faulques got to know and respect Jack, who became the conduit between the competing contingents.

In mid-January 1961 Alastair had another proposal for Jack. He had several more charters that he needed, but he was interested in a more formal involvement in Rhodesian Air Services. He liked Jack and wanted to be able to count on the

9 'The New Mercenaries' by Anthony Mockler, published by Corgi Books. ISBN 0-552-12558-X.

entrepreneurial aviator to provide air charter services in the Congo. The idea appealed to Jack who was keen to have the support of someone, not just with money behind them, but also with a need for charters. In the end they came to an agreement which resulted in Alastair being appointed as an Executive Officer of Rhodesian Air Services.[10] Jack was pleased, but knew he was now locked into dangerous mercenary flying, and that came almost immediately.

On January 12th Jack and Alastair were back in the Congo. It was a long four-day trip and their first destination was Bakwanga deep in the heart of Baluba territory. Just like Luluabourg, the town carried the same scars of war and had the same trigger-happy soldiers who shot at the aircraft as they came in to land. Fortunately, they seemed incapable of actually hitting anything too important, although they did put more 7.62 mm holes in the side panels that needed to be plugged.

From there they flew to the vast Katangese military base at Kamina. With Alastair's direct involvement in Rhodesian Air Services, Jack was accepted as part of the team and included in the discussions. The first person he met in Kamina was Mike Hoare. Jack hardly recognised him in his crisply pressed military uniform. There was no doubt that Mike was in charge of operations of the newly formed 'Compagnie Internationale', which was a group of almost one hundred Belgian, French, British, South African and Rhodesian mercenaries.

During these meetings Jack got to know some of the other men serving Katanga. They included 'Black Jack' Schramme. Schramme was a Congolese settler who had dedicated himself to fighting the ANC after they had brutally murdered his wife and children. He was tasked with leading the Katangese defence forces and worked closely with Mike Hoare who led the mercenary contingent.

Later that afternoon a government delegation arrived at Kamina to discuss the military situation with Mike and Alastair. To Jack's astonishment he was introduced to the famous Katangese leader, Moïse Tshombe himself. Tshombe sincerely thanked Jack for his support of the Katanga cause. Tshombe was polite, well-spoken and obviously highly intelligent. He also seemed to be a good listener who appreciated the advice of his multiracial team. The next day Jack sat in on a planning session with Tshombe. Several times the Katangese

10 Personal correspondence and documents provided by Ian Dixon, March 27, 2008.

President sought his advice on questions of aerial support and logistics. Having studied the Berlin Airlift and Chennault's aviation theories, Jack felt confident that he was able to give good advice.

At the end of the trip Jack retrieved the 'advisors' who had been working in Bakwanga and flew them back to Kamina where there was a lot of preparation to be done for the coming war. While there, Jack was introduced to some of the other mercenary leaders including Siegfried Mueller, a South West African veteran of the Wehrmacht SS who led a group of about thirty other ex-Nazi mercenaries.

At the end of January 1961 Jack had his next Congolese charter. This time he needed to deliver his first planeload of mercenary recruits into the Congolese war zone. The men he was bringing in were the initial core of Alastair's army. They included the usual mix of trained soldiers and petty criminals who were in the charge of one Jeremiah Puren. They flew directly to Elisabethville where they landed late that night. The recruits were driven to their training camp at a deserted mine at Shinkolobwe, to begin their induction into jungle warfare, while Jack and Alastair checked into Elisabethville's 'Grand Hotel Leopold the Second' – nicknamed 'Leo Deux' for their planned audience with Tshombe in the morning.

Tshombe was impressed with 'Colonel' Puren and after some consideration appointed Jerry Puren and Jean Zumbach to build the new Katanga Air Force. Both men had solid air force credentials; Puren had served in the South African Air Force while Zumbach was the ex-Wing Commander of 303 Squadron – and an accomplished diamond smuggler. Mike Hoare found it much more difficult to work with these competing swashbucklers and over time relied ever more on Jack Malloch to coordinate his aviation needs.

For the next ten days Jack flew a grueling schedule of flights around Katanga, diplomatic shuttles to Ndola and more recruitment flights to Johannesburg. As Rhodesia had not officially recognised Katanga, rather than use his Rhodesian Air Services branded Dakota, Jack mostly flew the aircraft that Tshombe had at his disposal including a Dove and a large DC-4. It was the first time Jack had flown a four-engined aircraft and it was exactly the sort of experience he was wanting. However, he couldn't put any of those flying hours in his logbook, as he did not want the Department of Civil Aviation in Salisbury to see where he had been flying. On those various flights Jack got to know President Tshombe well. Although they were from completely different cultures and backgrounds there was a chemistry between the two men.

With the demands of the Vilanculos run and the fact that his own DC-3 was parked while he was flying Tshombe's planes, Jack realised he needed a second crew to keep the holiday route alive. But with more staff came more overhead, and most of the money Jack had received from his last Katanga trip had gone into paying off the aircraft. His cash-flow was still very tight, but Alastair was confident that there was going to be a lot more business coming their way. He placed a few small carefully worded advertisements in the Rhodesia Herald and the Bulawayo Chronicle, looking for "experienced white police officers who may be interested in a well-paid alternative."

On 21st February, a week after Jack's return from Katanga, the United Nations, who were alarmed by the number of mercenary soldiers arriving in Katanga, passed a resolution on the breakaway province. UN Council Resolution 161 called for the removal of all foreign military troops in Katanga and gave their own forces the authority to carry this out. Jack was stunned. Just a few years earlier he had been training to fight on behalf of the United Nations. Now suddenly they were a hostile occupying force apparently rounding up anyone who was prepared to fight against Russian-armed marauders.

Instead of protecting civilians, the mission of these UN forces was to hunt down and expel any foreign military advisors in Katanga. This included Mike Hoare's growing contingent, the French officers who had recently arrived and the group of local Belgians who had switched allegiance to Katanga. This was a major threat to Alastair's recruitment operation and wasn't going to be good for Jack's charter business either. But it wasn't just his business that Jack was worried about. Considering he had also given Tshombe military advice Jack feared he was now a target as well.

Although the UN resolution caused concern, the mercenary commanders quickly found ways of keeping out of sight while still trying to meet their mandate. But this made defence of the country more difficult, as now almost every street corner was being patrolled by hostile forces trying to arrest the defenders. It was a classic perversion of a global organisation trying to force their politically correct, but distant, view on a complex and volatile local situation. In the end, apart from their freedom of movement, the only significant loss for Katanga was the French leader, Colonel Trinquier, and he wasn't even caught by the UN. Instead he resigned due to infighting with the Belgian Katangese. Most of the other French officers stayed on in Katanga, with Faulques becoming their leader.

Described by Jerry Puren as "an excellent and honest soldier" Faulques commanded a great deal of respect from his men and attracted a growing number of recruits around him. One of these men had been an NCO in the French Marines, prior to which he had been a policeman serving in Morocco and Algeria. By the time he arrived in Katanga he was going by the name 'Bob Denard'. Denard quickly became Faulques's right-hand man and started to build an army of French mercenaries. 'Four Commando', which comprised mainly of ex-Legionnaires, was soon referred to as 'Les Affreux' (the frightful ones), and for good reason. As for Mike Hoare and Alastair Wicks they were busy building their own army. This had initially been known as 'La Compagnie Internationale,' but to separate themselves from the Belgian and French mercenary groups, they began calling themselves 'Five Commando.'

In mid-March 1961 Jack flew Mike Hoare and another contingent of recruits from Johannesburg into Katanga. This brought the ranks of Mike's commando up to more than one hundred well-trained volunteers. It was time to start delivering on their contract to defend Katanga, and over the next couple of weeks they achieved remarkable victories. Split into two groups they recaptured Manono and pushed the Baluba and Sendwe rebels back across the Lukuga River. By the end of March they had recaptured all of northern Katanga, except for the last stronghold of Kabalo.

After several more clandestine trips into Katanga in support of Five Commando, Jack spent the end of March and early April catching up on his Vilanculos and Johannesburg holiday runs. As always, the contrast between the two destinations disturbed him, but the money made up for it. In his flying logbook he recorded a total of ninety-six flying hours for the months of February and March 1961. In reality that was little more than half of what he actually flew.

In April the action in South-eastern Congo ratcheted up with the UN forces taking a much more active role against Katanga. Having got wind of a planned mercenary attack against the town of Kabalo the UN prepared a trap, which very nearly netted Jack himself. Early in the morning of Friday April 7th Jack landed the packed DC-4 at Kabalo airport. Unopposed, the men enthusiastically stormed out of the plane and headed off into the town. Jack was worried about the eerie silence and with a strong sense of foreboding took off heading back for Kamina. Behind him the men walked straight into the carefully laid ambush. Two large river boats of Katangese reinforcements were also attacked before they could dock, one being sunk. In the fighting several Ethiopian UN soldiers were killed and about thirty of Mike's mercenaries were captured.[11]

The repercussions were serious. The terrifying Jeunesse surged back with a vengeance, and Tshombe and the mercenaries stopped trusting the Belgians who they suspected of leaking information. It then came out that Captain Richard Browne, who had led the disastrous assault, was the brother of an English MP[12] This caused acute embarrassment for the British Government and further hardened their resolve against Rhodesia, who they blamed for recruiting the mercenaries in the first place.

Having barely escaped from Kabalo Jack realised the real dangers of the business he was involved in. But it had earned him enough to pay off the final instalment on his DC-3. With his debt now paid in full Jack felt he could start investing in the proper expansion of his airline.

A week later Tshombe asked Jack to fly him and his Katangan entourage to a peace conference in Coquilhatville in the Presidential DC-4. The flight was delayed when the UN seized control of Elisabethville airport. They wanted to fly in reinforcements for the coming 'final solution' so, inevitably a firefight broke out between the UN troops and the Katangese Gendarmes, turning the airport into a battlefield. Tshombe eventually got to the conference two days late.

The conference was a failure and after several days of fruitless discussion Tshombe decided to leave but before he could he was arbitrarily arrested and imprisoned. The UN Secretary General Dag Hammarskjold was pleased and

11 'Mercenary Commander' Colonel Jerry Puren as told to Brian Pottinger. Published by Galago Publishing. ISBN 0-947020-21-7.

12 'The New Mercenaries' by Anthony Mockler, published by Corgi Books. ISBN 0-552-12558-X.

predicted that without Tshombe, Katanga would collapse within a matter of weeks.

To prove himself right in mid-May Hammarskjold unleashed his troops in Katanga. In coordinated pre-dawn raids they swept through the mercenary barracks and bases across the country, arresting anyone they could find. The only major group of mercenaries to escape was Mike Hoare and his men who were training at the small rural army base of Nyunzu. They were able to hold off the UN troops until nightfall when they quietly melted away into the jungle.

At the end of May Jack was chartered to fly a couple of planeloads of Five Commando soldiers back to Johannesburg after they had been released and their contracts terminated. Jack made more flights into Katanga in the first few weeks of June, discretely repositioning some of Mike's dedicated volunteers back into the troubled province.

After a huge ransom had been paid, in late June Mobutu agreed to release Tshombe who arrived back home to a hero's welcome. The entire city of Elisabethville lined the streets from the airport to the Prime Minister's residence waving and shouting their enthusiastic support. The huge public celebration and the outpouring of public approval did not go unnoticed by the watching UN, not that it changed their attitude.

The UN then decided that a more effective strategy was to sort out the other provinces first and then tackle Katanga from a position of strength. To buy off Kivu province Antoine Gizenga was welcomed back to Leopoldville as the new Vice-President. This meant that the Russians were also back in favour. Quickly their embassies were reopened and planeloads of Soviet 'advisors' started pouring back into the capital. Although this didn't bode well for the country's future, it did give Tshombe a much-needed breather to frantically rearm and rebuild his defences. Consequently, in July Jack did several overnight flights into Katanga bringing in men and equipment in anticipation of the coming invasion.

While the Congo was in chaos, the political situation in Rhodesia was not going well either. Ever since the mid-1950s there had been a growing stand-off between the Federal government and the British who were committed to giving independence to all of their African colonies as quickly as possible. Independence was exactly what Rhodesia wanted – and what had been promised back in 1923, but as the Federal government was primarily white that was unacceptable to Britain. They secretly started negotiating with Banda, Kaunda and the others leaders of the black revolutionary movements, looking for a more politically acceptable option.

At the end of July 1961 the people of the Federation of Rhodesia and Nyasaland went to the polls in a referendum on the Constitution that Britain had proposed for the three countries. The Rhodesian voters accepted the constitution because they had been led to believe that they would be confirming their desire for independence along the lines of New Zealand and Canada.

They had been tricked.

According to Kenneth Young, "It was some time before the Rhodesian electorate at large comprehended that something had been slipped into their Constitution after they had voted upon it which in effect took away most of the benefit they had hoped for. But when it became generally understood it caused deep doubt of British good faith and it had a strong effect on white Rhodesian minds in all that followed in 1964 and 1965. Suspicion haunted future discussions, and fear of the legalistic double-cross replaced the once blind faith in Britain. This was perhaps the greatest tragedy of the 1961 Constitution."[13]

On the positive side one of the other points of the referendum was to determine what the white voting population thought about the idea of bringing blacks onto the voters roll. This would ensure that black politicians, and the black majority who voted them in, would have real political influence and a direct say in the running of the country. It was approved by an almost seventy percent majority of the white electorate.

At the same time a little-known action was playing out in Nyunzu in northern Katanga, from where Mike Hoare and his men had recently made their escape. A force of UN soldiers quietly surrounded and isolated the town. Their pretext was to separate the local pro-Tshombe community from the Balubas, but without access to their lands the people were being starved to death. A passionate American Seventh-day Adventist minister named Len Robinson took up their cause and, with the permission of Tshombe, used one of the Katanga Air Force

13 'Rhodesia and Independence' by Kenneth Young, published by Eyre & Spottiswoode, London.

The long envisaged 'Entertainment and Water Sports Centre' that Jack and Joaquim finally built on Paradise Island.
Picture from Jack Malloch's private collection. © Greg Malloch.

Doves to deliver food to Nyunzu airfield.

But when the aircraft landed the British UN contingent refused permission for either the critical supplies to be taken into the town, or for the people to come to the airfield to collect it. The reason given was 'orders', at which Robinson exploded, and after a long 'fire and brimstone' tirade, the cleric ended with a calm but very sincere warning, "Captain, I will return to Elisabethville with this little mercy mission. I will then send telegrams to my church in the US, the relevant authorities in the Western governments, to the UN Secretariat and to certain journalists in the Western media. I will tell them, Captain, that UN troops under your command have surrounded a tiny defenceless flock of Christians and are starving them to death…"[14] With little alternative, the British Army Captain allowed the pitiful tribesmen to collect the small quantity of supplies from the aircraft.

Although Jack was getting busy with his Katanga charters again, traffic to Vilanculos had also been steadily increasing. During the first two weeks of

14 'Mercenary Commander' Colonel Jerry Puren as told to Brian Pottinger. Published by Galago Publishing. ISBN 0-947020-21-7.

August Jack did four more holiday flights. The Rhodesian Air Services office on Paradise Island was opened and quickly became the busy 'entertainment and water sports centre' that he had envisaged. Jack and Joaquim had invested a considerable amount in all the equipment, boats and fishing tackle that their guests would need. Now they were hoping that their investment would start to pay off.

But Jack's reconnection with his holiday route didn't last long and by the end of August he was back in Katanga, and things were not looking good. The number of UN troops had increased dramatically. They were everywhere, nervously peering out of their heavily fortified positions at every strategic point they could find.

While in Katanga Jack met with Colonel Faulques and his flamboyant second-in-command, Bob Denard. Jack had heard a lot about Bob, but contrary to his expectation, he liked the large, moustached Frenchman, who, with his slightly theatrical character, seemed to be the complete opposite of the battle-hardened Faulques. Both men were worried about when the United Nations would attack.

Sure enough, early on the morning of Monday 28th August while Jack was heading for Vilanculos with a load of holidaymakers the UN pounced. They had carefully drawn up a list of all the Europeans serving in the Katangese military, and were trying to remove all five hundred and twelve of them. In a lightning, country-wide sweep, more than four hundred of these targets were arrested including Alastair Wicks, Jerry Puren and Black Jack Schramme.

By mid-September Alastair had been released and deported to the U.K. but Jack was still very worried about his many other friends trapped in Katanga including Tshombe himself. And it wasn't just his friends in the Congo that he was worried about. Many of his Air Force colleagues had been deployed to Ndola and were now anticipating having to fly in combat against the Hunters and Canberras of the Swedish and Indian Air Forces. The opposing forces were equally matched with the Rhodesians having Provosts armed with machine-guns and tear-gas, rocket-armed Vampires and bomb-loaded Canberras.[15] As the Rhodesians strengthened their border to stop the Congo conflict spilling

---

15 'A Pride of Eagles' by Beryl Salt, published by Covos Day. ISBN 0-620-23759-7.

over the situation was quickly becoming a dangerous international stand-off.

As soon as he landed in the U.K. Alastair reconnected with his old friends Julian, Billy and David. They were a powerful group; Julian Amery was the British Under-Secretary of War, Billy McLean was a conservative Member of Parliament and David Stirling was the famous founder of the Special Air Service. In the late 1950s, to reinforce Britain's influence and counter the communist threat, these influential Tories founded the British Mercenary Organisation.[16] This was a secret arm of the government's foreign policy that specialised in recruiting mercenaries to undertake messy international assignments that they did not want Cabinet to know about. In his debriefing Alastair went into a lot of detail about Rhodesian Air Services and Captain Jack Malloch. Alastair strongly recommended that Jack be 'brought onboard.'

At 4 a.m. on Wednesday 13th September, with the mercenaries finally out of the way, the United Nations launched their military strike against the state of Katanga. It was, in effect, a UN coup d'etat. In this, the 'First Battle of Katanga', the United Nations forces seized control of all remaining strategic points in the main centres of Elisabethville and Jadotville.

Their initial objectives were to capture the Katangese government ministers, the remaining white advisors and 'anyone else with leadership ability'. The UN had presumed that the Katangese would crumble quickly, especially as they were significantly out-manned and out-gunned. But the gendarmes, with the support of the entire civilian population bravely defended their 'home ground' in the face of overwhelming odds. According to Jerry Puren, "The unexpectedly fierce resistance by the defenders was mirrored in countless fire fights at street strong points, across golf courses, from the gardens of private homes, from parks and rooftops and the vast Union Minière workshops…"[17]

Taking advantage of the UN attack, the Congolese National Army swooped down on Katanga's northern border. A fierce battle broke out between the Katangese gendarmes and two attacking columns of ANC. Although the Katangese were also at war with the United Nations, they managed to hold their ground in the north, pushing back the incursion.

---

16 War PLC: The Rise of the New Corporate Mercenary by Stephen Armstrong.

17 'Mercenary Commander' Colonel Jerry Puren as told to Brian Pottinger. Published by Galago Publishing. ISBN 0-947020-21-7.

Having quickly regrouped, the next day the Katangese gendarmerie counter-attacked the United Nations positions. They were supported by the few old aircraft that Jerry Puren had managed to save. According to Anthony Mockler this rag-tag Air Force "...consisted of two aged Fougas, a Dornier of First World War vintage, and a helicopter from which the pilot tossed hand grenades."[18] With their fanatical patriotism the Katangese were able to drive the UN forces back to the safety of their fortifications and their bullet-proof armoured cars.

Knowing he was outnumbered and in an effort to try and prevent further casualties, Tshombe requested a meeting in Northern Rhodesia with the UN leadership to try and resolve the situation. Hammarskjold himself suggested that he and Tshombe meet the following evening in Ndola to agree on a ceasefire. Within minutes Jack received an urgent request from Tshombe to get to Ndola as quickly as possible. Without question he agreed and confirmed that he would be in the Copperbelt border town by mid-morning the next day. Zoe was not so sure about this trip and had a nagging feeling that there was going to be a plane crash. Jack assured her that he would be okay.

By mid-afternoon on Sunday 17th, with the war between the Katangese and the UN still raging across Katanga, a large crowd of delegates and dignitaries assembled in Ndola. They included Tshombe and his team, Jack Malloch, Jerry Puren and several other 'advisors'. While Tshombe was preparing to meet Hammarskjold he received unexpected news of victory in Jadotville where the Katangese forces had captured the entire Irish garrison. Although Tshombe wanted peace with the UN, the news of this victory strengthened his hand.

Despite Tshombe's assurances the UN were afraid that Hammarskjold's aircraft would be attacked by the Katangese jet fighters so was carefully avoiding Congolese airspace. This caused a significant delay and in the end the delegation was due to land at about twenty minutes past ten that night. At ten minutes past ten, the pilot of the DC-6 sent the message, "Lights in sight, overhead Ndola, descending…" It was the last message he ever sent.

The next day the wreckage of the aircraft was found some ten miles from Ndola airport. There were no survivors. While it has since been proven that the accident

---

18 'The New Mercenaries' by Anthony Mockler, published by Corgi Books. ISBN 0-552-12558-X.

was caused by pilot error the United Nations never officially discounted the theory that somehow Tshombe and the Rhodesians had been responsible for the Secretary General's death. After some brief exploratory discussions Tshombe headed back to direct Katanga's battle for survival. There was a lot of frantic diplomatic shuttling to be done and Jack flew a full schedule to almost every landing strip in Katanga over the next three days as the fighting slowly simmered down.

By the end of September Jack was able to get back to his own business. Since the middle of 1960 he had been working on trying to gain an international licence with which he could open up a passenger route between Salisbury and Europe. Having done his research he had decided that Luton Airport, north of London would be the ideal destination. It was smaller than Heathrow and newer than Gatwick, making licences easier to obtain, and it was also located within the UK public transport hub. At the beginning of October Jack got a charter to Frankfurt. It was the perfect opportunity that he needed to get across to Luton and lobby for his licence.

Jack spent Sunday 8th and Monday 9th of October in Luton meeting with various people, one of whom was Bill Armstrong, the owner of Lutair Handling Services which was the airports official ground handling agent. Jack had set up the meeting to discuss possible ground handling options for his aircraft, but quickly discovered that Bill was also Managing Director of Autair International Airways.[19] As a former RAF Squadron Leader Bill had a lot on common with Jack and liked his entrepreneurial spirit. Their afternoon meeting extended into dinner later that evening. Although Bill wasn't involved in the allocation of landing licences for the airport Jack had made a very influential friend.

Learning from their embarrassing defeats the United Nations realised they needed overwhelming firepower to subjugate the Katangese. As the fighting ended so the next massive rearmament airlift started. In an attempt to slow this down in mid-October Tshombe signed a formal and 'final' ceasefire with the United Nations. It did not help; the huge American transporters continued to fly in ever-increasing amounts of troops and materiel into Katanga in direct contravention of the agreements that had been signed.

---

19 'Colours in the Sky: The story of Autair International Airways and Court Line Aviation' by Graham M Simons, published by GMS Enterprises. ISBN 9781904514701.

But it wasn't just the UN that Tshombe had to contend with. The Congolese Army, the Baluba rebels and the swarming Jeunesse had all made territorial gains in northern Katanga, slaughtering anyone they suspected of being a Tshombe sympathiser.

To help drive back the invaders Jack Malloch and Jerry Puren started to work on an aerial ground attack capability with the few remaining aircraft they had. Jerry's two Doves were fitted with machine-guns and home-made bomb racks. The bombs were actually milk-crates carefully packed with hand grenades and an elaborate rope of strings connected to the ring-pull of each grenade's pin. The idea was that this 'rope' was yanked hard by the pilot to pull the pins out before the whole dangerous contraption was released over the unfortunate target below.

Jack was nervous at the thought of having live grenades rolling around the back of his aircraft so he devised a more effective and controllable forty-four-gallon drum 'bridge buster' which could be tossed out of the rear door of the Dakota. Essentially it was just an oil drum filled with blasting dynamite and nails. The bulky home-made bomb was then sealed and primed with either grenades or traditional blasting fuses, depending on the contraption's expected 'fall time'. This was usually very short as Jack liked to come in as low as possible over his targets.[20]

With the effectiveness of the Katanga Air Force and their dangerous arsenal of home-made bombs, the Katangese Gendarmerie were able to push back the ANC. Jack's last mission in this northern area was the destruction of a road bridge over the Lubilash River. Jack made a couple of low passes over the length of the bridge while some of his cumbersome forty-four-gallon drum bombs were pushed out of the open side door of the Dakota, as Jack screamed from the cockpit, "Now!! Now!! Now!!" The heavy drums exploded on the narrow bridge leaving the structure slumped and broken.

When Tshombe heard about these exploits he was very grateful. In return he appointed Jack as the 'official' pilot of his personal DC-4 and awarded him the contract for all non-military flying required by the Katangese government. This guaranteed regular and well-paid charters for Jack's Rhodesian Air Services.

By the middle of November 1961, with Jack's support, the Katangese had

20 Interview with Jerry Puren, Durban, September 1999.

managed to repel the ANC forces, driving them back across the northern border. As they retreated towards Stanleyville the national army soldiers passed through the town of Kindu on the banks of the Congo River. There, the ANC rabble took their frustration out on a small civilian contingent of Italian UN airmen who had just landed in the town, devouring thirteen of them.

According to Jack Starr who was a reporter for the Mail and who visited Kindu soon after the incident, a traumatised representative of the World Health Organisation who was in the town at the time of the atrocity reported that the airmen had been 'tenderised' with a prolonged, almost ritualised beating at the hands of the National Army soldiers before finally being killed. The next day he described seeing Caucasian limbs for sale in the local butchery. This was independently confirmed by Martin Bangubangu who was living in Kindu at the time. In his broken English he stated, "…I ate the flesh of Italians in Kindu. I believe that this nightmare will pursue me until my death." Once the airmen had been killed, according to Bangubangu, "The hungry threw themselves on the remains, cut them with machetes and knives. The human flesh was sold in the market. Inedible leftovers were thrown into the River. The soldiers kept their fingers as trophies."[21] Many years later when asked whether cannibalism was quite so rife in the Congo, the French mercenary leader Bob Denard confirmed that it was, saying, "I can tell you, if the Balubas got hold of white flesh it went straight into the tribal cooking pot. I'm not joking."

As so often happens in times of war, necessity breeds strange bedfellows, and Jack was stunned when in mid-November the United Nations office in Salisbury contacted him requesting a couple of charter flights to reposition their troops. Jack wondered whether the UN knew of his level of involvement in Katanga. Were they offering him this work to entice him away from Tshombe, was it a trap, or were they were genuinely ignorant of his clandestine activities…?

As Alastair was no longer that involved in Rhodesian Air Services and was now based back in the UK, Jack decided to take on the UN charters primarily for the premium price he could earn. After he received the deposit payment it seemed he had no reason to be worried. Although after discussing it with his

21 Les générations condamnées. Déliquescence d'une société pré-capitaliste (Democratic Republic of Congo. Generations condemned. Failure of a pre-capitalist society), by Jean Kanyarwunga published by Publibook, Paris, 2006.

crew they decided that Jack shouldn't go on the charter just in case he was still on the United Nations' wanted list.

Early on the morning of Wednesday 22nd November the RAS crew met at the airport to prepare for the first of their UN flights. There was three of them, Captain Larry Owen who was leading the flight, First Officer Neil Stewart who was just getting used to his DC-3 First Officer duties and the attractive hostess, twenty-three year-old Lena Crosby. Jack had also arrived early to brief the crew before they set off. He wanted to be sure everything was going to be okay.

Once the crew had boarded Jack watched the aircraft start up. It taxied out and stopped short of the threshold of Runway Six, while waiting for their clearance. After a few moments the red and silver Dakota turned onto the runway. It stopped briefly while take-off power was applied. Then the brakes were released and it began to accelerate down the long runway.

Jack turned and went back towards his office as the sound of the aircraft receded into the distance. But moments later there was a booming explosion. With surging dread Jack ran out of the hanger and saw the plume of black smoke almost a mile away at the far end of the runway. Leaping into his car he raced towards the crash-site which was some six hundred yards south-east of the end of Runway Six.

Bouncing over the rough grass verge he got as close as he could to the flaming debris. As Jack leaped out of the car desperate to find his crew a figure emerged from the smoke holding the unconscious body of Lena in his arms. Without a word he gently passed the barely breathing hostess over to Jack and disappeared back into the flaming wreckage to try and find the pilots. Unfortunately, both had been killed instantly as the aircraft nosedived into the ground. It was only by a miracle that Lena had survived.

Aircraftman Kawilila had been working near the Royal Rhodesian Air Force bomb dump at the end of the runway when the DC-3 had tried to take off. He watched it climb. Then the port wing dipped, pulling the aircraft around into a left turn. As the turn tightened, he knew there was a problem. He was already sprinting as hard as he could towards the DC-3 as it rolled over and ploughed into the ground.

Less than a week after the crash Jack and his brother-in-law Ted Kruger were both pall bearers at Larry and Neil's emotional funeral. The Rhodesia Herald covered the tragic accident with a long article, in which they said "the Dakota that crashed last week was probably the most well-loved aircraft in Africa and certainly the most photographed. During its lifetime it carried thousands of folk to the sunshine and peace of Paradise Island. It also played its part in more than one national emergency…"[22]

A commission of enquiry to investigate the crash of VP-YRX concluded that the probable cause of the fatal crash was that "…the pre-take-off rudder trimmer check was not carried out correctly and the aircraft took off with full left rudder trim applied. Once airborne this was misinterpreted as port engine failure. The port propeller was feathered resulting in critical speed yaw."[23] It also seemed that the rudder ground locks may not have been removed before they tried to take off.[24]

Jack was devastated by the loss of his friends, but he also had his business to rebuild. He needed to quickly find a replacement aircraft, and he had to return the UN's deposit money which didn't help either.

Having heard about the accident Jack's friend Bill Armstrong from Autair quickly found an old Dakota for him and helped expedite the sale. In was a godsend and on December 5th, just two weeks after the crash Jack took ownership of the aircraft on the tarmac in Luton. After signing the papers and shaking hands, Jack filled the fuel-tanks and immediately took-off for the long flight home.

When he made his first refueling stop in Nice he heard that the United Nations had launched their next 'final' offensive against Katanga. In Elisabethville, once again fierce gun-battles erupted at all strategic points across the city, including the airport where the Katangese Gendarmes and the UN troops were locked in savage hand-to-hand combat. The 'Second Battle of Katanga' had begun. Jack knew he had to hurry. Tshombe would be needing him.

A day and a half later having snatched as little sleep as possible along the way Jack arrived at Salisbury airport. Zoe and the kids were there to meet him. After just an hour the new aircraft was refueled and he was on his way again, leaving

22 The Rhodesia Herald edition of Tuesday November 28, 1961.
23 Flight Safety Foundation's Aviation Safety Network accident description of the crash of Rhodesian Air Services Douglas C-47A-75-DL on November 22, 1961.
24 Personal correspondence with Ted and Blythe Kruger, March 30, 2009.

a very concerned Zoe fighting back the tears, knowing that Jack was heading straight into a very nasty war.

With Elisabethville airport in enemy hands and the city engulfed in fierce house-to-house combat, Jack spent his time flying in and out of Ndola to small remote airstrips across Katanga. His mission was to deliver desperately needed supplies and military equipment to the beleaguered Katangese soldiers and civilians alike.

According to the Prime Minister of the Federation of Rhodesia and Nyasaland, "The European quarter of Elisabethville was subject to prolonged and indiscriminate shelling by the UN forces equipped with both mortars and 75mm recoilless guns. …many atrocities were committed. This was no clean-up of a handful of mercenaries. This was total war, brought to Africa by the armed forces of the United Nations, in whose eyes the Katangese had committed two sins: they wanted to be independent and they preferred a partnership of races."[25]

By the middle of December 1961, the outnumbered and poorly armed Katangese were forced from their shattered capital. But in Jadotville, Kolwezi and Kipushi the Katanga Gendarmes tenaciously held their ground against the United Nations. A week later a truce was signed and the second Battle of Katanga was over. Apart from many unnecessary deaths it had achieved nothing. Tshombe was still in power. The Katangese were still defiant.

But the Katanga Air Force had been badly mauled. They came out of the conflict with little more than a Dakota and a Dove. Added to this were Tshombe's personal DC-4 and a civilian Piper Cub. With these extra aircraft at his disposal and the bombers and fighters of the UN at least temporarily out of the way, Jerry was able to concentrate on trying to push the ANC back north again. Every time the Katangese were distracted by the UN, the Congolese Army would retake northern Katanga, and this time when they recaptured Kongolo they celebrated by butchering twenty-three missionaries. This was certainly no place for the faint-hearted.

On March 9th, 1962 Tshombe called for a meeting with Jack in Kolwezi during which the President briefed Jack on the plan to make the DC-4 available to the

25 'Welensky's 4000 Days' by Sir Roy Welensky P.C. K.C.M.G., published by Collins Books, St James Place, London.

Air Force. But Tshombe was worried about how long it would survive once the United Nations started bombing the airfields again.

Pausing, Tshombe considered Jack for a moment. Unlike some of the mercenaries, Jack had always been loyal to him and he liked the Rhodesian. Choosing his words carefully Tshombe suggested that it might be better if he actually gave Jack his DC-4. Apart from clearing the outstanding debt, the idea was that as a Rhodesian-registered aircraft it would be less likely to become a UN target. The only condition was that while Jack could use the aircraft for his own business to recover his outstanding fees, Katanga's needs would take priority. Jack was stunned at the offer, but willingly accepted it, pledging Tshombe his full support.

After registering the DC-4 in Rhodesia, Jack removed all the seats to improve cargo space and deployed the Skymaster to the food airlift for the beleaguered northern town of Kongolo. Although the Katanga army had recently liberated the town from the Balubas the jungle road had been cut leaving the population surrounded and at risk of starvation as their food reserves quickly ran out. Initial efforts to re-supply the town by air had been greeted by a blockade of aggressive Swedish Air Force jets. When he heard about the blockade pastor Len Robinson, followed through on his threat and wrote to everyone he knew in churches and governments across the world accusing the UN of "interrupting the flow of food to starving people". The pressure did the trick and the UN 'peacekeepers' grudgingly agreed to allow humanitarian flights into the enclave. For the rest of April Jack and Clive Halse, who had recently joined RAS as a DC-4 captain, flew almost daily food flights into Kongolo. It was tiring, hard work, but Jack felt good knowing that they were keeping people alive.

But it wasn't just about food. Jack heard the stories of the ANC's atrocities and saw the wounds of the people he was feeding. As the UN had cut off all military supplies to Kongolo it was a foregone conclusion that the defenders would be out of ammunition soon. Jack felt that without military support this whole 'humanitarian' airlift was a waste of time as the people were going to die anyway. Jerry Puren felt the same, and between them they started carefully smuggling in desperately needed military supplies. The United Nations inspectors at Kamina had become bored with searching the aircraft on its daily flights, so according to Jerry, "In between the loads of skimmed milk and protein rations being dispensed by Reverend Robinson, we flew in arms and ammunition to the Gendarmes."[26]

Initially Jack only allowed the weapons to be smuggled onboard if he was personally flying the route. But after a while, one or two of his other crewmen approached Jack and suggested that maybe they should help the Katangese at least with ammunition. It was plainly obvious that food was just one element of survival. From this almost incidental clandestine action, so Jack's gun-running career began, and it wasn't long before he was flying consignments of arms and ammunition into Katanga from Angola.[27]

In May 1962 the French mercenaries moved to Kolwezi and Jack got to know their leader Bob Denard quite well. When their busy schedules allowed, they would often share a meal together to catch up on what was happening across the country. Bob's overpowering personality had built up the formidable reputation of 'Les Affreux'. Yet Jack saw through his tough exterior and appreciated Bob's patriotism and their shared fear of Communism.

On some occasions Bob's commander Colonel Roger Faulques joined them. Faulques was impressed with Jack and liked his professionalism and his reliability. What Jack didn't know was that the Colonel was involved with the French intelligence agency, the SDECE and had started mentioning Jack in his reports back to Jacques Foccart and his deputy Mauricheau-Beaupré. Foccart was a very influential adviser to the French government and had recently founded the Service d'Action Civique (SAC) which specialised in covert operations in Africa. Jack's reputation within the shadowy underworld of military contractors was growing.

But there wasn't much time for socialising with the French. Almost every day Jack flew the freight shuttle in and out of Kamina and Kongolo, often twice a day until 25th June when he returned to Salisbury. He left the hard-working aircraft in the hands of Clive and the other RAS co-pilots to keep the Katangese supply lines open. Although there was growing UN activity throughout Katanga, Jack was confident that they would be safe as they were doing the aid flights with the UN's permission. Considering the work pressure, Jack was relieved

26 'Mercenary Commander' Colonel Jerry Puren as told to Brian Pottinger. Published by Galago Publishing. ISBN 0-947020-21-7.

27 Personal correspondence with Ian Dixon, March 27, 2008.

that he was no longer a 'one-man, one-aircraft' operation, and could hardly believe that in just over six months since losing his only aircraft, he now had a fleet that included a four-engined DC-4, a DC-3 and a Dove.

After doing more than one hundred humanitarian and relief supply flights into Kongolo Jack needed to have the DC-4 serviced again. In mid-July the aircraft was flown back to Salisbury and was replaced by the smaller DC-3. As soon as the DC-4 was ready Jack phoned the DC-3 crew and told them that their last flight would be Saturday 28th and they could fly home once they had made their last delivery. They were very relieved as the military tension was high and it seemed that the UN were about to launch another full-scale attack.

Mid-morning on that Saturday 28th an urgent radio call came through from Salisbury Air Traffic Control. Jack was told his DC-3 had been hit by anti-aircraft fire and was making an emergency landing in Manono.

Jack hurried over to the control tower where he could talk directly to the crew. Apparently over the jungle between Kongolo and Kabalo the aircraft was hit by machine-gun fire that had disabled the port engine. The crew had ditched all the arms-laced cargo into the vast Congo River before making an emergency landing in the little town of Manono. Just as Jack was able to establish that the crew had landed safely a pack of heavily armed ANC soldiers burst into the cockpit and escorted the tasty looking white men off the now suspiciously empty aircraft. Jack was left not knowing what had happened to his crew. Although fortunately before lunchtime a detachment of Ethiopian UN troops arrived and took custody of the airmen.

Relieved that at least the cargo had been dumped Jack contacted the Department of Civil Aviation and informed them that his civilian-registered aircraft had been downed in the Congo. In consultation with the Ministry of Foreign Affairs it was agreed that Jack and a DCA representative should immediately go to Elisabethville to press the UN for the immediate release of the crew.

The very next day The Times in Britain ran the story, under the dramatic headline 'RHODESIAN PLANE FORCED DOWN IN THE CONGO – DEMAND TO U.N. FOR EXPLANATION.' The article quoted Jack as saying, "…the aircraft was holed in the port engine and the starboard propeller was shot away. This cowardly attack was utterly unprovoked, and the pilot saved the lives of the crew only be jettisoning the urgently needed food supplies," It went on to say that he intended to press for full reparation for damage and the immediate release of the crew, closing with the comment, "We have no alternative but to hold the United Nations responsible for this brutal act of piracy."[28]

The report in the New York Times was much more ominous, "The crew of a Katanga-chartered Rhodesian Air Services DC-3 that landed at Manono Airport have been taken prisoner. The United Nations was studying today whether the crew of the plane should be handed over to the Congolese Government. Premier Cyrille Adoula had made an informal demand that the crew be handed over to Congolese authorities as 'mercenaries' if it were found that the men had been flying strategic material."[29]

Three days later on Wednesday 1st August a Red Cross relief aircraft was also shot at in the same area. With the failure of the clumsy attacks on the relief flights and the political embarrassment they had caused, on Monday 6th August the United Nations decided it would be easier to just ban all non-UN flights in and out of the breakaway province. With the jet fighters of the Swedish Air Force there to enforce the ban, there was little anyone could do about it. Three days later the Central Government announced an immediate and total suspension of all telecommunication and postal services to and from Katanga. This was followed shortly afterwards by the United Nations who imposed sweeping economic sanctions. The noose was tightening.

Although Jack had the UN's permission for the relief flights and had complied with their demand for inspections, with the combination of his Dakota having been shot down and the flight ban, his Kongolo contract was effectively terminated. Within a few weeks the Kongolo defenders ran out of ammunition and were overrun. Within a month Len Robinson's entire flock were either dead or disseminated.

But Jack still needed to find his crew who were being held 'somewhere in northern Katanga.' While fighting to get information out of the UN – who Jack was convinced had orchestrated the attack in the first place – he was asked to do a flight for the Katangese Government in one of their DC-3s. The UN refused

28 The Times (UK), edition of July 30, 1962.
29 The New York Times, edition of July 29, 1962.

to accept that the ANC had encroached into Katanga or were responsible for any aggression. To force an acknowledgement of what was essentially an invasion of their territory, the Katangese Government decided to take the UN representatives on an aerial reconnaissance of the area.

The flight lasted four hours, and Jack made a point of swooping low over any concentrations of ANC troops that they saw. Twice they were shot at, and the second time it was particularly heavy, with bullets loudly pinging through the fuselage. The terrified UN monitors quickly decided they had seen enough. But Jack took his time, teaching them exactly what his crew felt like as they were being shot out of the sky just a few weeks earlier.[30]

Eventually in mid-August having got an assurance that his crew were at least alive, Jack finally returned to Salisbury. While there, he was approached by an Austrian-based freight company called Aero-Transport. They were wanting to run a cargo service from Europe to South Africa via Salisbury and needed a handling agent. To take on Aero-Transport, Jack decided to register a separate handling agency. He called it 'Trans African Air Service', although it was based in the RAS offices it offered a separate, dedicated ground handling service, for which Aero-Transport was more than happy to pay.

On Thursday 23rd August the United Nations forces in Manono finally released Jack's crew, although their Dakota would remain parked on the side of the Manono airfield for another two years before they were able to retrieve it. Alastair Wicks had also returned to Salisbury in response to Tshombe's pleas for help. Tshombe needed more mercenaries in anticipation of the next war with the UN and the ANC, both of whom were busy regrouping. Alastair quickly set up a recruiting operation which was run very discretely with the help of Kate Woolard, the wife of one of Jack's newly employed captains. Unfortunately, it wasn't long before "one of the senior controllers had a few jars too many and started blabbing" and the English reporters broke the story of Alastair's busy little enterprise.[31]

This messy breach highlighted the need for absolute secrecy. As a result, Jack always made sure that no single individual ever knew the full story of his

30 Interview with Jerry and Julia Puren, Durban, September 1999.
31 Interview with Kate Woolard, July 2003.

Captain Jack Malloch (left), Clive Halse (middle), Alec Hasson and Alastair Wicks (right) along with the RAS air hostess, having just landed the DC-4 on the tropical island of Mauritius in August 1962.

Picture from Jack Malloch's private collection. © Greg Malloch

'secrets' and what he was really involved in. Over time Jack would eventually run his clandestine operations like giant jigsaw puzzles. Each person involved knew just their individual 'piece' and never saw the complete picture. This discretion earned Jack the respect and trust of almost everyone he dealt with, including clients, governments and even intelligence services such as the CIA, the British BMO and the French SDECE.

But, discretion aside, by mid-August Jack was concerned about the real possibility of not being paid for his Kongolo contract. To try and make up for it he focused on developing new charter contracts. Since the closure of Hunting Clan he had wanted to establish an international route to Europe for which the DC-4 would be ideal, although he knew it would take a very long time to get a scheduled route set up, but he was able to set up a charter route to Mauritius.

The crew that Jack selected for the first trip was Clive and himself in the cockpit, Alec Hasson (who had handled 237 Squadron's flight admin back in Italy) and an air hostess to look after the cabin, plus Alastair Wicks who came along for the ride. The flight took eight and a half hours each way and although Jack didn't like wearing his uniform again, he was pleased with the viability of the route.

Clive and Alastair took their wives along and spent most of their time relaxing on the beach. But Jack had trouble reconciling the horrors of the Congo with the idyllic beaches of Mauritius. He was withdrawn and disturbed about what he had seen in the Congo and was worried about the growing turmoil in his own country and where that might lead.

By the time Jack landed back in Salisbury a few days later, the Prime Minister of Southern Rhodesia had banned the Zimbabwe African Peoples Union due to widespread unrest. The military was then brought in to bring the situation under control. Firstly, almost a million leaflets were dropped into various 'trouble-spots' before the SAS were deployed. The Rhodesian Special Air Service had a fearsome reputation and first-hand counter-insurgency experience from the jungles of Malaya. This made them the ideal regiment to flush out the ZAPU agitators, especially in the forests of the Eastern Highlands. Over the next week they did numerous parachute drops into the most strife-torn areas.

While the last of these SAS drops was taking place, Jack was in the middle of another one of his 'top secret' flights taking more mercenary recruits back into southern Katanga. The new schedule was to fly them into Ndola late at night, from where they were sneaked across the Katanga border and trucked to their bases far from the prying eyes of the UN. By dawn the DC-4 was always back in its parking bay at Salisbury airport, exactly where it had been the night before, just as if it hadn't flown at all.

Finally, after almost a year of negotiations, in late September Jack secured a route licence between Salisbury and London Gatwick. On Tuesday 9th October 1962, having sorted out Alastair's latest 'collection and delivery' charters, the first scheduled Rhodesian Air Services flight to London took off from Salisbury with Jack and Clive Halse at the controls. Three days later they returned with a full cabin. Jack was ecstatic, and in addition to this he had also managed to sign up a fortnightly flight between Salisbury and Mauritius.

By the middle of October the army had brought the situation in Southern Rhodesia under control. But in Katanga tension continued to escalate throughout

October and November. Surrounded and cut off from the rest of the world Jack knew the end of the defiant nation was drawing ever closer. Yet he continued to shuttle in men and military equipment and to fly out the wounded from the few remaining 'safe' Katangese airfields.

By this end-stage Jack was flying as much for Tshombe's cause as he was for the money and the payments from the break-away government were becoming erratic. With the UN's massive military build-up, it was obvious the final purge was drawing nearer by the day. As Jack didn't want to lose any aircraft or crew in the next all-out assault, he started reducing the amount of time his aircraft and crew were spending in Katanga. Sir Roy Welensky shared Jack's view, stating that "...no kind of settlement was wanted by those in control. Time and money had run out: all they sought was a quick kill."[32]

Tshombe was well aware of the situation and at the end of November chartered Jack for a two-day trip to Angola. First they went to Texeira de Sousa, a small Angolan town just west of the Katangese border. It was an ideal fall-back position. From Texeira de Sousa they flew to the capital Luanda where Tshombe met senior government and military leaders to discuss the possibility of sanctuary for Tshombe's 'government in exile'.[33]

While Tshombe had been trying to build a federation, Britain were trying to dissolve Rhodesia's. In early December they officially announced that Nyasaland would be allowed to secede from the Federation of Rhodesia and Nyasaland. This announcement was made without consultation and the Federal Prime Minister bitterly attacked Britain for bad faith. According to the British, Northern Rhodesian would be next to go. Then it would all be over, save for ensuring a Black government in Southern Rhodesia. So much for the dangled carrot of independence for Rhodesia on the Australian model.

On Friday 14th December 1962 Rhodesians went to the polls again. The public outrage at Britain's announcement of the break-up of the Federation had a significant influence on the results. In a surprise election upset voters cast their vote for Winston Field's new Rhodesian Front party. It was a protest vote, but the RF's better organisation and consultative approach was also appealing,

32 'Welensky's 4000 Days' by Sir Roy Welensky P.C. K.C.M.G., published by Collins Books, St James Place, London.

33 Jack Malloch's personal flying logbook entry.

especially as it was clear that the Federation's days were numbered and that Southern Rhodesia would have to 'go it alone'.

The bewildered Rhodesian Front suddenly had thirty-five seats and a Parliamentary majority, but little more than a month to take over the government. One of their biggest challenges was that, except for Ian Smith, none of the elected candidates had held office before. So, one of the first things that the new Prime Minister did was to appoint Smith, the founder of the party, as his Deputy PM and Minister of Finance. Jack who had been watching Ian's political career develop was very pleased for his old 237 Squadron friend.

Towards the end of December Tshombe set off on a European tour to try and get somebody to hear reason. But it was too late. On Sunday 23rd, after weeks of build-up, skirmishes broke out between the UN forces and the Katangese Gendarmerie. Kolwezi was awash with refugees, but they all knew that the town wouldn't be safe for long. Instead of preparing for Christmas, the Katangese dispersed their aircraft and frantically began digging their defences.

As part of these 'final preparations' Tshombe arranged another meeting with his trusted friend Jack Malloch. The Prime Minister said that he fully expected this to be the last battle and that with the overwhelming forces ranged against Katanga, there was little chance of survival, not just of the country, but of all Katangese, including himself. Once again Tshombe sincerely thanked Jack for his loyalty and advised him to get himself and his aircraft out of Katanga as quickly as possible. Tshombe then apologised that he had been unable to clear his accumulated debt with Rhodesian Air Services, but if Jack would accept it, Tshombe offered him his own personal Heron aircraft in lieu of payment. As with the DC-4 the Heron was worth much more than the money Katanga owed RAS. As it would almost certainly be destroyed on the first day of the UN assault, Jack accepted it. His challenge now was to get the aircraft out of Katanga before it was swept up in the maelstrom.

On the evening of 27th December, just a day after Jack had flown the Heron to Salisbury, the UN handed an ultimatum to Tshombe's Government. They were given just thirty minutes to end the secession and withdraw their troops. It was impossible, and with the limited communication options available to them, by the time they had contacted Tshombe in Europe, the deadline had passed. Tshombe knew it was just a pretext for a pre-emptive strike and warned everyone to brace for an imminent attack. He then immediately organised to fly back to Katanga as quickly as possible.

Before dawn on Friday 28th, the UN launched a full-scale attack. Key points were seized and armoured cars crushed whatever opposition was brave enough to stand against them. The Third Battle of Katanga had begun, and by the end of that first day, the shattered and smouldering remains of Elisabethville fell to the combined armed forces of the United Nations.

According to two foreign journalists still based in Elisabethville the situation was dire; "...the streets were filled with rubble and lined with blasted palm trees and shattered cars. The UN were bombing and pounding the city with mortars. They hit the beauty shop, the French Consul's apartment, the Sabena Airways office, the Roman Catholic Cathedral, the museum, the zoo and many other 'strategic' targets…" "…the UN troops looted all abandoned property and distributed shot and shell with equal abandon. The Congolese army, the dreaded ANC, simply went on an uncontrolled rampage. The Balubas continued to sever and consume remaining supplies of human genitalia while most of the other tribes seized the moment to settle old scores."[34]

On the first of January 1963 Jack flew Tshombe to Luanda as he desperately tried to finalise his retreat. Two days later Jadotville fell. But not before Jack and his dynamite-packed forty-four-gallon drums had cut a strategic bridge to delay the U.N. advance.[35] Although the mercenaries and the Katangese Gendarmerie fought a brave rearguard action, they were being relentlessly squeezed back towards Kolwezi and the Angolan border.

In Kolwezi most of the population fled as the mercenaries arrived to prepare for their last stand. There was Bob Denard's French contingent and the remnants of Jerry Puren's Air Force, who were joined by 'Black Jack' Schramme and the rag-tag survivors of Alastair Wicks's group of mercenaries. At the last minute they were reinforced by a thousand loyal Katangese soldiers who drove a large military convoy against all odds across UN-held territory.

---

34 'Banana Sunday, Datelines from Africa' by Christopher Munnion. Published by William Waterman Publications. ISBN 1-874959-22-6.

35 Interview with Ian Dixon, Durban, September 1999

On January 13th Shinkolobwe fell to the United Nations. Kolwezi was all that was left. Defeat was now certain and the next day Tshombe briefed his military and mercenary leaders to become an army in exile. Five thousand troops under Schramme and Denard with as much equipment as they could carry, started relocating to Texeira de Sousa in neutral Angola. Jerry Puren was given the task of flying out the heavy equipment, the remaining airworthy aircraft – and the national treasury.

The UN pursued the refugees right to the border and then, poised just six miles from Texeira de Sousa they gathered in force. The Angolan government warned the United Nations not to invade and reinforced their defences. The world held their breath until January 23rd when Tshombe finally signed a declaration ending Katanga's secession, calling off the UN warmongers.

After almost exactly three years the tenacious Katangese, whose military had never exceeded more than seven and a half thousand, had been defeated. They had been overrun by one hundred and twenty thousand United Nations soldiers, supported by squadrons of jet fighters and bombers, along with one hundred and eighty thousand ANC soldiers.

The UN closely supervised the administration of the province as the Central Government finally got their hands on the mineral wealth which had always been at the heart of the conflict. The UN had achieved their goal, although it still remains one of the most costly and one of the least remembered, of any UN deployment. Two hundred and fifty UN soldiers lost their lives, the majority of them in combat – at least a couple of whom met their end to the home-made drum bombs pushed out of the back of Jack's Dakota.

Yet the end of the war in Katanga did not mean the end of dangerous combat missions for Jack...

CHAPTER 7

Yemen, Congo and the Mercenaries Revolt: 1963 to 1967

The war in Katanga was finally over.

Tshombe had survived, as had Jack, although Katanga, as an independent country had not, along with a big slice of Jack's most profitable charters. But even with that loss Jack was surprised how his business had grown over the last three dramatic years. Although his Dakota was still stuck in Manono, he had managed to come out of the war with three reliable aircraft, the DC-4, the Dove, and the recently acquired Heron. Jack also had five captains working for him; Clive Halse, Gordon Brown, Paul Pearson, George Cock and Doug Lock. They were being kept busy with not just Vilanculos and Mauritius, but now the new Gatwick route as well. But these were all relatively big aircraft and weren't suitable for smaller business charters. To service this niche Jack had the confidence to buy a six-seater Piper Aztec. He was indeed a collector of aircraft.

Although the war was over Jack still did whatever charters Tshombe needed. In early February 1963 he was away for a full five days shuttling the ex-Prime Minister around central Africa. Reporting on this, the New York Times made several references to "the Rhodesian Air Services aircraft" that was always at Tshombe's beck and call.[1]

For the rest of February and March, things became more settled and routine. The regular regional route of Mauritius was operated with the DC-4 and Vilanculos by the DC-3, while the Dove, Heron and Aztec did local charters around the Federation. For a brief moment Rhodesian Air Services was truly legitimate with no hidden agenda.

1 The New York Times edition of February 9, 1962

But there were plenty of hidden agendas between the leaders of Britain and the Rhodesian Federation. In December 1962 the British had stated their view that Nyasaland should be given the right to secede from the Federation and began grooming the Nationalists. Three months later in March 1963, without the agreement of the Federal government, the British announced that "...any Territory must be allowed to secede..." This effectively killed the Federation. Sensing victory, Banda and Kaunda mobilised their supporters to agitate as much as they could before the final dissolution that was set for 31st December 1963.

With unrest brewing across all three countries of the Federation Jack's attention was once again taken by Katanga. At the end of April Tshombe chartered the Dove to shuttle some of his provincial administrators around.[2] Considering that the war was over Jack was surprised how haggard Tshombe looked. After the flights Jack wished the obviously unwell statesman the best of luck. As his Heron and Skymaster had been gifts from the ex-President, he also pledged his continued support. Tshombe appreciated Jack's sincerity and assured his white pilot friend that there was still a lot that they would do together.

True to his word, in the middle of May, Tshombe booked another charter and first thing on the morning of Saturday 18th, Jack and Doug Lock headed off for Katanga. Their first destination was Ndola where they picked up Tshombe and his entourage. They then landed at Kipushi to collect a few more people before flying across to Vila Luso in Angola where they spent the night. In the morning they flew to Texeira da Sousa and spent the next twenty-four hours partying and reminiscing with Puren, Schramme, Denard and the other military leaders who were maintaining the Katangese 'army in exile'.

Bob Denard was particularly pleased to see Jack and gave the Rhodesian a giant bear-hug. In his broken English, Bob said that he had been wanting to contact Jack about a job that he and his men had been offered to help the ousted King's forces in the Aden. Slapping Bob on the back Jack said that he would always be willing to help, although he didn't really expect anything more to come of it. They got to bed very late that night.

By the middle of June, unable to manage the relentless persecution any longer, Tshombe decided to go into formal exile. He arranged for Jack to fly him and

2 Jack Malloch's and Doug Lock's personal flying logbook entries.

his family from Kipushi to Salisbury. From there they took a UTA flight to Paris. It seemed that the era of Moïse Tshombe was finally over.

Although the Vilanculos and Mauritius routes were the scheduled 'bread and butter' flights of the RAS operation, Jack was now worried about the overall profitability of his airline. Without the danger-money that he had come to rely on he was finding it difficult to cover the expenses, including the inevitable fuel bill and a dramatically increased payroll. With demands from his creditors, and in some instances, advance payments, Jack was beginning to have doubts about whether he could keep the crews he had recently employed.

According to Bill Brown's wife Maureen, "In 1963, the first year we were there, Jack faced serious financial difficulties three times. But he was very honest about it and issued letters to Bill and the other staff warning them that they may be about to lose their jobs. It got so bad that I remember pleading with Bill to ask Jack if he could give us, even just five pounds so we could buy some groceries." When asked why people continued to work for Jack under those conditions, Henry Kinnear, who joined RAS in 1964, said, "He was a wonderful man, and great to work for. We would have done anything for him. He just had such a good way – he really gave us confidence that everything would get sorted out. Jack was a great boss – to a fault."[3]

In July they flew numerous flights into various European cities including Athens, Milan and Dublin, but it was taking its toll on the aircraft. At the beginning of August, ten minutes after take-off one of the engines had a fire warning. The flight to London was delayed by twenty-four hours which incurred even more costs. The Skymaster was due for a major service but that was going to cost a lot of money. As Jack was mulling over his limited options Bob Denard contacted him about doing the clandestine fights into the Yemeni desert that they had first spoken about back in May. It seemed that the operation was being coordinated by the French Ministry of African Affairs which was reassuring. As the money was good Jack jumped at the opportunity.

On Sunday 7th August, Clive and Doug took the DC-4 on an overnight charter to Mauritius, returning at lunchtime on Monday. With just an hour for a quick clean-up and refueling the waiting UK passengers were loaded. But the return

3 Interview with Henry and Maureen Kinnear, Boksburg, Johannesburg. November 7, 2003.

flight was going to take a different route altogether and Jack had chosen his crew carefully. He needed men of courage, discretion and loyalty.

They were getting back into the gun-running business.

As soon as they got the passengers to their final destination, the crew removed all the seats, storing them in some empty hangar space. They then did a quick flight to Dublin where they picked up freight for Frankfurt. There, Jack met up with Pierre Laureys, the arms supplier for the secret Aden mission. It was no surprise that he was a friend of Bob Denard.

According to one of Jack's hand-picked crewmen Ronnie Small, "From Frankfurt we set off for Sophia and then flew on to Prague in Czechoslovakia behind the Iron Curtain. I never left the aircraft as I was on a South African passport, and I can't imagine that the name 'Rhodesian Air Services' across our fuselage did us any good either. Jack and Pierre went into town to sort out the deal and a military guard was assigned to look after me while I did the servicing on Number Two engine which was giving us trouble. Then all the soldiers arrived. They loaded huge crates of Czech guns and ammunition. In the end the whole plane was full right up to the ceiling from the front to the back bulkhead."

"The weapons were Czech 9 mm Samopal submachine guns. They were small, reliable and very easy to handle – ideal for Bob's mercenary infiltrators. Once the guns were loaded, we took off, but Number One engine started backfiring. We set the mixture to rich as we knew we couldn't return with that cargo. We got to altitude and there was still the occasional backfire. But we were flying into Africa so there wasn't much chance of sorting it out. We had to just take our chances."

"It was pitch dark as we crossed the north African desert. The Automatic Direction Finder was out, so Jack had to navigate by dead-reckoning. It was worrying though as we didn't know where we were. There was just the vast expanse of black desert below. The auxiliary tanks were finished, and we were beginning to run out of fuel. As usual though Jack seemed to know exactly where he was going and was always very calm and confident. It was as if he has a sixth sense when he was in command of an aircraft."

"Eventually at about two or three o'clock in the morning we picked up Djibouti.

Jack Malloch in his Rhodesian Air Services DC-4 delivering weapons to Bob Denard in the remote Yemeni desert during the civil war in Aden in 1963. *Picture supplied by Greg Malloch. © Greg Malloch.*

The troublesome engine started backfiring again but being so low on fuel we had to land. When the tractor came with the steps I told the guy to go away and that we just needed fuel and oil. We hadn't told the authorities in Djibouti that we were stuffed full of machine-guns."

"I also needed to change the carb before we took off again, so I set up our ladder by the engine and took the cowlings off and put them onto the wing. It was difficult working in the dark with no light and I had to hold a little hand-torch in my mouth." Once the repairs had been made Jack submitted a new flight plan and was given clearance to take-off. Their cover story, which they continued to use for many of the flights, was that they were doing aerial mapping of the Yemeni coastline.

Ronnie takes up the story again, "It was daylight by the time we took off. As we flew out across the Gulf of Aden there was strict radio silence and we didn't answer any calls – all the switches were off and there were no beacons. Jack flew along the Yemeni coast to a certain position and then dropped down to about five hundred feet to try and find the mercenaries on the ground. Once we'd found them, we searched for a bit of flat desert without any dunes where we could land. We had no idea of the wind speed or direction which added to the risks. Jack approached as slowly as he could and tried to touch down right at the start of the flat patch so we would have as much space as possible to take off again."

"The worry was the thin nose-wheel snapping off when it dug into the sand, so Jack planned to hold the nose up as long as possible. But as soon as we touched down the wheels dug into the sand throwing the nose down hard and we came to a halt very quickly. Fortunately, the nose wheel survived, but seeing how all the wheels had sunk into the sand we were very concerned about whether we would ever be able to take off again. When we opened the back door I realised that we didn't need the steps to get out because the wheels had sunk right up to their axles in the fine, powdery sand."

"The mercenaries offloaded the weapons very quickly, loading them straight onto their camels. Once the aircraft was empty Jack started up the engines and gave a bit of power, but we didn't move at all. Eventually we were at full power with the brakes off, but the aircraft wouldn't budge. The plane was shaking and the engines were screaming. The cylinder-head temperature was right in the red at 232 degrees. Once you start moving you can cool the engines by opening the engine cowlings, but you need momentum. Eventually the aircraft started shaking loose from the sand and slowly started to roll forward. But the sand was sucking us in and we couldn't get up enough speed. The dunes were approaching, and we couldn't turn around."

"Jack had sweat running down his face, so much so that I gave him a wipe on the forehead to try and stop it going into his eyes. We just couldn't get to lift-off speed and we were almost right on top of the dunes now. Finally, Jack called out "Gear up!" The wheels tucked but instead of taking off, with just the very minimum of speed the plane seemed to sink down a little closer to the ground."

"I remember looking out of the cockpit window and the props were actually skimming the deck sand-blasting their tips. Another inch or two lower and it would have been over for us all. The engines were also still right in the red and could have seized at any second, but I dared not open the cowlings by even a fraction as it would have dropped us like a stone."

"As we raced up to the dunes Jack tweaked the control wheel back and we skimmed over the top of the first dune but sank back to ground level on the other side of it. We just didn't have the momentum to pull up. There was another stretch of flat ground ahead of us and we picked up a bit more speed and a little more height. We must have been about ten feet off the deck when I opened a tiny crack in the cowlings. We dropped a bit, but it started bringing the engine temperature down and eventually Jack was able to start slowly climbing out of the clinging desert. As soon as he could he banked and turned back towards the sea. I remember looking down and seeing the dark line of loaded camels and the French mercenaries all in their robes just like local Bedouins walking towards the mountains. There was only one guy in the world who could have landed in the desert – and that was Jack Malloch. No one else was mad enough!"[4]

"We landed back in Djibouti, filled up with fuel and hurriedly flew back to the UK to collect our passengers. That was the first of the trips into the desert that we made. I was on two of the flights, and Bill Brown was on one. I'm not sure how many Jack did altogether. There must have been quite a few. I know Jack piloted every one of them," Ronnie concluded.

By the time they had landed back in Salisbury the success of their daring flight into the desert had come to the attention of Johnny Cooper, Jim Johnson and his team of SAS soldiers hiding out in the Yemeni mountains. They also desperately needed re-supply, so Johnny contacted his commander at the British Mercenary Organisation and it wasn't long before David Sterling realised that this was the same Jack Malloch that Alastair Wicks had been recommending. A discrete message was quickly delivered to Jack requesting re-supply flights for the Special Air Service as well. Seeing that he was already committed to these dangerous trips, Jack agreed to help the British as well.[5] He squeezed in two overnight trips to Mauritius before setting off on his next 'military mission' on Friday 6th September 1963. Once again, he took his ex-Korean War veteran fighter pilot Doug Lock with him as First Officer.

With each trip Jack gained ever more experience. Soon he was landing with the absolute minimum amount of fuel to lighten the load and would carefully time take-off to the cold pre-dawn when the air was still and lift was better.

4 Interview with Ronnie Small, Jet Park, Johannesburg, South Africa, March 2, 2004.

5 'The SAS Savage Wars of Peace' by Anthony Kemp published by Penguin Books. ISNB 13579108642.

Another load of Czech weapons being delivered to some remote corner of the Yemeni desert. This time they were for Jim Johnson's 21 Squadron of the British SAS who had a few vehicles at their disposal. Jack is seen in the foreground walking in front of the truck that is being loaded.
Picture from Jack Malloch's private collection. © Greg Malloch.

But this meant landing and taking off in the dark without lights. According to Doug Lock, even with his Korean dog-fighting experience, these trips into the Yemeni desert were by far the most terrifying missions of his entire life.[6]

Over the next few months Jack did numerous flights into the Yemeni desert. He collected weapons from both Prague and Budapest and delivered them to Denard and his Legionnaires and Johnson and his SAS teams, as well as fitting in airdrops for the Imam's army. Several years later Johnson, who rose to the rank of Colonel, revealed that, "a little-known freight company, Rhodesian Air Services, owned by Jack Malloch, an old associate of David Sterling, was the company subcontracted to deliver these arms supplies."[7]

It wasn't long before the Yemeni revolutionaries heard about Jack's supply missions and were on the lookout to intercept him. To minimise the number of flights it was suggested that some of the weapons be delivered in fishing dhows to discrete coves in the dead of night instead.

6 Interview with Kate Woolard, July 2003.
7 'Britain and the Yemen Civil War, 1962 – 1965: Ministers, Mercenaries and Mandarins: Foreign Policy and the limits of covert action' by Clive Jones. Published by Sussex Academic Press 2004. ISBN: 1-903900-23-9.

A photograph taken by Jack Malloch of pro-Royalist paratroopers in Aden. Based on the evidence it seems likely that they were deployed out of the back of Jack's civilian Dakota.

Picture from Jack Malloch's private collection. © Greg Malloch.

Although Jack didn't have to make so many risky flights into the desert he still had the contract to bring the weapons into Djibouti. The problem was that his DC-4 wasn't always available and sometimes the consignments couldn't wait for his next regular UK charter. Jack needed a European-based aircraft with a crew he could trust. He got in touch with his ground-services client and old friend Marian Kozuba-Kozubski at Aero-Transport in Austria. Marian offered to charter Jack one of his Constellations to carry the weapons from Europe to Djibouti. It was a good arrangement as the Constellation had twice the cargo-carrying capacity compared to the Skymaster.

But the problem was that the contraband now had to be offloaded in Djibouti, transferred to the port and repacked into boats. This had security implications with a lot more people knowing about the operation. Jack was very uncomfortable with this. After the first three or four Constellation flights, he regretted having got involved in the 'boat plan' and expressed his concern to his British and French 'clients'. Jack wanted to revert to direct flights, but it was too late.

The Constellation was impounded on its very next flight into Djibouti and fifteen hundred Mauser 7.92 mm rifles and twenty MG34 machine-guns were found on board. A few days later a newspaper article appeared in the Austrian press under the headline 'Arms trafficking to the Yemen with an Austrian charter plane.' This exposé was a huge blow and a major embarrassment for the owners of Aero-Transport, who turned out to be well-known Austrian politicians. Consequently Aero-Transport was shut down several months later.

With all this drama in the middle of November, Zoe realised that she was pregnant again. Although it was a little unexpected, they were very excited to be having another child. With this news Jack felt he should refocus on legitimate business and concluded a deal to provide extra pilots and aircraft to Wenela in Bechuanaland. They were looking for the support for their busy year-end period flying mine workers back home for the Christmas holidays. Jack was also always shopping around for the cheapest servicing for his aircraft and as a result of the Wenela deal he was able to get discounted rates on maintenance which helped the cash-flow.

While Jack's Dakota was being used for the Wenela contract, Sterling's British Mercenary Organisation contacted him about another 'little job' they needed. They were having trouble in the Sudan and had secretly deployed some special forces into the country who needed discrete air support. Jack was a reputable 'operator' and was already flying into Khartoum and Wadi Halfa, so wouldn't arouse suspicion. The operation was based out of Addis Ababa in Ethiopia, from where they were to fly into small military airfields dropping off urgently needed supplies for the special forces.

Four days before Christmas Jack and John Woolard, who had extensive experience in Ethiopia and the Horn of Africa, carried out their first mission in the Sudan. It was a success, but the DC-4 was running rough. The technicians in Addis Ababa had a look at the ailing aircraft. They picked up a couple of major problems with two of the engines, one of which was clearly beyond repair. Jack and the crew were used to flying on three engines, but two just wouldn't be enough.

The problem was that a new DC-4 engine was going to cost about twenty-five thousand pounds. In the end, after a long and sleepless night, Jack decided to give his father a call. After a ten-minute discussion Vic was clear on what he had to do: Firstly, find twenty-five thousand pounds and a Pratt & Whitney R2000 radial engine. Then have it shipped out to Addis Ababa as quickly as possible.[8]

Without the Skymaster, it meant that Jack's sole surviving Dakota needed to handle more routes and charters. Of his fleet of four aircraft, two were now stuck on the ground; the DC-4 was stranded in Addis and the flak-damaged DC-3 was still rotting away in Manono. In the end it was mid-January before Vic and Jack managed to get the new engine financed and delivered to the Ethiopian technicians where they fitted it under Jack's close supervision. How Jack and Vic managed to organise the money no one knew, but it put them both into serious debt. Nevertheless, once the Skymaster had been repaired it was quickly put back into action, for both the clandestine British re-supply flights, and the European and Mauritius routes.

By February 1964 Jack had had little to do with the Congo, although things were beginning to come to the boil again in the vast, troubled country. The feathered Bafulera tribesmen triggered a rebellion in the Kivu and Kwilu provinces which quickly spilled into northern Katanga. With their magical potions and raw savagery, the rebellion swept aside the undisciplined ANC and unleashed terror on the civilian population. With the support of Ghana and the Soviet Bloc, what had started as a 'minor disturbance' was growing into an unstoppable tide.

There was also drama in Rhodesia, although in the more civilised setting of their Parliament. By mid-April due to the lack of any sort of positive progress with Britain the Rhodesian Prime Minister Winston Field resigned and Ian Smith was chosen as his successor. The British were horrified and placed their troops in Aden on immediate standby to fly to Salisbury in case of a declaration of independence.

With all this turmoil going on around them, Zoe was due to give birth towards the end of June. Jack planned his flights to make sure that he would be in Salisbury. He flew until the 25th when he returned from Mauritius. He had still cut it a bit fine as the very next day Zoe went into labour. On Friday 26th Jack and Zoe's third child was born. It was another baby boy and they christened him Gregory. This time Jack had a full three days off before his next short internal

8 Personal correspondence with Dennis Rawson, March 18, 2008.

charter, and a week before his next overnight flight.

While the Malloch family were celebrating life, death was hard at work in the Congo. Albertville on the shores of Lake Tanganyika sank into an orgy of unrestrained violence at the hands of the terrifying Bafulera. The bodies of hundreds of unfortunates were dumped in the harbour which was stained a dark red for weeks.

With their witch-doctor's magic potions, from their north-eastern strongholds Gizenga's rebels had spread out across the country gaining control of almost half of the Congo. From Albertville, the town of Uvira was overrun and the rebels' next major target was Luluabourg in Kasai. With the Congolese National Army retreating in disarray, and horrific savagery sweeping across the 'heart of darkness', the situation was becoming desperate.

And desperate times called for desperate measures. In a totally unexpected move President Kasavubu, faced with imminent defeat, invited his old enemy Tshombe back from exile to help turn the tide. The announcement caught most people completely by surprise. Jack was pleased, for two reasons. Firstly, he knew that Tshombe was probably the only person capable of bringing order back to the Congo, and secondly, he knew this would probably mean a lot more work for him. He was right on both counts.

Tshombe was offered the position of Prime Minister, with jurisdiction across the entire Congo, as well as responsibility for defeating the rebels and bring order back to the vast, troubled country. On Tuesday 30th June Moïse Tshombe arrived in Leopoldville. Ironically, he landed just in time to see the last of the United Nations troops sheepishly leaving the country – which was now in a far worse situation than when they had first arrived.

Tshombe's initial strategy was to try and negotiate with the rebels. Predictably this was futile and by the middle of July the rebels had also taken control of Baudouinville, Coquillatville and the city of Stanleyville. Tshombe knew the political pitfalls of employing white mercenaries, but with his national army deserting *en masse* he couldn't see any alternative. By the end of July, Tshombe managed to get the reluctant approval of Kasavubu and Mobutu to start building a white mercenary force.

Without a moment to lose, Tshombe had instructed his old loyalists Wicks (who was still in partnership with Jack), Puren and Schramme to quickly establish a mercenary army to stop the rampaging hordes of rebels bearing down on the last bastions of the Establishment. The first person that Jerry brought onto the team was Mike Hoare who was appointed 'Commander-designate' of the armed forces while Jerry was made 'Commander of Air Operations'. Alastair Wicks was already there, and Mike made him his second-in-command. Within days Alastair was back in Salisbury setting up a mercenary recruitment centre. He also warned Jack to expect the first Congolese charters to start coming through as soon as they had shortlisted the volunteers.

This first charter for Tshombe was on Thursday 20th August. With the details confirmed and the deposit paid Jack felt that old twinge of excitement coming back. The flight was from Salisbury to Johannesburg where Jack picked up the first thirty-six mercenaries. He flew them directly to the ex-Belgian military complex at Kamina where Mike Hoare and Alastair were ready to start training.

Jack was stunned at the scale of the operation. In Katanga where they had fought together less than two years earlier, everything had been done on a shoestring in defiance of the might of the United Nations. But now they actually had the same American C-31 transporters flying for them. The Americans were busy relocating the two Katangese armies under the command of Schramme and Kaniki who were bolstering the defences of Luluabourg. Although Mike and Alastair appreciated this 'heavy lift' capability of the US Air Force, they knew when it came to bringing in the politically-sensitive mercenaries, Jack was their only option.

The target was to build a brigade of two hundred mercenaries to lead the attack against the rebels. Over the last week of August Jack did three more flights delivering volunteers to Kamina. As a result, in August he clocked almost eighty hours of flying time, almost all of which was in Tshombe's old Skymaster.[9] At last Jack's billing was up and his cash-flow eased slightly.

The challenge now was keeping up with the Mauritius and UK charters along with numerous, short-notice shuttles between Johannesburg and Kamina. In the middle of all this, after three consecutive midnight take-offs Jack had to do his DCA 'Periodic Flight Test.' The timing couldn't have been worse. Although

9 Jack Malloch's personal flying logbook entries.

The Rhodesian Air Services DC-3 VP-YUU on the dirt strip at Chiredzi airport in November 1964.
Picture from Jack Malloch's private collection. © Greg Malloch.

Jack passed, the examiner noted "…On the whole a competent performance by a tired captain under adverse conditions."[10]

With the growing number of mercenaries under his command Mike's 5 Commando were able to meet and slowly start pushing back the rebels. But to crush the rebellion it was felt that a strike right into their heartland was necessary and plans were drawn up for a lightning attack on Stanleyville. While these plans were being formulated two other things happened. Firstly, Jack's old Gascon friend Bob Denard returned from the Yemen to fight again for Tshombe, and secondly the CIA established 'Operation Wigmo'. Wigmo was essentially the American's air service in the Congo. It was staffed by exiled Cuban pilots who flew a fleet of DC-3 transports, T-28 fighters and B-26 bombers. In time Wigmo took over all of the functions of Jerry's Congolese Air Force. As Jack was already doing a lot of air transport work for Tshombe, Wigmo would also have an impact on him – and in more ways than one.

With the UN finally out of the Congo Jack quickly retrieved his old Dakota from Manono, although it did require a major overhaul before it was able to

10 Documents and papers belonging to Clive Halse provided by Chris Halse.

rejoin the fleet some eight weeks later.

Jack mainly used this Dakota for domestic charters and juggled the Skymaster between the demands of Mauritius and the Congo. While Mike Hoare's 'Wild Geese' were having remarkable success, the old ANC regiments were still a soft target for the rebels, who started using terror tactics to break their morale. One of Jack's flights was to retrieve a planeload of wounded ANC soldiers from the front lines. These 'walking wounded' were all limping with their heads bandaged. Apparently they had been caught by the Balubas who had chopped their ears and testicles off. Then the rebels just took their ammunition and handed their empty guns back, letting them go as a stark warning to anyone else who dared to stand in the way of the Baluba. The strategy worked and soon hardly any ANC would risk venturing out of their barracks.

With the Federation dissolved, on July 6th, 1964 Nyasalaland was granted independence becoming the new nation of Malawi. In Southern Rhodesia the political 'death spiral' continued to be played out in a series of talks, proposals and counter moves between the British and Rhodesian governments. This was complicated by the British general election, in which the Labour Party managed to gain a knife-edge majority of just a few seats. On 26th October, just ten days after the announcement of Labour's victory, Northern Rhodesia also gained independence, becoming the Republic of Zambia.

Back in the Congo, at the end of October Mike Hoare's 5 Commando were ready to launch their campaign to liberate Stanleyville and to ultimately defeat the rebels. On Sunday 1st November Mike chartered Jack to fly his officers and men from Kamina to Kabalo in the old DC-4. From Kabalo 'The Wild Geese' with the support of a column of Congolese infantry and engineers started their 'Stanleyville Column' to try to save the civilians who were being held captive in the bloody Simba capital. They were led by Mike Hoare and Alastair Wicks, who, as well as being second-in-command, took on the role of 'air liaison officer'.

Although Jack had been doing a lot of flights in the Congo, there was a growing amount of unpaid debt with his Congolese 'client' and he was having trouble keeping up with his fuel, insurance and salary payments. He knew that Tshombe would always honour his debt, but now that orders had to be channelled through the Central Government's miles of red tape, Jack was not so sure if he would ever get paid. Yet he didn't want to pull the plug on Tshombe, especially as they were friends, and Jack knew Mobutu who was just waiting for the chance to discredit the new Prime Minister.

Away from this intrigue Mike and Alastair were having remarkable success and had certainly turned the tide on the rebels. Their relentless campaign culminated in late November with the liberation of Stanleyville as they drove the Simbas ever further into the far north-eastern corner of the jungled country. But there was still a lot of work to be done, and in mid-December Jack was flying more mercenary recruits from Johannesburg into Kamina. It was a twelve-and-a-half hour night flight in the DC-4, and these shuttles would continue for at least the next twelve months. According to Jerry Puren, "Jack was flying mercenaries into Kamina with at least one full flight every two weeks."

Yet the Stanleyville victory was actually a major problem for Tshombe. The reason was that now that the country had been saved, Kasavubu and Mobutu no longer had a reason to share power with their old enemy. The plots against Tshombe started to be hatched.

After a brief holiday with the family over Christmas the demands on Rhodesian Air Services ramped up even more and in February and March Jack Malloch, Clive Halse, Paul Pearson and Henry Kinnear, were flying almost continuously across the length and breadth of the Congo. They moved mercenaries for Mike, they did general cargo for Air Congo and they did 'Operations from Leo' for Tshombe. In March Jack flew to Luluabourg, Albertville, Bunia and Stanleyville. He also did his first charters back into Elisabethville.[11] The old capital city was still lying in ruins after the UN's last brutal assault.

In March 1965, Jack flew almost one hundred hours, all of it in the DC-4 and all of it on behalf of the Congolese Central Government. Jack's other pilots were flying almost as much. With this level of involvement in military, passenger and cargo flying, Jack had come to the attention of Wigmo, who, over the last six months had been progressively taking over all flying duties in the Congo. Considering the strategic importance of the work Jack was doing, they felt

11 Entries from the personal flying logbooks of Jack Malloch, Clive Halse, Paul Pearson and Henry Kinnear.

they needed to get more control over it, especially the mercenary and freight flying. They began watching Rhodesian Air Services very closely. According to Jack's flying crew, the CIA would track them wherever they went. "We would enforce radio silence as soon as we crossed the Zambezi, but whenever we landed anywhere, a USAF Hercules would fly in and land about half an hour behind us. They would only be on the ground for about ten minutes, just to photograph us on the ground and then they would fly off again. Apparently, there was a 'Herc' in the air when they heard we were on our way and they would satellite track us to wherever we landed,"[12]

It wasn't long before representatives of the CIA set up a meeting with Jack to discuss their 'working relationship'. In this meeting Jack agreed that the Rhodesian Air Services contracts would become an extension of the Agency's Wigmo operation. Although he was now tied into the CIA Jack agreed to this arrangement due to the rising level of tension between Mobutu and Tshombe and the likelihood that RAS would eventually be targeted by the Mobutu faction.

As Jack proved himself to the CIA he become ever more involved with the American Secret Service. For Jack, these CIA contacts were to prove very valuable in the years to come.

With the growing demands of the overseas passenger route, Alastair's clandestine midnight flights and Wigmo's CIA contracts, Jack realised that he needed another large aircraft for his fleet. His lone DC-4, with all its mechanical problems just couldn't be stretched far enough any longer. Jack had been impressed with the Super Constellation that he had chartered from Aero-Transport, but there were not many in Southern Africa and this would make servicing and spares a challenge. He therefore decided to start looking for another DC-4. Although the DC-4 had less of a payload, this was probably a better option as it would avoid the need for crew conversions, and the aircraft could share spare parts.

Jack contacted his friend Bill Armstrong from Autair to see if he knew of any second-hand DC-4s that might be on the market. Bill immediately offered Jack one of his own ex-USAF Skymasters. With the strained and ever-worsening political tension between Rhodesia and Britain, and the bubbling rumours of

12 Interview with Ronnie Small and Henry Kinnear, Jet Park, Johannesburg, March 2, 2009.

Jack's DC-4 outside Bill Armstrong's hanger at Luton airport in 1965 prior to its delivery. Although the registration had not been changed when this picture was taken Bill had branded the aircraft Air Trans Africa. Jack wanted to be anonymous and removed the name as soon as he received the aircraft.

Picture provided by Dave Welch. © Dave Welch.

an imminent Unilateral Declaration of Independence, Jack though it prudent to try and stagger payments to Autair over a period to time. He wanted to be sure that if his profitable Gatwick route was terminated, he would be able to return the aircraft without a huge financial loss. Bill Armstrong not only agreed to this type of structured deal but was reputed to have actually invested money into Rhodesian Air Services.[13] The 'buy-back' deal that Jack eventually signed for the new DC-4 was much better than he had ever hoped for and Bill even included delivery of the re-registered aircraft to Jack's hanger at Salisbury airport.

As soon as Jack received the aircraft he stripped off all its markings except for the small 'VP-YYR' near its tail leaving it a bare metallic silver. This was intentional as Jack wanted to be discrete, especially as neither the Rhodesian government nor Wigmo's CIA commanders wanted an overtly Rhodesian aircraft flying around the Congo.

The new Skymaster was on the ground for less than twenty-four hours before heading off on its first mercenary charter. That round trip was more than seventeen hours which gave Jack plenty of time to get to know how the twenty-year-old

13 Interview with Henry and Maureen Kinnear, Boksburg, Johannesburg November 7, 2003.

aircraft handled. It was good and Jack was pleased. With the new DC-4 picking up on the demanding Congo flights, the older one could concentrate on their overseas and Mauritius routes. By the end of August Jack was fully committed to the mercenary and CIA flights in the Congo, relinquishing the overseas routes to his other crews. But there was no let-up in the pressure. In September Jack logged more than one hundred and ten hours flying in the DC-4s, half of which was at night due to the clandestine nature of his flights.

Now that he had two DC-4s Jack applied for a licence to operate a regular flight from Salisbury to the tropical Indian Ocean islands of the Seychelles. Landlocked Rhodesians loved exotic islands, so he had been planning this route for a long time, but just hadn't had the aircraft available to do it. The initial fortnightly flights to Victoria on the island of Mahé began in early October 1965. Jack had managed to win licences and contracts for all his aircraft and at last it looked like a good healthy income was secured for the business.

Yet while Jack's future was looking good, the country's future was looking ever more uncertain. Britain was insisting on 'majority rule' prior to independence and the Rhodesian government was ever more convinced that the only rational option was to break away from Britain altogether. By the end of September, reflecting the extreme exasperation felt by almost everyone, Ian Smith said, "If the British Government would not make concessions, well then Rhodesia has no alternative but to go its own way regardless of the consequences. This decision has been taken with regret, with open knowledge of the dangers involved."[14]

And it wasn't just in Rhodesia that things were coming to a head. In the Congo President Kasavubu and Mobutu's 'Binza Group' started moving in on Tshombe. The problem was that the Katangan had become hugely popular in the process of defeating the rebels and seemed almost certain to win the upcoming elections. Mobutu and his CIA backers agreed that Tshombe needed to go – permanently.

At the end of September on the eve of Mike Hoare's attack against the rebel strongholds of Fizi and Baraka, Kasavubu announced that the Congolese Parliament would be assembled within the next few weeks. It was clear that this was going to be the end of Tshombe, as, with the liberation of Fizi and Baraka, the rebellion would finally be over. According to Mike, "Mr. Tshombe

14 The British Evening Standard newspaper, September 23, 1965 edition.

asked us to press on as quickly as we could, even though he saw in this a threat to his own office. The future of the Congo was the paramount consideration. It was typical of Mr. Tshombe that he should put his country above his personal ambition, and I had a presentiment that the end was near for him."[15]

By the beginning of October Jack began to sense a growing indifference towards Tshombe by the CIA operatives at Wigmo, and this worried him. The contracts kept coming in though and Jack had a lot of flying to do in support of the Wild Geese who launched their final attack on the rebel strongholds along the shores of Lake Tanganyika. Mike Hoare and his force of two hundred mercenaries made a surprise attack on the rebel-held port town of Baraka while Alastair Wicks, his one hundred mercenaries and three hundred of the best hand-picked ANC soldiers, attacked the town of Lulimba from the south, causing a diversion.

After a fierce battle, Baraka was wrestled from the enemy in a desperate action reminiscent of the Normandy landings with the mercenaries having to fight for every inch of the exposed beach before gaining a foothold in the town. This was one of the last battles that Che Guevara's Cuban advisors directed, and it certainly showed in the ferocity of their defence.

The next day, Alastair and his four-hundred-strong army arrived having cleared the towns and villages to the south. With the extra men, Mike was able to reinforce Baraka and regroup for the next push onto the fortress town of Fizi. After a couple of days clearing the enemy from the surrounding villages, on Sunday 10th October 1965, 5 Commando attacked Fizi, only to find it completed deserted. With the disappearance of their Cuban leaders, the rebels had decided to retreat northwards into the bush from where they planned to launch a classic guerrilla-style war, for which Che had trained them well.

Three days later on the 13th Jack heard the news that Tshombe had been dismissed by President Kasavubu during a session of the Congolese Parliament. The reason Kasavubu gave was that with the final defeat of the rebels Tshombe's task was over. Tshombe, ever the pragmatist, gracefully accepted his ousting and turned his attention to campaigning for the coming elections. Jack, knowing how things worked in the Congo, worried about the safety of his good friend and of all those who supported him, including Alastair and the numerous Rhodesian

15 'Mercenary' by Mike Hoare, published by Corgi Books. ISBN 552-07935-9.

Air Services crewmen who were still in the Congo.

With the ill-considered manoeuvrings in Leopoldville President Kasavubu encroached on Mobutu's military jurisdiction and the Commander-in-Chief was furious. To pacify him, a few days later Kasavubu promoted Mobutu to the rank of Lieutenant-General. But it was too late. Having just got rid of Tshombe, with his new-found power Mobutu decided that Kasavubu would have to go too. And so the palace-drama continued…

Meanwhile after Wilson's threat of military action against Rhodesia had been leaked, the tension between Britain and the self-governing colony couldn't have gotten any worse. When asked how he viewed the threat of an armed invasion in the case of a declaration of UDI, the Rhodesian Prime Minister firmly replied, "We believe the dangers attached to doing nothing are worse than the dangers attached to UDI. If anyone puts a foot in our country and has no right, he must take what is coming his way. If we have to get out of our country, we would rather go down fighting than crawling on our hands and knees."[16] The die was cast.

But Wilson thought Smith was bluffing. He thought that the Rhodesian business community and middle class, who were very patriotic to the Crown, would not accept UDI. He was wrong, and at the end of October Wilson made another PR blunder when he was quoted as saying that he was "obliged to lead Mr. Smith up the garden path." This further hardened Rhodesian public opinion against the British. The disastrous talks ended with Wilson threatening to destroy the Rhodesians if they were to go ahead with the threat of UDI.[17]

Like many other Rhodesian businessmen, Jack was gravely concerned about the future and the impact sanctions would have on his airline. Although he now had the new Skymaster, with the Congolese contracts and the overseas routes, his original DC-4 was still fully committed. But Jack was having more and more trouble finding and affording the spare parts to keep the old aeroplane in the air.

As a result, with every long-haul flight, especially the UK charters, Jack's flight engineers would take a long list of spare parts for the ailing DC-4 with them.

---

16 'Rhodesia and Independence' by Kenneth Young. Published by Eyre & Spottiswoode, London.

17 Ibid.

According to one of the engineers, they had to be as self-sufficient as possible, "With our bucket of bolts we really worked our guys to bring that plane home – there was always something to worry about. Often when I did my repairs on the aircraft they were strictly illegal, but we just had to keep the plane flying." The passengers were unaware of what was really happening behind the scenes and didn't realise that they were all flying 'on a wing and a prayer'.

Meanwhile Rhodesia wasn't only being threatened by sanctions. The extremists saw their chance to topple the government and unleashed their gangs of agitators and intimidators, flooding the townships and vulnerable rural communities with their brutal 'commissars'. A wave of violent attacks, torchings and murders followed. Faced with the onslaught, on Friday 5th November the Rhodesian Government declared a State of Emergency. Army units were dispatched to trouble spots around the country, all Royal Rhodesian Air Force squadrons were placed on alert and controls were placed on imports to try and limit the impact that the imminent sanctions would have on the country's external reserves.

In the back of the military commanders' minds were also Wilson's threats of military intervention. Consequently, they began dispersing their assets and strengthen the defence of their installations. From his hanger Jack watched the barbed wire being unrolled around New Sarum and the military aircraft taking off in pairs for the outlying bases. There were dark storm-clouds on the horizon and Jack could hear the distant rumble of thunder. In Katanga he had seen the air force dispersing before, and he had seen the destruction of war. He felt hollow inside, although at least this time Rhodesia had jet fighters and bombers which would be a bit more effective than Katanga's Dakotas and crop-dusters.

Faced with no attempt at reconciliation and just tougher conditions from the British, Rhodesia's twelve sombre Ministers gathered on Thursday 11th November 1965. After lengthy consideration the decision was made. There was no future in continuing the negotiations with the British Government who clearly had no intention of honouring their obligations to the country that had been consistently promised over the last forty-two years. They adjourned to the Phoenix Room and signed the fateful Unilateral Declaration of Independence.

It was announced that the Prime Minister would address the national at 1.15 p.m. At the Rhodesian Air Services hangar, a radio was organised and at lunchtime

Jack and his staff, many with their sandwiches in hand, gathered. With the entire nation listening, Smith informed the country that the Cabinet had decided to declare independence and gave the reasons why.

Smith ended the announcement saying, "I believe that we are a courageous people and history has cast us in a heroic role. To us has been given the privilege of being the first Western nation in the last two decades to have the determination and fortitude to say 'So far and no further.' We may be a small country, but we are a determined people who have been called upon to play a role of world-significance. We Rhodesians have rejected the doctrinaire philosophy of appeasement and surrender. The decision which we have taken today is a refusal by Rhodesians to sell their birthright and even if we were to surrender does anyone believe that Rhodesia would be the last target of the communists? We have struck a blow for the preservation of justice, civilisation and Christianity and in the spirit of this belief we have this day assumed our sovereign independence. God bless you all." The announcement ended with the playing of "God Save The Queen." Across the country, in stores, offices, factories and workshops people stood in respect for the Queen.[18]

Everyone was worried though. Some worried about an attack by Britain. Others feared an attack from the countries to the north and most worried about internal attacks by ZANU and ZAPU. As for Jack and most other business owners they were worried about the imposition of sanctions, and what that would do to their livelihoods.

With Tshombe having been sidelined Jack wasn't counting on much future business in the Congo. That meant the survival of his airline now depended on the international routes to England, Mauritius and the Seychelles, all of which were now in jeopardy. He had two DC-4s, two DC-3s, a Heron, a Dove and the Aztec plus a significant number of staff. Yet the only route he could count on was Vilanculos and, as he well knew, that could be serviced by a single Dakota.

While Britain was considering the military option, they quickly put their threatened sanctions into force. Rhodesia was expelled from the Sterling Monetary Area and the country's assets in London were frozen. Preferential

---

18 'Rhodesia and Independence' by Kenneth Young. Published by Eyre & Spottiswoode, London.

trade arrangements were cancelled and the importation of Rhodesian sugar and tobacco into Britain was banned. Harold Wilson, in his characteristic ill-informed over-confidence announced that the measures would bring Rhodesia to its knees in "weeks rather than months".

According to Dudley Cowderoy and Roy Nesbit, "Sanctions busting began the day sanctions were imposed. It was to grow into a swashbuckling, cloak and dagger industry in which great risks were taken but in which there were correspondingly profits and losses."[19] Although Jack Malloch never really considered himself a 'swashbuckling sanctions-buster', to keep his business alive he certainly worked hard to find a way around Britain's sanctions. And it wasn't long before they started to bite…

Within two weeks of UDI, Jack's landing licence at Gatwick, his most profitable route, was revoked and Rhodesian Air Services was banned from British airspace. Just as Jack had feared he was one of the first victims of sanctions.

While Jack was wondering what to do with his new DC-4, on Thursday 25th November, General Mobutu, backed by the CIA, carried out a coup d'état and took over leadership of the Congolese government. Tshombe, realising that his life was in danger, decided to go into exile again.[20] The ex-Prime Minister contacted Jack, told him of his imminent departure and advised him who he could safely deal with in Leopoldville, but warned him to be very careful. Tshombe then wished Jack all the best and promised that he would do his best to return.

On Monday 6th December, Britain withdrew Rhodesia's Commonwealth Trading Preference, extending sanctions to cover ninety-five percent of the landlocked country's exports. Then on Friday 17th the British announced an embargo on oil supplies to Rhodesia and quickly intercepted an oil tanker on its way to offload oil into Rhodesia's pipeline. Rhodesia immediately felt the pinch and realised that it needed to conserve whatever fuel supplies it had left. Ten days later, a coupon system of petrol rationing was introduced. This was to last, on and off, for the next fifteen years.

With his UK route cancelled and a growing number of creditors snapping at

---

19 'War in the Air. Rhodesian Air Force 1935 – 1980 by Dudley Cowderoy and Roy C. Nesbit. Published by Galago Publishing. ISBN 0-947020-13-6.

20 'Mercenary Commander' Colonel Jerry Puren as told to Brian Pottinger. Published by Galago Publishing. ISBN 0-947020-21-7.

his heels, by the beginning of 1966 Jack knew he wouldn't be able to sustain the airline for much longer. To make matters worse, with the imposition of sanctions, his new route to the Seychelles had also been blocked. Jack was faced with stark choices. He could either sell the airline or declare bankruptcy and shut it down.

Although he was scuffling for every bit of financial support he could find, Jack just couldn't sustain the business and at the end of January 1966 he was forced to liquidate.

Jack's Dakota VP-YUU and the Dove were both sold to Jack's rivals at Central African Airways. With these two aircraft CAA also purchased the air service permits to Mauritius and Jack's 'Champagne flight' to the Victoria Falls. The second Dakota was sold to NAC in South Africa along with the landing rights at Vilanculos. NAC had long planned to take over the lucrative 'island holiday' route from Rhodesian Air Services and had at last got it. Jack had been flying into Vilanculos for more than ten years and that loss hurt him the most.

The new DC-4 was then given back to Bill Armstrong at Autair. Although to help see Jack through the difficult transition Bill left the aircraft in Jack's care, allowing him to use it as he needed for a couple of months before his crew travelled down to Salisbury to retrieve it.

And that wasn't Jack's only lucky break. Ironically, just as he was in the throes of collapse and left without any options, he was able to find an investor. It was David Butler, a famous Rhodesian Olympic yachtsman and one-time leader of the opposition. Although his passion was still in competitive yachting, he was involved in numerous business ventures including a small air charter service, so had long known and admired Jack.

With Dave's backing, Jack managed to retain Tshombe's old DC-4 with which he established their new air charter business. For the new business, Jack still had the paperwork and company registration documents for the dormant ground handling business 'Trans African Air Services' which he had set up to handle Aero-Transport back in 1962. With Dave, it was agreed that they would use that existing registered business and just rename it. For the new name Jack shuffled the words around a bit, eventually settling on 'Air Trans Africa.' Several weeks later, Dave bought the Dove back from Central African Airways and with it,

Jack took off once again.

Much to his delight, Dave also suggested that if they were to pursue long-haul flights they should start looking at buying a bigger aircraft. Over the years of flying the DC-3 and DC-4, Jack had fallen in love with Douglas aircraft and had been wanting to upgrade to the larger and more powerful DC-7. Now, literally out of the ashes of bankruptcy, it seemed he might have the chance. Although the collapse of Rhodesian Air Services had been traumatic, at the last minute, things had turned out much better than he could have ever imagined.

After a month of searching Jack signed a purchase agreement for an Italian DC-7. Unfortunately that deal was cancelled at the last minute, blocked by the ever-widening trade embargo against Rhodesia. Even though Jack seemed to be one of the main victims of sanctions, he wasn't one to give up and decided to ask for help from his CIA friends at Wigmo. It wasn't long before they found a second-hand DC-7 for him. Having successfully organised the finance, in mid-March Jack arrived in Florida to take custody of the Ex-PanAm aircraft.

US Aviation rules stated that an American crew had to fly the aircraft out of the country. Through his CIA contacts Jack was introduced to Derrick 'Red' Mettrick. Jack was impressed with the American's flying skill and offered him the position of captain for the flight back to Rhodesia. Red agreed and gathered the rest of the crew.

The first leg of the trip was from Miami to Nassau, the capital of the Bahamas. From there they flew south-east over the Dominican Republic and the string of tropical islands of the Lesser Antilles before picking up the Brazilian coastline just east of French Guiana. Following the coast, they eventually landed at Recife on the very eastern tip of Brazil. There they refueled and restocked in preparation for the three thousand-mile flight across the south Atlantic.

After getting their clearance they taxied out and started their take-off run. But just as the aircraft reached full power and was accelerating down the runway the fire alarm on Number 3 engine went off. Immediately the captain throttled back and braked hard. They stopped near the end of the runway, turned and taxied back. They were all painfully aware that there were no mechanical facilities at Recife.

Ronnie Small opened up the engine and quickly discovered that it was a serious problem which would have resulted in an engine fire. He had to replace the Power Recovery Turbine unit. Luckily they were carrying a large stock of spare parts so he was able to do the repair within a couple of hours. But with every passing hour Jack became ever more nervous as every minute on the ground increased their chances of being caught.

As soon as Ronnie gave the thumbs-up they quickly taxied out and requested clearance for take-off again. This time the tower refused permission. They were instructed to return to the parking area. No reason was given. Jack and Red went to find out what the issue was. They were told that somehow their clearance out of Miami was a problem and until this was resolved they had no clearance and couldn't take off. Jack was very worried that they had been tracked down and that he was about to lose the aircraft.

According to Ronnie Small, "That evening we went to the hotel, then spent the whole of the next day waiting at the airport – to no avail. The worst thing was that Salisbury didn't know where we were. We had no way of telling them anything. There were no phone lines to Rhodesia and to add to the complication there was a carnival going on, and the whole country had shut down. Eventually one night while we were all having dinner the whole crew decided that the next day we would tell the tower that we needed to do a ground run, but instead we would take off and escape. We hadn't seen any Air Force so we felt we had a good chance of making it – even Red and the American crew were keen on the plan, as by now we were all worried that we were going to be arrested for breaching sanctions."[21] However, when they arrived at the airport the next morning ready to make their escape their clearance had been reissued and they were able to take off without having jet fighters scrambled after them.

After some twelve hours flying due east across the Atlantic they landed at Luanda on Africa's west coast. As soon as they were on the ground, Jack contacted the Air Trans Africa office in Salisbury to let them know that they were almost home. Then as soon as the aircraft was refueled they took off again for the last leg to Salisbury, another five hours away.

Within hours of landing in Salisbury Jack started the reregistration process and just two days later the new aircraft was heading off on its first charter to

21 Interview with Ronnie Small, Jet Park, Johannesburg, March 2, 2004.

London. With no Rhodesian livery and a flight plan submitted from Luanda no one at Gatwick questioned the routing or where the aircraft had originated from. Although Air Trans Africa was still a very young operation, Jack was pleased with progress. He had got his first 'Seven' and he had managed to open up a route back into the UK right under the noses of the British authorities.

Jack, with his impeccable discretion was also appreciated by his friend the Rhodesian Prime Minister, who, through the Central Intelligence Organisation, started using Jack more and more, as Ronnie Small recounted; "I remember once I had to go and do a pre-flight on a Dakota at 4 a.m. for Jack who was going to do a solo flight. It was quite unusual. Jack said that he would go from the hangar which was even more mysterious. We also needed to have the plane back for an 8 a.m. scheduled flight to Chiredzi. Once the plane was ready and started up, an African gentleman climbed into the right-hand seat and Jack flew to Blantyre and back. It later turned out that it was the Malawian President Hastings Banda himself who had been on a secret trip visiting Ian Smith."[22]

Having been operating for well over ten years, by the mid-1960s Jack was well-known in Southern African aviation circles. It didn't take him long to rebuild the charter business that he had relinquished with the closure of Rhodesian Air Services. But this time he was very focused on squeezing every moment of airtime out of his aircraft before he succumbed to the temptation of buying more aeroplanes. One of Jack's crew later commented, "In those days there was no such thing as flying limits. That only came in later. There used to be two guys in the cockpit and one in the bunk. The second guy was there to just check that the pilot didn't fall asleep from exhaustion. We flew all the time – keeping the aircraft in the air was the big thing for us."[23]

Although there was a steady market for passenger traffic between Salisbury and London, Jack had also been getting increasing freight requests, and they began 'splitting' the load on some of their trips, especially the Mauritius route which Jack had managed to keep. As the freight was only one-way, the passengers and crew quickly discovered that the empty half of the plane on the return journey made a good dance floor. "Those Mauritius flights were fun. I remember the

22 Interview with Ronnie Small and Henry Kinnear, Jet Park, Johannesburg, March 2, 2004.
23 Interview with Henry Kinnear, Boksburg, Johannesburg, November 7, 2003.

one trip we did the front half of the plane was full of pig carcasses and the passengers were at the back. It was an eight-hour trip each way and on the way back without the freight we had a major dance party on the empty cabin floor at the front."[24] Certainly not something modern load masters or IATA regulations would permit.

Although British economic sanctions targeted Rhodesia, the country's northern neighbours, especially Zambia were suffering even more as they had been cut off from their biggest trading partner. According to Henry Kinnear, "After sanctions were applied we actually did a lot of flying in support of our neighbours as they were also suffering." And there was a lot of flying to be done. To be able to pick up these contracts Jack re-registered the old DC-4 in Bechuanaland, although much of its flying remained on standard Air Trans Africa (ATA) routes. With this extra work it seemed as if the airline was finally establishing itself and, although they were still flying for 'Wigmo' in the Congo, Jack felt he was finally getting out of the shadowy world of clandestine military flying.

But Jack was operating in Africa and there was never a shortage of drama. On 28th April 1966 Nigeria's second military coup took place as the country's Muslim northerners deposed the Ironsi military government. With this a massive tribal purge erupted, mostly against the Ibo who lived in the eastern delta area known as Biafra. It was later estimated that up to one million people, mostly civilians, lost their lives in the aftermath of the July coup. In the months that followed, more than two million Ibos from across the country fled back to their eastern tribal homeland. It wasn't long before the mass of Ibo started to question why they should remain in the Nigerian federation considering that the rest of the country just seemed intent on slaughtering them all.

Meanwhile in Brussels, Tshombe was horrified by how many of his people had been killed in the ill-fated 'First Katangese Revolt' that had played out in April and May 1966. In desperation he commissioned Jerry Puren to come up with a better plan that would succeed in bringing the Katangese back to power in the Congo. In his plans, when considering air support Puren noted, "Bracco and Libert were still circulating in Portugal and together with Jack

---

24 Interview with Henry and Maureen Kinnear, Boksburg, Johannesburg, November 7, 2003.

Malloch, I reckoned we would have sufficient pilots. I would alert them to be on stand-by."[25]

However, at that time Jack was unaware that he was being worked into another revolution and was trying to sort out a few challenges of his own. The DC-7 was having a major overhaul, so Jack had to deploy the old DC-4 to the Gatwick route. At least with its new Bechuanaland registration it was legitimate. But it was a strain trying to keep up with the passenger routes and charters without the DC-7, especially with the growing demand for freight charters. It was obvious that they needed to upgrade their fleet. So, together with Dave Butler they decided that they should buy another DC-7. There were a couple of second-hand ones for sale in the UK and Jack quickly finalised the deal. Unfortunately, once again, it got blocked by the anti-Rhodesian authorities.

Although Jack really appreciated Dave's financial strength and his willingness to invest in the business, he was growing uncomfortable with Dave's liberal political views. This became acutely embarrassing for Jack at the end of August 1966 when Dave wrote letters to every Member of Parliament asking them to reject the Constitutional Amendment Bill and seek the resumption of talks with Britain. This led the Prime Minister to subtly question what side Jack was really on. After assuring Ian of his loyalty Jack realised that in politics even business affiliations could be damaging.

As if to prove his commitment to the Rhodesian cause, in the last few months of 1966 Jack fully immersed himself in the lucrative cargo run to breach Britain's sanctions. According to Paul Pearson, "We were heavily involved in sanctions-busting, with a regular service flying passengers into Europe (Spain, Holland and Germany). Then we would remove the seats and flying goods back, before returning to bring the passengers home."[26]

Although at the time Jack didn't consider himself a 'sanctions-buster.' He was just trying to run a successful air charter business and was accepting orders from clients who were wanting him to bring in goods – although he did appreciate the importance of these goods to his strangled country and was proud to be able to help. He believed in the righteousness of his country's cause, much as

25 'Mercenary Commander' by Col. Jerry Puren as told to Brian Pottinger. Published by Galago Publishing. ISBN 0-947020-21-7.

26 Personal correspondence with Paul Pearson.

he had believed in the righteousness of Katanga's cause, and being a man of principle, Jack always stood by the things he thought were right.

Although Jack was away from home a great deal, he was a very committed husband and father and took every opportunity he could to teach his children the importance of these principles. When his young daughter Alyson was just eight or nine years old, she told Jack that she would mow the whole lawn (and it was quite a big one) for ten cents. He agreed but they only had an old-fashioned manual lawn mower and soon the little girl was exhausted. When she had mowed over half the lawn Alyson asked her father if she could just get five cents even though she had mowed more than half of the agreed area. "He said that our agreement was the whole lawn for ten cents and that is what I must do otherwise I wouldn't get anything. I did a bit more but didn't finish it, but my Dad stuck to his word. He wasn't at all mean and probably later he gave me money or bought what I had wanted, but the lesson stuck. You have to stick to your word no matter what!"[27]

By October 1966 the level of violence in Nigeria had subsided. But no-one believed the problems had been resolved. Most people – at least in Nigeria – saw the lull for what it was: a fleeting chance for each side to arm up for the inevitable civil war. Just before the end of October Alastair Wicks, who had recently had his Congolese contract terminated, met up with Jack. He presented all of the gun-running charters that Biafra needed. Knowing that Jack usually flew for a cause he believed in, Alastair went to great lengths to convince his partner of the righteousness of the Biafran cause. They were a small nation being victimised by a central socialist government. It was almost identical to Katanga and had the same emotional appeal. Jack was interested, but was worried about the risks, especially as ATA was establishing itself as a legitimate airline. Skeptically Alastair asked Jack how long he really thought it would last, considering that every flight plan that they submitted to British Air Traffic Control was technically illegal. Jack conceded the point and said he would at least think about Biafra.

1966 ended badly for Rhodesia. The UN had voted on tighter sanctions, the oil pipeline was shut down and Wilson was resolutely courting the radical

27 Personal correspondence with Alyson Dawson, May 5, 2019.

nationalists. Although Jack had managed to survive the first year of sanctions, 1966 ended badly for him too. The deal on the next DC-7 had fallen apart, and after the excitement of the rebirth of Jack's new airline the confidence of his creditors had begun to wane. They were all starting to squeeze for money. With the growing frequency of in-flight emergencies Jack also needed to invest in serious servicing and repair work. Once again cash flow was becoming critical.

To make matters worse the Tax Department were onto Jack for a fifty-thousand-pound tax liability and were threatening to shut the business down if the account wasn't paid in full. Jack brought in a professional auditor and after a few days their accountant discovered that somehow the finance payments on the DC-7 had not been put through the books. After the necessary adjustments the year end accounts for 1966 reflected a loss of fifty-thousand-pounds. This meant that there was no pre-tax profit, so the tax claim was reversed.[28]

But the business had still made a loss and the lack of cash-flow had caught up with them. With little choice, Jack called Alastair and set up a meeting to discuss what opportunities there really were in Biafra. What came of this meeting there is no record, but on Wednesday 18th January 1967 the Rhodesia Herald ran a front-page article titled "SA and Rhodesian pilots ferrying arms to Biafra." It specifically mentioned Alastair Wicks and "a Salisbury-based airways company". Although Jack denied any involvement, it was an obvious reference to Air Trans Africa.

It does seem likely that Jack did do at least a few arms deliveries for Biafra in early 1967 based on the fact that he was able to pay the outstanding salaries and catch up on some of his creditors. He also renewed his search for another bigger aircraft. While he wanted another '7', a dealer offered him a Lockheed Super Constellation which Brazil's national airline was wanting to get rid of. Although Jack had never flown the L-1049G it was certainly a good deal.

Jack's biggest problem was that his financier Dave Butler had lost interest in Air Trans Africa. There were two main reasons for this: Firstly, the tension that his outspoken political views were causing and, secondly, he had come to realise that there would not be a reasonable financial return on his significant investment in the airline. As a result, Dave wasn't willing to make any further

28 Interview with Dan Remenyi, April 8, 2010.

investments in the business.

Exploring every possible option Jack set up a meeting with his Prime Minister friend Ian Smith. Jack asked whether the government would be able to help him out in some way, considering that he was already involved in breaking sanctions for the good of the country. To his surprise Ian, who was secretly pleased with the growing split between Jack and Dave, was quite accommodating. Although Smith didn't offer to pay for any new aircraft, the Prime Minister recommended a very sympathetic banker, who did. The deal on the 'Super-Connie' went through in March 1967 and in early April the new aircraft arrived in Salisbury, quickly catching up on the backlog of freight contracts.

In early April Jack also managed to pick up another supply contract for Zambia. This time the 'fuel airlift' contract came through Botswana National Airways. BNA had been foundered by none other than the Autair owner, Bill Armstrong back in 1965.[29] Although Bill now had little to do with the day-to-day running of the airline he was able to suggest that the charters be subcontracted to Air Trans Africa as BNA couldn't fulfil the request as they had only one DC-3.

To be able to take on the sub-charter it meant that Jack had to get another Botswana registration number for the DC-4. Although he secretly retained the aircraft's Rhodesian registration as well, as one of his crewmen recalled, "I remember a time when we had the aircraft flying on two different registrations which was highly illegal. We didn't tell the registration office in the US as they would never have permitted it."[30]

The British Government was paying Botswana National Airways for the fuel airlift. Yet the main contractor was a Rhodesian sanctions-busting airline. It was a dangerous arrangement, but quickly the flights became 'clock-work' as the men fought to maintain their target of four deliveries a day. Henry Kinnear described the operation, "It was forty-five minutes flying time to Livingstone, and the best turnaround time we managed to get was just ten minutes. In Livingstone the Royal Air Force did the off-loading, and it was a very fast operation. We would take about forty drums of fuel and bring back between sixty and eighty empty drums.

29 'Colours in the Sky: The story of Autair International Airways and Court Line Aviation' by Graham M Simons, published by GMS Enterprises. ISBN: 978-1-904514-70-1.

30 Interview with Ronnie Small, Jet Park, Johannesburg, March 2, 2004.

"We had this brilliant African chap Tex, and what the RAF would do was drive a forklift up to the dispatch door and by the time we had taxied into place Tex had the cargo net down. As the door opened, he would roll the drums straight onto the forklift. They would then just tip the forklift forward and roll the drums away out under the aircraft. We would do this from sun-up to sundown every day."[31] Jack loved the slick efficiency of these super-fast turn-rounds. He was convinced that aircraft engine troubles were aggravated by the expansion and contraction of heating and cooling. To avoid this his airline had to master the art of fast turn-rounds. It was to become a skill that Air Trans Africa and Affretair would become famous for.

Unfortunately, payment from the Botswana National Airways was a major problem from the start and once again Jack's cash-flow was threatening to shut him down. By mid-May he had to suspend the flights until he at least got written purchase orders. Although the flights resumed Jack was not happy with the arrangement or the trustworthiness of his client. But the BNA general manager, a fellow by the name of Dave Morgan had looked him in the eye and promised that payment was on the way. For Jack a man's word was his bond, so, nervously he gave Morgan the benefit of the doubt. It was a mistake.

The lean times did teach Jack how to save money though. During one of these episodes he was in the cockpit of the DC-4 on a return leg from England. They had just taken off from Nairobi with full fuel tanks when number one engine failed and they needed to make an emergency landing. Douglas regulations stated that the DC-4 should not be landed with the wings full of flammable fuel. The procedure was to dump the fuel first. But having just paid for it, Jack couldn't afford the loss. Commenting on this later the Flight Engineer said, "Actually I don't think we ever dumped fuel on the DC-4. We just didn't have the money to waste. But Jack did a perfect, very, very soft landing. You couldn't feel it touch down. Jack could fly by the seat of his pants. There was no one who could come near him. He was the best pilot I ever knew."[32]

But this time no amount of flying skill could get Jack out of the financial jam he was in. And the tension seemed to be building up everywhere. At the end of

31 Interview with Henry Kinnear, Boksburg, Johannesburg, November 7, 2003.

32 Interview with Ronnie Small and Henry Kinnear, Jet Park, Johannesburg, South Africa, March 2, 2004.

May, Colonel Ojukwu declared that the Eastern state of Nigeria was to break away from the Central Government as the independent country of Biafra. Enugu was to be the capital and Ojukwu was sworn in as Head of State. Meanwhile Jerry Puren was finalising his coup plan to bring Tshombe back to power in the Congo. Through careful negotiation he had managed to get both Schramme and Bob Denard to commit to the plan. If they were to be successful this time, everyone had to be onboard – and on the same side.

All of Jack's problems, however, were financial. In early June he took the Heron to Francistown to plead with Morgan for any sort of payment. In addition to paying his fuel and salary bills, Jack knew that he needed to urgently overhaul the DC-4's number four engine. It was running rough and was well overdue. On Monday 5th Jack returned home empty-handed. From experience he knew it was now just a matter of time before his airline was going to collapse.

A few days later Jerry Puren stopped over in Salisbury to see Jack. They met in private. "We want the Heron and the DC-4 for an operation towards the beginning of next month" Jerry stated. "Problems with the DC-4's one engine, but it will be ready for you," Jack replied. According to Jerry, Jack knew better than to ask questions.[33] The truth was more likely that he had bigger things to worry about.

The following Thursday disaster struck. On their second trip back from Livingstone Captains Dave Alexander and Ron Mackie suffered the long-expected engine failure on the DC-4. It was the troublesome number 4 engine which had to be shut down. They flew on to Francistown on three engines, but with virtually no service capability in Botswana, they ferried the aircraft to Salisbury where it could be properly repaired.

The damage was bad, and the DC-4 was going to be out of action for a while. Jack tried to contact Morgan in Botswana, desperate for any money he could get. When Jack finally did manage to track the BNA Managing Director down, Dave Morgan flatly refused to pay. Jack had been fleeced. As a Rhodesian company he could never sue for payment for a British-funded contract and as Autair had withdrawn their interest in the Botswana operation, there was little

33 'Mercenary Commander' by Col. Jerry Puren as told to Brian Pottinger. Published by Galago Publishing. ISBN 0-947020-21-7.

Bill Armstrong could do about it either.

According to Henry Kinnear, "Britain paid Botswana National Airways for all the flights, and Air Trans Africa did all the servicing on the BNA Dakotas. But Botswana National Airways never paid Jack. Dave Morgan kept all the money. We never got paid a cent for all that hard work. Field's did the repair work on the failed engine. But because they heard that Jack was in trouble they held onto the aircraft until the bill had been paid in full. Jack had to mortgage his house to get the money to pay for the engine. Then to top it all Shell said that the ATA account had expired, so they also needed to be paid up front as well."[34]

This meant Jack had his Skymaster back, but he didn't have the cash to be able to fly it – or any of his aircraft for that matter. Jack was broke and Air Trans Africa was grounded.

A few days later, just as Jack was preparing to inform the bank that he had failed, Jerry Puren showed up. He wanted to discuss the plans to oust Mobutu and reinstate Tshombe, and he needed Jack's help in recruiting more mercenaries for the job. When Jerry heard about Jack's situation he quickly contacted Tshombe and "within a few days the money arrived."[35] As for Jerry's mercenaries, "In six hours Malloch pulled them in from all corners of the Rhodesian capital. They knew absolutely nothing about the coup. All they knew was that they were returning to the Congo, that there would be fighting, and that there were good prospects for money and loot."[36]

With Shell paid off Jack had a small reprieve and was able to do another passenger flight to Europe in the DC-7. This brought in a bit more profit and he was still able to take on Tshombe's charter. But without David Butler's financial support it wasn't enough to change the fortune of the airline. Faced with no alternative Jack contacted Alastair and informed him that if he could get work flying weapons in for Ojukwu he would take it.

Alastair was pleased and through his French Secret Service network contacted Pierre Laureys, the Parisian restauranteur/arms dealer who they had worked with on the Yemen mission. Laureys was also pleased that Jack was onboard. He was

34 Interview with Henry Kinnear, Boksburg, Johannesburg, November 7, 2003.
35 Interview with Jerry and Julia Puren, Durban, April 16, 2001.
36 'Mercenary Commander' by Col. Jerry Puren as told to Brian Pottinger. Published by Galago Publishing. ISBN 0-947020-21-7.

reliable, resourceful and discrete, exactly what the Biafrans needed. It didn't take long for Pierre to convinced Ojukwu, and his friend Félix Houphouët-Boigny, President of the Ivory Coast, that, unlike other gunrunners, Malloch was a man of principle and the right person to establish a clandestine arms airlift.[37]

A week later, on Wednesday 28th June Jack loaded up his planeload of mercenary recruits and just before three o'clock in the morning they set off to Luanda. The plan was to meet up with Tshombe in the Angolan capital before regrouping in Punia for the start of the coup. Only four of Jack's passengers that night would return alive.[38] When they arrived in Luanda they were directed to a far corner of the airport where officers of the PIDE, the Portuguese secret police, met them and arranged for their weapons to be loaded. According to Jerry, "The Portuguese still had virtually the entire Katangese armoury and as we watched, truck after truck began arriving at the air base for loading. It was the same material we had shipped out so precipitously in those last hasty days before the Katanga secession ended in 1963: FN rifles, rocket launchers, machine pistols, 30 calibre machine-guns and boxes of 7.62 mm ammunition."

But there was no sign of Tshombe. He had been delayed in Madrid. Although Jerry was extremely unhappy with the change of plan, it was decided that they should deliver the weapons and return for Tshombe later. Finally, on the evening of Friday 30th June Tshombe left Madrid for Luanda. But over the Mediterranean a double agent in Tshombe's team of Spanish bodyguards commandeered the aircraft and delivered the ex-President to his archenemies in Algiers. The pilot was a 'Wigmo old hand', and with the level of organisation and planning that was involved, the CIA, who had long backed Mobutu were strongly implicated in the kidnapping.

Jack was stunned by the news and Puren and Schramme were devastated. Without their leader they knew the planned coup was destined to fail. They then heard that Mobutu had dispatched his crack 3rd Parachute Regiment to firstly disarm Denard's 6 Commando, and then to re-establish authority over Punia and Schramme's 'Eastern province'. Now war was coming to them, whether they wanted it or not. With little choice and events spiraling out of

37 'Shadows, Airlift and Airwar in Biafra and Nigeria 1967 – 1970' by Michael Draper. Published by Hikoko Publications. IBSN 1-902109-63-5.

38 Interview with Jerry and Julia Puren, Durban, April 16, 2001.

Weapons from Katanga's national armoury being unloaded at Schramme's estate in Eastern Congo at the start of the Mercenaries Revolt. Schramme's 10 Commando Leopard insignia can be seen on the side of the truck.

Picture from Jack Malloch's private collection. © Greg Malloch.

Jack (left) and Jerry Puren in Punia just before their attack on Kisangani on 5th July 1967.

Picture from Jack Malloch's private collection. © Greg Malloch.

their control, Puren and Schramme decided to go ahead with the coup anyway. It was a desperate decision, but they hoped that if, by some miracle, they were able to snatch power, maybe they could establish a 'caretaker' government which would be able to force Tshombe's release.

Late the next morning, once the DC-4 had been unloaded in Punia, Jack said his good-byes and good-lucks to Puren, Schramme and the other 'Leopard Group' leaders and headed back for Salisbury in his empty, strangely melancholic Skymaster.

At dawn on Wednesday 5th July 1967 Schramme's three columns of combined mercenaries and Katangese troops attacked the cities of Kisangani (which Stanleyville had been renamed), Bukavu and Kindu. Kisangani and Bukavu quickly fell, but the ANC had already reinforced Kindu and the attack bogged down. As each side dug in, fierce street fighting ensued. At the same time in West Africa the Nigerian Federal army attacked the break-away state of Biafra, starting another horrific war in which millions of people would die.

Back in eastern Congo Mobutu's paratroopers counter-attacked Kisangani. With overwhelming numbers, they pushed through the defences right into the heart of the city. In the confusion, Bob Denard was shot in the head while Jack was heavily involved shuttling reinforcements and supplies wherever they were most needed. On more than a couple of occasions he found himself flying right into the thick of the fighting.

At one small airfield he needed to make a 'hot evacuation'. Jack landed in an old DC-3 as the group of mercenaries he was trying to rescue, with several wounded and some civilian refugees in tow, rushed up towards the aircraft with the hordes of hungry ANC hot on their heels.

Quickly the men, women and children clambered aboard the aircraft, assisted through the already open door by one of Jack's crewmen. Meanwhile, a couple of the mercenaries lay down 'suppressing fire' to hold off the enemy as Jack quickly turned the aircraft for their takeoff run. The last few men leapt into the back of the aircraft as Jack started accelerating down the runway, with bullets smacking into the thin fuselage. One last mercenary stood firm, emptying his magazine at the enemy before flinging his weapon down and sprinting as hard as he could after the Dakota as his comrades screamed for him out of the aircraft's rear door.

The man was almost within reach of the outstretched arms of his friends when the aircraft started pulling away from him. Knowing his fate, the running man shouted up at the plane, "Shoot me! Shoot me!" Eventually, leaning out of the door, one of the mercenaries let off a long burst of automatic gunfire into his friend, cutting him down into a crumpled, bleeding heap on the dirt runway. The loud clatter of submachine-gun fire and flying shell cases reverberated through the aircraft. In horror everyone knew how the chase had ended.

The DC-3 lifted into the sky and the door was secured. Behind them, machete armed Simbas swarmed over the lifeless body of the abandoned mercenary. Inside the cabin, amidst the stench of sweat and blood, the civilians were in tears, as were a few of the soldiers, who quickly turned their attention to tending their wounded.[39] It had been a dramatic rescue which was eventually immortalised in Daniel Carney's book, and the subsequent Hollywood movie 'The Wild Geese'.

Delivering the rescued men back to Kisangani, Jack quickly transferred to his Heron and headed back for Salisbury as fast as he could. Behind him the fighting closed in around the airfield. Within hours of Jack's escape the airport fell to the advancing ANC paratroopers. He had only just managed to escape in time. It wasn't that Jack had lost his nerve, but Alastair had confirmed their first flight into Biafra and that was a contract Jack didn't want to lose.

A day later in the confusion of Kisangani with both paras and mercenaries locked in battle, several of the wounded mercenaries including Denard himself had been captured by the ANC. The men, all still on their hospital stretchers, had been taken to the airport where the plan was to fly them as trophies back to Mobutu in Kinshasa. In a daring raid one of Denard's deputies, Jean-Louis Domange, forced his way onto the Air Congo aircraft that had already been loaded with the wounded prisoners. With a handful of desperate mercenaries and a few civilians who had joined them earlier, Jean-Louis commandeered the aircraft and forced the pilot to fly them to Rhodesia. This desperate act made Jean-Louis one of the world's first hijackers and no doubt saved the lives of

39 Personal correspondence with Judy Chapman, November 11, 2008.

everyone on board.[40]

As there was heavy secrecy surrounding the event and the authorities wanted to ensure that no-one knew the location of the passengers, the media were told that the aircraft had landed at Kariba. Which it had.[41] However what the media were not told was that the aircraft was quickly refueled and flew on to the quiet, unmonitored airstrip at Mount Hampden. From there Bob and the other wounded soldiers were quickly spirited away to Salisbury General Hospital. Over the next week the civilians were repatriated by their governments, except for a young Congolese girl in her late teens who didn't have anywhere else to go. She remained in the Mount Hampden reformatory until Bob Denard had fully recovered. She then travelled to Belgium with him, and interestingly, they were later married.[42]

With Tshombe having been kidnapped and the mercenaries' revolt having bogged down, Jack hadn't been paid for any of his recent Congolese flights, and the deal with Biafra, due to the arms embargo against the breakaway state, was that he would only be paid upon delivery. The problem was that he literally didn't have a penny left to his name. He was fully mortgaged against the cost of the engine repairs and the initial deposit he received from Tshombe had been used up.

Once again Jack was faced with the very real prospect of having to shut the company down and liquidate. And this time it was all the more painful knowing that he had a confirmed charter into Biafra yet couldn't even raise the money to buy fuel to make the delivery and collect the profit. There was no point trying to plead with Dave for any support as he had withdrawn from the business completely in bitter objection to Jack's involvement in the mercenaries' revolt.

Although Jack did have one more card to play.

For a while now Bill Armstrong of Autair had been expressing an interest in gaining a stake in Jack's operation. The conversations had started with the purchase of the second DC-4 just a few months prior to UDI. While the idea

40 The Rhodesian Herald article 'Congo plane with wounded aboard lands at Kariba' published July 8, 1967.

41 This has been confirmed by Ian Dixon who was the Station Manager of Kariba Airport at the time.

42 Personal correspondence with Judy Chapman, November 11, 2008.

appealed to Jack, he had held off, knowing there would likely be challenges for a reputable British airline to invest in a Rhodesian operation.

With no alternative Jack contacted Bill and sounded him out on some sort of partnership. Bill was very pleased at the prospect and obviously felt bad about how the Botswana deal had turned out. He was definitely interested in getting involved in Air Trans Africa but said that considering the need for delicate discussions with the other Autair shareholders he would need a bit of time before a decision could be made.

Time was not something that Jack had. Although he couldn't tell Bill, the truth was he needed cash in his hand right now. After the high drama of the last week, Jack knew it was over. While he appreciated Bill's support the reality was that the collapse of his airline had just been delayed, and the hole he was in now was deeper than ever.

Sadly, he called together the crew he had selected for their first flight into Eastern Nigeria. They were Clive Halse, who had been with Jack through almost all the dramas, Paul Rex, Henry Kinnear and Bill Brown. Jack told the men that unfortunately with the non-payment of both the Botswana contract and the disappearance of Tshombe he had run out of money. He literally couldn't even buy the fuel they needed to get to Biafra.

It was over. Jack thanked the men for their loyalty, and then gave them notice that their current pay-cheques were their last.[43] After the meeting he went back to his office. He didn't know what to do next. He had no options. Not only was he about to lose his Biafran contract, he couldn't even rescue his friends on the battlefields of the Congo.

Suddenly there was a knock on his office door. Right at that very last moment, something completely unexpected happened…

43 Interview with Henry Kinnear, Boksburg, Johannesburg, November 7, 2003.

CHAPTER 8

Defeat in the Congo and imprisonment in Togo: 1967 to 1968

Jack looked up. Paul Rex was standing at his office door.

"What can I do for you Paul?"

"Well, I don't have a lot of savings..." Paul began. 'The poor guy needs a loan, and I don't have a single penny to give him,' Jack thought to himself. He felt tired. That deep dog-tiredness that comes with defeat.

"But..." Paul started again hesitantly, "I think I've got enough to buy the fuel to at least get us to Luanda... If it will help...?"

Jack wasn't quite sure if he had heard correctly.

"You are offering to pay for the fuel we need...?"

"Yes boss." Paul replied, firmer this time.

After a quick five-minute discussion, it was agreed. Paul would draw the cash, they would fuel-up and leave as quickly as they could. Jack was overwhelmed. He assured Paul that as soon they received the money for the delivery he would be refunded in full.[1]

On the morning of Sunday 9th July 1967, the hand-picked crew boarded the empty Skymaster and prepared for takeoff. Their families had come to say good-bye, and were all lined up outside the hangar, waving as the aeroplane taxied out towards the runway. Everyone knew how important this desperate 'last' flight was, yet no-one really knew what to expect or what they were really flying into.

They landed in the Angolan capital just as dusk was gathering. But there was little time to consider the dangers ahead and by 8 o'clock that evening having refueled the aircraft on Pierre Laureys' account they took off again for an

1 Interview with Henry and Maureen Kinnear, Boksburg, Johannesburg, November 7, 2003.

overnight flight to Portuguese Guinea, on the western tip of Africa. From there, with another load of complimentary fuel they flew on to Lisbon. In total it was more than twenty hours flying time, and although Clive was the captain, Jack spent almost the entire time 'resting up front' in the cockpit.

Early on the morning of Tuesday 11th the Air Trans Africa crew were back at Lisbon airport to supervise the loading of their cargo. It was a full consignment of arms that, according to the flight crew, included canisters of napalm. As soon as the cargo was strapped down onto the cargo pallets, the aircraft took off again, heading back to Bissau where more Portuguese-financed fuel was taken on. From there Jack and his unmarked DC-4, stuffed full of weapons, flew south-east, skirting the coastline of Africa. As they neared Ghana they turned further south out over open waters towards the jungled island of São Tomé where they landed and spent the night.

The next morning they flew due north for the Biafran capital. Knowing the country was in a state of war, and having been on the receiving end of trigger-happy airport guards before, Jack was more than a bit nervous landing at Enugu airport. He made sure that air traffic control was fully aware of their approach and had given all the necessary acknowledgments and permissions before they made their slow and obvious approach. Fortunately the landing was uneventful, although Jack did notice the numerous anti-aircraft emplacements along the length of the runway, several of whom tracked the aircraft as it taxied to a halt at its allocated parking bay outside an empty hangar.

The hangar doors were opened and a tractor pulled the aircraft inside. Quickly the awaiting solders started unloading the precious cargo. Just as the crew started to relax a loud rattle of heavy calibre machine-gun fire drowned out the sound of an approaching aircraft. More guns joined the fray, including the loud popping of some larger anti-aircraft artillery.

Expecting that they were under attack the startled crew ran to the hangar entrance in time to see a Swiss-registered Dassault Mystère trying to land ahead of a hail of crossfire. As the intense 'friendly fire' died away the pilot of the executive jet nervously taxied back from the end of the runway and parked near the same hangar where the DC-4 was being unloaded.

As the Mystère's door opened Jack's old friend Pierre Laureys stepped out, relieved to have survived their final approach and landing. Jack, who had been expecting Pierre, immediately thanked him for sorting out their fuel bills. The two men then went straight into a meeting to discuss Biafra's needs and what they could do to help Ojukwu. The Biafran military were pleased with Jack's successful operation and that evening, having paid Paul back for his 'start-up' loan, Jack treated the crew to a celebratory dinner at the Intercontinental.[2]

While Jack and the Biafrans were celebrating the first successful delivery of clandestine arms, on that evening of July 13th, it had been a very tough day for Schramme and his men. Fighting for their lives they punched their way out of Kisangani and melted into the surrounding bush. Schramme and many of his men knew the area intimately and although they numbered in the thousands, they were able to disappear completely, leaving Mobutu's paratroopers with an empty, smouldering shell of a city.

The next morning, Friday 14th, five days after leaving home, Jack and Clive flew back to Portuguese Guinea. In the capital Bissau they refueled and were provided with a detail of Portuguese Air Force personnel who carried out some essential maintenance on the Skymaster while more military hardware was loaded onto the aircraft. Again, neither the servicing nor the fuel were charged for.

On the 15th they made their second delivery to Enugu. But the aircraft was not performing well and although they had another consignment to collect in Lisbon, Jack was worried about whether they would make it. Fortunately his new Portuguese friends came to the rescue again. As soon as they landed in Lisbon on Monday July 17th the aircraft was put in for a whole week of servicing. Jack was very relieved to have been able to get a top quality service for the old workhorse free of charge.

The lull in the flight schedule also enabled Jack to finalise the agreement with Bill Armstrong who had spent the last few weeks leaving messages for Jack. Autair indeed wanted a stake in Jack's operation, although the whole arrangement needed to be handled extremely discretely so as to avoid any embarrassment for the British airline. Speaking about the deal after his retirement Bill vaguely confirmed, "...with money in hand, we found ourselves

2 Interview with Henry and Maureen Kinnear, Boksburg, Johannesburg, November 7, 2003.

looking at the fixed-wing field again, this time taking over from David Butler's Rhodesian Air Services and forming a successor company, Air Trans Africa with Captain Jack Malloch as Managing Director."[3] And so, on the back of their first delivery into Biafra, and with the support of the Autair deal, for the first time in a long time Jack's financial situation started to improve.

With Bill's help Jack was also able to make a bid to buy another old Super Constellation which was going at a very good price. According to Henry Kinnear, "Bill Brown, John Hodges and Bunny Warren went to go and get the Connie. It was an ex-TAP aircraft that was already in Lisbon. Towards the end of July they ferried it to Salisbury and used it for spare parts."[4]

While his crew went home in the new Connie, Jack stayed behind, spending the week cultivating his contacts within the Portuguese PIDE, which was their International and State Defence Police. Apparently the deal he agreed with them was ten thousand US dollars for each successful delivery of arms from Lisbon into Biafra. This was a lot cheaper than the twenty two thousand dollars that Hank Wharton, Biafra's other gun-runner was charging.[5] Due to the volume of both weapons and food deliveries Hank continued to compete with Jack for most of the airlift, although Jack was definitely preferred by both Portugal and France. Pierre Laureys introduced Jack to the SDECE office in Paris who were responsible for Biafra, although they already knew of Jack through Bob Denard.

On Monday July 24th, after a week in dock, the Skymaster was ready to go again. Jack recalled the crew back to Lisbon while the Portuguese loaders tried to fit two huge Bofors anti-aircraft batteries into the back of the DC-4. The guns were massive, mounted on a heavy chassis with four articulated wheels. Considering the trouble the Portuguese had getting the heavy artillery into the aircraft, Jack's crew were worried about getting them out at the other end. Paul Rex spent most of the time on the HF radio trying to get a message to Enugu to organise a ramp. When they landed an enormous wooden ramp had been specially built and the guns were unloaded with no trouble at all.

---

3 'Colours in the Sky: The story of Autair International Airways and Court Line Aviation' by Graham M Simons, published by GMS Enterprises. ISBN: 978-1-904514-70-1.

4 Interview with Henry Kinnear, Boksberg, Johannesburg, November 7, 2003.

5 'São Tomé and the Biafran War (1967–1970)' by Gerhard Seibert, published in the International Journal of African Historical Studies Vol. 51, No. 2 (2018).

After catching up on some sleep, late the next morning, Thursday 24th, Jack and the crew left Enugu, heading back for home at last. After the long flight they eventually touched down in Salisbury at lunchtime on Friday. For Jack it had been almost three weeks since he had last seen his family, and Zoe brought the children out to the airport to welcome him home. Unfortunately he could not stay long and needed to get the Heron up to Port Harcourt as quickly as possible for a whole series of internal charters that Ojukwu needed.

After less than an hour on the ground Jack headed off again. It was hard to say good-bye to Zoe, Alyson, Ross and baby Greg, but as he explained to Zoe, the money was good and this could be their chance to get the airline financially stable once and for all. Although she missed Jack terribly Zoe was as understanding as ever.

It was just getting dark by the time Jack landed back in Luanda. As he shut down the engines his old friend Jerry Puren came running up to the aircraft. Jerry had been stranded in Luanda for almost three weeks and was desperate for any news of what had happened in Kisangani. Schramme's entire army seemed to have just completely disappeared. Jerry begged Jack to do a recce over Eastern Congo to try and find them.

Jack really did not have time for this diversion, but he was also very worried about his missing friends. He also felt a little bit guilty that the Heron he was flying had originally belonged to Tshombe and Jack had promised that it would always be available for him. Although Tshombe was languishing in an Algerian prison, Jack felt that this was still his mission. After a quick discussion with the crew, Jack agreed that they would do the reconnaissance flight. The only problem was the cost of the fuel, but that was quickly taken care of by the sympathetic Portuguese who provided full tanks for the excursion.

Early the next morning they gathered at the airport, and there was a lot of them. Most of Jack's crew came along for the trip, in addition Jerry had one of Tshombe's aides, Naweji with him, plus the two pilots, Libert and Bracco, who were old Katangese 'faithfuls'. Jerry knew of a couple of ex-Katanga Air Force T-28s that had been left in eastern Congo which, if possible, he wanted the two KAF pilots to bring back to help support the crumbling Mercenaries Revolt.

They flew from Luanda firstly to Henrique de Carvalho near the Congo border where they filled up with more Portuguese fuel. From there they continued across the border northeast towards Punia. Arriving over the town they made a few low passes. The buildings in the middle of the town seemed to have been gutted, with their charred and jagged roof rafters pointing skyward and blackened rubble spilling out across the streets around them. There were few people to be seen and no sign of the mercenary column.

With everyone intently scanning the ground below, Jerry asked Jack to take them to the nearby airfield to see if the aircraft were still there. As they approached they saw the burnt-out wrecks of the T-28s. The aircraft had been torched. From the airfield they turned and flew several miles out of town to Schramme's estate. The farmhouse was completely razed and most of the outbuildings looked ransacked and gutted. The place, which had until so recently been the de facto seat of Eastern government, looked completely abandoned.

Naweji suggested they fly south towards Kindu to see if Schramme and his men were on their way to Katanga to spark the planned uprising there. It seemed a reasonable suggestion and Jack followed the weaving dirt road out of Punia. He was getting worried about their fuel situation.

Just twenty five miles south of Punia they flew over a huge column of ANC troops and armour blocking the road. The entire column opened fire on the low-flying Heron and several bullets smacked into the wings and fuselage as Jack tried to get away. It was obvious that Schramme couldn't have gone south, which meant he must have headed east for Bukavu, near the Rwanda border.

But they were getting very low on fuel. Then Jack remembered that he and Jerry had hidden fuel at a homestead near Lubutu a couple of years earlier. Gambling that it might still be there Jack cut across the green jungle until, to everyone's relief a cluster of tin-roofed buildings came into view. After a few low passes to make sure the place was not in enemy hands, Jack landed on the small strip behind the farmhouse.

The place seemed completely deserted. There was nothing but an eerie, ominous silence. Jerry, with his submachine gun in hand, Jack and a few of the others went off to see if they could find the buried fuel drums. The homestead had been completely ransacked, but buried beneath the rubble in the back yard, Jerry and Jack found the forty-four gallon drums of fuel. Knowing that the ANC in

Lubutu would have been alerted to their arrival, the men knew they had limited time, so feverishly dug up the drums and quickly rolled them over to the Heron. One of the crew recounted, "Jerry dug up six drums of fuel. But we could hear firing in the distance which made us all nervous. We took the drums and stood them on the wings and poured them into the tanks by hand."[6] After a long, anxious hour on the ground, anticipating the arrival of enemy troops at any moment, the Heron was eventually refueled and they were able to take off again as dusk was beginning to gather. By the time they landed back in Henrique de Carvalho it was well after ten p.m. and the Portuguese had given them up for dead.

Although they had not found Schramme, Jerry was sure he knew where they were. So, without further delay Jack flew back to Luanda and then headed north for Biafra as quickly as he could. Their first stop was Libreville where Pierre Laureys had set up a meeting between Jack and the Gabonese President Leon M'ba to discuss 'areas of cooperation.'

When Jack arrived for the meeting he was informed that M'ba had taken ill and that he would be meeting with the Vice-President Albert-Bernard Bongo instead. As both Jack and Albert-Bernard had Air Force backgrounds, the two men immediately found commonality. Within days of this meeting President M'ba was diagnosed with cancer and, to Jack's benefit, Bongo succeed him.

By the time Jack got to Enugu he had messages confirming that Schramme's column had been found. They were fighting their way towards Bukavu on the Rwandan border but were desperately short of ammunition, fending off continual attacks and ambushes. Jack was desperately needed to fly supplies to the beleaguered column. Their situation had also been complicated by a huge convoy of hundreds of civilian vehicles that were moving with the mercenaries in an attempt to escape the terrible retribution of the vengeful Congolese Army.

Jack immediately headed back home. He spent just one day in the office catching up on paperwork, before heading off with Paul Rex, Geoff Mason and Henry Kinnear on Tuesday August 1st. They flew from Salisbury to Swartkop Air Force base in South Africa where they collected a load of arms and ammunition for Schramme, delivering it to Angola's forward military base at Henrique de

6 Interview with Ronnie Small and Henry Kinnear, Jet Park, Johannesburg, March 2, 2004.

Carvalho. The day before another ATA crew had flown a consignment of .303 and 7.62 mm ammunition out of Waterkloof Air Force base, also destined for Schramme. The two wars were stretching Air Trans Africa to the limit.

A week later, while Jack was making his third arms flight into the Biafran capital, Schramme managed to outflank Mobutu's elite battalion of paratroopers and captured the fortified town of Bukavu. The next day Tshombe's aide Colonel Monga proclaimed the creation of a 'Government of the People' based in Bukavu and gave Mobutu ten days to resign "...or be driven out of the country."[7] In response, Mobutu vowed to kill them all.

On Saturday 12th Jack made his fourth arms flight into Enugu and on Tuesday 15th a fifth, building up the Biafrans' military stockpile. With it he was also building up his reputation and in mid-August Silva Cunha the Portuguese Minister of Defence himself instructed the Governor of São Tomé, Silva Sebastião to transfer weapons from their Air Force aircraft into Jack's DC-4 for delivery into Biafra.[8] The Portuguese wanted to keep their operation discrete so trusted Jack to make the deliveries on their behalf. Of course, for the money Jack was more than happy to oblige.

Although ATA were making more frequent deliveries, the demand was also increasing. The Biafrans had invaded southern Nigeria while the Nigerians had invaded northern Biafra, so there were battles on all fronts. When the Soviets announced massive military backing for the Federal government Jack realised that he would not be able to keep up and asked Bill Armstrong to start looking for additional aircraft.

Schramme was also fighting battles on all fronts. Bukavu was now surrounded by the Congolese Army and the ragtag defenders had almost run out of ammunition. Jack needed to do an urgent resupply. It was a dangerous mission, but the lives of thousands hung in the balance. Early on the morning of Friday September 1st Jack flew a planeload of ammunition from Swartkop Air Force based in South Africa to Henrique de Carvalho from where an air drop was hastily organised for that same evening over the mountainous terrain near Bukavu.

---

7 'Mercenary Commander' by Perry Juren. Published by Galago Publishing. ISBN 0-947020-21-7.

8 'São Tomé and the Biafran War (1967–1970)' by Gerhard Seibert, published in the International Journal of African Historical Studies Vol. 51, No. 2 (2018).

Ronnie Small, who was on the flight, described what happened:

"Re-supplying the mercenaries at Bukavu was the hairiest flight I ever did. The first flight was in the middle of the night and there was a massive thunderstorm right over our target so we had to abort. Then on the second flight the next morning the Congolese T-28s chased us out. As Jack approached the drop zone in the lumbering DC-4 we stumbled across the Congo Air Force fighters who were also looking for Schramme. Recognising Jack's old DC-4, the fighters swooped down on us firing wildly."

With tracers skimming past his cockpit Jack remembered the times he had tangled with German fighters over Italy. He instinctively took the same evasive manoeuvres. Only this time he was in a four-engined aircraft stuffed with highly explosive cargo. Diving into a jungle valley, Jack took the Skymaster down as low as he dared, weaving in and out of the steep-walled chasms to shake off his attackers who, he realised, were his old CIA Wigmo pals.

"The scariest part was when Jack looked up out of the cockpit window and stared straight into the dense green mountainside that we were flying right into. He immediately pulled back on the stick and applied maximum boost to avoid stalling as we climbed hard. It was a terrifying minute or so as we got closer and closer to the mountain and eventually skimmed right through the treetops at the summit before we could get out." Although they were all almost killed in the process, they were able to lose the fighters. Michael Draper later recorded that according to Jack's crew, "...VP-YTY returned with green propellers and the oil coolers full of leaves."[9]

With another war also desperately needing weapons, Jack had no choice but to offload the crates of ammunition and fly to Lisbon as quickly as he could to pick up a new Portuguese consignment, this time for Biafra. Six days later having covered almost ten thousand miles, he delivered it to Enugu. It was Air Trans Africa's seventh successful delivery. Jack had completed his first contract and was now established as Biafra's 'prime military importer.' He now had a string of confirmed charters from both the Portuguese and the French.

Jack and his crew spent the night in Enugu, but Jack was nervous about his

9 'Shadows, Airlift and Airwar in Biafra and Nigeria 1967 – 1970' by Michael Draper. Published by Hikoko Publications. IBSN 1-902109-63-5.

white-topped aeroplane parked out in the open with enemy aircraft on the prowl looking for targets. Hence, early the next morning they headed back to Henrique de Carvalho where they reloaded the weapons and ammunition for Schramme which they had abandoned almost ten days earlier. Jack wondered if Schramme had managed to survive without it for so long.

Once again fate got in the way and by the time Jack and Paul Rex were approaching Bukavu just before midnight, there was another heavy thunderstorm and they had to abort, returning with the load of vital supplies undelivered for the third time in a row. It was almost dawn by the time Jack got to bed, but he could not sleep. He really did not feel well and kept coming over in a hot clammy fever. Although he didn't know it he had contracted a serious strain of malaria in Enugu and it was now beginning to infect his entire system.

After a few restless hours Jack gave up trying to sleep and decided to try and make the delivery again. This time they arrived over Bukavu late morning in glorious sunshine. The sky was cloudless and the lake was sparkling blue. Quickly they made several runs over the target drop zone as the crew in the back of the aircraft frantically pushed out the crates of mortars, mortar bombs and small arms ammunition. After thirty minutes they had delivered almost the entire planeload of supplies.

As there had been no enemy ground fire Jack had concluded that the ANC must have withdrawn. But just as they were about to go, the parachute on one of the last crates of mortar bombs failed to open and it crashed to the ground with a massive reverberating explosion. This woke up the ANC. First there were a few blasts of anti-aircraft fire, then the whole front opened up at the Skymaster. Hot red and white tracer hemmed in the slow-flying aircraft as the pings of small arms fire punched into the wings and underbelly. With the last crate thrown out and the parachute successfully deployed, Jack quickly turned west into the hills and got out of range.

By the time they landed back in Henrique de Carvalho Jack was almost unconscious and had to be carried from the aircraft. In the end he spent more than a week in bed at home. It was almost the end of September before he was well enough to fly again. This was the beginning of a long and bad patch for Jack's health. According to Alyson, Jack's daughter, "It seemed to me that he was always unwell and that was just how it was." Initially he thought it was just the relapsing malaria that he couldn't shake off, but as the symptoms got worse and his whole body became pained, Jack wondered if he had cancer. Finally after months of slow degeneration he had to be rushed to hospital. There it was discovered that his gall bladder had failed and had been progressively poisoning him over a period of years. He was sent straight into emergency surgery, and the effect was immediate. According to Alyson, "the next day we went to visit him in hospital, and I had never seen him look so well."[10] Jack credited the doctor for not just saving his life, but saving him from all the worry about having cancer.

Although Jack still had plenty of other things to worry about and by the time he was back in the cockpit, the Battle of Enugu had begun. The Nigerian Federal Army were closing in on the city and the Air Force were pounding it with daily bombing raids. During one of these sorties President Ojukwu's personal HS-125 jet was badly damaged. Ojukwu immediately contacted his Rhodesian friend about finding a replacement. Having just been awarded another arms contract, Jack decided to make his own Heron available to the Biafran President. Originally he had wanted to lease the aircraft, but considering the likelihood of it being shot down or caught in another bombing raid Jack thought it more prudent to sell the aircraft outright. While the negotiations got underway, Jack organised for it to be delivered to Enugu as quickly as possible.

The Heron had been based in Luanda where it was being used for support missions for Schramme who was still surrounded and under constant attack. But as it was almost impossible to get any more supplies to the besieged defenders and their surrender was inevitable, on Friday September 29th Jack flew the aircraft from Luanda to São Tomé. From São Tomé Jack then took a quick trip across to pay a visit to his new Gabonese friend President, Bongo. At the meeting Jack was introduced to Bongo's new military advisor, a Frenchman by the name of Colonel Jean Maurin. The uniformed Frenchman stepped forward with his hand outstretched and a broad knowing smile. It was none other than Bob Denard! Bob and his knot of faithful followers, including Jean-Louis Domange, had managed to get involved in training the country's armed forces.

10 Personal correspondence with Alyson Dawson, March 30, 2020.

One of Bob's first recommendations to Bongo was to bring Jack on board, which, with the blessing of the French Intelligence agency, the SDECE, he was more than willing to do.

While this was going on one of Jack's crew delivered the Heron to the besieged Enugu airport. Unfortunately the very next day it was peppered with shrapnel during another Nigerian Air Force raid. There were several holes in the nose and one of the cockpit windows was broken. This needed attention before the Heron could fly, but with the Nigerians now just a few miles away Jack decided to abandon the aircraft and evacuate his crew as quickly as possible. He managed to get them out just before the city fell to the federal forces on October 4th. The Heron, which did not make a single flight for the Biafrans, was the first of Jack's losses in Biafra.

Meanwhile with their friends still fighting for their lives on the Rwandan border, neither Jack nor Bob Denard had quite finished in the Congo. During the first week of October 1967, Bob managed to get a radio message to Schramme informing him that a DC-4 would be making another parachute drop of supplies. At ten o'clock the following morning, Jack was over the smouldering city with his crew heaving pallets of arms, ammunition and medical supplies out of the rear cargo door.

This time there was heavy anti-aircraft fire but having recovered from his malaria, Jack felt much more in control. As they finished the last run, the radio crackled in Jack's headphones. It was Jerry Puren who was now in the thick of battle. He asked Jack to tell his wife that he loved her very much. It was a disturbing message, but Jack tried to put a positive spin on it when he finally managed to get a phone connection through to Julia from Luanda late that evening.[11]

With the fall of their capital city, most analysts predicted that Biafra would crumble within a matter of weeks. But having a first-hand understanding of how people are prepared to defend their homeland, Jack wasn't so sure. He moved his operational base to Port Harcourt and started making longer-term plans. Although the Nigerian forces had been driven away from Biafra's second city, there was still the very real danger of 'friendly fire' as Mike Hoare described:

11 Interview with Jerry and Julia Puren, Durban, September 1999.

"In matters of aviation there was no man like Jack Malloch. Over the years I had seen him in action in various parts of Africa, and Europe too. Jack was the most fearless aviator I had ever met. One time he was transporting a highly unstable cargo of mortar bombs, rockets, that type of thing, into Port Harcourt. We were all on edge as he waited to pick up the beacon which was to be switched on for exactly thirty seconds at 0300 hours. He found the beacon and a few miles onwards a sudden flare-path erupted into flame. The moment the wheels touched, firing broke out along the length of the runway, exactly as predicted. Bullets crashed through the fuselage and only by the grace of God failed to ignite the explosives we were carrying. We juddered to a halt. We were safe. 'Well done, Jack.' I said thankfully, wiping the sweat from my brow. 'Bastards,' he said, 'they do it every time!'"[12]

As most international banks did not recognise Biafra, the country had to make their foreign payments in cash. Fortunately their oil reserves generated a lot of it. Jack did not mind getting paid in these 'bricks' of banknotes, just as long as he was being paid. He used the cash to pay his fuel bills, crew salaries and suppliers. He then deposited the rest into his Rhodesian bank account where it was gratefully received to prop up the country's foreign currency reserves. What Jack didn't like about the abundance of cash was that he was often asked to carry large amounts of it in stuffed briefcases, sometimes accompanied by diplomats, and sometimes just entrusted to the crew. Jack knew this could only lead to problems...

Henry Kinnear relates one such incident; "Once I remember some money went missing. I wasn't on the flight but Captain Klaus[13] and Jim Townsend were. Apparently they loaded the US dollars in Abidjan and flew it to Libreville, but when they got there some of it was missing. The rumour was that Klaus had taken the money. Apparently some years later Klaus went back to Libreville on holiday with all his diving equipment. I was told that 'He dived successfully. But he didn't leave the bay...'."[14] Although it was not just Jack's crew who were implicated. Pilfering was rife with the other 'opportunists' – as was the retribution. Apparently the particularly greedy were tossed out of aircraft over

12 'The Seychelles Affair' by Mike Hoare. Published by Bantam Press. ISBN 0-552-12890-2.
13 The real identity of 'Captain Klaus' has been withheld by request.
14 Interview with Henry Kinnear, Boksberg, Johannesburg, November 7, 2003.

the Bight of Biafra with "cement shoes on."

Wealth could be amassed even just with legitimate money and by the end of October, Jack had committed all of his aircraft to the Biafran airlift. The Heron had been lost in Enugu, but the Super Constellation, the DC-4 and the DC-7 were all flying regular arms shuttles into Port Harcourt. But with the ever increasing demand Jack knew he needed more aircraft if he was to keep the arms contracts to himself.

While ATA was trying to hold down their Biafran contracts, the pressure was on Schramme and his beleaguered column in the fortified ruins of Bukavu. Knowing what was about to happen they prepared themselves for the inevitable 'final assault' by the massed ANC forces surrounding them. On Sunday October 29th, 1967, the long-anticipated attack was finally unleashed. Tens of thousands of Congolese National Army soldiers launched a heavy and coordinated assault on all three sides of Bukavu.

By Saturday November 4th, after a week of heavy fighting, the rebels had been pushed right to the banks of the Ruzizi river and were under extreme pressure with their ammunition running very low. The next day after one hundred days of continual siege, Schramme, Puren and their entourage of men, women and children retreated across the Cyangugu Bridge into Rwanda where they surrendered.[15] Jack was relieved that most of his friends had survived the siege and in mid-November the Red Cross deported the whites to Europe and the blacks back to the Congo. For those unfortunates Mobutu followed through on his promise and killed them all.

Jack tried to put this out of his mind and turned his attention to a DC-7CF that he wanted to add to the fleet. It was owned by Sudflug in Germany who were more than happy to turn a blind eye to the UN sanctions and the sale went through quickly and easily.

With this bigger fleet and larger staffing Jack was no longer able to manage every little detail of the operation. One such detail was a box of twenty 9mm automatic pistols that was accidentally left on-board the Constellation. The box had been pushed under one of the crew seats so had been missed when

15 'Mercenary Commander' by Perry Juren. Published by Galago Publishing. ISBN 0-947020-21-7.

the aircraft was unloaded. As the ATA crews had been designated Biafran Air Force pilots when they were in the country, the men decided to share the guns out between them for their own self-defence. Alex Forsyth was given one, and later someone gave him a box of bullets for it, although he never actually fired the weapon. The rest of the guns were left hidden in the back of the aircraft. When the flight engineers learnt a few weeks later that the Constellation was going to be serviced in Europe they stowed the last remaining pistols onto the new DC-7 as that aircraft was the next most likely to go back to Rhodesia.[16]

It seemed a harmless enough decision at the time.

While Biafra was able to hold its own on the battlefield, food was beginning to get scarce. By the end of 1967 the Red Cross, the World Council of Churches and the Catholic Caritas Internationalis had all started raising concern about "A serious protein deficiency in Biafra." In a very short space of time this protein deficiency would become wholesale starvation. But the Nigerians didn't have the patience for starvation so on Wednesday January 3rd, 1968 they announced their latest plan to bring down Biafra.

This time it was economic. They announced that Nigerian banknotes would be withdrawn and replaced – in just nineteen days. This meant that the Biafrans had less than three weeks to cash in their old notes and introduce new Biafran ones. They had already ordered new banknotes, but if they could not convert the tons and tons of old Nigerian Pounds that filled their bank vaults the country would become bankrupted.

Suddenly the trickle of cash out of Biafra turned into a flood, as everyone scrambled to get as much money as possible out of the country before the deadline. The Biafran Government turned to Jack. But this time it was not the usual suitcase or two of money, it was a whole planeload of cash that they needed to launder. With few details, but knowing how important it was for the Biafran cause, Jack agreed to help.

After a few days at home at 4.40 a.m. on the morning of Sunday January 7th, 1968 Jack and John Aldridge took off from Salisbury on their 'Money Run'. But Jack felt uneasy. Zoe had helped him pack and had said good-bye, but the children were asleep when he left for the airport so Jack just kissed them in

16 Interview with Alex Forsyth in Greyton, South Africa, August 2003.

their beds. As always he would miss them all terribly.

At six fifteen they landed in Beira and filled the tanks with high-octane avgas. Due to sanctions this fuel was not available in Salisbury and Jack felt he needed the extra performance for this assignment. According to Jack's logbook they then flew directly to São Tomé, landing on the Portuguese island at half past four in the afternoon. In truth they had gone via Port Harcourt where they had taken on board nine and a half tons of banknotes all sewn into large, unmarked hessian sacks. In total they had seven and a half million Pounds' worth of cash stuffed into the back of the aircraft. The first thing they did once on the ground in São Tomé was organise a couple of armed guards to make sure no one came near the aircraft, then, exhausted from the long day of flying, they checked into their hotel.[17]

On Monday 8th Jack spent most of the day on São Tomé waiting for instructions from the Biafran Ministry of Finance. Although the money had been successfully taken out of the country, it still needed to be converted before the Nigerian deadline. It was quite late in the evening by the time the instruction eventually came through.

At 3.45 a.m. the next morning they took off with their load of cash for Lisbon, landing in the Portuguese capital just before half past seven that evening. In Lisbon a military guard was assigned to protect the aircraft and her secret cargo. The next afternoon they were requested to deliver the sacks of cash to Basle in Switzerland. This they did but Jack was becoming very concerned about the time it was taking to have the 'hot' cargo off-loaded. Jack's feeling of unease grew over the next two days while they waited in cold, wintry Basle. Although the money had been destined for the Banque Populaire Suisse, it seemed that there were now middlemen who were cutting their own deals to sell off the heavily-discounted banknotes. Yet nothing had been taken off the DC-7.

On the morning of Saturday January 13th more instructions came through for Jack and his old partner Alastair Wicks, who by now was directly involved in the assignment. It seemed that someone had bought the seven and a half million pounds of Nigerian banknotes, but needed them taken back to Portugal, so they

17 Interview with Alex Forsyth in Greyton, South Africa, August 2003, and entries in Jack Malloch's and Alex Forsyth's flying logbooks.

One of the millions of Nigerian banknotes that Jack flew out of Biafra in January 1968.

Original banknote provided by Henry Kinnear.

returned to Lisbon. At last Jack felt the 'money flight' was almost over and, expecting that they would soon have the DC-7 back in circulation, he booked the 'Connie' in for an overhaul.

Frustratingly, it was to be a full week before the loaded DC-7 would fly again and to make matters worse the DC-4 was also due for maintenance. By this stage Jack's worry had turned into full-on premonition but there was nothing he could do. The operation was controlled by a 'Mr. Woodnutt' who seemed to be an intermediary between the Biafrans and the money buyer, although during their wait in Lisbon Jack discovered that Dr. Kurt Wallersteiner, an influential German financier, had organised the charter. Apparently Wallersteiner (likely with Woodnutt) had bought the banknotes for one tenth of their face value, and they were now desperately looking for someone to sell the expiring cash to. The world of gun-running and arms dealing was comparatively small and over the years Jack had built up a wide network of contacts so already knew Wallersteiner, not that it gave him any particular comfort.

On Thursday January 18th, Jack and Alastair Wicks had a meeting with Kurt Wallersteiner and the mysterious Mr. Woodnutt. In this meeting it was agreed that the consignment would be flown to Lomé, capital of Togo on Nigeria's western border. From there the buyers planned to smuggle the money back into Nigeria before the deadline on the 22nd of January. According to a sworn statement that Jack issued sometime later, apparently, he had been shown a copy of the contract to deliver the cash to Lomé and it included permission and approval from the Togolese Government. He also said that the charterer had confirmed the arrangements with a banking representative in Togo for the cargo to be offloaded in Lomé.

Eventually they were cleared for take-off late in the afternoon on Friday January 19th. But as they accelerated down the runway a fire warning lit up on engine number two. They had to abort. It wasn't a good omen. The repairs took about eight hours. While that was being done Jack asked Alex Forsyth to alter one of the registration letters on the fuselage, changing it from VP-WBO to ZP-WBO. According to Jack's official statement this was a request made by the Togolese authorities to avoid any embarrassment if the press were to see a Rhodesian-registered aircraft making a delivery into their country.

At about 4 a.m. on Saturday 12th they were finally able to take off. In all there were nine people on board: Jack Malloch, John Aldridge who was officially captain of the flight, Paul Rex who was First Officer, a Brazilian navigator Vasco Luis de Abren, John Deegan and engineers Alex Forsyth and Bill Keating. Plus Alistair Wicks and Kurt Wallersteiner who were there to oversee the transaction.[18]

Shortly before reaching Portuguese Guinea Paul Rex suddenly developed severe stomach pains. The decision was taken to land and get him to a hospital. At 1.30 p.m. they took off again, leaving Paul having emergency appendix surgery. They followed a course quite far off-shore so as not to alert any of the hostile countries along the way. According to John Aldridge, "seventy miles south of Lomé, I called the tower and asked if they had any knowledge of our anticipated arrival. The controller replied that he had not been notified…"[19] John was immediately suspicious, questioning why, if they had all the necessary clearance, the

18 'Shadows, Airlift and Airwar in Biafra and Nigeria 1967 – 1970' by Michael Draper. Published by Hikoko Publications. IBSN 1-902109-63-5.

19 Part of a statement made by Jack Malloch to the British Aviation Insurance Company as part of a claim for the loss of VP-WBO, as reproduced in 'Shadows, Airlift and Airwar in Biafra and Nigeria 1967 – 1970'.

tower was not aware of their arrival. Wallersteiner said that his buyers should be at the airport waiting for them and would be able to sort everything out.

They landed in Lomé at 6.20 p.m., shortly after dark. There was no one there to meet then.

In Jack's report he takes up the story, "We were marshalled in and Dr. Wallersteiner then left the aircraft to make the necessary arrangements for the offloading. After about twenty minutes it appeared that something was not in order. Wallersteiner had no explanation but told me we should arrange to take off immediately with the load..."

According to John Aldridge, "We were all milling around on the ground waiting to be unloaded when someone in authority arrived. This person thought that there was something fishy about the flight and a petrol bowser was parked in front of the aircraft so that we could not escape."[20] Jack tried to file a new flight plan with ATC, but it was refused. That in itself would not have stopped Jack. But the bowser did.

Inevitably the Togolese authorities decided to search the aircraft. When they discovered literally tons of cash on board they became even more suspicious. According to Alex Forsyth, things then took a turn for the worse. "When they were searching the plane they found the box with the remaining handguns in it. Then they found a couple of the bullets in the bottom of my briefcase, and they became completely enraged. They were shouting and screaming saying that we would all get the death sentence!"[21]

"We were told that we must go into town until things had been sorted out. We were put in the back of an army vehicle with the soldiers. But instead of going to the hotel we arrived at the gates of a prison. Armed guards immediately surrounded the truck and we were herded in at gunpoint. We were taken upstairs to a large concrete-floored cell. There was nothing in the room at all – no bedding, chairs or anything. We had our suitcases and flight bags but that was all. Lying on a bare, concrete floor certainly makes you aware of how many bones you have. At the far end was a single armed guard who was sitting on the floor with a bottle of wine busy singing to himself and getting thoroughly drunk whilst

20 Personal correspondence with John and Lyn Aldridge, November 25, 2008.

21 Interview with Alex Forsyth, Johannesburg, December 2001.

The police station in Lomé, where Jack and his crew where initially imprisoned and scheduled for execution on January 29th 1968. The truck in the foreground is likely the very vehicle they were driven there in.
Picture from Jack Malloch's private collection. © Greg Malloch.

playing with his rifle."

John Aldridge recalled their first interrogation, "After a while we heard a loud clatter of hobnailed boots rushing up the stairs, and in came the soldiers with fixed bayonets pointing at us. Eventually the officer in charge came in with a chair and sat down in front of us. The officer couldn't speak English so only Alastair and Vasco could understand the interrogation. The officer wanted to know where the money was from and who owned it. Under Alastair's whispered advice we kept saying we were merely the drivers. "We know nothing," we kept repeating to the torrent of French questions being fired at us."

"Bill Keating, was first up and had a full body search. Bill had difficulty in controlling himself and I could see his fists clenched and I just prayed that he wouldn't do anything. Thankfully he didn't, but Bill was mortified by the search – as were the rest of us. After Bill only maybe one or two others were searched but when nothing was found the whole thing petered out. Fortunately

I wasn't searched nor were my bags. The next morning Jack and one of the engineers were then taken back to the aircraft so that all the panels could be opened and searched."[22]

When Jack and Bill were taken to the aircraft it was one of the only times that Jack was separated from the rest of the crew. He was still in the guard of the soldiers who had threatened to kill them, and according to a couple of sources, the soldiers decided to 'show the Togolese people what a real Rhodesian looked like'. Forcing Jack to strip down to his underpants they frog-marched him through the main street pushing their bayonets into his back all the way. The crowds of people, who had become used to public capital punishment, started baying for Jack's death. After a terrifying and humiliating march through the hostile streets, during which Jack expected to be killed, either by the guards or the crowd at any moment, he was allowed to dress and was returned to the rest of the crew.[23]

Later, according to Alex Forsyth, they discovered that, "The two local Lebanese bankers that Kurl Wallersteiner had arranged, hadn't paid off the right people. They ended up in jail with us too, and I think they had already been detained before we landed. Our fate was sealed before we even got there…"[24]

The prisoners were then informed that they were going to be executed the next morning.

Alex recalled their desperate situation; "We were all jammed into a small cell together while they were preparing the gallows outside – we could look out of a little window and watch them. They were going to hang us…" Understandably the men didn't sleep well that night. Apart from the prospect of imminent execution, they were savaged by clouds of hungry mosquitoes that swarmed through the barred window. Just before dawn the next morning they were startled by the loud crackly sound of Tom Jones singing 'The green, green grass of home' over the prison loudspeakers. The song added to the poignancy of the moment.

Within minutes a troop of soldiers arrived and with their fixed bayonets prodded the stiff and groggy men down the stairs into the dim courtyard below where

22 Personal correspondence with John and Lyn Aldridge, November 25, 2008.

23 Interview with Blythe and Ted Kruger, January 1998, and personal correspondence with Blythe Kruger August 21, 2008.

24 Interview with Alex Forsyth in Greyton, South Africa, August 2003.

they were lined up in front of the silhouetted gallows. After a while an officer arrived and the prisoners held their breath. An order was barked and, to their relief, the men were herded back to their cell. They were told that there had been some mistake and they weren't going to be executed that morning. It was going to be the next day instead.[25]

The mental strain and physical exhaustion began to take its toll. Most of the men spent the day dozing on the floor trying to get comfortable lying on their spare clothes while the blaring music was played over the public address system. "I Left My Heart in San Francisco" gnawed away at John while Jack could never listen to 'The green, green grass of home' again.[26]

Later that afternoon the gallows were tested again in preparation for the executions. Although they didn't want to, most of the men watched from their second floor cell window.

Just before dawn the next morning it was the same drill. They were woken to the jarring music and marched down to the gallows. There they stood in breathless anticipation for half an hour or so before being marched back to their cell for the next round of interrogations.

A few days later, while languishing in their crowded cell, a tall well-dressed African man happened to be walking down the corridor past them. He stopped to look. A group of smelly unshaven white men was definitely out of the ordinary, especially as they were talking to each other in English.

"What are you doing in here?" the man asked, carefully putting down his briefcase. Suddenly he had everyone's attention.

"We are the Air Trans Africa aircrew and we were detained about a week ago." Jack quickly replied, keeping an eye on the police escort.

"Do you need a lawyer?" The man asked.

"Definitely!" Jack replied.

The man's name was Dr. Santos and it turned out that he was a very well-known local lawyer who had been visiting another client in the prison. Within a day he was formally retained by Jack and began acting on the crew's behalf

25 Personal correspondence with Alyson Dawson, August 19, 2019.
26 Personal correspondence with John and Lyn Aldridge, November 25, 2008.

immediately.[27]

Although the currency conversion deadline had passed and the banknotes were now worthless, the airmen remained locked up in the grim prison until Thursday January 25th, 1968 – Alex Forsyth's birthday. That day the men were transferred to an empty block in an army barracks on the outskirts of the city. It was a huge relief, as they were now essentially held under house arrest and "... there was no longer the imminent threat of execution as there had been in the police jail."[28] This transfer was likely the result of their new lawyer's lobbying.

Soon after arriving in their new confinement there was an unexpected guard inspection and most of the barrack guards were caught sleeping. As punishment they were immediately beaten. Jack was shocked at just how pervasive corporal punishment had become in this little dark slice of West Africa. Next time the men saw the Lomé contingent arriving they quickly woke up all the guards to make sure they weren't disciplined again.[29] Quickly the appreciative guards become much more friendly and the conditions improved significantly.

Just over a week after being transferred to the barracks the prisoners were taken to the Courthouse in Lomé where they were interrogated and formally charged with the illegal importation of 'merchandise'. Jack, as the most senior member of the crew, was also charged with the illegal importation of firearms. Their lawyer then requested that the case be adjourned to give the men time to organise their legal defence.

A week or so later the British representative in Lomé visited the prisoners to check that they were being fed and were not being maltreated. The men had hoped that something positive would come from the British, but unfortunately not, as John recalled; "The British representative was absolutely useless and all he did was take our passports, which we never received back even after we had been cleared of any wrongdoing." But at least they were able to get messages out via the Ambassador.

Meanwhile with the incarceration of their Managing Director along with a significant portion of crew, non-payment of the last 'money' charter and three

27 Interview with Reg Smith, Isle of Wight, UK. May 17, 2014.

28 Interview with Alex Forsyth, Jan Smuts Airport, Johannesburg, December 2001.

29 Personal correspondence with Alyson Dawson, August 19, 2019.

aircraft out of action, Air Trans Africa was in deep trouble. Bob Nisbet who had taken over the management of the business was battling to keep the operation alive. Staff were encouraged to leave and those who chose to stay were paid what little the gutted company could scrape together.

As usual Jack's family was at the end of the queue. Without any regular income and little savings the family quickly started running out of money. Fortunately many of Zoe's relatives were farmers who would regularly bring over fresh produce, so with careful planning she was able to keep the family life as normal as she possibly could. Through it all she never complained, focusing instead on keeping up her strength and the morale of her three children. But there were many nights, when alone, she cried herself to sleep. This extreme stress also took a physical toll on her and by the end of it she had developed a serious stomach ulcer.[30]

For Jack in addition to missing and worrying about his family, one of the worst aspects of their confinement was the relapse of his malaria. He was provided with basic medication but spent weeks sweating and shivering on his bunk trying to fight off the deadly disease.

Towards the end of February 1968 the men were able to make contact with their families via the Red Cross who had negotiated for letters to be delivered. Jack's first letter home was dated the 24th and in it he talked about the fact that none of them had done anything to be ashamed of, that there was no case against them and that he hoped they would be home by Easter. He said how much he was missing the family and talked about taking them all away on holiday in their caravan to the mountains of the Eastern Highlands where it was cool, as it was so hot and humid in Lomé. Although he said they were treated well, the food was good and the accommodation was fair, he said they were all suffering from depression.[31]

Although the correspondence to and from the men was not censored, serious precautions were still taken to avoid anything which could complicate their release. It meant that everything that was written had to be carefully considered. Later, Jack's daughter Alyson, who was eleven years old at the time, recalled

30 Personal correspondence with Alyson Dawson, May 5, 2019 and March 30, 2020.
31 Personal correspondence with Alyson Dawson, March 30, 2020.

how difficult it was as a very worried child, "I remember the letters we wrote to my Dad while he was in jail. We had to be very careful not to mention anything that would trace us back to Rhodesia. We wrote quite a few letters and we got six back from him during those long six months."[32]

By the middle of April a court date was set and in the pre-trial negotiations, through their lawyer, Jack managed to secure the release of the two youngest members of the crew, Alex Forsyth and John Deegan, both of whom were suffering from the experience. Jack was also able to get Alastair Wicks released, arguing that both Alastair and John were not officially members of the crew and had just come along for the ride. The early release of the three men was secured at a bail of three thousand six hundred US dollars. The Togolese magistrate also agreed that the men did not need to return for the final trial due to the time they had already spent in jail. This was a very encouraging sign and Dr. Santos felt that, if necessary, it could be used as a precedent in their final defence.

In reality Jack's main motivation for getting Alastair out was so that he could start reviving ATA and re-establishing their lost Biafran contracts. Although Alastair was released as an innocent passenger, according to a report in the New York Times on June 14th, he was described as "An executive of the Lisbon-based Air Trans Africa."

The trial of the ATA crew finally started in Lomé on Tuesday May 4th, 1968. Most of the first day was spent recapping the pre-flight arrangements and how the planeload of cash had come to land in Lomé. Over the previous five months much of the blame had shifted to the two Lebanese bankers, but the prosecutor was still trying to place as much guilt onto the airmen as possible. Throughout the day Dr. Santos continually corrected the prosecutor's interpretations of the men's English answers back into French for the judge. He consistently noted that the interpretation either missed the point, or was blatantly incorrect to the detriment of the accused.

Although Santos was clearly an outstanding lawyer even he had trouble explaining away the modified registration letter on the aircraft. Although the point of 'saving embarrassment' for Togo did seem to gain the Judge's sympathy. But the box of pistols couldn't be explained and no one accepted the excuse that

32 Interview with Alyson Dawson, Fish Hoek, South Africa, August 31, 2003.

they were for self-defence. At the end of the first day the proceedings were adjourned and the men were told the verdict would be given the following day.[33]

At nine o'clock on the morning of Wednesday June 5th the men were back in Lomé's High Court for closing arguments. After an hour there was a short recess and then the judge handed down the verdict. Jack was sentenced to a three month jail term and fined the local equivalent of just under a hundred US dollars for tampering with the registration of the aircraft. It was a small fine in comparison to the bail amounts for Alastair, Alex Forsyth and John Deegan. All other charges were dropped. Jack was also released with the others in lieu of the amount of time he had already served in detention, which was more than his final sentence.

The men were then returned to the barracks to collect their possessions. According to John Aldridge, "When we finally left the barracks the burly African commander was on duty and bear-hugged Jack, kissing him on both cheeks saying how happy he was that we were being released." From the barracks they were driven back to Lomé where Santos booked them into a local hotel for the night. He gave them airline tickets for the first flight out of Lomé the next morning and warned them to stay locked in their rooms. He was concerned about a last minute conspiracy to have them re-arrested. This meant that Jack had to abandon the DC-7, although he fully intended to retrieve it later when things were a bit safer.

Their experience over the first five months of 1968 affected all of the crew in different ways. They all lost weight. That was easy to put back on. The psychological scars on the other hand remained, and a couple of the crewmen never fully recovered from their trauma. The one thing they all agreed on though was how good their local lawyer was. "Señor Santos turned out to be an outstanding lawyer who took on the controversial case and defended the scruffy group of white men he found at the back of the jail with tenacity and dedication."[34]

Although he had been warned against going back to Togo, Jack did make a couple of trips to Lomé over the course of the next year, fighting hard to get his aircraft back. According to Alyson, "I remember being worried that he would

33 Personal correspondence with John Aldridge, November 25, 2008.
34 Ibid.

This picture of the abandoned DC-7 at Lomé airport was taken on June 6th 1968 on the tiny spy-camera that Prime Minister Tshombe had given to Jack. He snapped the image from the window of the commercial flight that he and his crew were flown out of Togo on.

Picture from Jack Malloch's private collection. © Greg Malloch.

dare to go back in case he got captured again."[35]

Unfortunately it was to no avail and in the end he had to leave VP-WBO parked on the side of the runway until it just eventually rotted away. Many years later an observer noted, "The plane, a very valuable asset, had stood a good while on the edge of Lomé airport, until someone with a bulldozer decided it was in the way. He simply rolled the aircraft over and dumped it on a heap of rubbish."[36]

Although the dangers of Lomé would prove to be nothing compared to the dangers of Biafra and the maelstrom of war that Jack was about to be sucked into…

35 Personal correspondence with Alyson Dawson, August 19, 2019.

36 Personal correspondence and notes provided by Geoff Cartwright, December 7, 2009.

CHAPTER 9

The Rise and Fall of Biafra: 1968 to 1970

After his release Jack's first full day back home with Zoe and his three children was Saturday June 8th, 1968. Although Jack had a business to rebuild, he spent that whole weekend at home with his family. He had missed them dreadfully and really wanted to catch up on everything that had happened over the last six months.

Jack also caught up with what had happened in Biafra. The breakaway nation had lost a lot of ground since he had been incarcerated. Port Harcourt had fallen, and the remaining enclave was reduced to a small heartland completely surrounded by the Nigerians. Cut off from the rest of the world everyone in the dwindling territory was starving to death. The only means of getting supplies in was to via a dangerous night flight into a couple of improvised landing strips. The main one was called 'Airstrip Annabel' near the village of Uli. It was little more than a straight strip of highway, widened to handle cargo aircraft.

With this dire situation Jack realised that the opportunity to rebuild Air Trans Africa was still in Biafra. Sure enough, within minutes of being back at his desk Jack's old SDECE friends contacted him with a lucrative offer to fly into Uli.

Although he was still recovering, with safe havens in Gabon, Ivory Coast and São Tomé, along with a willing financial backer, Jack took the contract – and the deposit that he so desperately needed. This significant inflow of cash jolted the company back to life. After the stress of the previous six months, everyone, especially Bob Nisbet, heaved a sigh of relief. Repayment plans were quickly worked out, and with the available cash they were able to start catching up on the back-pay that was still owed to the remaining staff.

But, unfortunately, there were some things money could not fix.

While Jack had been in jail, his father, who took the whole episode very badly, had become unwell. Initially the family thought it might just have been due to the stress. But with Jack's release Vic didn't get any better. Although he was preoccupied with rebuilding his life and getting back into Biafra, Jack was worried about his father.

Within three weeks of getting out of jail Jack had signed a couple of contracts with both the French and the Portuguese and was ready to give Biafra another go. By that stage two thousand Biafrans were dying of starvation every day. Most of them were children under the age of ten. But it wasn't just a lack of food that was killing the Biafrans. With the fall of Port Harcourt and the military stockpiles that they had been hoarding there, the defenders had very little ammunition left to protect themselves. Sensing victory the Nigerian army surged forward on all fronts, slaughtering thousands. Few prisoners were taken and most were killed. Word quickly spread that surrender was not an option. This was going to be a fight to the death.

With his Christian upbringing Jack had a strong humanitarian streak so was glad that the Red Cross and the World Council of Churches were making an effort to feed the desperate civilians. Yet he felt that without allowing the Biafrans to defend themselves there was little point in feeding them. The same attitude was articulated by Gustav von Rosen who said "I soon realised that every priest, every doctor, every black and white man in Biafra was praying for arms and ammunition before food, because the idea of feeding children only to have them massacred didn't make sense."[1]

The situation was almost identical to Katanga and its northern enclaves, and once again Jack felt it was his moral duty to get involved, and he had all the connections to do so. He knew Albert-Bernard Bongo the President of Gabon and Felix Houphouet-Boigny, the pro-French President of Ivory Coast very well – along with their French military advisors which included Jack's friends Jacques Foccart and Bob Denard. Rolf Steiner, having gathered several ex-Katanga mercenaries to serve under him was also there. These, and many of the other tough fighters who Jack counted amongst his friends now filled the ranks of the Biafran and Gabonese Special Forces.

1 'The New Mercenaries' by Anthony Mockler. Corgi Books. ISBN 0-552-12558-X.

Sadly, while working on his plans, Jack was reminded, tragically, of the dangers of the airlift. On the night of Monday July 1st, 1968 during a violent tropical storm a Super Constellation belonging to Jack's rival Hank Wharton crashed on final approach into Uli. There were no survivors. The captain was August Martin, a Tuskeegee Airman and Jack's friend and ex-employee Bill Brown was the flight engineer. When Jack had been stuck in prison Bill had been forced to find work elsewhere and this was how it ended.

Bill and the rest of the crew were buried in a small cemetery on the outskirts of Uli village. More than one hundred and fifty others would join Augie and Bill in the cemetery before the war finally came to an end. Jack was devastated by Bill's death, especially as he had just started recruiting again and had wanted to get his trusted crewmen, including Bill, back to Air Trans Africa. Bill's wife Maureen lived in Salisbury and Jack knew her well. Realising that she wouldn't be receiving any insurance pay-out and was now in desperate need, he offered her a job at ATA which she gratefully took. She ended up working for the company for several years before eventually marrying Jack's faithful long-serving lieutenant Henry Kinnear.

By the end of the first week of July Jack had secured hanger space with the Gabon Air Force and his first shipment of weapons was ready for collection. But first he needed to find out as much as he could about 'Airstrip Annabel' near the little settlement of Uli. Due to the growing risk of prowling enemy jet fighters the strip only operated at night. But the approaches were challenging. In addition to the undulating ground, it was in the middle of a plantation of tall palm trees. It certainly was not going to be easy flying. Jack decided to make the first couple of flights into the airstrip to ascertain the best way of getting in and out.

With just a rough hand-drawn map, Jack made his first approach down into the pitch-black forest where Annabel was supposed to be. Having an uncanny sense of where he was, Jack only had to make the slightest adjustment as the runway lights were briefly flashed on for him. With his usual calm confidence few people believed that it was his first flight into the tree-lined landing pad. Once on the ground Jack was directed into the nearest parking bay, where he turned the aircraft around to face back down the runway. He throttled back feathering the propellers, but kept the engines running. There were no starters or batteries at Uli, and he wanted to be ready for a quick get-away. The German mercenary Rolf Steiner was waiting on the ground for them. He was desperate to get ammunition to the nearest battlefields where every single bullet was needed.

The flight was a success and Jack committed to the contracts, carefully briefing his crews on the route and the best procedure for landing in the darkness. According to Anthony Mockler, it was Monsieur Jean who personally organised Jack's first arms flight into Biafra; "'Monsieur Jean' had hired Jack Malloch, the ex-Spitfire ace from Rhodesia, at the time forty-nine years old, to organise these dangerous missions. The first plane loaded with arms and ammunition landed at Uli on July 13th; and thereafter every night arms and ammunition were flown in from Libreville…"[2] Quickly Jack and his crews adapted to a nocturnal life-style with exhausted sleep from early morning to mid-afternoon and high tension flying from sunset to sunrise.

Three weeks later, the bombing of Uli started.

The first attack was a daylight raid and the results were devastating. The air traffic control centre was the main target. It took a couple of direct hits and by the time the dust had settled it was clear that most of the radio equipment had been completely destroyed. As a result of the raid, which quickly became a daily routine at Uli, the Biafrans decided to hide the control 'tower' away from the airstrip, deep within the palm trees. Although this new position ensured that the installation would survive, it had no view of what was really going on which made air traffic control all the more challenging.

According to one of Jack's crewmen; "we understood that the 'control tower' was actually a bunker, several metres underground and perhaps a kilometre away from the runway, hidden to avoid the daily bombings. As the Nigerian Air Force knew about the airlift, the 'airport' equipment and Non-Directional Beacon were regularly relocated, either after being damaged by daytime bombing or to avoid being destroyed permanently."[3]

As the situation deteriorated, even with the combined aircraft of Jack Malloch and Hank Wharton, they couldn't keep up with the demand for military supplies,

2 'The New Mercenaries' by Anthony Mockler. Corgi Books. ISBN 0-552-12558-X.

3 Personal correspondence with Mike Gibson, August 25, 2009.

never mind food and medicine. The two rival gun runners just had too few aircraft. To address this the French, who preferred dealing with Jack, started working on ways to subsidise his fleet.

In an unnoticed transaction an ex-USAAF DC-4 belonging to TransportFlug was sold to Gilbert Bourgeard. Bourgeard was, in fact, Bob Denard. Soon after the sale the aircraft disappeared off the register, though it appears to have been given to Jack to replace his old DC-4 VP-YTY which was still stuck in Woensdrecht waiting for its overhaul to be paid off. This aircraft was operated by ATA until 1970 when it was scrapped.[4]

Two days after the sale of this DC-4 the German Ambassador in Libreville informed the British that "…it is common knowledge that a DC-3 is carrying arms and ammunition and is being loaded in secret at an Air Force hanger." According to Michael Draper, Air Trans Africa was operating this DC-3. With clandestine deals Jack had increased his nightly delivery capacity by two more aircraft, both given to him by the French.

But what Jack really wanted was his DC-7 that was still impounded at Lomé airport. He contacted his trusted West African lawyer Señor Santos and they arranged to meet up in Johannesburg to discuss the case. With hindsight South Africa was not the best choice for their meeting and Jack was acutely embarrassed that due to the local apartheid laws he was not able to meet his close friend in the same hotel that he was staying in. But the meeting was productive. Over the next few months the two men made several trips to Togo arguing that as Jack had served his three month jail sentence there was no legitimate reason for the authorities to withhold the aircraft. It was to no avail, and as it was clear on his last trip that the authorities were running out of patience with him Jack decided to abandon the aircraft. With the evidence of his efforts to recover it he decided to try and make an insurance claim on it instead.

Jack submitted his claim, but it was immediately rejected. He was told to simply go and get the aeroplane. He provided the background, but the insurance company was even less inclined to consider it once they discovered that Jack had been convicted of a crime which they rationalised led to its 'negligent loss.'

4 'Shadows, Airlift and Airwar in Biafra and Nigeria 1967–1970' by Michael Draper. Published by Hikoko Publications. IBSN 1-902109-63-5

Understandably no insurance company wanted to make a full replacement payment on a perfectly serviceable aircraft.

But Jack was not one to give up, especially on a matter of principle so he turned to an English insurance broker by the name of Reg Smith who was recommended for difficult cases like this. After meeting with Jack and looking at the case Reg agreed to take on the claim. It was going to be difficult though, so Reg found a French lawyer who specialised in aviation insurance cases and went out to see him a few times in Paris to discuss the best way forward. Although it was going to take a while for the case to be heard, and there was going to be a long appeal process, Reg felt confident, and reassured Jack that they "had a couple of good ideas on how they could justify the claim."[5]

By September Biafra was almost bankrupt and the shrinking nation was forced to abandon the city of Aba. It had been their administrative capital and largest remaining city, but they had run out of ammunition and were simply unable to continue its defence. Together with other losses this reduced Biafra's territory to less than five thousand square miles, or one-sixth of the state's original size. Less than a week later the Nigerian Army's 15th Brigade make a fast dash towards the town of Oguta and again the Biafrans were unable to stop them due to their critical shortage of military supplies. By September 12th Uli itself was almost within range of the encroaching Nigerian artillery and the vital airstrip was abandoned. Once again it seemed that Biafra was about to collapse.

With Uli out of action and their supply situation worse than ever the Biafran government begged Jack to fly as many military flights into the battered Red Cross airstrip at Obilagu as he could. A week later this airstrip was also overrun by the Nigeria Army. But within hours of Jack's first resupply flight on the night of Friday 13th, the Biafran army was able to regroup and once again start to push back the Nigerians. Their focus was on Oguta and on the 15th the Nigerians retreated from the embattled town, allowing Uli to reopen and more supplies to be flown in. But this victory meant a compromise elsewhere and the very next day on the other side of the tiny country the city of Owerri was lost to Federal Forces.

Meanwhile, as Jack was working his flight schedules to go back into Uli, in

5 Interview with Reg Smith, Isle of Wight, U.K., May 18, 2014.

Holland, Aviolanda finally released his DC-4 and his Super Constellation, having at last been paid for the overhauling of both aircraft. The DC-4 was flown to Libreville where it was re-registered with a Gabonese registration, TR-LNV. This was Jack's first 'Tango Romeo', and within a day of arriving in Gabon it made its first arms shuttle into Uli.

At the end of September Jack personally went to collect his Super Constellation from Woensdrecht. It was also registered in Gabon. Although for its first week of operation every night Jack and Clive flew tons of military hardware into Biafra from the Ivory Coast in a huge triangular flight path taking them from Abidjan to Uli, Uli to São Tomé and back. During this time Jack and the crew stayed in the luxurious Presidential Palace in Abidjan.

Just when and how Jack established his friendship with President Félix Houphouët-Boigny of the Ivory Coast is not known. But either way, they certainly did have a close friendship as reflected by this luxury accommodation in the President's compound. There they "…dined with the best French crystal and gold-plated cutlery." Something that was unheard of for any other aircrew.[6]

By the beginning of October 1968 Uli was Biafra's only lifeline. This made it critical for aircraft to be landed, unloaded and turned around as quickly as possible to enable as much food and military hardware to be delivered and dispersed before the inevitable dawn bombing raids. In total darkness this was always an extremely dangerous exercise.

The danger started as soon as they crossed the Nigerian coastline. They always kept an altitude of at least ten thousand feet to keep out of range of the Nigerian anti-aircraft positions. Jack's Intelligence friends informed him as to what AA artillery the Nigerians had so he knew how high they needed to fly. Although it was unsettling for the crews to watch the bursts of muzzle-flashes firing up at them.

Arriving over Uli, due to the build-up of air traffic the pilots were usually ordered to join the top of a spiraling holding pattern, often in pitch dark, stormy conditions. This was made up of a stack of incoming aircraft, all impatiently waiting for their turn to land on the strip of bomb-cratered highway. As there was so little space on the ground outgoing flights would also have to be handled

6 Interview with Henry Kinnear, Boksburg, Johannesburg, South Africa, November 7, 2003.

and coordinated to make room for the next ones. And with all this, there was the added danger of air, or in the latter stages of the war, ground attack by Nigerian forces.

Sometimes they would be in the turbulent holding pattern for as long as half an hour as they slowly worked their way down through the whirlpool of aircraft. Eventually, once the aeroplane ahead of them had taxied off the runway they would be cleared for landing. Less than a mile from touchdown they had to confirm they were on final approach by quickly flashing on and off their landing lights before the few runway lights that were still working were switched on. Jack was famous for his uncanny knack of always being perfectly aligned, even on moonless, cloudy nights. In the chaotic darkness most pilots found it difficult to judge their actual position especially as Uli's weak non-directional beacon was often overwhelmed by violent tropical thunderstorms.

As soon as the aircraft had touched down the sparse runway lights would be switched off and they would quickly taxi to a paved area on the side of the main strip to get out of the way of the next incoming aircraft. In a complete blackout the pilots carefully picked their way along with just their own nose-wheel lights and a couple of waving flashlights that the Biafran ground personnel had.

When the engines were shut down the flight engineer would open the cargo doors, and emaciated bodies, often stripped down to the waist and sweating in the tropical heat, would appear with ladders. They would then start offloading as quickly as possible to make way for the next aircraft, and the next, and the next... before dawn would cut off the lifeline yet again.[7]

One night in early October while jostling for apron space the cockpit of a German Church DC-7 was struck by the wing of a Red Cross DC-6. Both aircraft were damaged and hidden under piles of palm fronds and tree branches to escape the daily bombings while spare parts were sourced and flown in. The Red Cross DC-6 was able to survive but the DC-7 took a couple of direct hits from the marauding MiGs and was completely destroyed. It was a sober reminder to Jack's crews to be particularly careful in the crowded confusion they had to face each night.

Although Jack's main concern wasn't the congestion on the ground it was being

7 Personal correspondence with Mike Gibson, August 25, 2009.

bombed on the ground. Sure enough, on the evening of Wednesday October 23rd, he had just landed a few minutes after nine and was standing on the tarmac discussing requirements for his next few flights with the local commanders. Suddenly a droning air raid siren went off and instantly everyone scattered, running for cover into the trees at the sides of the busy airstrip.

Although no bombs fell that night, during the first week of November the Nigerians adapted a Dakota based out of Benin City as a night-bomber. With a white mercenary crew and the call-sign 'Intruder,' they started nightly bombing sorties over Uli. Predictably their first victim was a Church DC-7 which was delivering a cargo of dried stockfish. Twelve Biafran ground crew were killed and Father Desmond McGlade, the captain and the first officer were all badly injured. Then, less than a week later a couple of Nigerian MiGs screamed out of the night strafing Uli's runway and punching a string of holes into a Red Cross chartered C-160.

Still, there was some good news for Biafra. As the country was broke the French agreed to use its Secret Service fund to source and supply over two million Pounds worth of arms to help Ojukwu. "By linking itself to Paris' subterfuge, South Africa also got involved. The plan was orchestrated by Jacques Foccart, the Élysée's shadowy éminence grise in charge of African affairs. France persuaded Pretoria to provide the secessionists with arms and ammunition… The South African Army eventually gave Ojukwu hundreds of tons of ordnance as well as a squad or two of special forces…"[8] Of course Jack was involved in not just flying the weapons in, but with the special forces themselves, further deepening his relationship with the South African military establishment.

By mid-November Jack was back in Salisbury. He needed to recruit more crews, and he was worried about his father who seemed to be getting worse. He flew down to Fort Victoria and after the expected objections managed to get Vic to the family doctor. The verdict wasn't good. As soon as the specialist in Salisbury got the results he immediately booked Vic into hospital. As Blythe recalled, things did not go well, "...an operation followed. But he was riddled with cancer. We were distraught. After the operation Jack and Zoe took my

8 'War Dog, Fighting Other People's Wars' by Al J. Venter. Published by Casemate Philadelphia. ISBN 1-932033-09-2.

mother and father back home to Fort Victoria. Once back home my Mum did a great job looking after him. But we did not realise how weak he had become…"[9] 1968 had been a very tough year for Jack, as with the stress of jail, the stress at work and the stress of his dying father, he felt completely exhausted. As he prepared to leave home to go back to war, in the pit of his stomach he knew worse was still to come.

Once back 'in theatre', considering the rash of night-time bombing raids Jack pushed back their flight schedules to ensure that none of his aircraft arrived at Uli before 9.30 p.m. Over time this became an honoured agreement between the non-Nigerian pilots on both sides of the conflict. "The arrangement was that they wouldn't bomb the airfield after nine o'clock, so we just made sure we never arrived before nine thirty. Sometimes we would get there and there would be burning aircraft because they had arrived too early. But it was an easy rule to follow. The Nigerian bombers were generally expats and most didn't really want to do us harm. It was a gentleman's agreement."[10]

By the beginning of 1969 it was obvious that ATA still couldn't keep up with the growing demands of the Biafran High Command. Jack needed more aircraft, and his old friend Bob Denard was more than happy to help. This time he bought Jack an ex-Air France DC-4 from the French Domestic Postal Service. To hide its ownership the old French registration numbers were left on the aircraft and the crews actively fueled conflicting rumours about who owned it.

In mid-January Jack headed back to Salisbury. He needed a few days off and wanted to negotiate the purchase of another DC-7. With the help of his French supporters, who were now very involved in his business, Jack was put in touch with a man by the name of John Squire. John was the Managing Director of an Irish company called Aer Turas that had an ex-KLM DC-7C for sale.

John, who was 'SDECE approved', wasn't a fan of the British so was more than happy to work around their sanctions. The deal was quickly concluded and the aircraft was ferried to Salisbury and on to Libreville where it was re-registered as TR-LOK. Although for most of its gun-running career the aircraft didn't carry any registration letters at all. It was only recognisable by the faded old

9 Personal correspondence with Blythe Kruger, June 27, 2008.
10 Interview with Henry Kinnear, Boksburg, Johannesburg, November 7, 2003.

ex-KLM name 'Yellow Sea' that was still visible on its nose.

Aer Turas had four other freight-configured aircraft, but only needed two. They asked Jack if he might be interested in buying the other couple as well. As the price was very reasonable Jack confirmed he would take them but staggered over the next few months to give him time to train his crews on the larger aircraft.[11]

By this stage Jack had staff based permanently in both Lisbon and Libreville. In Libreville where they were delivering war material and in Lisbon where they were collecting war material. Alastair Wicks and Pierre Laureys were still very involved in both sides of the operation, as revealed in mid-January by the Rhodesian Herald; "South African and Rhodesian airmen based in Lisbon have now taken over as the main operators of the arms supply routes between Europe and Biafra. The men are under the command of a Captain James Wicks. All are said to be contracted to a Salisbury-based airways company which, since Biafra broke with the Nigerian Federal Government, has been operating several grey-painted Super Constellations on supply runs from Lisbon into Biafra... This mission is believed to be the head of a Europe-wide arms-buying campaign working through a Lisbon-based Frenchman, Mr. Pierre Lorez..."[12] Although the Herald got Alastair and Pierre's names slightly wrong, they, along with ATA were all definitely implicated. After this unwelcome publicity Jack tried to avoid São Tomé and its snooping reporters, preferring instead to deliver the military hardware from the Libreville Air Force base directly into Uli.

Being old and over-used, Jack's aircraft were in constant need of service and attention. With little choice, towards the end of March the old Connie was recalled for yet another service, and to get the growing number of shrapnel holes patched up. According to one of the technicians at Field's who were based in the hanger right next to Air Trans Africa, "We always knew when ATA had aircraft back at Salisbury Airport, as the various departmental supervisors would come into the section, waving their pink job cards saying, 'Get over there quickly – they want to fly tonight!' Then we would see a stream of sheet-metal

11 'Shadows, Airlift and Airwar in Biafra and Nigeria 1967 – 1970' by Michael Draper. Published by Hikoko Publications. IBSN 1-902109-63-5.

12 'S.A. and Rhodesian pilots ferrying arms to Biafra' front page article in The Rhodesian Herald, edition of January 18, 1969.

'tin-bashers' quickly going off to repair the bullet holes."[13]

While this repair work was being done Jack was pleased to be back in Salisbury and catch up with the family for a bit. He was very worried about his father so between his long flights and meetings he managed to fly down to Fort Victoria to at least help a little. Vic, who by now was gaunt, frail and continually coughing, was wracked with pain and seemed to be fading fast. When Jack arrived at Breezy Brae he could hardly recognise his father. The cancer had permeated his entire body and Jack realised that he needed to prepare himself for the inevitable.

But there were still the demands of his business to look after. On March 13th, having been serviced as best as possible the ageing Constellation returned to Libreville via the South African Air Force base of Waterkloof. There it was loaded with just over ten tons of South African weapons. These were delivered into Uli the following evening.

By the beginning of April 1969, even with the massive airlift, there was just too little food to keep the country alive. Almost all of it was going straight to the main population centres to keep essential services going. Many of those in outlying areas were simply left to die. And die they did, by the thousands. Children were particularly vulnerable and with no other alternative many were abandoned at the doors of the various mission stations and churches. The desperate priests, nuns and missionaries suddenly found themselves surrounded by throngs of crying, disorientated and emaciated children. As most of the aircraft of 'Jesus Christ Airways' (which the Joint Churches Aid aircraft had been dubbed) were returning to São Tomé empty, the churches quickly set up a transit camp on the island for the starving children. Quickly this facility was overwhelmed, and many kids were placed into institutions in other countries around the region.

Although Jack was not directly involved in the relief flights and didn't want to compromise his French and Portuguese clients, he was extremely concerned about the orphans. Whenever he could, he would make his outgoing flights available to carry loads of the agonised children out to safety.

That was traumatic in itself.

There were tens of thousands of the skeletal children trying to stagger their way

13 Personal correspondence with Mike Daly, July 2008.

One of Jack's unbranded ex-Aer Turas DC-7's which became the mainstay of his nightly arms airlift into the besieged airstrip at Uli during 1969.
Picture from Jack Malloch's private collection. © Greg Malloch.

to the overcrowded airstrip before the Nigerian army caught up with them. As there were no seats or safety-belts they would have to sit huddled together on the hard steel cargo floor of the aircraft, often sobbing or just staring blankly ahead, numbed by the pain of starvation. When they landed those who could, slowly and painfully shuffled down the crew ladder. And every time there was always a few left behind who had died on the way. Their little bodies were wrapped in blankets by the solemn priests who buried them with all the dignity and rites they deserved.[14]

In April 1969 ATA received the second DC-7 from Aer Turas. It was a cargo-configured DC-7CF and was registered in Gabon as TR-LOJ. The third DC-7 was also on its way and was just waiting for its final service before delivery. Jack desperately needed these aircraft as his old ones were failing. A week before TR-LOJ joined the roster the Super Constellation suffered a major hydraulic failure just as it had crossed into Nigerian airspace. The crew managed to nurse it back, but its gun-running days were over.

Jack got the news of this loss as he sat at his father's deathbed in Salisbury General Hospital. His father was in a coma and there was nothing left to do but

14 Interview with Colin Miller, Bulawayo, Zimbabwe. January 1998.

wait. Several hours later, after a long and torturous struggle Vic finally passed away. The next day was Good Friday.

It took Jack a couple of weeks before he could get back to work and by then the congestion in the turbulent night sky above Uli was even worse. "On occasions as many as twenty aircraft were circling simultaneously, some of which were assigned the same altitude by the unqualified Biafran controllers. One Swedish pilot, Ulf Engelbrecht, claimed that 'if all the pilots were to turn on rotating beacons and clearance lights, a dozen of them would die of fright at their proximity to each other!'"[15]

The Biafran army couldn't hold with their deliveries being held up in the queue at Uli so asked Jack to start flying their supplies into the lesser known Uga strip some fifteen miles northeast of Uli. Although Jack was an exceptional pilot, even he found Uga challenging. After his first flight into the rough strip in mid-May he recommended that only the smaller DC-4s land there. But Jack's crews didn't just have to deal with the rough, short landing strip but also the ever-present threat of enemy bombers. At about midnight on the night of May 20th Mike and his father Johnnie Gibson arrived over Uga for their sixth flight into the tiny strip. Usually the last of the Nigerian bombers had long since gone to bed. But not so that night…

"We approached normally and began descending in the holding pattern, having been informed there may be an enemy bomber in the area. This turned out to be true and that night the DC-3 was armed with incendiary bombs. Seconds before touchdown, we saw a large flash on the ground ahead of us, a little to the left of the runway, and then what seemed like a few seconds later just as we touched down, there was another explosion on the right, but just behind us. We had actually landed through a line of falling bombs."[16] After another day of relentless pounding Uga was put out of action for the rest of the war.

The Nigerians were now resolved to end the succession and completely destroy the enclave. This ushered in a much more deadly phase in which Uli, and anyone brave enough to land there, became a prime target of the Federal forces. In the first week of June 1969 in a MiG raid on Uli a humanitarian DC-6 was strafed

15 'Shadows, Airlift and Airwar in Biafra and Nigeria 1967–1970' by Michael Draper. Published by Hikoko Publications. IBSN 1-902109-63-5.

16 Personal correspondence with Mike Gibson, August 20, 2009.

with rockets and canons just as it was landing. Then just three days later a pair of Nigerian MiGs, piloted by a South African Ares Klootwyk and an Englishman Mike Thompsett, shot down a Red Cross DC-7. The American captain and his crew were all killed trying to deliver their cargo of rice.[17]

All humanitarian flights were cancelled that night. But Jack didn't fall under the jurisdiction of the Red Cross or the churches, and knowing how desperately needed the military supplies were, he chose to personally fly in the next load of arms and ammunition. As they started their final descent they passed over the still smouldering remains of the downed mercy flight. Everyone was silent.

But the challenges of Uli weren't just from the Nigerian Air Force. The tall palms remained a continual hazard. "I remember one night, John Hodges was very pissed-off with Clive Halse, who had skimmed the palm trees on the downwind leg of their approach. John was swearing and showing him the evidence which was lodged in the undercarriage. After that Clive was given the nickname 'Twiggy!'"[18]

With the enemy closing in on all sides, Jack realised the Biafrans needed better quality weaponry if they were to hold their ground. Tapping into his network of arms dealers he quickly formulated a plan. Due to his extreme discretion most people only saw Jack as a hard-working cargo airline operator, but this was far from the truth. With his extensive secret service contacts he was directly involved in organising many of the undercover deals themselves. The arrangement he organised for the Biafrans was just one such example.

The operation involved all three ATA DC-7s, with Jack personally leading them. They flew around the bulge of Africa via Abidjan and Faro in Portugal all the way to Tel Aviv in Israel. There they collected more than forty-five tons of cutting-edge military hardware. They were in the Jewish state for a full day while the fleet of aircraft were being loaded. Jack took advantage of this time to meet with his suppliers, knowing full well that he would be needing them again.

The next day the three aircraft flew back arriving in Libreville on the evening of Wednesday June 11th. That was the first of several such multi-aircraft shuttles

17 'Shadows, Airlift and Airwar in Biafra and Nigeria 1967–1970' by Michael Draper. Published by Hikoko Publications. IBSN 1-902109-63-5.

18 Personal correspondence with Mike Gibson, August 20, 2009.

that Jack organised between Israel and Gabon,[19] and as soon as they were on the ground the weapons were off-loaded and warehoused. Over the next few days almost all of it was delivered into Biafra. But not all of it.

In mid-June the last consignment of brand-new Israeli weapons where loaded onto Jack's DC-7, but instead of heading for Uli, once over the Gulf of Guinea, Jack turned south. Eight hours later he landed in Salisbury, delivering his first plane-load of weapons to Rhodesia in direct contravention of the United Nations arms embargo against the country.[20] A significant portion of the weapons ended up being shared with South Africa, although the Rhodesians kept a good selection for themselves, including crates of rockets and Uzi submachine guns. These were carefully studied, and it wasn't long before they had their own home-made versions.

In addition to bringing weapons into Rhodesia, Jack was also interested in finding ways of exporting goods out of the country.

Tobacco was one of the country's main exports and according to John Graylin, the chairman of the Tobacco Export Council, "Sanctions disrupted our tobacco industry terribly... Then we started to sell it 'under the counter'." And that was where Jack came in. Through his friends in Gabon a deal was struck for Rhodesian tobacco to be exported to Libreville and processed into cigarettes for sale on the international market. Shortly thereafter Peter Stuyvesant cigarette packs appeared stating that they had been manufactured in Gabon, a country that didn't even grow tobacco.

But there was little time to think about Rhodesia's needs, as Biafra, squeezed into a thin strip of land around Uli, was fighting for its life. During the last week of June Jack had a lot of military hardware to deliver and all his available aircraft were fully deployed. Yet he felt uneasy and knew that just one little slip in the chaos and confusion of Uli could spell disaster. Already his crews were operating right on the cusp of disaster, as one of their logbook entries reflects; "Low and slow looking for the airfield. Flew into the tops of the palm trees with gear down and approach flaps. Once again green propellers and branches

---

19 Jack Malloch's and Henry Kinnear's personal flying logbooks and personal correspondence with Mike Gibson, August 19 2009.

20 Jack Malloch's personal flying logbook.

in the undercarriage."[21] Clive Halse was at the controls of this particular flight which didn't do his 'Twiggy' reputation any good.

On the night of Thursday 26th, June the weather was perfect. But it was too good. Tshombe's old DC-4 was the first in the air, leaving Libreville just after nine o'clock that evening. The entire cargo was made up of hundreds of stacked boxes of ammunition. As they crossed the coastline they were caught in the bright silver moonlight of a huge full moon. With no cover they were extremely vulnerable to enemy fighter aircraft and had to turn back. Eventually they got into Uli at 4.30 a.m. just in time for a frantic unloading and a panicked escape before the arrival of the marauding MiGs.[22]

The next night it was mortar bombs, land mines and rocket propelled grenades. In contrast to the night before the Biafran air traffic controllers were warning of dangerous thunderstorms. They couldn't afford any more weather delays so as soon as they reached their 'safe time' the aircraft took off in staggered waves, starting with the slower Skymaster. Although everyone managed to make their deliveries and survived the night Jack couldn't shake his nagging premonition.

As ammunition was now absolutely critical all the aircraft were loaded with hundreds of heavy boxes of .303 and 7.62mm bullets for their deliveries on the night of Saturday 28th. Unfortunately, the unloading time in Uli was taking ever longer as starvation sapped the strength of the ground crews. This and the later take-off times meant that the aircraft could each only make one delivery per night which didn't help.

That night Captain Jack Wright had command of the Katangan DC-4 and Jack was flying one of the DC-7s. Jack had positioned the aircraft in São Tomé late in the afternoon so he could land in Uli as soon after the 9 p.m. 'curfew' as possible.

At quarter to seven that evening the old Skymaster took off from Libreville. The French DC-4, F-BBDD was loaded, ready and waiting for the crew to return.

In São Tomé Jack was in the cockpit of the DC-7 monitoring progress. In Algeria Tshombe was crying out for help in his prison cell. Over Uli Intruder was in the air looking for targets. Below the orphans were cowering.

---

21 Henry Kinnear's personal flying logbook.
22 Ibid.

Things were converging…

The landing at Uli was uneventful and there was no sign of the Intruder which was a relief. The DC-4 taxied to the side of the main runway to be unloaded. Knowing he had to make another flight in F-BBDD before the end of the night Jack Wright was anxious to leave, and as soon as he got the thumbs up that the cargo was clear he immediately started taxing forward in readiness for a fast take-off, requesting clearance from Air Traffic Control.

Then for some inexplicable reason they turned the wrong way onto the runway.

As they reached V2 speed and lifted the nose off the ground they saw a wall of dark green trees in the landing lights up ahead. As they were just inches off the ground the Captain knew they would never clear the tall palms. Instinctively he cut the power and slammed on the brakes. Seconds later the fast-moving aircraft ploughed into a low reinforced bunker ripping away its starboard undercarriage. Crashing down onto its belly the crippled Skymaster careered into the tree-line and burst into flames.[23]

"Even before the aircraft came to a halt the crew were out of their seats and running towards the rear of the empty fuselage. As the undercarriage had collapsed all three men managed to get out… As so often was the case in the Biafran War there was a final twist of irony that night. When Jack Malloch flew back to Libreville for breakfast, news was just breaking that Moïse Tshombe had died that night in an Algerian jail. Somebody went over and told Malloch the news. Malloch just shrugged and quietly remarked, 'His aircraft just died with him…'."[24]

The truth was that Jack was very upset by both the loss of his favourite aircraft, and the loss of his trusted old friend.

The next day Jack flew back to Salisbury. It had been a tough few weeks that had ended particularly badly. He needed a break. But there wasn't much hope of that. After a brief overnight with his family, Jack made the first of a couple of flights from Salisbury to Durban to meet with Mike Hoare to discuss setting up 'special forces' training. According to Mike, who was retained for a time by

---

23 Notes from Jack Malloch's and Henry Kinnear's personal flying logbooks and details related by Henry Kinnear, Boksberg, Johannesburg, November 7, 2003.

24 'Shadows, Airlift and Airwar in Biafra and Nigeria 1967 – 1970' by Michael Draper. Published by Hikoko Publications. IBSN 1-902109-63-5.

Ojukwu, some eighty mercenaries were hired by Biafra, mostly from mid-1968 to mid-1969. Apart from a very few, Ojukwu wasn't impressed with them and by August 1969 almost all of their contracts had been ended.

Although Ojukwu did trust the French and they convinced him that certain specialised military operations and training assignments needed foreign experts, they didn't want to be caught deploying their own forces into the war zone. The French turned, once again, to their South African friends for help. In response a team of South African Special Forces was put together led by a former Rhodesian SAS major by the name of Ian Carpenter. This man, whose real name was Jan Breytenbach, kept his true identity from all but his SDECE handlers, Jack Malloch and Ojukwu himself. In time he would reach the rank of Colonel and would rise up to legendary status within the ranks of the South African Defence Force.

While operating in West Africa Jan and his highly trained colleagues were assimilated into the ranks of the French Secret Service and all connections back to South Africa were carefully hidden. The SDECE facility in Libreville was a nondescript, bungalow right on the beach in a quiet residential suburb. This became Jan's rear base, from where the operation to set up and train the guerrillas of the Biafran Organisation of Freedom Fighters was run.

Zoe was not highly involved in Jack's business and focused on trying to ensure a normal life for their children. Although she was more aware of the intrigue that he was involved in than most people realised. As Jan recalled, she was known to the French secret service and sometimes traveled with Jack.

"Just before we were deployed the French organised a special dinner for Jack and Zoe at the Intelligence facility. That was when my men and I were introduced to the legendary 'Captain Jack'. The French considered the Mallochs 'VIP visitors' so they were provided with special accommodation in the only decent hotel in the city. Jack Malloch was an impressive guy. He was obviously a man with plenty of guts and was dedicated to Rhodesia and furthering his country's cause. He was definitely a born leader in the military mould and someone who would not hesitate to put his own neck on the block. His pilots all had very high regard for him... We used his wife's name 'ZOE' as the code name for our particular team as a token of our regard."[25]

The very next night Jack flew Jan and his team with their heavy packs of equipment into Uli. They were squashed in amongst the loaded palettes of ammunition in the back of one of the DC-7s. Every Thursday night thereafter ATA flew in supplies and rations specifically for the 'BOFF' operation and Jan would always be waiting in the darkness on the edge of the bomb-scared runway to collect the vital consignments.

By mid-August the Nigerians were closing in on all sides. Leaving his two fully committed DC-7s and the French DC-4 to keep making their nightly deliveries, Jack headed off to Faro to replenish their stockpile of Portuguese munitions. It was a desperate relay race to keep the system working and Jack was personally involved in every part of it. The suppliers needed to keep committing. The weapons needed to be cleared and ready for collection. The boats needed to keep sailing from South Africa and Jack needed to keep aircraft flying in from Portugal and France. The hangar in Libreville needed to be kept full, and the roster of flights into Uli needed to keep happening. And all of this needed to happen night after night, come hell or high water – and with the torrential rainfall and Nigerian gunners they often faced both.

The only thing Jack didn't have to worry about was cash-flow. Having struggled to balance his books for so long this was a huge relief. All the bills were paid, and there was plenty of profit. They were even able to increase salaries and allowances. According to Jack's crews those were their 'hay-days'. Although most of the money was paid across to Jack by his SDECE handlers it was collected from the French, Portuguese and South Africans who were all involved in the operation. A high ranking South African Defence Force officer later recalled "... the SADF, indirectly financed, via the French, much of Jack's sanctions-busting operations and his flights into Biafra in support of Ojukwu's army."[26]

By the end of August 1969 the gun-running operation and the nightly 'gauntlet' was well honed, slick and efficient. According to one of the commentators at the time, "Jack's DC-7s were ideal aircraft and his aircrews were the only ones who could clandestinely fly war material into Biafra under the most dangerous

25 Personal correspondence with Jan Breytenbach, January 28, 2003.
26 Ibid.

and adverse conditions, right under the noses of the International Red Cross and the Roman Catholic humanitarian flights."[27]

But no matter how many nightly flights they were able to make, Jack knew it was too little, too late. Biafra's defeat was just a matter of time. To see ATA through the inevitable 'transition phase' once the collapse came, from mid-August he started cultivating new business opportunities. For this Jack considered the main products that Rhodesia needed to export. These where its mineral wealth, which was too heavy for air transport and its tobacco, which was a too light for air transport. Then there was Rhodesia's world-class beef, which, being perishable, was ideal.

Jack knew the Chief Financial Officer at the Cold Storage Commission (CSC) who was a fellow Spitfire Ace by the name of Corry van Vliet who had also flown against the Germans in North Africa and Italy. With the help of this old comrade Jack was able to get into the government-owned organisation and propose the idea of using Air Trans Africa to export Rhodesian beef.

Nick Spoel who ran the CSC, along with his Board of Directors, were intrigued by the proposal. Jack didn't just have the aircraft to export the prime beef, but he also had a buyer – the Gabonese themselves. With the help of Bob Denard and Jean-Louis Domange, a contract was prepared for the supply of top-quality Rhodesian beef to the Gabonese High Command. As the deal was paid in desperately needed hard currency and at a good price, the Cold Storage Commission jumped at the opportunity, and Jack's first 'Meat Run' was prepared.

Just before dawn on the morning of Wednesday 15th October 1969, after all the palettes of Triple-A grade beef had been loaded and the interior of the DC-7 had been brought down to a frigid few degrees above freezing, Jack and Mike Gibson took off, heading north. They flew directly to Libreville where about half of the consignment was offloaded. The other half was then delivered to Port Gentil, one hundred miles south-west of Libreville.

From Port Gentil they refuelled with high-performance avgas on São Tomé. The ground crew knew that the aircraft was a gunrunner, but this time there was a strong smell of blood in the empty cargo hold. They knew better than

27 Personal correspondence with Michael Draper, August 2, 2003.

to ask questions, but a rash of wild rumours briefly did the rounds.[28] The Cold Storage Commission and the client were both very happy and started planning more deliveries.

Jack did the second 'Meat Run' on October 28th and his third delivery on November 5th. With their initial success the conversation with Bob and Jean-Louis then turned towards setting up a meat importing and wholesaling business in Libreville. A business that would eventually become known as Soduco. Jack knew this was the beginning of something big.

With the desperation of the Biafran High Command for any additional munitions they could get, and the potential of the new Meat Run, Jack asked his friend Bill Armstrong to find another DC-7 for the airlift. Bill had already proven his worth to Air Trans Africa and according to Graham Simons, "Aircraft came and went through Luton, disappearing into darkest Africa." But they didn't all make it.

In early November Bill bought an ex-Caledonia Airways DC-7 for Jack, but the 'sanctions-police' found out about the deal and wouldn't allow the aircraft to leave the country. According to Bill, "…it was then flown from Stansted to Shannon in Ireland for 'short term storage'. However, the UDI crisis deepened and extended well beyond the aircraft's 'fly-by date' and not one revenue earning hour was flown by the time it was finally abandoned. In purchase and other costs we suffered a tremendous loss. She remains in Ireland to this very day – for me a continuing reminder of the perfidy of politicians. Some you win and some you lose! I suffered no lasting bitterness, as I was confident that there were many 'winners' to come – however for now this was an omen of even more disaster as the UDI crisis caused continuing chaos…"[29]

Meanwhile by the beginning of November 1969 Jack's old Super Constellation was finally ready to fly again. It had been slowly repaired out on the tarmac in Luanda since its double engine failure back in April. Many of the engine parts it needed had been scavenged by Jack's innovative ground crews from the numerous dead and dying Constellations that littered the airfields of West Africa. By mid-November 1969 it was air worthy and Jack flew the aircraft

---

28 Personal correspondence with Mike Gibson August 25, 2009, and notes from Jack Malloch's and Henry Kinnear's personal flying logbooks.

29 'Colours in the Sky: The story of Autair International Airways and Court Line Aviation' by Graham M Simons, published by GMS Enterprises. ISBN: 978-1-904514-70-1.

back to Salisbury. There Jack had the aircraft repainted and its seats refitted. He wanted to get back into the passenger business.

With the severity of Nigeria's final push to crush Ojukwu's oil-rich state, Uli's nine p.m. 'gentleman's agreement' began to crumble. The nightly bombing was more intense and lasted longer into the evening. To compensate Jack pushed back his flight times to ensure that no-one arrived over Uli before ten o'clock. But this meant faster turn-around times especially for the later crews as the MiGs always struck with the first rays of dawn.

Airstrip Annabel was now the eye of the storm. It was jammed with hundreds of thousands of uprooted civilians, all in various stages of starvation, with tens of thousands of desperate soldiers locked in hand-to-hand combat, right at their backs. This all-consuming cyclone of violence and death was converging on the little battered airstrip, now known through the world's newspaper headlines simply as 'Uli'. It was the last remaining symbol of hope for all of them.

In a last-ditch effort the Joint Church Aid increased their number of food flights as much as the limited hours of darkness and their stretched pilots would allow. By the end of November they managed to deliver twenty-two flights a night into Uli, and in-between them, squeezed in the Canadians and as many of Jack's military flights as he could.

Well-known war correspondent Al J. Venter described what Uli was like in those desperate last days; "None of us will ever forget the heat and the noise that cloaked us like a sauna. Time meant nothing. You were simply too awed, too overwhelmed by what was going on, and the musty, unwashed immediacy of it all. Our senses were constantly sharpened by the stutter of automatic fire along the runway. The priests in their white cassocks, the rattle of war, the roar of aircraft, the babble of voices shouting in strange tongues and the infants hollering all made for a surreal assault on the senses."[30]

Conditions in the air were not much better. According to Henry Kinnear by mid-December, they were subjected to anti-aircraft fire over the entire area of what little was left of Biafra. Then in the pre-dawn hours of Tuesday 16th their luck nearly ran out. After delivering a cargo of ammunition they tried

30 'War Dog. Fighting Other People's Wars. The Modern Mercenary in Combat' by Al. J. Venter. Published by Casemate, Philadelphia. ISBN 1-932033-09-2.

to restart their engines but discovered that the old DC-7s batteries were flat. Dawn, and the inevitable MiGs, where less than an hour away. Things were suddenly very tense.

Captain Davis discovered that his friends in a Gabonese 'Appolo' DC-6 were still on the ground and were prepared to lend the ATA crew their own batteries. As fast as possible the batteries were removed from the 6, loaded in the 7, the engines were fired up, and then the batteries had to be removed and refitted into the DC-6 again. By the time the transfer was complete the eastern sky was turning purple and pink with the arriving sun.

Itching to leave, the breathless ATA crew waited for the DC-6 to start. Once started the old aircraft taxied out for take-off. Although the DC-6 was moving as quickly as it could, for the wide-eyed men in TR-LOK it felt like an eternity. As soon as he could Captain Davis turned onto the runway, while the terrified men scanned the horizon for the in-coming fighters. By the time they finally lifted off the deserted bomb-scared tarmac, the ground crews were all hiding in their shelters and the sky was the bright blue of morning.[31]

For some reason their prayers were answered and that morning the daily Nigerian air raid didn't happen.

There were no spare DC-7 aircraft batteries in West Africa, but they had to keep flying. From then on, they always keep one engine running while on the ground so it could be used to start the others. This added to the already extremely dangerous situation on the ground. A few nights later, with the Nigerian ground forces closing in, the drama reached fever pitch. Going for the kill, the 'Intruder' bomber would drop bright flares to identify targets and improve their aim.

And it worked. With the runway lit up as bright as daylight the bomber made a series of runs over the busy airport. High explosive bombs landed amongst the scurrying ground crews who were trying to unload as much food and ammunition as they could before they were killed or the precious cargos destroyed. On the Dakota's last pass, a bomb fell directly on a Canadian Super Constellation. The aircraft exploded in a huge fireball showering the entire area with flaming debris. The ground crews rushed forward with buckets of water to try and extinguish the flames, while the Nigerian bomber circled overhead spraying

31 Henry Kinnear's personal flying logbook.

them with machine-gun fire.

One of Jack's DC-7s was there delivering a load of ammunition. Knowing his batteries were flat Captain Miller kept a couple of the engines running, but in the darkness and confusion from the bombing and strafing a Biafran handler ran under the wing to help put out the fires – straight into the spinning propeller. He was instantly decapitated. His headless body flung across the runway. There was no record of his name. He was just another senseless casualty of the war. Recalling the mayhem many years later Colin dryly commented, "…that night there was both green and red on our props."

On Sunday 21st December, a few nights after the loader had been killed, fuel stocks on São Tomé ran out completely. Jack's aircraft could refuel in Libreville with the lower octane Gabonese fuel. But the aid flights were strangled. The next day the long-awaited Nigerian 'final push' was launched. The strategy was to cut Biafra in half with an all-out assault.

Jack was flooded with desperate orders for military supplies and quickly flew back to Libreville from Salisbury in his DC-7 TR-LNZ to get at least another aircraft into theatre as quickly as he could. The Biafran army needed everything, and anything that Jack and his crews could deliver and it was all immediately thrown into the crumbling frontlines. Although France, Portugal and South Africa continued to pour as much military hardware into Biafra as they could, everyone knew the end of Ojukwu's Biafran state was now just a matter of days away.

The first week of January 1970 saw frantic fighting throughout Biafra as the remnants of the Biafran army tried to regroup and fight their way back into defendable positions around the resupply airstrips of Uli and the military airfield at Owerri. By the end of the week Uli was a major centre of evacuation. But getting aircraft in and out of the airstrip was ever more challenging. By January 8th, due to the incessant air raids some five hundred metres of Uli's runway was completely out of service because of the large number of irreparable bomb craters.

On the morning of Friday 9th Ojukwu summoned 'Ian Carpenter' to his Headquarters. He informed the special forces commander that Biafra had finally collapsed and defeat was imminent. He wanted the South African teams to evacuate that night before they were caught by the Nigerians. Jan immediately radioed Jack for urgent extraction then give orders for the dispersal and future operations of their guerrilla students.

As darkness fell Jan and his SDECE operatives joined the tens of thousands of people converging on the airstrip. Only seventeen aircraft landed at Uli that night and after hours of being 'entertained by the sound of artillery fire uncomfortably close to Uli', it was the early hours of the morning before the South African's evacuation flight arrived. It was Jack's TR-LOK captained by the Vietnam-vet, and supposedly CIA operative, Ed Davis. It was broad daylight on the morning of Saturday 10th January by the time they landed back in Libreville, very relieved to have made it out alive.

Although air traffic control at Uli had been abandoned the French Secret Service wanted to make another flight into Uli. They needed to get a message to Ojukwu and wanted to try and rescue some French doctors and their large group of sick children. The flight was, of course, in one of Jack's DC-7s. The plan was to fly in a cargo of ammunition and petrol, and hopefully fly out the children. Jan and one of his trusted commandos volunteered to 'ride shotgun' and after a few brief hours of troubled sleep the crew and soldiers readied TR-LOK for their last 'flight into Hell'.

While the DC-7 was being loaded at Libreville airport, Uli airport was being savagely strafed and bombed. The raids damaged the last few remaining landing lights and cratered the length of the runway. Facing certain defeat and imminent death, once again the exhausted and starving ground crew got their shovels and spades and tried to smooth out the smouldering blast holes as quickly as they could, not knowing if anyone else would be coming to help them. The sound of artillery and machine gun fire was a steady rumble in the background.

With the panic and confusion a single brave priest went back to the 'control bunker' and switched on the equipment. In as calm a voice as he could he warned any last incoming flights of the damage, lack of order and likelihood that the airfield would be overrun by the Nigerian army at any moment. With no Air Traffic Control, hardly any landing lights and the airstrip now within artillery range, only a couple of aircraft landed, the last of which was TR-LOK.[32]

32 Personal correspondence with Jan Breytenbach, January 29, 2003.

Although it was dark the crew could see the whole area was dotted with fires, punctuated by the bright explosions of impacting artillery shells. After making a few low passes over the airfield they could see the roads were jammed with cars and terrified refugees. Even though there was another aircraft on the tarmac with a throng of vehicles and people around it, they decided to attempt the landing.

It was bouncy due to the latest scattering of repaired craters, but they got down okay and taxied into the nearest parking bay, where a scurry of wide-eyed loaders quickly started emptying the aircraft. They kept all the engines running, ready to escape at a moment's notice, while Jan disappeared into the crowd to try and find someone who could get his message to President Ojukwu. He found a senior ranking officer who led him to a small collection of vehicles at the side of the runway, where to his astonishment he found Ojukwu himself with some of his senior staff. Rocked by the continuous blast of incoming artillery, Ojukwu shook Jan's hand and thanked him for his concern, assuring him that he was about to leave. His Constellation was already lined up on the runway with its props turning.

At the far end of the runway there was a loud rip of machine-gun fire that panicked the crowd of mostly women and children. Jan knew that their time was up. Running back to the DC-7 he found it surrounded by a mass of people, many of them armed soldiers trying to fight their way onboard. They were trying to commandeer the aircraft to fly out the relatives of some of the fleeing government officials and their piles of luggage. The fact that they were wanting to take luggage while leaving children disgusted the ATA crewmen.

Blocking the open cargo door at the back of the DC-7, the other SDECE agent was trying to hold back the surging mob. Seeing Jan's predicament, with a loaded pistol in his hand the agent screamed at the crowd telling them that the aircraft would not be going anywhere unless they made way for the 'pilot' to get back on board. Presuming that Jan was the pilot the crowd reluctantly allowed him to climb up the flimsy ladder into the rear fuselage. The thin aluminium ladder was the only means of entering the aircraft, which was good for crowd control, but difficult for the critically frail children.

There was no sign of the French doctors and their sick kids, but amongst the throngs of pleading people were some Roman Catholic nuns who were trying to evacuate a large group of terrified orphans. Captain Miller, Jan and the crew decided to help them instead. It was two o'clock in the morning.

"When Ojukwu took off it seemed to increase the frenzy of the crowd. The Nigerians were attacking the far end of the runway and artillery shells were falling dangerously close to the aircraft, although we were too busy trying to get the women and children onboard to notice. Some of the soldiers scrambled past the children to force their way on board, but the flimsy ladder collapsed under the heavy load. We backed a truck up to the rear entrance and the nuns tried to organise the children onto the roof of the truck but suddenly what sounded like AK-47 fire started from very close quarters. The plane was now under direct fire. We had to go. We rapidly taxied out, followed by farewell shots from the frustrated crowd. We were the last plane out of Uli."[33]

Leaving the scattering throngs of refugees behind and leaping over fresh artillery craters, the aircraft with its terrified passengers and perforated fuselage scurried away, disappearing through a curtain of falling mortar bombs. What became of the last piles of supplies left on the side of the runway and of those terrified women and children running in all directions, no-one ever knew.

Forty-eight hours later Major-General Philip Effiong, the highest ranking Biafran army officer still alive broadcast an unconditional surrender. The war was over. As was the largest civilian airlift in history.

With defeat, the futility of trying to save Biafra and her people was devastating. Thirty years later Steve Cook summed it up, "A hastily assembled cast of smugglers, dreamers, mavericks and ministers came together on a stage where a tragedy of life and death was played. For two years, daring fliers carrying mercy supplies in rickety machines roared into the dominion of Hell itself. Though most of the pilots survived, millions of those they were trying to save perished. It was a noble effort that would end as an exercise in futility, now nearly forgotten."[34]

As with Katanga, Jack had once again thrown his lot in with the losers. It had been good for business in that every flight was paid for, and Jack had made some very important friends along the way. But he was sad that yet again the

---

33 Personal correspondence with Jan Breytenbach, January 29, 2003.

34 'Ghosts of Sao Tomé' by Steve Cook, Flight Journal, December 1999.

underdogs who were trying to do the right thing for their people had been abandoned by the international community and left to the mercy of their Soviet-supported central governments.

The trend didn't bode well for Rhodesia.

With the establishment of his sanctions-busting 'meat run', helping Rhodesia was where Jack now turned his attention...

CHAPTER 10

Affretair and the Sanctions War: 1970 to 1974

Jack's Super Constellation VP-WAW in its Afro-Continental Airways livery, parked on the side of Salisbury Airport's main runway in early 1971.
Picture from Jack Malloch's private collection. © Greg Malloch.

The collapse of Biafra had basically come down to a simple matter of logistics – no army, no matter how committed, could win a war with empty rifles and empty stomachs. Unfortunately, no matter how hard he tried Jack just couldn't deliver enough supplies to keep them going. The lesson was that to keep a country alive you needed to plan ahead, cultivate your supporters and secure your trade and supply routes.

Knowing this Jack had already started thinking about how he could use his international and secret service connections to help Rhodesia. Unlike Katanga and Biafra this was now his own country, and it was struggling to survive the blockade that Britain had imposed on it back in the mid-1960s. By the beginning of 1970 Jack had developed a new trade route for Rhodesia to export its prime beef to Gabon for valuable hard currency. Just before the fall of Biafra he had built this business into a regular weekly delivery to the Gabonese army bases in Libreville and Port Gentile.

The day after Biafra surrendered Jack captained another 'meat run' into Gabon. The flight gave him an opportunity to debrief his aircrews and meet his 'French Connections' to plan the future. From Libreville Jack refueled in São Tomé, drawing from the last of their high-octane fuel stocks. There were more than fifteen humanitarian aircraft all parked and loaded with food and medicine, waiting for permission from the Nigerians to deliver the aid to the starving population in the Delta region. That permission was never granted and the dying Biafrans were left to their fate.

One thing that the Nigerians did do though was to plough up Father Joe Prendergast's cemetery at Uli. By the end of the war it contained one hundred and fifty-seven carefully tended graves, at least until the bulldozers came. Without any remorse the Nigerian engineers scraped everything away, purging anything that could keep the memory of Biafra alive.

Fortunately, while Jack had been immersed in Biafra, on both the political and military fronts 1969 had been a quiet year for Rhodesia. The government had focused hard on trying to develop a moderate black middle class who could help keep the extremists at bay, boost national productivity and maintain economic stability. Looking back Ian Smith later recalled, "…a number of British MPs conceded how much more we had done for our black people than had been done in all the surrounding countries. We had provided better schools, better hospitals, better houses, better recreation facilities, and a higher standard of living. We also had peace, which was exceptional and almost unique in the world, and a declining crime rate. Yet the U.N., with the support of both Britain and the USA, had passed a resolution declaring that Rhodesia was a 'threat to world peace'."[1]

But that peace was about to be broken as the Rhodesian 'bush war' started to heat up. This time irreversibly. With renewed resolve the first large-scale Zanla incursions into Rhodesia took place in mid-January 1970. These attacks, which included the machine-gunning of the Victoria Falls airport, were better organised and the guerrillas were better equipped and trained. It was a wake-up

1 'The Great Betrayal. Ian Smith. The memoirs of Africa's most controversial leader.' By Ian Smith. Published by Blake Publishing Ltd, England. ISBN: 1-85782-1769.

call for Rhodesia.

A month after the fall of Biafra, Jack was having his own wake-up call as Air Trans Africa was heading for a crisis. During the airlift they had been extremely busy and had been stretched to the limit. But it didn't really matter as there was plenty of money to hold the business together. The aircraft were paid, the insurance and fuel were paid, the salaries and even the S&Ts were paid. But with the abrupt ending of the Nigerian Civil War, once again, Jack's cash flow quickly dried up. By the end of January all he was left with was the weekly meat run and a bloated operation that didn't have the best management and control systems.

Deep down Jack knew that he wasn't the right person to be able to implement the proper processes and regulations. He was a maverick and knew that his aircraft could perform perfectly well far beyond the limits set by IATA or even the manufacturers themselves. Yet the world of aviation was getting more regulated all the time. This frustrated him, but he conceded that if his airline was going to become a legitimate operation he would have to abide by the rules.

Grudgingly, he decided to employ someone who was a stickler for rules, and the obvious choice was John Aldridge. It wasn't an easy decision as Jack knew many of his pilots, especially those who had flown in Biafra with him, did not like restrictive regulations either. Yet, having received Jack's assurances that they were committed to doing things properly, John duly accepted the position of Chief Pilot,[2] much to the trepidation of the 'old hands'. Although John was an exemplary pilot, his uncompromising standards were not taken the way they were intended. It wasn't long before tensions started to rise. The more senior pilots like Ed Davis and Clive Halse didn't have to fly with John, but the first officers and flight engineers didn't have a choice. John soon gained a '*bête noire*' reputation amongst the crews.[3]

Although the Biafra airlift was over, Jack's gun-running days weren't. Constrained by an arms embargo and a simmering insurgency Rhodesia had to start strengthening its armed forces with weapons designed for modern counter-insurgency warfare. Through the SDECE and people like Jan Breytenbach

2 Personal correspondence with John Aldridge, November 25, 2008.

3 Personal correspondence with Mike Gibson, August 25, 2009.

Jack knew the arms dealers in South Africa, most of whom were very sympathetic to the Rhodesian cause. A deal was finalised and in mid-March 1970, having just returned from a 'meat run', Jack flew down to Waterkloof military base to collect a load of weapons. For the first time the weapons were 'his' and within five hours they were back in Salisbury unloading them. Jack timed his arrival to be in the evening once most of the ground staff had left, leaving just a small team of trusted senior staff to unload the crates of automatic rifles. John Aldridge was not amongst them.

Jack was disturbed that everyone at Waterkloof seemed to know that it was an Air Trans Africa operation. That common knowledge was going to be a problem if they wanted to operate internationally as any association with Rhodesia would be unacceptable. That combined with the growing financial challenges they were facing made Jack seriously think about mothballing ATA and reforming it as something completely different. What he wanted to establish was a truly international operation based outside the country. He already had hanger space in Libreville and most of his aircraft were registered there, so it made sense to base the new business out of Gabon. Jack discussed the idea with his French Secret Service contacts who were not just supportive, they wanted to be involved. They recommended that Jack talk to Bob Denard who was now their key operative in the area.

As Bob had a high-profile mercenary reputation Jack did not think it wise to have him involved in the business. He suggested that Jean-Louis Domange take an executive position with the business instead. Jean-Louis was loyal to his French controllers and had become influential within President Bongo's inner circle which made him ideal. Jean-Louis agreed and all that was left was to decide upon a name. Between Alan Clements and Jean-Louis they suggested that they call the business Affretair, using the French verb 'affréter' as an abbreviation of the official name 'Compagnie Gabonaise d'Affrètements Aériens'.[4] Jack liked the name and it was quickly approved.

They then considered who else should be involved. In addition to locking in the interests of the French through Jean-Louis, Jack wanted to ensure both

4 Personal correspondence with Jean-Louis Domange dated April 2, 2019, and personal correspondence with Alan Clements dated August 10, 2008.

a long-term market for their Rhodesian beef as well as the support of the Gabonese Government. For the market they appointed a Frenchman by the name of Gerard Durand as a director. Durand already held import licences and was well connected in the Gabonese meat wholesaling industry which made him ideal. Jack also wanted to give his friend President Albert-Bernard Bongo a stake. Bongo was keen, but they all agreed that he shouldn't be named in the company paperwork, so Mboumba Celestin was appointed as his proxy.

With Durand and Celestin as the two directors, the business was registered on May 27th, 1970. The business of the company was noted as being 'a common air transport carrier and representative of other transport companies as well as being an importer and exporter of goods.' The registered capital of the business was five million CFA Francs[5] and the day-to-day management was left to Jack and Jean-Louis, neither of whom were mentioned in the company documents.

Jack also wanted to tie the Rhodesian government into the operation and after a discussion with Prime Minister Ian Smith it was decided that Brigadier Andrew Dunlop would become a co-director of the business. As a high-ranking officer in the British Army Andrew had earned a DSO during the Second World War, but it wasn't his bravery that led to his nomination. Along with Ian Smith he had been a founding member of the Rhodesia Front Party and up until just a month earlier, he had been the country's Minister of Transport and Power.

According to the U.N. Security Council, "as Minister of Transport he was chiefly responsible for breaking the international oil embargo imposed against the régime in Southern Rhodesia and for numerous other actions contrary to the mandatory actions imposed by the Security Council."[6] In fact Andrew was on record as saying that sanctions were "of great use to our country" and "they gave a tremendous fillip to secondary industry" greatly stimulating the local manufacturing sector. It was exactly that sort of positive, 'can-do' attitude that Jack appreciated.[7] Unfortunately though Andrew's tenure with Affretair didn't

5 Confidential memo from the American Ambassador in Libreville to the US Secretary of State in Washington dated August 31, 1973.

6 United National Security Council, sixth report of the Security Council Committee established in pursuance of Resolution 253 (1968) concerning the question of Southern Rhodesia, dated January 9, 1974.

7 'Unpopular Sovereignty: Rhodesian Independence and African Decolonisation' by Luise White, published by the University of Chicago Press, ISBN-13: 978-0-226-23519-6.

last long. He was well into his sixties by the time he joined the operation, and his health was already ailing.

Once he had got everyone onboard Jack then transferred ownership of the three DC-7s to Affretair, leaving Air Trans Africa with the Dove. To preserve the integrity of the new business any sanctions-busting flights, particularly the 'meat run' were kept on ATA's books. Any legitimate international work, particularly onward flights from Libreville into Europe were then handled by Affretair, even though both businesses used exactly the same aircraft. Jack intentionally made no effort to brand the aircraft and left them with their old pre-Biafra markings and the faded reminders of their previous owners. Confusion was exactly what he wanted.

According to Henry Ellert, "with Malloch's assistance the Rhodesian Ministry of Foreign Affairs established a low-key diplomatic presence in Libreville and later in Abidjan. The Rhodesians had orders to foster trade, and soon plane-loads of beef, clothing, textiles, shoes and fresh produce were arriving in Libreville."[8] Considering the involvement of Bongo and the focus on building Rhodesia's trading partnerships it was more than coincidental that "...the offices of Affretair in Libreville were conveniently located in a building on Boulevard de la Mer, next door to the Gabonese Foreign Ministry!"[9]

With the establishment of a legitimate operation Jack felt that the main challenge for the freight side of the business had been addressed, but he was still very aware of the demand for passenger services. Since late 1969 he had been planning a passenger role for the Constellation and by mid-1970 with the tightening financial situation of the business he revived those plans. Once the long-running repairs on the Super-Constellation had been completed he registered a new business called Afro-Continental Airways (ACA). In September he transferred ownership of the Connie over to the new operation which was granted a licence to operate a scheduled weekly passenger service between Salisbury and Windhoek in South West Africa from the beginning of 1971. Although, as always Jack's ambition went far beyond the regional capitals. In

8 'The Rhodesian Front War. Counter-insurgency and guerrilla war in Rhodesia 1962 – 1980.' by H. Ellert, Published by Mambo Press 1989. ISBN: 978-0869224366.

9 'Neo-colonialism: France's legacy to Africa.' by Mahmoud Yahya published by Emwai Centre for Political and Economic Research (1994). ISBN: 9783247808.

Passengers on Jack's inaugural Afro-Continental Airways flight from Salisbury to Windhoek in late January 1971. The Rhodesian flag can be clearly seen on the central tail.

Picture from Jack Malloch's private collection. © Greg Malloch.

a newspaper interview he boldly announced plans to operate charter flights to the U.K. in defiance of the British travel ban.[10]

What Jack didn't mention in his interview was that just three days earlier during an air-test to Lake Kyle the auto pilot amplifier on the Connie had exploded.[11] The old aircraft was certainly getting to the end of its useful life, yet it was being touted as a reliable passenger work-horse. Jack's plan was to prove the financial viability of the passenger route and, if it was indeed profitable, he could always deploy one of the DC-7s onto it. The Connie just had to last for another year or two. But things didn't get off to a good start and they had to abort their very first take-off out of Salisbury due to an engine failure.

Sadly, it wasn't just the Constellation that was giving trouble. Less than a week after the engine failure, the latest DC-7 that Jack had bought had to abort two attempted take-offs due to zone one fires. Ten days later the same aircraft had to abort again due to a zone one fire warning and in mid-March, with its bald tires, the aircraft 'severely aquaplaned' across the drenched Libreville runway. Then in May while flying back from Libreville Jack also had an engine failure and they had to make the trip on three engines, taking more than eight hours

10 The Rhodesian Herald interview with Jack Malloch, January 31, 1971.

11 Henry Kinnear's personal flying logbook.

over hostile territory to get back home.

A growing number of the aircraft were needing serious servicing but without his French and Portuguese clients Jack just didn't have the money. The big challenge was getting over the massive debt that had accumulated since the end of the Biafran airlift. It was simply too much and with the threatening tone of his creditors Jack began to consider the real possibility that he might end up going back to jail.

Fortunately, his insurance broker was at last seeing some success with the claim for the DC-7 that had been abandoned in Lomé. Reg Smith later recalled, "I remember when the claim was finally settled and we came out of the hanger, it was a beautiful evening with a deep blood red sunset." I said to Jack, "You've won. So, what now?" Jack looked at me and replied, "I'm not going to fight the war like this anymore. I need a DC-8." I looked at him and said, "But that will be eight million dollars, and this pay-out will hardly cover your debts." Jack replied, "I know. Will you help me?" I was mesmerised. I had never seen anyone so intense. I had no choice, 'Yes.' I said."[12]

Although Jack's long-term plans always saw beyond the immediate short-term challenges, those that the airline was facing were severe. The undivided attention of Jack's outstanding technicians was able to keep the old DC-7 TR-LNY limping along until early July. Then, in the space of just two weeks the aircraft suffered a slew of serious mechanical failures. It needed at least two new engines and significant parts for its landing gear.

With no choice Jack reluctantly contacted his old SDECE-approved friend John Squire at Aer Turas again, and asked if he had an old DC-7 which he would be prepared to sell for scrap. John was more than happy to help and as the aircraft was being sold to Affretair, a legitimate Gabonese-registered business, there were no sanctions hurdles to get around. Left in its previous red-striped livery, save for its new Gabonese registration TR-LQC, the DC-7 was delivered from Shannon Airport to Libreville on the tenth of August.

The next day Jack flew it down to Salisbury.[13] He was pleased as the insurance had paid off the debts and covered the deposit on the new aircraft. As that

12 Interview with Reg Smith, Isle of Wight, U.K., May 18, 2014.
13 Henry Kinnear's personal flying logbook.

sale had gone through so easily Jack wondered what additional aircraft he should purchase before MI6 and the CIA realised the link between Affretair and Rhodesia. Jack discussed the idea of upgrading to a DC-8 with his shareholders. The challenge this time was going to be sneaking a large, modern jet through the sanctions net. President Bongo said that it would be no problem as he would simply verify the purchase, and obviously no-one would question the wishes of the President.

With the Connie committed to the South West African route, Jack needed to keep the DC-7s busy so was always on the lookout for new business. In September he was able to confirm a daily meat run into Elisabethville. Jack was a bit nervous about going back into the Congo, or Zaire as it had been renamed, but his captains felt they would be safe considering they were now essentially Gabonese. Jack agreed, although he was painfully aware that neutrality hadn't helped the Italian airmen who had been eaten in Kindu.

The two DC-7's TR-LNZ and TR-LOJ were committed to the Congo shuttle which started in early October. Although TR-LNZ had got over its technical troubles, they were just beginning for TR-LOJ and the third flight nearly ended in disaster. Soon after take-off number three engine had to be feathered due to a loss of engine pressure, a zone one fire warning and a landing gear warning. Fortunately they managed to return and emergency repairs were made.[14] The next day the flight engineer discovered much more serious issues deep within the engine. The decision was made to ground the aircraft and use it for spare parts to help keep the rest of the fleet going.

Although Jack had managed to keep his business alive and transition it from the intensity of the airlift through to main-stream commercial services, 1971 ended badly for him with the long-anticipated crash happening at the end of December.

On final approach into Libreville airport just as the landing gear was being lowered TR-LNZ lost all hydraulic pressure. The aircraft made a heavy crash-landing, bursting three tires on impact. Reverse thrusters were applied, but number four engine failed. This caused the aircraft, loaded with tons of AAA Rhodesian beef, to swerve to the left and plough into the soft sand on

14 Henry Kinnear's personal flying logbook.

Initial rudimentary efforts to move TR-LNZ after it slid off the runway at Libreville airport in December 1971.

Picture from Jack Malloch's private collection. © Greg Malloch

the edge of the runway.[15] With the lack of proper equipment it was a difficult and dangerous recovery that continued until almost dawn. According to Henry Kinnear, "We got it out of the way after 16 hours. While lifting the aircraft in order to put some borrowed DC-6 wheels in place, the crane's sling broke and the aircraft fell back onto the ground. Bob McIntyre and I had just got out from underneath it when this happened. If the sling had gone while we were undoing the wheel nuts, we would not have lived to tell the tale."[16]

As soon as he heard about the crash Jack flew to Libreville in the Super Connie to find out what happened. It would be almost three months before TR-LNZ was able to rejoin the flying roster. To make up for the lost capacity the Affretair ground technicians quickly got the 'scrapped' DC-7 TR-LQC up to flight readiness. In just over a week it passed its air tests and stepped up to the meat run. But the old aircraft was not really up to it. On its first trip to Libreville it suffered an exhaust fire on number three engine. This damaged the PRT unit which only became apparent on its next leg to Luanda. A week later, on a charter to Negage in Angola it had a speed-brake and undercarriage warning problem. This was

15 'Shadows, Airlift and Airwar in Biafra and Nigeria 1967 – 1970' by Michael Draper. Published by Hikoko Publications. IBSN 1-902109-63-5 and details in Henry Kinnear's personal flying logbook.

16 Personal correspondence with Henry Kinnear, January 19, 2004.

followed a few days later by the complete failure of number two engine.

To add to the challenge not all of the 'meat runs' that Affretair were doing involved carefully butchered plastic-wrapped beef carcasses. On some of the flights the cattle in the hold were still very much alive. Several large cattle ranches in Angola were looking at upgrading their herds and needed new breeding stock to be flown in. This was especially challenging for the load masters who had no idea how to herd cattle. Things did get better once one of the Cold Storage Commission herd-boys taught them how to do the 'herders' whistle.'[17] All the flights to Negage in 1972 involved live cattle, and in March Jack picked up another contact for daily flights to Nova Lisboa to build up a prime herd there as well.

It was soon after these Nova Lisboa flights started that Jack's relationship with John Aldridge ended. John had been growing ever more frustrated by the corner-cutting and although his concern was safety, his efforts didn't go over well. According to John Fletcher, "John was quite a difficult chap and didn't really fit in to our culture. We were at war after all!"

One morning the cattle had been loaded into the aircraft, but John was reluctant to fly. Jack went down to see what was going on. John demanded to know whether the cattle had been weighed.

"We have an approximation…" Jack answered.

"I'm telling you! You haven't got a clue!" John exploded, wagging an accusing finger in Jack's face. Jack, who didn't like being challenged in front of his staff lost his patience.

"Sure, we can lighten the load…" he said, pulling the plug on the crew drinking water which drained out onto the tarmac. Speechless John stormed off. Through clenched teeth Jack called over to John Fletcher who had witnessed the exchange.

"Please phone Mrs. Malloch and tell her I'll be late." Without another word he climbed into the cockpit and flew the consignment himself. The next morning John was fired.[18]

In early 1972 President Bongo set up a meeting with the US Ambassador in

17 Interview with Nori Mann, Thakeham, West Sussex, May 8, 2019.
18 Interview with John Fletcher, Johannesburg, South Africa, May 16, 2002.

Libreville and mentioned that he would like a Gabonese company, Affretair, to acquire a DC-8 from the United States. Neither Bongo nor Jack were aware that they were under suspicion at the time. The CIA knew Jack from his activities in the Congo and had already put Affretair on their watch list.[19] Things were about to get a lot more difficult.

When pressed on the purpose of the aircraft the President said that it would be used for "his official travel, and for commercial purposes inside and outside Gabon." Knowing the background Ambassador McKesson was surprised that the national President himself was lobbying for the aircraft. He said that the sale would require U.S. government approval and that he would need written assurances from both Affretair and the Government of Gabon that the aircraft would not trade with Rhodesia. The Office of the President provided both of these documents to the Ambassador and they were followed by assurances from the Gabonese Minister of Transport. These commitments were compelling, although the US Department of Commerce was still suspicious.[20]

It was at about this time that Jack's daughter Alyson, who was fourteen, started working at Affretair. Jack's three kids had been spending time at the hanger since they were young, "running around and climbing on the scaffolding." Alyson loved those weekend trips as Jack allowed her drive from the entrance gate to the hangar and back. Although he restricted her to the private aviation area as he remembered all too well the fright of being caught by the police for driving under-age when he was a boy back in Umtali.

Alyson loved spending time working with her father. It started as weekend work, "answering the phone and doing odd jobs in the office so he didn't waste time having to do it. Usually it was just me and him in the office and he used to spend quite a bit of time in the hangar too, getting involved in the maintenance work. Little by little I did more and more jobs…" She was paid for the hours that she worked, and Jack warned her that he would treat her more strictly than the other staff as he didn't want them to think she was being favoured. Alyson was fine with that as she definitely did not want to be seen as "the boss's daughter" yet

19 Confidential memo from the US Secretary of State in Washington to the American Ambassador in Lagos, Nigeria, dated May 4, 1974.

20 Ibid.

she really wanted to get involved and contribute.[21]

Ever since he had opened up the Mozambique coast in the 1950s Jack had appreciated the potential of tourism. With Mozambique facing a major Communist insurgency in their northern provinces the seaside appeal of that country was waning. Yet Rhodesia now had its own inland sea with the massive Kariba Dam along its northern border. Some hotels and resorts had been built, but Jack knew there was still plenty of opportunity. The problem was that there were no roads down the length of the lake's shoreline and the remote wilderness, high hills and steep gorges made access almost impossible. This meant that if people from Salisbury wanted to visit fishing spots like Binga in the lower reaches they had to drive almost a thousand kilometres.

Knowing Jack's interest in tourism, in late 1971 his old friend Clive Halse offered him an opportunity to invest in a new shipping company that Clive had recently set up with a young engineer by the name of Bev Portman. They felt that the obvious way to open up Kariba's tourism potential was to run passenger ferries down the length of the waterway. Jack, along with Ming Longmore and a few other senior staff at Affretair jumped at the opportunity and invested whatever they could into Clive's new Lake Shipping Company (Pty) Ltd.[22]

The immediate need of the business was for a couple of ferries to ply the route between Kariba and Binga and Bev started to work on designing and building them. But as that was estimated to take a few years, the Lake Shipping Company shareholders ordered a large passenger hydrofoil from Seaflight S.P.A. of Italy. At a quarter of a million dollars it was a massive, and quite risky, investment for the group, a couple of whom sunk their entire life savings into the venture.

Once built the 54-seater hydrofoil was shipped whole as deck cargo. After sneaking its way through the British warships that were enforcing their blockade against Rhodesia, the vessel arrived in Beira in early April 1972. Secured onto its massive transporter it then slowly made its way to Salisbury, inching around numerous obstacles along the way.[23] Once in Kariba Bev fitted the foils and in mid-May the press were taken down Sanyati Gorge to witness the

21 Personal correspondence with Alyson Dawson, May 5, 2019.

22 Personal notes and papers belonging to Clive Halse provided by Chris Halse.

23 Reuters article, 'Rhodesia: British-built hydrofoil craft on way to Lake Kariba after evading British sanctions blockade' issued on May 3, 1972.

launch of the 'blockade-busting' ship. It was a remarkable feat for a landlocked country and reflective of the 'can-do' attitude of the Lake Shipping Company shareholders. Within another two years the first car ferry, the MV *Sealion*, was also completed and entered service.

While the launch of the *Seaflight* in early 1972 was a pleasant distraction, Affretair was barely limping along. As Brigadier Dunlop had left the business Jack decided it was time to get more serious financial involvement and went back to Ian Smith to explore the options. After a broader discussion involving several other people it was decided that, considering the strategic nature of Affretair, there should be greater government involvement. This time two directors were appointed; Cecil Roberts, who was the head of the Reserve Bank of Rhodesia, was appointed as Chairman of the Board, and Alec Bartrum became the Financial Director.[24] Alec had been a Wing Commander in the RAF during the War and, according to John Fletcher, "was a great businessman who was brought in to keep an eye on Jack's expenditure."[25]

Jack, who had the official title of Operations Director now certainly had the financial expertise he needed. He just needed to come to terms with the advice and direction that these astute men gave. Apparently, Roberts would regularly put the brakes on Jack's spending, but the bigger issue was a difference in their vision for the business. "It was not a very happy relationship as 'Robbie' Roberts was too staid for Jack and didn't approve of all the '007 / funnies' we got up to. Instead he felt we should concentrate on making the airline profitable and sustainable." Jack's intense patriotism would simply not allow for that.[26]

Through this change, the operation continued to hustle for as much work as they could while battling with the frequent mechanical issues and growing number of in-flight emergencies and engine failures that plagued the operation. The grim reality was that even if they had the money for spare parts the U.N. sanctions would have blocked the sale anyway. Consequently, the Air Trans Africa engineers had to make continual compromises and take continual risks often just to manage the work they already had.

---

24 Interview with Nori Mann, Thakeham, West Sussex, May 8, 2019.

25 Interview with John Fletcher, Johannesburg, South Africa, May 16, 2002.

26 Personal correspondence with Ian Hunt dated April 15, 2010 and with Donald Mackie dated March 30, 2010.

According to an airframe fitter from Fields one of the DC-7s was being serviced in readiness for its scheduled overnight delivery, but just as the work was done the electrical element on one of the engines shorted on a propeller blade and melted the de-icing boot. The stone-damaged propeller needed to be removed so the boot could be replaced, and the blade repaired. But there was no time and the ATA shift-boss said they had to fly that evening. He suggested simply taking off the faulty propeller.

"The prop will be out of balance," the fitter objected.

"So, take the opposite one off," the shift-boss shot back.

"Then there will be no de-icing," the exasperated techie argued.

"We never use de-icing," the ATA manager explained. "The engines are way over their 'time life' so we cannot engage the exhaust driven turbo blower for altitude, so we never fly above ten thousand feet. Take the props and boot off!" The technician did, and the aircraft flew that night.[27] Neither IATA nor John Aldridge would have approved.

By August 1972 Jack knew that all the DC-7s were on borrowed time and if they were to grow to the next level, they needed to press on with the new aircraft they had been negotiating for. In September, with the reluctant approval of the American Government, an Affretair delegation flew to the United States to buy a DC-8 jet freighter. The group was led by Jack and included Alan Clements, Reg Smith and a couple of senior UTA staff.

Commenting on this Reg said, "The French were very helpful. They provided the training for our ground staff, and they lent us their own people to go with us into the US to select and check the aircraft." And it was no ordinary aircraft that they were looking for; "We had to find an aircraft that could operate at high altitudes. Plus, it needed to have cargo doors and a robust undercarriage that could handle the airfields that Jack was flying in and out of." On Friday 13th October they settled on a six-year-old DC-8F Model 55 'Jet Trader' from a subsidiary of the Flying Tiger Corporation. They did a rigorous three-hour test flight over the Pacific coast and everything seemed fine. Upon landing, after a quick discussion with the French, Jack confirmed the sale and signed all the paperwork.

27 Personal correspondence with Mike Daly, July 4, 2008.

The aircraft cost US$5.45 million. Although it was a very reasonable price Jack didn't have that sort of money and borrowing it was difficult. According to the US State Department, due to the suspicions of Rhodesian involvement EXIM, the Export-Import Bank of the United States, which was the country's official export credit agency, refused Gabon's application to finance the sale. Consequently "the Gabonese financed the acquisition themselves" which surprised the Americans.[28] Apparently Jack organised this through an American aviation finance company, Aerodyne International Incorporated of Chicago,[29] this finance company having been recommended to Jack via 'a Swiss contact.' This person seems likely to have been the President and main shareholder of Jet Aviation in Basle, Carl Hirschmann himself, who coincidently was also Chairman of a Zurich-based bank.[30] Through Affretair's new Chairman, no doubt the Rhodesian Government provided the necessary assurances to seal the deal.

The connection back to the Flying Tigers is very perplexing, especially as Jack did have some involvement with Chennault back in the late 1950s. This seems to be confirmed by the comment made by the Sunday Times in 1982, when they wrote; "Malloch's connections with the famous Flying Tigers, led by American Claire Chennault in support of Chiang Kai-shek, gave him friends in Washington."[31] Exactly who those 'friends' were is unclear, but it does seem that they gave Jack a remarkable degree of support. According to the January 1974 edition of the Africa Report, "The Flying Tiger Corporation was fully aware that Malloch was a white Rhodesian acting for the illegal regime and therefore deliberately connived in breaking U.N. sanctions against Rhodesia."[32] Obviously they wouldn't take that sort of risk for just anyone.

Wasting no time at all, the day after the sale was concluded they flew the DC-8 out of the United States. The crew was Captain Alan Clements, Flight Officer Heyko Schroedl, two flight engineers, Jules Vasseur and G.Trahan who were

---

28 Confidential memo from the US Secretary of State in Washington to the American Ambassador in Lagos, Nigeria, dated May 4, 1974.

29 Personal correspondence with Alan Clements, November 23, 2001.

30 Correspondence between the US Embassy in Bern and the State Department in Washington dated April 19, 1973.

31 Sunday Times (Zimbabwe) article in their May 30, 1982 edition.

32 Declassified communication from the United States embassy in Addis Ababa to the Secretary of State in Washington dated October 18, 1974.

both from UTA, along with two ex-United Airlines crew who were included 'as observers'. Schroedl had flown with Clements in the Congo, Vasseur was a UTA crewman who was 'on loan to Jack' to set up his maintenance department at Affretair while Trahan was on loan to assist in training Affretair's flight engineers on the DC-8. Also on board were Jack Malloch, Harry Hersey, Jack's engineering manager and Bob Morris who worked as an aircraft broker for 'a firm' in Switzerland (likely Hirschmann's Jet Aviation).

The route they flew was north over Winnipeg in Manitoba and east over Hopedale in Labrador. From there they flew out over the North Atlantic south of Iceland, passing over Cork in Ireland before landing in Paris some eleven hours later.[33] At last in a UTA facility, Jack felt the aircraft would be more secure while they sorted out the transfer of ownership. In Paris, while all the seats were removed and it was being configured to freight, Jack and Alan Clements, who was fluent in French, went to see the Minister of Aviation. They wanted to get his approval for Affretair to operate the DC-8 between Gabon and Paris. Jack was also wanting to get access to better maintenance facilities which they did not have in Libreville. The Minister gave his approval and granted Affretair permission to use any civil airport in France.[34]

Meanwhile Reg was busy sorting out the necessary clearances and coverage to enable them to get the aircraft home. But he was nervous. He had to get the aircraft insured before they could take possession of it and was worried about the person he was using. He had a grave foreboding that they were being set up. At the last minute he decided not to risk a trap. But he needed an alternative. Reg knew of a fellow[35] that had gone to the same school as him who worked at Lloyds. "We had seen each other at Lloyd's and had nodded to each other, but we had never really spoken." Reg recalled, "But once I had the papers ready I decided to take them to this chap instead. He took one look at them and shook his head. Then he smiled, signed them and said, "You had better take these and get out of here." We were so lucky we found a good contact who was prepared to help us exactly where and when we needed. There were many coincidences

33 Personal correspondence with Alan Clements, dated October 26, and November 13, 2001.

34 Personal correspondence with Alan Clements, dated August 10, 2008.

35 Name withheld by request,

like that."[36]

As soon as Reg was back in Paris with the paperwork Jack quickly assembled the crew. He had got wind of an attempt by the British to impound the aircraft and wanted to get away as quickly as he could. Everything was wrapped up and the French hastily arranged a farewell party for their Rhodesian friends. At this well-attended event the airline manager himself gave a farewell speech wishing Jack and the crew the best of luck.[37] It reflected the esteem with which the French regarded Jack. Over time, with the encouragement of the SDECE this relationship with UTA grew from strength to strength.

According to the staff in Libreville, "…we had a coded message ready to send back to Salisbury; 'Pegasus Flies' meant that Jack had made it to Gabon, whilst 'Old Ford' meant a failure. We'll never forget seeing his beautiful bird on its landing circuit at Libreville Airport. We were on the tarmac when the DC-8 was brought into its allotted space, the door opened, and Jack appeared with a great smile on his weather-beaten face. He descended to the ground and limped over in some pain. But he was very happy. This, to us, was Jack's finest hour."[38] The reason why Jack was limping was that his old Second World War leg injuries were giving him trouble again.[39]

The next day they flew on to Salisbury, finally taxiing into the Affretair hanger right on the chimes of midnight on 22nd October, giving plenty of time for the aircraft to be hidden away before it attracted any attention. And it wasn't just the aircraft they delivered, "we also brought back to Salisbury a lot of ground equipment, plus a flight engineer on loan to us from Seaboard World Airlines."[40] This link to Seaboard is perplexing considering they were involved in Jack's next DC-8 deal and would eventually be bought out by The Flying Tigers themselves.

The first thing that Jack wanted to do as soon as they got home was to get his license to fly the DC-8. So along with Captains Palmer and Morrist, and Flight Engineer Kinnear, he went back to San Francisco for the rest of October to do his conversion training. Although Jack always struggled with academics, he

---

36 Interview with Reg Smith, Isle of Wight, U.K., May 18, 2014.
37 Ibid.
38 Personal correspondence with Derek van der Syde, July 17, 2008.
39 Personal correspondence with Alyson Dawson, April 4, 2020.
40 Personal correspondence with Alan Clements, dated November 13, 2001 and December 6, 2008.

Jack and the Affretair crew taking off in a United Airlines DC-8 during their conversion training in the United States in October 1972.
Picture from Jack Malloch's private collection. © Greg Malloch.

was very excited about captaining a four-engined jet, and according to Reg, "It was remarkable because he was on the phone to us every night, and he was in the classroom every day. He actually got his license very quickly."

Although they only had one DC-8 Jack needed at least three qualified crews to keep it in the air. Delta had offered crew conversion training and in January 1973 another group of Affretair pilots went out to Denver for the second DC-8 conversion course. The pilots on this course included Chris Higginson, along with Gus Tatersall, Horse Sweeney and a handful of other seconded Air Rhodesia captains who were also looking to upgrade to jets. According to Chris, "We had an American pilot join us on the course, but he was just a CIA spy sent to check up on us. He was likeable and he did not pull the plug on us."[41] One has to wonder if the reason why he didn't expose the Rhodesians was due to Jack's own personal influence within the Central Intelligence Agency.

While more Affretair staff were being converted to jets the airline had a critical and immediate need for experienced crew. On his next trip to Amsterdam Alan Clements heard about a German cargo operation called Atlantis that had

41 Personal correspondence with Chris Higginson dated November 17, 2007

recently gone bust and had aircrews looking for work. To ensure positions for captains coming up through the ranks, he employed six German co-pilots and six flight engineers, all current on the DC-8. Some of the seconded Air Rhodesian pilots, especially those who had fought in the Second World War were initially uncomfortable with Germans. But the men proved their worth and Jack was particularly grateful for the experience and work ethic they brought to the operation.[42] He was also amused by the wild speculation that spread about the mysterious 'Germans pilots'.

In addition to qualified crew Jack also needed paying contracts to cover the cost of the financing. Although Affretair was doing more meat-runs into Lumbumbashi, the obvious opportunity was Europe. Clearly the quality of Rhodesian beef was outstanding, and the landed price was well below the usual market-price. There were also plenty of people sympathetic to the Rhodesian cause who were prepared to overlook U.N. sanctions to turn a profit. A Greek meat wholesaler in Athens by the name of Stavros Tsonis was one of the first to see the potential of this.

Within a month of the new aircraft being registered in Gabon the first delivery of the country's highest-grade beef was successfully delivered into Athens at the end of November 1972. The Greek authorities didn't have any problem with a Gabonese registered aircraft delivering 'South African' beef. The Rhodesian Cold Storage Commission was happy to be moving greater volume and the country was very appreciative of the foreign currency it earned. As for Jack he now had a profitable international route for the Eight and the buyer was pleased. In-fact over the next six months the orders ballooned to over sixty tons a week. Incredibly, over such a short space of time, this accounted for a quarter of all meat being imported into Greece.

To get around the fact that the beef was Rhodesian, by leveraging his South African government connections Jack was able to arrange original South African veterinary department documents stating that the meat was from South Africa. As the embargo against South Africa was not yet as tight as it was against Rhodesia this South African source was ideal. The only challenge was collecting the original certificates in Pretoria, which kept the old ATA Dove busy.

42 Personal correspondence with Alan Clements dated November 7 and December 2, 2008.

Affretair did need to diversify its routes though, and through Jack's Swiss contacts they started flying into Zurich on a regular basis. Unfortunately, with this good news the military situation in Rhodesia was deteriorating and there seemed to be a growing tide of heavily armed insurgents now destabilising the western and north-eastern border areas. The reason was the establishment of nationalist bases in Botswana, increased infiltration by ZIPRA forces from Zambia and a growing tide of Zanla insurgents from northern Mozambique. The country was now fighting a war on three fronts. Jack, who was well connected with regional and international arms dealers, spoke to his friend the Prime Minister, then he met with some people in the Ministry of Defence. Soon thereafter a South African Air Force Hercules C-130 was doing regular deliveries of war material directly into the Air Force hangers at New Sarum.[43]

Although the passenger route to Windhoek had settled into a profitable scheduled service for Afro-Continental Airways,[44] at the beginning of 1973, with the success of Greece, Jack's attention turned to growing his freight business into Europe. The main problem that he needed to solve was not just tapping into the profitable business of moving freight around Europe, but to find regular consignments to bring back to southern Africa in the otherwise empty aircraft. To help with this, through a mutual RAF fighter-pilot friend, Jack recruited Claude Milan, a French businessman. It was Milan's job to find trading partners in Europe for Rhodesia and he was exceptionally successful at this. Eventually, according to Pierre Péan, Milan was working with almost every country that had signed the U.N.'s Resolution 253 against Rhodesia.[45]

There was a lot of business moving freight around Europe and one of the main hubs was Holland and on January 18th Affretair's DC-8 made its first landing in Amsterdam.[46] Soon afterwards the airline applied for landing rights at Schiphol. John Fletcher who was heading up the commercial side of Affretair was invited to have lunch with one of the senior airport executives to negotiate the deal. John was told that if KLM and Martin Air were given landing rights in Libreville, which they had been battling to get for years, Affretair could have

43 'War in the Air. Rhodesian Air Force 1935 – 1980' by Dudley Cowderoy and Roy C. Nesbit. Published by Galago publishing. ISBN 0-947020-13-6.

44 Flight International editorial dated March 22, 1973.

45 'Affaires Africaines' by Pierre Péan, published by Fayard (1983). ISBN: 2-213-01324-1.

46 Henry Kinnear's personal flying logbook.

them in Amsterdam. Jack had a quick word with Bongo and the rights for the Dutch airlines were granted immediately. True to their word Affretair was then given all the legitimate rights they wanted at Schiphol. The only condition was that they never carried arms or ammunition into Holland.[47] This too was the start of a long and very beneficial relationship.

Meanwhile the two surviving DC-7s were growing their trade routes in Central Africa with Negage in Angola and Lumbumbashi in Zaire dominating.[48] According to the Rhodesian Herald since the beginning of 1972 Air Trans Africa had carried over four and a half thousand live cattle to Angola for breeding purposes, returning with their cargo-holds full of coffee beans and frozen fish.[49] These lucrative cattle flights continued until Angola's final collapse.

With plenty of business available in Europe Jack and his friend President Bongo felt they could easily sustain a second DC-8, especially if they were able to expand their routes to the Far East. They started to put their plans together. While Jack was growing his airline and dreaming of all the possibilities, the tension between Rhodesia and her hostile neighbours was getting worse. Zambia had been openly supporting the nationalist insurgents, and with the spike in terrorist activity Rhodesia had threatened to take more severe action. The situation was tense. Then Zambia complained to the United Nations that Rhodesia had bombed them with chemical weapons. The claim was clearly ludicrous and was written-off as melodramatic propaganda although, looking back, it does seem that Affretair might have unwittingly had something to do with it...

In early May 1973 one of the DC-7s was having trouble on its way home. They had suffered an engine failure about half an hour after take-off, having already aborted their first attempt due to a fire warning. They should have aborted again, but the crew decided to continue. "We were trundling along nicely for the first two hours, but then, well past the 'point of no return' a second engine had to be feathered. Luckily, we still had one good engine on each wing to feed the hydraulic system for landing gear, flaps and brakes, although control was more difficult, we had to continue. As we lumbered along in the dark across Zambia, we began losing speed which meant having to let the aircraft drift to

47 Interview with John Fletcher, Johannesburg, South Africa, May 16, 2002.
48 Captain George Dyer's personal flying logbook.
49 The Rhodesian Herald editorial in the Monday April 2, 1973 edition.

an ever-lower altitude. However, it became apparent that we would not make it over the Escarpment to Salisbury. We couldn't divert to Lusaka as we weren't even supposed to be in their airspace. We managed to let Kariba know we were coming, and the Air Force guys there arranged goose-neck flares along the runway, and Land Rovers with their headlights positioned at each end. The payload was only a couple of tons and relatively easy to jettison. It was Streptomycin pesticide powder in 10-pound bags. Dave Goldsmith and Alan Partington threw the bags out of the two rear emergency hatches to lighten the load, over, what was likely – and hopefully – an uninhabited area of Zambia."[50]

Less than a week later Zambia logged their complaint to the U.N.

Of much greater concern was a change in Zanla tactics. Seeking more recruits for military training outside Rhodesia, its members undertook the first mass kidnapping of school children. These abductions marked a turning point, and the insurgents increasingly began to terrorise the civilian population in order to force their compliance.[51] While this drama was playing out Jack was busy flying aid charters for the German government into Niamey in Niger. The cargo on these flights was, "medicaments, protein foodstuffs, powdered milk etc., intended for the population in the distressed area." Jack appreciated this business and always liked helping people in critical need. When questioned about this later the Germans were equally unapologetic, stating that, "Since urgent humanitarian assistance measures are always given priority and since neither the German Air Force nor Lufthansa were in a position to undertake the flights, the services of a foreign carrier had to be used. Only Affretair was prepared to undertake the transports, in view of the urgency of the situation."[52]

Media reports in both the London Daily Telegraph in February and in the South African aviation magazine Wings in May 1973 stated that the DC-8 was known as 'the Sanctions-Buster.' To try and get away from this dangerous label Jack christened it 'Sitatunga.' But the name that stuck was 'Tango Romeo' being the first two letters of its Gabonese registration. The diplomatic chatter within the

50 Personal correspondence with Mike Gibson, August 20, 2009.

51 'A Pride of Eagles', by Beryl Salt. Published by Covos Day Books. ISBN 0-620-23759-7.

52 United National Security Council, sixth report of the Security Council Committee established in pursuance of Resolution 253 (1968) concerning Southern Rhodesia, dated January 9, 1974.

AUGUST 26 1973 No 7837 Price 9p

THE SUNDAY TIMES

THE FOLLIES OF THE FAMOUS
Beginning serialisation of the latest diaries from CECIL BEATON 25

ENJOYING THIS BRITAIN
A Bank Holiday guide to the Areas of Outstanding Natural Beauty 8

TOP HOLE!
A rare golfing excursion with P G WODEHOUSE 27

This is Tango Romeo, Rhodesia's cheekiest sanction-buster

After the long sanctions-busting flight by way of Libreville, cut-price Rhodesian beef for Greek tables is unloaded at Athens airport

Now bombers

Special report by Paul Eddy

THE PICTURE above shows Tango Romeo, a DC8 cargo jet which for the past five months has been operating the most audacious sanction-busting operation devised by Rhodesia. Twice, sometimes three times a week, Tango Romeo (registration TR LQR) flies 30

American and British intelligence services started referring to both the DC-8 and Jack Malloch himself as 'Tango Romeo'. But it was the British Sunday Times that truly established Jack's famous *nom de plume*. A British journalist was able to join the dots between Jack Malloch and Affretair and started discretely monitoring the aircraft to see what he could find out. Quickly he realised that he had uncovered a massive exposé of sanctions-busting, intrigue and international collusion. With the detailed information he had he was able to sell the story to the Sunday Times who felt it warranted front-page coverage.

Two days before the story broke the British and American intelligence services were informed about it. The US State Department were particularly concerned about the "alleged violation of Rhodesian sanctions" by the US government who had approved the sale of the DC-8 the year before.[53] While Scotland Yard and the CIA were prepared for the story, Jack was certainly not. When he was informed about it, it came as a huge shock. The editorial was run in the Sunday Times and

53 Confidential memo from the US Secretary of State in Washington to the American Ambassadors in London, Casablanca, Libreville and Abidjan, dated August 24, 1973.

in the London Observer. The Sunday Times detailed Jack's sanctions-busting flights while the Observer discussed how America had circumvented sanctions by selling Jack the DC-8 in the first place. These accusations were taken very seriously by the US State Department who consequently clamped down on anything involving Rhodesia.

With his careful, almost phobic, focus on discretion and secrecy, this unexpected exposé was Jack's worst nightmare. Reeling, he could only imagine that this was the end of his entire operation and that all his clients and the business that they had built up over the last few years would now be over. To make matters worse Jack and his family were in Paris at the time and, for some inexplicable reason, there were no deliveries of the Sunday Times to Paris that day so he didn't know exactly what had been reported. Eventually Claude Milan flew someone from his office all the way to London to bring back the newspaper.

It was clear that everything would now become much more difficult and that every move they made would be under intense and hostile scrutiny.

On this Jack was correct and for the next seven years it seemed that his entire operation was thwarted at every turn. This started almost immediately. As part of their efforts to get their own house in order, the State Department in Washington wrote formal letters to the Governments of Gabon, Greece, France and the Netherlands asking what steps they were taking to address the "grave violations of UN sanctions."[54]

Yet, it appears that the Americas were well aware of everything Jack was up to at least six months before Eddy's article appeared. According to hearings before the US Foreign Affairs Subcommittee on Africa back in March 1973, "The largest customer for Affretair's Rhodesian beef is a one-time Salonika butcher, who has an eye for a good spare rib – and a bargain…"[55] Their comprehensive information went right down to exactly how much the beef was being sold for. None of this was made public at the time.

Within a day of the article being published the Greek Ministry of National

54 Confidential correspondence between the US Secretary of State and the US Ambassador in Libreville dated 31 August 1973 and the declassified report to the US Mission at the UN detailing the Rhodesian Sanctions committee meeting on September 4 1973.

55 Hearings Before the Sub-committee on Africa, March 20, 22, April 6, 1973. Published by the United States House of Congress, Foreign Affairs Committee.

Economy sent a letter to the United Nations Sanctions Committee reiterating their statement that the "Commercial Industrial Chamber of Greece has never approved any invoices for the import of meat and other products from Rhodesia. Therefore, the report in the Sunday Times of London, is incorrect."[56] Gabon on the other hand was slower and more considered in their response. Jack was kept informed of these developments and tried to assure these supportive governments that greater discretion would be taken in future. Although it seemed hollow in light of the huge international embarrassment that had been caused.

In addition to all this, Jack was also facing the usual technical challenges from the old, tiring DC-7s, especially TR-LNZ which hadn't really recovered from its crash in Libreville. Plus, he was also worried about Captain George Dyer and the next batch of Affretair trainees who were in the middle of their DC-8 conversion course in Denver. There were swirling rumours that the men were about to be arrested and detained.

It seemed as if everything was falling apart. With all this stress, when Jack got back to his office in Salisbury his new secretary, Nori Mann noticed blood on the back of his shirt. Jack tried to brush it aside but Nori and one of the other P.A.s insisted that they check his back and wash his shirt. Reluctantly he took off his shirt. Nori was shocked. "There was an oozing wound in the middle of his back and a huge scar as if he had been cut in half. Apparently the long scar was from when he had had his gall bladder removed. The doctor was nicknamed 'The Butcher' and I could see why. The bleeding wound apparently was from where he had been stabbed in the back with a bayonet while in Togo. The bayonet was rusty and the wound never healed properly, so would periodically flare up again."[57]

Within a week George and the rest of the team were back safely, it seemed that Jack had managed to hold onto both the Gabon and Greek deals and, remarkably, the orders from Amsterdam seemed to be picking up. In fact, it seemed that business generally was up. Looking back Jack recalled, "I got a bit of a fright at first, but it turned out to be a false alarm and surprisingly there was very little reaction. In fact, it was one of the best advertisements I've had in my life.

56 Declassified report to the US Mission at the UN detailing the Rhodesian Sanctions committee meeting on September 4, 1973.

57 Interview with Nori Mann, Thakeham, West Sussex, May 8, 2019.

Offers of charter work flooded in from all over the world, and we took it."[58]

Somehow, they seemed to be getting through the situation, yet, there was still plenty of diplomatic chatter about Jack and Affretair. At the end of October the American Consulate in Johannesburg described him as a "...rakish formed RAF Spitfire pilot, former gun and currency smuggler and airborne sanctions-buster." They went on to say that "his technique and security are good enough that, despite his notoriety, British and Dutch efforts to block his operations or catch him violating sanctions have failed so far."[59]

As the media excitement around Affretair subsided Jack was relieved to be able to quietly slip out of the spotlight and concentrate on the new business that had been generated. Many of these new clients were opportunists looking for discounted goods and cut-rate deliveries. Although it did help keep the aircraft busy and they were able to generate valuable foreign exchange to bring back home.

One thing that did stick as a result of the Times editorial though, was the nickname 'Tango Romeo.' According to Rowland White, "As nicknames go, 'Tango Romeo' is a pretty good one, especially when it's been coined by a newspaper based on the call-sign of your gun-running cargo plane. Buccaneering Jack 'Tango Romeo' Malloch established an extraordinary succession of aviation companies... They don't make them like Jack anymore."[60]

After a couple of months of lying low Jack and his friend President Bongo had regained their confidence and felt it was time to restart their plans to buy a second DC-8. There was even more business coming their way and they wanted to capitalise on the profit potential of it all. Through his 'friends in Washington' and his supporters at United, Jack had found another DC-8, this time from Seaboard World Airlines. It was one of their 63 CF models and it was in very good condition. But to buy the aircraft and get it out of the United States they needed U.S. Federal government approval. Once again President Bongo took on this responsibility and in early December he met with the American Ambassador and mentioned that he wanted to purchase another aircraft.

58 Interview with Jack Malloch published in the Zimbabwe-Rhodesia Sunday Mail published on March 9, 1980.

59 Official memo from the American Consulate in Johannesburg to the Secretary of State, Washington dated October 31, 1973.

60 'Cleared for Takeoff: The Ultimate Book of Flight' by Rowland White, Published by Chronicle Books (2016). ISBN: 1452135509.

The Ambassador was surprised and recounted the recent negative publicity. The President brushed the concerns aside as inconsequential and went to lengths to explain why another DC-8 was in the national interest. In his report back to Washington the Ambassador said that, "In light of past difficulties I do not recommend that we help Gabon acquire another DC-8. In view of Bongo's insistence however it is obviously not going to be easy to turn him down."[61]

The Americans did turn down Affretair's requests for spare parts though. Having received six different emergency requests for various spare parts for the DC-8 including a wheel assembly and critical engine parts, at the end of January 1974 the U.S. Department of Commerce blacklisted both Affretair and Air Trans Africa. As the reason for the parts was 'to be used to repair a grounded aircraft at Schiphol Airport,' it seemed that this lack of spare parts would finally cripple the DC-8.

Yet, just ten days later, the U.S. Embassy in the Hague reported that, "...far from being grounded, the aircraft arrived at Schiphol on the evening of February 11th, loaded fuel and cargo and departed. The aircraft was in fully serviceable condition and appeared to have a new Pratt & Whitney engine recently installed in Paris during a service with UTA."[62] Once again the French had come to Jack's rescue.

But back in Rhodesia things were not as easy. In February 1974 fuel rationing was reintroduced and the length of military call-ups were increased as the country changed its posture from defence to attack. This attack was immediate with six strikes by Rhodesian Air Force combat aircraft into Mozambique in February alone. Although the war was raging in Mozambique's northern provinces, Rhodesia, working with her Portuguese ally, had managed to keep the worst of it out of their own country. But then disaster struck. In late April there was a military coup in Portugal and the new government was focused solely on getting out of their three African colonies as quickly as possible.

The long-term implications of this were not immediately obvious, and Jack's own attention was distracted by the final demise of his old Super Constellation.

---

61 Declassified correspondence between the US Ambassador in Libreville to the Secretary of State in Washington dated December 5, 1973.

62 Confidential correspondence from the US Embassy in The Hague to the Secretary of State in Washington dated February 14, 1974.

The Afro Continental Super Constellation arriving at Charles Prince airport at Mount Hampden in April 1974 where it was converted into a clubhouse. *Picture provided by Chris Knaggs. © Chris Knaggs.*

Two days before the Portuguese coup and on its way back from a meat run to Port Gentil the Connie landed in Luanda on three engines. After an initial inspection so many other problems were found that the ground crew took a week to get the aircraft flying again. On the 13th Jack did the next flight in the Connie with a load of live cattle to Villa Luso in Angola to make sure it was okay. It wasn't, and in addition to having another engine failure a flap also got stuck making control, especially during landing extremely dangerous.

What looked like crushed shrapnel was found in the engine filters and the same chunks of metal had jammed the flap mechanism. The problem was that legitimate spare parts were unavailable due to the sanctions blockade so Affretair's innovative engineers had used bicycle chains in the flap-tracks instead of the genuine diamond chains that were specified.[63] It was another week before the aircraft could be retrieved from Villa Luso, and by then Jack had decided to scrap it. There was no longer the demand for a regular flight to Windhoek, the other hoped-for passenger routes hadn't materialised and the mechanical issues were becoming life-threatening. As he had no need for the remaining

63 Interview with Henry Kinnear, Boksburg, Johannesburg, November 7, 2003.

parts Jack donated the aircraft to Charles Prince airport where it was converted into a novelty clubhouse.

Within three months of the coup, the Portuguese army in Mozambique collapsed leaving Frelimo in control of all but the main cities. It was a major disaster for Rhodesia who suddenly lost access to their main shipping port and their oil pipeline. Plus, they now had an additional one thousand kilometres of hostile, mountainous border to secure. It was impossible and with the flood of indoctrinated insurgents pouring through the forested highlands, attacks, murders and ambushes became a daily occurrence.

But the real disaster was that the collapse of Portuguese rule in Mozambique convinced the South African Prime Minister B. J. Voster that black rule was inevitable in Rhodesia. He decided to loosen ties with Rhodesia and seek a détente with Zambia and Tanzania. With a deadly strangle-hold on the country, Voster threatened to cut off all of Rhodesia's supplies, forcing Ian Smith to declare a ceasefire and agree to talks with the nationalists. It was another Great Betrayal, and, as expected, the agreements didn't hold. But there was now blood in the water and Zanla, ZANU or ZAPU surged in for the kill.

That wasn't the only disaster Jack was having to deal with. After a series of unanticipated issues, the Lake Shipping Company was in serious trouble. Firstly, with the increase in terrorist activity across the country the level of tourism to Kariba was significantly reduced which impacted revenue, and they had a couple of serious mechanical setbacks with the hydrofoil. A bearing failed which took it out of service for longer than expected and then it hit an unchartered rock in deep water. Unable to recover, the company went into liquidation and the shareholders, including Jack lost everything they had invested.[64]

Clive and Bev were both in serious financial trouble. Clive started working full time for Affretair but Jack didn't have a need for a design engineer. Although he was very impressed with Bev who clearly was a designer of extraordinary talent. Jack wondered if his skills could be put to better use and mentioned Bev to his Air Force contacts and it wasn't long before the young man was working on innovative new bomb designs with Group Captain Peter Petter-Bowyer. In this partnership Bev designed the remarkable bouncing Alpha bombs and the

64 Personal correspondence with Chris Halse dated January 14, 2008.

The original DC-8 in its old 1973/4 livery taking on a challenging cargo at Schiphol airport. In the foreground supervising the operation are Captain Eddie Morrist and Bob Libbrecht.

Picture from Jack Malloch's private collection. © Greg Malloch.

long-nosed Golf bombs for Rhodesia's Canberra and Hunter strike jets,[65] and later, in the 1980s, he went on to design South Africa's CB470 cluster bomb.

To make up for the financial loss Jack spent a bit of time focusing on a sideline business in the arms trade. While he was never an 'arms dealer' and his primary motivation was to ensure Rhodesia had enough military hardware to hold back the Communist tide, he did make money in shipping and moving the weaponry. How this worked was that Rhodesia used standard NATO inventory, but access to these supplies ceased with the imposition of sanctions in the mid-1960's. However, the country was very successful in capturing a huge harvest of Soviet and Chinese weapons from dead terrorists and arms caches in neighboring states. Many of the world's arms dealers were only too happy to barter new Communist munitions for NATO ones for a discounted commission, leaving plenty of room for mark-ups in the middle.

65 'Winds of Destruction. The autobiography of a Rhodesian combat pilot' by P.J.H. Petter-Bowyer. Published by 30° South Publishers. ISBN: 0-9584890-3-3.

The captured weapons were sorted out by the British South African Police (BSAP) armourers and initially offered to the South Africans who used them to arm regional destabilising groups such as UNITA and Renamo. Jack then flew the balance to Europe where it was exchanged for NATO-compatible supplies. The serial numbers of all the weapons passing through the system were carefully recorded and, over time, it became apparent that many of the AK-47s and RPD machine-guns went through this process of purchase, capture and redistribution several times before the end of the Rhodesian war, making many people very rich along the way.[66]

Meanwhile President Bongo, who had recently converted to Islam and changed his name to El Hadj Omar Bongo, was becoming frustrated by the lack of progress on his request for permission to buy another DC-8. The Americans did not want to alienate Gabon but were very uncomfortable with the request. To stall the discussion in late April the US deferred the decision to the Organisation of African Unity to "afford Africans the opportunity to sort the problem out among themselves." They conceded that if no objection was received from the OAU they would 'contemplate' approving the sale.[67]

To prove that there would be no possible use of the aircraft by Affretair or any Rhodesian involvement, Omar Bongo provided his colleagues at the OAU, and thereafter the Americans, with compelling, watertight paperwork. This was in the form of an original 12-page signed contract between the Government of Gabon and the French national airline UTA. The agreement covered two startling points: Firstly for "modifying the plane into a Presidential plane," and secondly "to entrust to UTA the technical and commercial management of the plane" which included the possibility of "being utilised on the commercial lines of UTA / Air Afrique."

According to the American Embassy in Libreville this contract provided "as explicit assurances as we could hope to obtain that the aircraft will be owned by the Government of Gabon and utilised by UTA on regular commercial

66 Personal correspondence with Ian Dixon, April 27, 1999.

67 Confidential correspondence from B.K.Huffman of the State Department to the American Consulate in Jerusalem dated May 4, 1974.

routes when not used personally by the President."[68] This signed agreement was an incredible achievement and reflected just how powerful and influential Jack's connections and supporters really were. Although Jack had established good contacts within UTA it is very unlikely the airline would have taken this degree of political risk, essentially just for the servicing of a couple of DC-8s owned by 'a friend'. In is much more likely that it was secured through the SDECE, and again, due to the audacity of it, it would have had to have been approved at the highest level. This was most likely Jacques Foccart himself who, as Secretary-General for African and Malagasy Affairs, considered Jack both a valuable asset and a personal friend.

So, to enable his aircraft purchase Jack was able to solicit the direct support of the President of one country, and the Advisor-to-the-President of another. Both of whom supported him without question, at significant personal and national risk. Clearly no other airline operator has ever had this degree of power and influence. But this high level of support did not stop with the securing of priceless paperwork, Bongo was prepared to go significantly further for Jack.

At the OAU conference in Mogadishu in early June Gabon asked for OAU approval for the aircraft purchase. When this didn't seem to be forthcoming the Gabonese Foreign Minister Paul Okumba stated that he welcomed the opportunity to provide the OAU with detailed information on all the other African countries trading with Rhodesia. At that point there was an immediate motion from Zaire and several other countries to have the entire discussion removed from the minutes. By that stage Affretair was making almost daily flights into Kinshasa and Lumbumbashi and the Zairean leadership appreciated how profitable it was becoming.

Gabon got the approval they were wanting[69] while Bongo got a pair of live cheetahs from Jack and a very grateful delegation from the Rhodesian Ministry of Foreign Affairs.[70]

Meanwhile, President Bongo turned his full attention to the Americans. In a

---

68 Confidential correspondence from the US Embassy in Libreville to the US Secretary of State in Washington, dated May 20, 1974.

69 Confidential report from the US Secretary of State to the US Ambassador in Kinshasa dated June 18, 1974.

70 Personal correspondence with Eddie Cross dated November 25, 2009.

telephone conversation with the U.S. Ambassador John McKesson he threatened to review his future dealings with U.S. firms if the DC-8 matter was not resolved. This included pending railway contracts, interests in Belinga Iron Ore, the extension of Libreville's Intercontinental Hotel, a possible PanAm contract and several U.S. proposals for off-shore oil concessions. All of this Bongo was happy to put on the table to help his good friend Jack Malloch.

There were obviously significant economic benefits for Gabon being a preferred trading partner with Rhodesia, which was a powerhouse in Africa at the time. Of course Jean-Louis, who, by this stage had married one of Bongo's daughters, would have been strongly advocating for this too. Yet the question remains how Jack Malloch as a white, English-speaking Christian entrepreneur from Rhodesia could have built up such a close and trusting friendship with a black French-speaking, Muslim president from Gabon, especially back in the early 1970s. The depth of this friendship reflects Jack's personal charisma, his trustworthiness and his sincerity. This is corroborated by the author Michael Draper who noted, "Jack's ability to forge a close relationship with many of Africa's black leaders speaks volumes about the manner in which he conducted his business."[71]

And the authorities in the Netherlands were also prepared to stick their necks out for Jack. The Dutch Permanent Representative to the United Nations responded to the UN Sanctions Committee saying that "neither Affretair, nor Air Trans Africa has yet violated existing legislative measures concerning UN sanctions against Southern Rhodesia." It was a polite 'push-off' and the Dutch continued to do business as usual, facilitating Jack as much as they possibly could.

But when it came to the export license for the next DC-8 nothing changed, and no decision was made. At the beginning of July 1974, the US Ambassador personally followed-up with the State Department chasing for approval of the sale. In his correspondence Ambassador McKesson said, "we can state that there is no evidence that the plane will be used for Rhodesian trade and there is a strong presumption that it will not. We have submitted every bit of evidence and data available to this end. It would be helpful if it were possible for the Department to pass to us any negative information holding up sale. It

71 Personal correspondence with Michael Draper, dated September 21 2008.

is also clear that export of the plane, if not illegal, would be in U.S. national interests."[72] There is no evidence that the Ambassador ever received a reply.

Two months after the change of government in Portugal, there was another change of government, this time in Greece where the right-wing military Junta was finally toppled. This also had a major and immediate impact on Jack's business.

In early June 1974 forty high ranking Greek officers were arrested and court marshalled. During these proceeding a special 'Meat Trial' was set up to investigate Affretair's rapid dominance of the Greek market and who amongst the Generals facilitated this lucrative business. According to court records a Greek CAA official confirmed that he was aware that Affretair was delivering Rhodesian meat and that the airline had a permanent office in Athens coordinating the operation. The new dispensation threw Stavros Tsonis in jail, cancelled Affretair's landing rights and no longer accepted any South African or Portuguese veterinarian certificates of origin.[73]

But as the Greek market was shut down so the Dutch market was opening up. It wasn't long before Affretair were flying a higher volume of Rhodesian beef to Amsterdam and other equally keen markets in Europe who had come to appreciate the extraordinarily high quality of the Rhodesian beef. According to one of the senior managers at the CSC, "the beef exports were based on high quality, vacuum packed beef cuts that had been boned in our factories. The prices obtained were always top of the range and could support the cost of air freight."[74]

All this furthered justified the need for another DC-8. At the end of July 1974 President Bongo instructed his Privy Counsellor, the Frenchman Jacques Pigot, to give the Americans a final ultimatum. Pigot phoned the U.S. Embassy and informed them that the President's patience was now seriously frayed and that

72 Confidential letter from Ambassador John McKesson to US State Department in Washington dated July 1, 1974.

73 Letter from the Permanent Mission of Greece at the U.N. to the Secretary General of the United Nations dated June 28, 1974. Declassified communication from the US Secretary of State to the American Ambassador in Athens dated September 20, 1974 and communication from the US Ambassador in Greece to the Secretary of State in Washington dated October 2, 1974.

74 Personal correspondence with Eddie Cross dated November 25, 2009.

he had set the deadline for resolution of the matter to mid-August. If the sale had not gone through by then apparently "Bongo planned to 'make other arrangements' and would, of course, be very displeased with the U.S. Government."

As further evidence that the aircraft would not be used by Affretair Pigot provided the Embassy with a letter from UTA confirming that it had already received at its Paris warehouse 'all the material necessary to give the aircraft interior VIP configuration.' Although the Embassy in Libreville had already been convinced by the first signed UTA contract this original letter on official letterhead clearly reiterated their justification for the sale. Pleading for the sale to be granted the US Embassy in Libreville asked the State Department to at least "note the purchase of VIP trappings for interior of aircraft, which lends further credence to judgement that Bongo intends second DC-8 for legitimate use. I submit it is farfetched to believe he would go to expense and bother of giving DC-8 plush interior with expectation of then ripping it out to give aircraft cargo configuration necessary for Rhodesian trade."[75]

Although this letter was original, the 'trappings for the interior' had not actually been ordered, received or warehoused, and there was no expectation from Bongo, Jack or the UTA senior management that such a refurbishment would ever be done. The contract and the letter were simply convincing props required to get the difficult American bureaucracy to issue the export license.

Yet, for all this effort it seems the U.S. Department of Commerce didn't budge. Jack and Omar, unaware of how hard the Embassy had lobbied for the deal, went ahead and made their 'other arrangements'. With his many contacts in the world of aviation Jack knew a Belgian fellow who ran an airline called Pomair that operated a couple of DC-8s out of Ostend, but as his business was going into liquidation he was looking for someone to buy his aircraft. One of them had been put into the UTA facility in Paris for some repair work to its undercarriage so Jack asked the service manager what he thought of the aircraft and whether it would be worth buying. With a comprehensive report in hand, Jack put in an offer and it was quickly accepted.

As soon as the deal was confirmed Jack wanted to hide the aircraft before either

75 Confidential correspondence between US Embassy in Libreville and US State Department dated August 1, 1974.

the British or Americans found out about it. But any change of commercial aircraft ownership and all the necessary insurance and paperwork that goes with it is both complex and public. It wasn't long before the Americans got wind of the deal, and they were not impressed. To severe their ties with Affretair someone from the US Embassy in Paris contacted Jack and told him that the London insurance company would be forced to cancel all his policies unless he immediately paid up the remaining balance on the first DC-8.

Within a day Jack made out a cheque for several million US dollars and delivered it to the flabbergasted Embassy contact. Reluctantly the man accepted it and said he would have it verified. As soon as he left the Embassy Jack put a call through to Alan Clements and told him to fly the aircraft out to Libreville immediately. Alan gathered the crew, filed the flight plan and quickly fueled up the aircraft for the long flight. He had just started the engines and was completing his pre-flight checks when a UTA official contacted him via the control tower and informed him that his flight plan had been changed and that he was now to go to Amsterdam. While odd, Alan accepted the change without a second thought as it was likely all part of covering their tracks.

As he was about to taxi out a large black embassy vehicle adorned with an American flag raced across the tarmac towards them. To the crew's consternation it pulled up next to the DC-8 and a suited man in dark sunglasses tried to get up the stairs. Fortunately, the UTA ground crew blocked him while the flight crew pushed the stairs away from the aircraft, enabling Alan to accelerate away and make their escape.

When requesting permission to land at Schiphol just over an hour later Alan did not tell Air Traffic Control that they were nine tons over their maximum allowable landing weight due to their brimming fuel tanks.[76] After a quick crew change Jack then had the aircraft relocated to Brussels, with several other misleading flight plans being filed to muddy the trail. From there, armed with more fictitious paperwork Colin Miller quickly headed off on the tense flight home before the Americans, or anyone else for that matter, were able to stop them.

This time, to ensure there were no leaks, Jack told no-one that they were coming, not even the Chairman of the Board knew that they had secured the

76 Personal correspondence with Alan Clements, dated November 4 2008.

aircraft. This implies that Jack didn't get the money to pay off the first DC-8 from Affretair. The only person who knew they were on their way was Nori Mann, Jack's trusted P.A. She didn't sleep at all that night, worrying endlessly that they may have been intercepted along the way. When the aircraft eventually landed at Salisbury in the pre-dawn darkness it was quickly hidden away far from prying eyes. For a few days it remained there while Jack and the Rhodesian Central Intelligence Organisation waited to see if any reporters had managed to break the story.[77]

Luckily everyone was completely distracted by the implosion of Angola and Mozambique so, at least in Southern Africa, no-one had the slightest interest in the comings and goings of a shadowy aircraft in the dead of night.

On 11th September with a rapidly deteriorating situation, a growing refugee crisis and panic in the streets, Frelimo troops marched into Lourenço Marques and took over the Mozambique Government. They were still dumbstruck by the unexpected and rapid withdrawal of the Portuguese army and were completely unprepared for the reins of power. In Angola the situation was much the same. On the 16th Captains Fleming and Phillips flew one of the DC-7s into Luanda. But the situation was extremely chaotic and unstable with no remaining administration and everyone desperate to get out before the enemy soldiers arrived.

Jack also made a flight into Luanda, but his was specifically a rescue mission to help get Rhodesia's diplomatic staff out before they fell into enemy hands. According to those on the flight, "there was a degree of urgency to take off and Jack was yelling at us to get into the plane. The wife of the Commercial Consul was running across the runway clutching belongings which, to her, but not to Jack, were most important and could not be left behind."[78]

Along with Angola and Mozambique, Portugal's other African colony of Guinea Bissau was also handed over to the Soviet-backed insurgents, but it was the loss of Angola that hurt Affretair most. Since 1970 they had built up significant business in Angola, and not only were all those contracts lost, but the airline was also banned from Angolan airspace. Unable to officially fly over Angola and Zambia made the route to Gabon much longer and more dangerous, especially

77 Interview with Nori Mann, Thakeham, West Sussex, May 8, 2019.
78 Personal correspondence with Judy Chapman dated November 11, 2008.

for the unreliable old DC-7s.

Once back from this Luanda distraction, Jack was relieved that still nothing had appeared in the newspapers about his second jet-freighter. But the Americas knew and information on the aircraft was sent right up to Henry Kissinger himself. On 17th September 1974 the Secretary of State sent a note to his Embassies in South Africa and Gabon. In it he mentioned an intelligence report that "indicates that the Rhodesians now have two – repeat two – DC-8s on Affretair's meat run to Europe. Although we were aware of Rhodesia's desire to obtain another DC-8, this is the first indication that one may have already slipped through the sanctions net."[79]

The aircraft cost eight and a half million US dollars, and there is no paper trail as to where that money came from. As with the first DC-8 it is more than likely that the bulk of it came from the Rhodesian Government, although Affretair would have been expected to repay the loan from trading income. President Bongo had also said that he would pay for it, but whether that was just to secure the export permit or not is unknown. It is also very possible that some of Jack's other 'partners' contributed towards it and it is rumoured that the South African Defence Force, through an international proxy, at least fronted the deposit on the aircraft.[80]

Strangely, all talk of the second DC-8 then died down completely. Bongo and his Ministers stopped harassing the U.S. Embassy for the export permit. It seemed they no longer had the slightest interest in their mid-August deadline, and in fact no longer seemed to have a need for the aircraft at all. All the diplomatic chatter dried up and Kissinger was left wondering whether his intelligence report was actually correct or not. The US Embassy in Libreville maintained a watch at the airport but did not report seeing a second DC-8. After a few weeks they stood down.

In mid-October two things happened. Pomair declared bankruptcy having disposed of all their aircraft and the issue of selling US-based aircraft to Affretair was formally ended when the U.S. Department of Commerce denied all U.S. export privileges to Affretair. The reason given was "because of its use of a

79 Declassified correspondence between US Secretary of State Henry Kissinger and US Ambassadors in Cape Town, Pretoria, Johannesburg and Libreville, dated September 17, 1974.

80 Interview with John Fletcher, Johannesburg, South Africa, May 16, 2002.

U.S.-origin DC-8/55F Jet Trader aircraft in export-import transactions with Southern Rhodesia, and its failure to answer interrogatories regarding the matter." Air Trans Africa was then also denied all their export privileges for being "associated with a denied party."

But the question remained, exactly where was Jack's second DC-8 and what was it being used for? The transfer of ownership of the aircraft was only recorded on April 26th and was registered in Gabon on May 24th – 1975. This was a full eight months after Kissinger heard that Jack had acquired it. Based on his track-record in Biafra Jack certainly wasn't adverse to keeping, and using, old registrations, especially if he needed to obscure the paper-trail, and the paper-trail on this particular transaction was extremely well hidden. Thirty-five years after Jack's death the only record of Pomair having been the previous owner of the aircraft was in declassified State Department documents[81] and even they contain no clues as to the aircraft's whereabouts for those missing eight months.

There is one last enticing clue to this whole mystery. It was a comment made by a Gabonese Civil Aviation official to a U.S. intelligence operative in which he said that they had been waiting for a long time for the aircraft to be registered seeing that it had been on-hand for so long. The agent noted in his debrief that this "possibly indicated foreknowledge."[82]

For all the drama of getting the second DC-8, the final victory was bitter-sweet. Jack had lost the lucrative Greek and Angolan markets. The Super Constellation had finally died, taking the passenger route to Windhoek with it, and Affretair's Gabonese cover had been well and truly blown.

As for Rhodesia, their closest ally was bullying them, and they now had a raging war igniting their entire Eastern border.

For Jack it was all horrible *déjà vu.* If they were to survive, he knew they would need another Affretair and another Gabon…

---

81 Declassified memo titled 'Rhodesian Sanctions: Affretair' sent from the US Mission to the U.N. to the US Secretary of State in Washington dated April 21, 1976.

82 Declassified memo titled 'Suspected diversion U.S. origin aircraft' sent from the US Embassy in Libreville to the US Secretary of State in Washington dated September 19, 1975.

CHAPTER 11

Cargoman and the Second Trade Route: 1975 to 1977

With Gabon having been compromised as a cover for his international operations Jack needed to find an alternative.

In early 1974 he discussed the problem with his fellow directors. Brigadier Andrew Dunlop spoke about the success he had had with a very well-placed contact high up within the Omani government. That contact was an ex-British military officer by the name of Timothy Landon. Landon had been operating in Oman since 1964 and, over time he had risen to become the head Intelligence Officer in Dhofar. Although his real influence was the fact that he was also a close friend and confidant of the Omani Crown Prince Qaboos. Having been credited as a key player in the 1970 coup that brought Qaboos to power, Landon had been given free rein by his ever-grateful sponsor. Yet, unknown to most, Timothy Landon's brother Chris was a rancher in Rhodesia. According to Brett Popplewell, Landon "had family relations who were under siege in Rhodesia and South Africa and here he was with his finger on the Omani oil tap."[1]

According to Dunlop, to facilitate the oil deal with Rhodesia, Landon had set up an oil exporting business called Transworld Oil. His partners in this business were Qais and Omar Zawawi. From the humble beginnings of this trade with Rhodesia, Transworld Oil would eventually become one of the world's largest oil trading firms,[2] making Landon and the Zawawi brothers extremely rich in the process.

Although Dunlop had resigned from his ministerial post he was able to set up a

1 'Life of the White Sultan shrouded in controversy' by Brett Popplewell published by the Globe & Mail on July 14, 2007.

2 'Oman: Oil entrepreneur extraordinaire' by D. Patrick Maley published by United Press International on October 1, 1994.

meeting between Malloch and Landon. That first meeting was held in Muscat and went very well, especially when they discovered that they had a mutual friend in the influential British politician Julian Amery. Jack wondered whether Landon had also been involved in Amery's British Mercenary Organisation.

Landon introduced Jack to his partners Qais and Omar. At the time Qais was the Omani Minister of State for Foreign Affairs while Omar was a special advisor to Sultan Qaboos Bin Said. It was obvious that both businessmen were much more influential than their titles implied. Jack instantly established a good rapport with the men, and they agreed to set up a new air freight business together. Based out of Muscat the business was intended to generate a profit for the local shareholders and provide the external base that Jack needed to keep Rhodesia's international trade-routes open.

Having just emerged from their own war against communist insurgents the Omanis were very sympathetic to Rhodesia's situation and were more than happy to bend the U.N.'s sanctions to help. According to 'an eminent Omani who held ministerial office', "The oil shipped to Southern Africa left Oman by sea, with Bills of Lading made out for Japan. But these were changed several times on the high seas. They also had a cargo plane which secretly flew other supplies down to Rhodesia and South Africa."[3]

The mention of this 'cargo plane' is intriguing. Could this possibly have been where Jack's second DC-8 was deployed for those seven months that it was unaccounted for? There is absolutely no trace of it from the time the CIA reported that it was in Jack's custody in September 1974 through to it finally being registered in Gabon in April 1975. Perhaps… It would certainly have made sense to prove the viability of the new business, show commitment to the partners in Muscat and start building up contracts before the formal change of ownership of the aircraft. One thing is for sure though, Jack was not one to waste any asset and it would have been extremely out of character for the vital aircraft to have just been hidden away in the back of some hanger somewhere while Rhodesia, Gabon and Oman were all begging for increased capacity.

Wherever the aircraft was, Affretair was being stretched to the limit trying to

3 'Oman: The True-Life Drama and Intrigue of an Arab State' by John Beasant, published by Mainstream Publishing (Edinburgh) Ltd. ISBN: 1-84018-607-0.

keep up with the meat flights to Amsterdam, Zurich and Zaire. While John Fletcher had been employed as Commercial Manager tasked with bringing in new business and developing new commercial routes, Jack personally retained the strategically important meat business. He dealt with Tony Hall from the Cold Storage Commission and oversaw the entire operation which, over time, had become slick and efficient, just as he liked it.

According to one of the senior managers at CSC at the time, upwards of one hundred tons of prime beef were being airlifted out of the country by Affretair every week from early 1974 onwards. For Affretair's freight consignments the meat had to be prepared according to required cut as well as final destination. In Gabon there were three destinations, Libreville, Franceville and Port Gentil and all of the meat for the European markets was also routed through Gabon. In Zaire there were two destinations, Kinshasa and Lubumbashi, although with Zaire after a few bad experiences with debt collection Jack changed the process. He flew the numerous buyers to Salisbury airport and the CSC literally sold the beef to them for cash straight off the tarmac. When the aircraft was full and the load had been paid, they were all flown back.[4] This worked extremely well as it was cash up-front and all costs were factored into the per kilogram price.

The orders generally comprised of rump, fillet, loin, topside, silverside, thick flank as well as hind and fore-quarters together with offal. There were also some unique requirements. The Swiss liked pickled ox-snout which they called 'ox maul'. This they regarded as something of a delicacy along with 'binden fleisch' which was similar to Rhodesian biltong.[5] Quickly the butchers at the Cold Storage Commission mastered the art of these unique preparations, and the orders kept coming. Each market also had their own set of specifications and those included things like the amount of beef fat thickness and the percentage of overall fat. Again, the Swiss market was particularly discerning and many of the cuts had to be physically measured to ensure conformity to their market requirements. So much top-grade beef was sold to Switzerland that by the late 1970s it was rumoured that if you wanted to eat great Rhodesian steak you just had to go to a Mövenpick.

4 Personal correspondence with Eddie Cross dated November 25, 2009.
5 Personal correspondence with Paul Sheppard dated October 21, 2009.

Once the orders had been confirmed the Affretair loadmasters issued the Cold Storage Commission with a palletization plan. This was needed to ensure the correct weight distribution on the aircraft and the correct sequence for off-loading. The CSC Manager that the ATA Traffic Office liaised with was Ian Anderson. He was an old Scotsman who had exceptional attention to detail, and that was exactly what was needed for the clandestine nature of the sanctions-busting business. To add complication all correspondence was in code, "C-92 was for Congo Brazzaville and woe-betide you if you every referred to it as Congo Brazzaville on an open telex or phone line."[6]

The CSC would prepare all the 'import back-door' documents based on the quantities of the various meat cuts and the 'sensitivity' of the destination. These documents were used to clear the load into the destination country. Meanwhile ATA would prepare the export documents for the Rhodesian Customs along with Export Control in the Prime Minister's office. This was handled by Mike Brough who would deliver all the necessary documents, duly stamped, every day – and night. All this preparation started about thirty-six hours before each planned flight so the CSC had enough time to prepare the pallets on the day of the flight.

Once prepared the freight pallets were then loaded in their pre-set order into the COLCOM-branded refrigerated pantechnicons and their twenty-two-ton tri-axled trailers. Under cover of darkness they were driven from the abattoir in Marandellas out to the airport. There was always the possibility of a terrorist ambush along the way which added to the tension.[7] The trucks arrived at ATA's off-loading platform by about six or seven o'clock in the evening. If there was no unanticipated drama, the pallets were retrieved from the Cold Rooms and loaded onto the aircraft. Once in they needed to be all strapped down and ready to go by two a.m. when the crew would begin their final pre-flight checks.

But there was lots of unanticipated drama, almost all of which could impact the aircraft's take-off weight and departure time.

There were any number of ways that things could unravel. Typically these would include challenging or changing weather conditions along the route and

6 Personal correspondence with Ian Hunt, March 1, 2020.
7 Personal correspondence with Paul Sheppard, October 21, 2009.

unexpected last-minute passengers, who were often government dignitaries who Jack was always willing to help out. Then inevitably Tommy Minks in Engineering would call the Traffic office and say they had an 'AOG' (aircraft on the ground) which urgently needed spare parts. These could be a spare engine, an undercarriage unit or any of a hundred and ten other heavy parts, which could easily add tons to the load. All this also had to be weighed and loaded by the two o'clock deadline.

The timing was important because in addition to maintaining secrecy and ensuring that the aircraft were not caught over hostile airspace in daylight, it was the coldest time of day. This provided an optimal 'QNH' which meant they could take off with heavier loads. 'QNH' was an old Morse-code term which meant atmospheric pressure adjusted to mean sea level.

Just before take-off the Load Masters would once again check the QNH. Any significant drop in air pressure or increase in air temperature could reduce the take-off weight by as much as two tons. This was a perpetual problem, especially during the summer months. Consequently, the aircraft were more often than not over their regulation take-off weight. If these variables all conspired to push the weight too far over the operating limits of the aircraft – or the comfort level of the designated captain, some of the cargo had to be off-loaded. This would mean that the back-door documents would have to be re-issued – by the CSC, and the destination would have to be advised of the short load. Again, this was tricky considering the time of day and the urgency of making the take-off 'window.'[8]

Jack, who never wanted to disappoint his important clients or their buyers, considered off-loading an absolute last resort. If he was the captain he would always try and take it all, carefully considering the mathematics to better understand the risk. It was a fine balance to ensure that safety was not compromised, and this is where Jack's knowledge and intuition of aircraft and their true limits came into play. Considering that the entire aviation industry was hardly three generations old at the time, Jack wasn't convinced that all the rules and regulations had necessarily determined the true operating parameters for every conceivable situation. As with his 'hot starts' for the Spitfires, Jack felt that with careful thought and some calculated experimentation, most limits could

8 Personal correspondence with Ian Hunt, March 1, 2020.

at least be challenged. And, remarkably, with the help of Horse Sweeney and a few others, they were successful in this endeavour. With faster take-offs they were able to lift increased payloads in the DC-8, especially at higher altitude airports such as Salisbury and Nairobi.

"Most of the accomplished captains, including the likes of Colin Miller and Mike Gibson, regularly took off three or four tons over the limit. Jack, who was the acknowledged 'overweight champion,' on one occasion did a flight that was ten tons over, but he was the only one who ever went that high."[9] But not all the pilots were comfortable with this. When Horse called a meeting to discuss the procedure the meeting ended rather abruptly when it became apparent that the process was not endorsed by the aircraft manufacturer.[10]

Although Jack did get exasperated by some of the pilots who vehemently stuck to the rule-book, he would never show his annoyance or even think of criticising any of them for it.[11] He still regretted how his relationship with John Aldridge had ended. Instead he would lead by example and by using the speed-technique he was able to quite regularly take-off up to eight tons over the limit. This involved setting the flaps to fifteen degrees, accelerating to one hundred knots and then lowering the flaps to twenty-five degrees.[12] Eventually, to the credit of Affretair's studious pilots, McDonald Douglas did approve their high-speed take-off technique for high altitude airports.[13]

While the high-speed take-off helped the DC-8, any sort of take-off was a challenge in the two surviving DC-7s. As they were both well past their expiry date there was always a lot of thick oil sloshing about in the bottom engine pots which had to be cleared first. The lower spark plugs would also be drowned in oil, especially after standing for a few hours. After anything up to fifty 'turns,' the first engine would start in a billowing cloud of blue smoke, and then settle down to idle, while the pilots tackled the next engine. With four engines to get going this could take some time. Once all of the engines were fired-up they would taxi off to the very end of the longest runway. And this wasn't just the

9 Interview with Ian Hunt, Gaborone, Botswana, April 14, 2010.
10 Personal correspondence between Tony Norton and Cacho Cabral, February 28, 2020.
11 Personal correspondence with Ian Hunt, February 6, 2020.
12 Personal correspondence with Cacho Cabral, January 28, 2020.
13 Personal correspondence with Cacho Cabral, February 23, 2020.

longest runway in Salisbury, at eleven and a half thousand feet it was actually the longest civilian runway in the world.

There was another long wait as they did a hundred other things before finally revving the engines up to full power. At peak power they would let it go and the monster would start lumbering forward. Eventually, just before the end of the runway it would claw its way over the perimeter fence and skim over the trees beyond. Every inch of the runway was needed as the worn-out old turbochargers no longer worked. The Tower would then confirm that they were cleared as the vintage aircraft disappeared into the darkness. Hardly anyone knew where they were going, and they did not maintain radio contact.[14]

To ensure that the meat would be accepted in its final destination and couldn't be traced back to Rhodesia the detail and integrity of the packaging was critical – and became quite an art form. The marketing staff from CSC made regular intelligence-gathering trips to other meat exporting countries, carefully copying every detail of the foreign carton design, print roller marks, veterinary labels and export stamps. These were then meticulously reproduced. It wasn't long before Rhodesian beef in almost perfect foreign packaging, often Argentinian, found its way into the European markets.[15]

With the extra tonnage that they were able to take off with, the CSC was still able to keep up with the demand. At the time the Commission was operating all six of their abattoirs to maximum capacity, processing upwards of two thousand cattle every day, so, for the hard currency, they were more than capable of cramming every flight out of the country.

And it wasn't just the loads that were pushed to the absolute limit. According to John Fletcher, with the fast turnarounds and continual flying Affretair broke the world record for the utilisation of the DC-8. During that busy period the aircraft engines were reputed to have never cooled down. Although to do it John admitted that they regularly exceeded the regulation Duty Hours. But no-one complained, and Jack ensured that he was always part of the effort. "Malloch would load pallets himself if need be. He worked so hard that everyone else did too."[16] It was all part of the extraordinary bonding of the tight-knit Affretair

14 Personal correspondence with Mike Daly dated July 4, 2008.
15 Personal correspondence with Paul Sheppard, November 19, 2009.
16 Interview with John Fletcher, Johannesburg, South Africa, May 16, 2002.

crew. "We all felt very proud to be part of his team. I think everyone in Affretair felt that they had joined a family and Captain Jack was the patriarch."[17]

A continuing challenge for Affretair was the freight volumes on the return flights from Europe to Salisbury and the cost of half-empty aircraft eroded profitability. To resolve this Jack and Bongo hatched a plan which the Gabonese President sold to the South African ambassador. In May 1975, Jack met with the South African Airways (SAA) Planning Manager, proposing a weekly cargo flight from Europe to Johannesburg and on to Salisbury. The aircraft used was to be the Affretair DC-8, but 'wet-leased' by SAA. In return for this concession, Bongo offered SAA the use of Franceville airport as a technical stopover. These elements, along with Safair's landing rights at Libreville for Armscor shipments, were consolidated in an agreement that Air Trans Africa and SAA signed in June 1975. After a couple of issues were resolved Affretair made its first landing in Johannesburg on July 17th, 1975.[18] The establishment of this critical freight route directly into Africa's most lucrative market, which became known as 'PG812', was instrumental in Affretair's long term success. Ironically, an English handling agent Kingsley Aviation were to become one of the main customers that utilised this service – making them the subject of several Sanctions Committee investigations.

While the Americans had tried to minimise their involvement in the 'Rhodesian issue', the CIA had certainly played their part in reporting on Jack's sanction-busting efforts. This had seriously complicated the purchase and servicing of the DC-8s. Yet it was more to protect America's reputation than to punish Rhodesia. Jack understood this, but was still surprised when, in mid-1975, a team within the CIA contacted him about doing some clandestine work for the Agency. It was part of their covert 'Operation IA Feature' to destabilise, and hopefully oust, the Marxist Angolan government.

Mobutu provided three infantry battalions along with the operational bases in southern Zaire for these attacks. Jack's job was to fly in the foreign 'military advisors' who, predictably, had been recruited with Bob Denard's help. Although Jack was very good at covering his tracks, there is a record that he made at

---

17 Personal correspondence with Jon Aird dated July 27, 2010.

18 'Apartheid South Africa and African States: From Pariah to Middle Power, 1962 to 1994' by Roger Pfister. Published by I.B. Tauris (2005). ISBN: 9781850436256.

least two DC-7 flights into Kinshasa in July 1975, delivering more than two hundred and fifty mercenaries for the operation.[19]

It was likely during the time of these military missions that Jack's crew had to jump-start the DC-8 with a fighter jet. They were flying into a remote military base in southern Zaire to collect a big consignment of AK-47 rifles along with another military hardware. As the facilities were very basic with no ground-power available the crew would usually carry a starter unit on a pallet inside the aircraft. They would put the exhaust out the door to start number one engine. Unfortunately the generator unit took up a lot of cargo space and on this particular flight the plane was full that they couldn't fit in the starter unit, so the plan was to keep one of the engines running. For some unanticipated reason they had to fully shut down which was a real problem as the airstrip was insecure and they needed to be out before dawn.

"Jack, who seemed to know everyone, got onto the radio and told them to go to the hanger and ask for the guy there and explain the problem to him. In the hanger there was some sort of military jet fighter, which they set up in front of number one engine to get the engine turbines moving. Jack knew it would destroy the engine, but it would be enough for them to start the other engines which would enable them to fly back home, which is what they did."[20] While it cost Jack fifteen thousand dollars to repair the engine, he was at least able to retrieve his aircraft and crew. According to John Fletcher who was on the flight, they came back the next night and did it all over again until the full consignment had been collected.

Ever since Jack had met with Claire Chennault back in the mid-1950s he had always been intrigued by the potential of the Far Eastern market and now that he had the second DC-8 he wanted to give it another try. But as the British were still very influential in the area the Rhodesians would need to be particularly careful. Jack knew he was too recognisable, so instead sent his chief pilot, Colin Miller, and Affretair's Commercial Director John Fletcher to investigate the market. John had recently returned from Paraguay, Paris and Muscat. Now it was time to go to Hong Kong.

---

19 Interview with Henry Kinnear, Jet Park, Johannesburg, March 2 2004.

20 Interview with John Fletcher, Johannesburg, South Africa, May 16, 2002 and interview with Ian Hunt, Gaborone, Botswana, April 14 2010.

The trip was meticulously planned with the help of Rick May, an agent from the Rhodesian Central Intelligence Organisation (CIO). He provided John and Colin with fake passports and carefully briefed them on what they could and couldn't do and who, if anyone, they could trust. This was clearly more of a spying mission than a business trip, and one that the airline men were not trained for.

The involvement of the CIO is interesting considering that some sources claim that "Malloch's planes and operational costs were funded by the CIO."[21] While this seems an exaggeration considering how much business the Cold Storage Commission were doing with Affretair, the Intelligence Service could still have been a significant contributor. And over time more circumstantial evidence has come to light to support this CIO theory. Apparently just before he died, Ken Flower, the former head of the Rhodesian CIO, confirmed that the spy agency were indeed Jack's financiers. He is quoted as saying, "If Jack Malloch wanted a new aircraft then he bought it, and the CIO was left to foot the bill." Apparently to keep tabs on this liability an ex-police officer was appointed by the secret service to keep an eye on Jack. The CIO was also behind the appointment of the private security firm that handled all security services for Air Trans Africa.[22] While the full extent of the CIO's involvement in Affretair will never be fully know, it does seem to have been much more than most people realised.

Before the end of July John Fletcher and Colin Miller, under their new aliases, arrived in Hong Kong, having caught a commercial flight from Johannesburg. They quickly started following up their connections, beginning with the Kai Tak Airport Authorities in Kowloon, then they moved on to the Civil Aviation Authorities and the Department of Commerce. Their initial request was for permission to make non-scheduled cargo flights from Hong Kong to Amsterdam and Lagos.

But the men had been compromised. Just before midnight on their first day John received a phone call in his hotel room. "I suggest you fly out first thing in the morning…" an anonymous voice said. It turned out to be a British MI6 agent who agreed to meet with John. After a few very late drinks the agent agreed to delay the arrest and give them a chance to escape. As they parted company John

21 'The Rhodesian War: A Military History' by Paul L. Moorcraft and Peter McLaughlin published by Stackpole Books. ISBN 978-0-8117-0725-1.

22 Personal correspondence with Peter Stiff dated April 25, 2002.

The CL-44, TR-LVO landing at Maastricht Airport on 22nd August 1975 while the Affretair crew were doing their conversion training on the aircraft. The 'swing-tail' hinges can be clearly seen just before the tail section.
Picture provided by Paul Hooper. © Paul J. Hooper.

was stunned when the nameless agent turned back and said, "…and when you get back to Salisbury tell Rick May I think he's a prick for letting you come!"[23] John was left in no doubt that there was some insider leak between the CIO and the British Secret Intelligence Service. John and Colin immediately packed up and got away as quickly as they could. Hong Kong formally declined Affretair's request for the flights and the U.K. put a travel ban on John Fletcher and Colin Miller, along with Jack Malloch and Andrew Dunlop.[24]

Less than a week later, in early August 1975 Bob Denard deposed President Ahmed Abdullah of the Comoros, replacing him with Ali Soilih. Just six months later Abdullah returned and retook his throne in a successful countercoup. And so, the drama of the Comoran 'coup-coup' islands began…

With the fragility of the old, over-worked DC-7s, and the consistent need for 'medium-haul' freight deliveries Jack had been looking for a new, more reliable aircraft. Since 1973 Affretair had been flying into Luxembourg and Jack had made some good connections within Cargolux Airlines, to whom he happened

23 Interview with John Fletcher, Johannesburg, South Africa, May 16, 2002.
24 Declassified memo from the US Mission to the UN to the Secretary of State in Washington titled 'Rhodesian Sanctions: Affretair,' dated April 21, 1976.

to mention the need for a DC-7 replacement. It was perfect timing as the lease on one of their CL-44s was up in mid-August and the aircraft was being returned to Cargolux. The main benefit of the four-engined turboprop was that it had a 'swing-tail' that could open up fully to take in almost any cargo. Within just two weeks the sale was finalised and the aircraft was transferred to Affretair. Luxembourg had no problem with Rhodesia and the deal, which included a replacement engine, was quick and easy.

Quickly the two new aircraft settled into the routine of the meat run. The CL-44 supplemented the routes into Johannesburg, Kinshasa, Abidjan and Libreville. While the second DC-8, registered in Gabon as Tango Romeo LVK, joined the original '8' in an intensive shuttle between Salisbury, Amsterdam and a whole slew of destinations in-between.

At the end of 1975 Jack's two nephews Dave and Mike Kruger both received their military call-ups papers. Dave joined the infantry while Mike decided to go for a Commission and joined the Air Force, becoming a pilot like his father Ted. Blythe, who was left with just her daughter Elza-Lynne, was terrified that her boys might not come back from the war. Jack was also very involved in the war and his clandestine flights were bringing in significant quantities of military equipment and hardware. Although the details of many of these flights have been carefully hidden from public record.

One of the biggest sanctions-busting deals that the Air Force pulled off was bringing in eighteen brand new Cessna 337s directly from the Reims factory in France. Having proven themselves in Vietnam these twin-engined aircraft, which the Rhodesians named the Lynx were excellent in the counter-insurgency ground-attack role. Considering the French connection, it is almost certain that Malloch was involved in this deal. The fact that at the end of January 1976 Jack delivered a DC-8 planeload of Lynx spares directly to the Air Force maintenance hangers at New Sarum[25] seems to confirm this.

'Above the board' Affretair had also established themselves as regular sub-contractors to both Air France and Sabena. According to their CIA 'watchers', "under charter to Sabena, Affretair aircraft have been seen in Brussels, Geneva,

25 'Rhodesian Air Force Operations' by Preller Geldenhuys. Published by Peysoft Publishing. ISBN: 9780994115409.

Zurich, Palma de Mallorca, Kano, Lagos and Kigali. While under charter to Air France they have been seen in Paris, Geneva, Zurich, Palma de Mallorca, Pointe-à-Pitre (Guadaloupe), Lagos, Nairobi, Djibouti, Dubai and Karachi." Rodney Davies also noted that "Air France would sometimes use Affretair's planes when their own ones were fully booked."[26] Most ironically, Affretair was also hired by the United Nations itself to provide air transport for humanitarian aid in the Sahel.[27]

This was all good for business, but Jack was concerned about the implications of Hong Kong. Clearly Affretair was compromised and needed to be replaced. By the end of 1975 Jack had a plan. The first thing they did, through third-party proxies that Bongo selected, was register a new business in Libreville. It was called Air Gabon Cargo. Affretair was then moved from Gabon into a new office in Johannesburg, and the Affretair branding was stripped off the DC-8s.

The Joburg office was run by Ming Longmore and Linda Ming who were very careful to hide any connection back to Rhodesia. They specialised in freight handling between South Africa and Europe. As a handling agent, technically they were able to use any airline or cargo service they needed to meet their clients' needs. They 'just so happened' to use a new freight company called Air Gabon Cargo based in Libreville. Air Trans Africa, with its head office at Salisbury Airport was then used as the official name of the business in Rhodesia where, at the time, few people had even heard of either Affretair or Air Gabon Cargo. Jack still had the Afro-Continental business, which he decided to keep under wraps, perhaps for more clandestine operations in the future.

These changes re-establish the illusion of neutrality for the Libreville-based business. This quickly enabled the opening of Air Gabon Cargo offices in Libreville, Amsterdam, Geneva and, in time, Muscat. It also ensured that the south-bound flights from Schiphol which arrived every Sunday evening in Johannesburg were full.[28] This dramatically improved the financial viability of the overall business.

To ensure that the demise of Affretair in Gabon looked as genuine as possible a few subtle leaks were given to Embassy staff to alert the British and American

26 Personal correspondence with Benjamin Davies dated October 12, and 22, 2009.
27 'Affaires Africaines' by Pierre Péan, published by Fayard (1983). ISBN: 2-213-01324-1.
28 Personal correspondence with Donald Mackie dated March 30, 2010.

intelligence services that Affretair had fallen out of political favour. Considering that Jack was not a spy-master his careful and considered approach worked very well. In May 1976 this culminated in an article in the leading Libreville newspaper that the Government of Gabon had decided to dissolve Affretair and incorporate it into the national airline, Air Gabon, as a division called Air Gabon Cargo.

The official reason that was given intentionally made no mention of Rhodesia. Instead it cited a desperate need for additional aircraft and the policy that required national civil aviation operations to be concentrated into one company. Both the people of Libreville and the US State Department were "divided between those who believed President Bongo had moved to end the controversial Rhodesian trade and others who thought the President will find new ways to continue this highly lucrative commerce."[29]

Malloch and Bongo also went to great lengths to blur the source of the beef being imported into Gabon. A timely Gabonese and Burundian trade summit provided them with the perfect cover. The US Ambassador in Gabon reported back to Washington that "The meeting of the Joint Commission in Libreville coincided with the dissolution of Affretair. The two events are linked according to local sources who believe that the Gabonese market will now be supplied by Burundi meat instead of Rhodesian beef."

This Burundi deal was followed several months later when it was announced that a contract between Soduco (the meat importing business that Jack and Bob had established in the early 1970s) and the Swaziland Meat Corporation had been signed. The agreement was for sixty tons a week of Swazi AAA-grade beef to be imported into Gabon conveniently "carried by Gabonese airplanes." Remarkably, the agreement was signed by the Swazi Minister of Mines and Tourism himself.[30] Yet Swaziland didn't actually have a domestic beef industry. It was all just another fantastically elaborate prop in Jack's web of intrigue, and, judging by the tone of the US Embassy, it was working.

---

29 Declassified correspondence between the US Embassy in Libreville to the US Mission to the United Nations in New York, dated May 7, 1976.

30 Article in the December 17, 1976 edition of the L'Union newspaper, Libreville, Gabon, and in the declassified memo titled 'Gabon to import meat from Swaziland' from the US Ambassador in Libreville to the US Secretary of State dated December 18, 1976.

Having re-secured their Gabonese-base Jack needed to turn his attention to Oman and his agreement with Landon and the Zawawi brothers. But both of Jack's DC-8s were fully committed to Air Gabon Cargo and were flying almost to the limit of their, and their aircrews', capacity, forcing ever faster and more efficient turn-arounds and loadings. If the Middle Eastern market was to be opened up it would need an 'Eight' of its own.

Again, Cargolux were more than willing to help. Considering how easily the CL-44 sale had been they suggested that Jack choose the DC-8 he wanted, they would buy it to legitimately get it into Europe. Then they would simply resell it to Jack, and everyone, except the U.N. Sanctions Committee, would get what they wanted.

Jack's old friends at Flying Tiger in Los Angeles had the perfect DC-8 for Jack and were more than happy to work through Cargolux to get it to him. It was an almost new, extra-long cargo-configured DC-8-63. As all the links back to Rhodesia had to be obscured, numerous commissions had to be paid to the fleet of 'middlemen'. These all added to the delivery price of just over ten million dollars. One of these 'middlemen' that Cargolux wanted to 'front' the sale where Greyhound Financial and Leasing that were based out of Zug in Switzerland.[31]

By the time 'Robbie' Roberts, who was Chairman of the Air Trans Africa Board, got to hear about this proposed sale Flying Tiger had already applied for an export permit and Greyhound had put in a temporary waiver request for urgent delivery. This was based on 'their client's critical need for the aircraft.' Based on their experience fighting for the second DC-8, pushing for this Emergency Waiver was intentionally done to try and minimise the depth of investigation into the sale.

With the deal all but inked, Roberts was livid. He strongly objected to the purchase and complained right up to the Prime Minister, raging that, not only had he been sidelined, but that the purchase was an irresponsible use of the country's extremely limited foreign currency. Reluctantly Ian Smith advised Jack to at least establish the business in Oman first to prove the need for a third aircraft before going ahead and buying it. For Jack it was the only way to properly establish the business and he was incensed that a 'petty bureaucrat'

31 Confidential 'Integrity and Reliability Check' memo between the US Secretary of State in Washington and the US Embassies in Luxembourg and Bern dated May 13, 1976.

was being so interfering.

The sale collapsed, as did the relationship between Jack and the Board Chairman. In protest Robbie Roberts resigned as the Chairman of the Board. He was replaced by Alec Bartrum who was more open to Jack's ambitious and unconventional thinking.[32]

Jim Torond was the Permanent Secretary for the Rhodesian Ministry of Transport and Power and Affretair fell within his portfolio. Consequently, over time he became the link between Affretair, Treasury and the Prime Minister, especially on matters of finance. It was Jim who argued for, and established, the Rhodesian government's subsidy of Affretair which helped finance the airline's operational costs.[33] This shifted ever more financial decision-making over to the government, although Jack appreciated that it ensured the survival of the business and he no longer had to worry about lurking debt-collectors and looming foreclosures.

While the loss of the DC-8-63 was a blow to the business, had they gone ahead with the deal, I believe it would have been a lot more difficult to pull off than Cargolux or Flying Tiger anticipated. The reason is that it appears both businesses were already on the CIA's 'watch list' and the waiver application and request for permission to export had been flagged as suspicious.

All this resulted in a full six months delay in Jack's Oman plans. This was embarrassing as the Business had already been registered in Muscat under the trading name 'Cargoman.' The four named directors of the company were the two powerful Zawawi brothers, Qais and Omar, Walid Zawawi who was Omar's teen-age son, and Angus Hume, a business manager from the Zawawi Group of Companies. Malloch and Landon both intentionally avoided being named in the paperwork.

With Rhodesia winning on the battlefield the South African government's hopes for an appeasement with Black Africa had come to nothing. In early 1976 the South African President asked America for help and Henry Kissinger began his famous shuttle diplomacy between Dar es Salaam, Lusaka and Pretoria. These

32 Interview with Ian Hunt, Gaborone, Botswana, April 14, 2010, and personal correspondence dated February 6, 2020.

33 Personal correspondence with Jim Torond dated August 3, 2010.

talks culminated in September 1976 with Smith meeting Kissinger and Voster in South Africa. Rhodesia had come to rely on the regular South African Air Force C-130 that delivered weapons to New Sarum Air Force base in Salisbury. To ensure Smith's compliance, in a classic 'quid pro quo' Voster cancelled the flights. With no choice Smith agreed to majority rule in two years and to the establishment of an interim government to work out a new constitution.

This was doomed when Robert Mugabe announced that ZANU and ZAPU were working towards establishing a united military front. Far from decreasing, the savage, violent incursions were stepped up. By early October there were daily attacks, with gangs rocketing farms, civilians being ambushed and killed, and landmines being sown everywhere. Disagreeing with Voster's handling of the situation, after a few agonising months Jack's supporters within the South African Defence Force let him know that they would still make the weapons available as long as he came to collect them, which he was more than willing to do.

Rhodesia quickly started looking beyond South Africa for a more reliable supply of arms. Crown Prince Leka, the deposed Albanian monarch and friend of P.K. van der Byl, Rhodesia's Minister of Foreign Affairs, turned out to be particularly valuable. He was living in asylum in Spain from where he ran his arms dealing enterprise. Through the Prince, Rhodesia was able to purchase one hundred and fifty thousand G3 automatic rifles and a hundred million rounds of ammunition. According to the paperwork the final buyer was South Africa, although it seems that Rhodesia was the main beneficiary. Soon after the shipment was made all of the remaining Rhodesian auxiliary and reserve defence force units had been upgraded to these 7.62mm NATO standard weapons.

While the 'Frontline States' where trying to oust the Rhodesian government, the French were thinking about how they could oust the Benin government. This secretive plan was dubbed 'Opération Crevette.' The intention was to overthrow the communist President, Mathieu Kérékou whose repressive anti-Western dictatorship was threatening to destabilise the whole region. France's 'man in Africa' who agreed to do all the dirty work was Jack's silent partner Bob Denard.

There were many supporters of this plot. According to Jacques Foccart, the coup was backed by President Bongo of Gabon, President Houphouët-Boigny of the

Ivory Coast, King Hassan II of Morocco and President Eyadéma of Togo. They were all allies of France, and all, except Eyadéma, were friends of Malloch. It also appears that Jack committed more than just moral and logistical support. According to Rodney Davies, a Rhodesian Foreign Affairs operative based out of Abidjan, "Money paid to Air Gabon Cargo …was used to partly finance the attempted coup d'état in Dahomey in 1976."[34]

The actual coup attempt took place on January 17th, 1977, but all the planning was done in the latter part of 1976. This was driven mainly by King Hassan II who was incensed by Kérékou's support of the Polisario Front. The preparations began in early November when Denard signed a contract with the 'Dahomey National Liberation Front' to reinstate the former Dahomey president Dr Emile Zinzou. Bob then started negotiations with Jack for the hire of one of his DC-8s and the outright purchase of one of his DC-7s. Apparently the agreed fee for Affretair's services was ninety-five thousand US dollars. According to Anthony Mockler, "the DC-7 and DC-8 which Denard had negotiated were from the charter company in which he himself had an interest."[35]

Bob then started recruiting his mercenaries. Once formed this 'Omega Force' started their training at a military base at Benguerir in Morocco. The plan was simple: Launch a surprise attack against Benin's capital city Coutonou, shock any opposition into inaction and capture or kill the President and as many of his Ministers as possible. The plan was slated for January 5th, but just three days before that date President Eyadéma of Togo pulled out, compromising the back-up invasion plan. It was not a good omen, but Bob pressed ahead anyway.

On January 12th the DC-7 did a run to the South African Air Force base at Waterkloof, returning with a full load of weapons for the Rhodesians. It then did a meat run up to Libreville, where it stayed. On the 14th Jack flew the DC-8 from Salisbury to Libreville. This was a positioning flight and the cargo hold had been reconfigured to passenger seating. Early the next morning Jack flew to Morocco and collected the first eighty men, bringing them back to the

---

34 Personal notes and papers belonging to Rodney Davies, as provided by Michelle Davies on January 15, 2010.

35 'The New Mercenaries' by Anthony Mockler. Published by Transworld Publishers 1986. ISBN: 0-552-12558-X.

Gabonese army base at Franceville.[36] After dinner, a thorough debriefing and a bit of sleep, the men and their equipment were crammed into the DC-7. As Jack did not want any of his pilots to be on the ground in Benin he hired a Swedish pilot Bjorg Isberg, who he knew from Biafra, to take the aircraft into Coutonou. When the old DC-7 finally took off just on one o'clock in the morning Jack fully expected it would be the last he would see of his old aircraft.

The attack got off to a good start and one of the assault team made it all the way to the Presidential Palace. Unfortunately, at the last minute, President Kérékou had changed his plans and was not there and the resistance, organised by a crack team of North Korean advisors was much tougher than anticipated. In the end the mercenaries were beaten back. They retreated to the airport and made a hasty departure before the national army was able to catch up with them.

Jack got his plane back and was able to maintain 'plausible deniability' as much of the international condemnation was focused on Denard and his mercenaries. France denied any involvement, as did Morocco and Gabon. Over time the outrage died down, although it does appear that the working relationship between the 'partners' continued. For quite a few more years Affretair's Johannesburg Manager coordinated a lot of military trade between South Africa and Morocco. Morocco purchased a fleet of South African armoured vehicles for deployment into Western Sahara and over the next few years Jack's aircraft delivered a lot of spares and equipment in support of them.[37] Bob Denard, no doubt with the encouragement of Jack, relocated to Rhodesia, where he helped with the command of a French-speaking, ex-Foreign Legion unit known as 7 Independent Company.

Within three days of the failed coup the DC-7 was doing another 'arms run,' this time collecting weapons from the South African armouries in both Bloemfontein and Waterkloof. As for the DC-8, the passenger seats were removed and it was sent to Muscat. The Oman Civil Aviation Department had issued a temporary operating licence so the business was, quite literally, cleared for take-off. The aircraft was registered in Oman and painted with its new Arabic livery. The

36 Jack Malloch's personal flying logbook. Although flight times and durations were noted, no landing destinations were included.

37 Interview with Ian Hunt, Gaborone, Botswana, April 14, 2010 plus personal correspondence dated February 6, 2020.

The Affretair DC-8 re-registered as A40-PA seen at Schiphol airport in its distinctive Omani livery.
Picture taken by Fred Willemsen on April 2, 1977. © Fred Willemsen.

business was registered in Muscat and Geneva with offices in Seeb near the airport. For the official launch of the business Jack invited Rhodesia's Foreign Minister P.K. van der Byl to Muscat to meet with Landon and the Zawawis.[38] Several reciprocal visits were made to Rhodesia as a result.

The sudden appearance of the DC-8 caused quite a stir in Oman, especially within the British intelligence community. They did some digging to find out who really owned the aircraft and that just added to the confusion. They concluded that, "The aircraft is owned by a Swiss company, 'Associated Aviation Enterprises.' It is operated by Air Gabon and leased to Cargoman Limited when required."[39]

Meanwhile, back in Rhodesia, since about 1974 several aviation enthusiasts within the Rhodesian Air Force had been wanting to renovate one of the old Mk. XXII Spitfires. There were a couple in the Military Museum in Gwelo and two that had been displayed on plinths at the gates of New Sarum and

38 Confidential memo from the British Foreign Secretary David Owen to the British Ambassador in Muscat dated December 1977.

39 Confidential memo from the British Ambassador to Oman, Charles Treadwell, to the British Foreign Office dated February 28, 1977.

In January 1977 Spitfire SR64 (PK350) was removed from its plinth and broken down into its main components ready to be renovated. Note the antique 'tommy tin helmet' worn by one of the retrieval crew.
© RhAF Photographic Section, New Sarum.

Thornhill air bases. After assessing their options, the team chose SR64 which guarded the gate at New Sarum. Remarkably that aircraft had been mounted fully intact. With very little flying time on its engine and airframe it was almost brand new. While the team were intent on getting the aircraft back into the air the official view was that it would be too expensive and should just become a static display in the museum.

Undaunted, at the end of January 1977 the project team carefully took the Spitfire off its plinth and stored the pieces in one of the hangers on the base. But before any serious work could be started on the renovation the project team were completely distracted by the upsurge in fighting. Enemy forces were pouring into the country and the Rhodesians had to fight back with everything they had. The project team simply had no time or resources for the Spitfire, and it was left, largely ignored, at the back of the hanger.

Although Jack had not officially been part of the Air Force effort, according to Spike Owens who was heading up the project he had been very influential in getting the senior commanders to agree to even allow the aircraft to be taken off the plinth.[40] The truth was that Jack had long been keen on renovating a Spitfire. Knowing how manoeuvrable they were and the awesome firepower they could deliver, besides the historical importance of the renovation, he felt that the Spitfire could become an effective counter-insurgency ground-attack aircraft. Although he didn't mention these thoughts to anyone else and instead just waited for the right opportunity.

He didn't have to wait long. Within a month there was a formal dining-in event at the Air Force Officer's mess at New Sarum. Jack waited for the after-dinner drinks to settle in and then brought up the subject of the Spitfire. According to Jack's P.A. at the time, "...he came in the next morning and said with a big smile, 'I've got myself a Spitfire!' He was so excited. He was like a dog with ten tails!"[41] In May 1977 a formal agreement was signed between Jack and the Ministry of Defence. It noted that Jack would renovate the Spitfire as a 'flying museum piece' at his own expense, while the Air Force would retain formal ownership of it, once complete, Jack could fly the Spitfire whenever he pleased. Jack asked to use the aircraft on combat missions but that was flatly denied. He decided to get the aircraft flying first before pressing the point.

As a result of van der Byl's meetings with Landon and the Zawawis, "in the spring of 1977 several British contract officers serving with the Sultanate of Oman's Air Force visited Rhodesia to brief Rhodesian Air Force crews on how to avoid Sam-7 missiles."[42] This was extremely valuable learning for the Rhodesians and was highly significant considering that the trainers were in fact British RAF officers.

And it wasn't just the Air Force who were learning new flying skills. Jack's daughter Alyson, who had trained as a medical lab technologist had been transferred to Umtali earlier in 1977. The hospital where she worked was close to the airport and, as she had a bit of disposable income, she thought it would be a good idea to give a few flying lessons a try. "I didn't tell my family and thought I would just go solo to prove I could do it. But I was bitten by the bug

40 'Malloch's Spitfire. The Story and Restoration of PK350.' by Nick Meikle, published by Casemate Publishers. ISBN: 978-1-61200-252-1.

41 Interview with Nori Mann on May 8, 2019 at Thakeham, West Sussex, England.

42 Secret memo to the British Foreign Secretary from the British Ambassador in Oman dated December 1977.

and when I returned to Salisbury I spent every cent on flying until I got my private licence. That was May 1977 just before I turned twenty-one."

Alyson's passion for flying exactly mirrored her father's; "The feeling of achievement, to get that aircraft into the air and down by myself, the feeling of leaving your problems behind and being free, defying gravity and soaring like a bird. You felt you were wearing the plane. I did some aerobatics as well and it was wonderful."[43] When Jack heard that Alyson had gained her private pilot's licence he was extremely proud of her and told everyone in the office.[44] Not content to just have her PPL Alyson quickly went on to qualify as a flying instructor.

Jack was seeing success too. By mid-1977 Cargoman had established itself as the official freight carrier for Oman, and Affretair had their 'second route'. According to Henry Ellert, "Malloch's achievement opened new vistas for the Rhodesians in their sanctions-busting operations and flights into the Middle East were to prove extremely important not only in monetary terms but also in support of the Rhodesian war effort."[45]

This support of the war effort was now of paramount importance as hordes of Soviet and Chinese-trained insurgents were swarming into the country across the borders with Zambia, Mozambique and Botswana.

With little option in this fight for survival, the war now became Jack Malloch's main focus, and he quickly ascended into the highest echelons of military power and decision-making.

43 Personal correspondence with Alyson Dawson, May 5, 2019.

44 Interview with Nori Mann on May 8, 2019 at Thakeham, West Sussex, England.

45 'The Rhodesian Front War. Counter-insurgency and guerrilla war in Rhodesia 1962–1980.' by H. Ellert, Published by Mambo Press 1989. ISBN: 978-0-869224-36-6.

CHAPTER 12

The Rhodesian War: 1977 to 1980

Jack's DC-7, TR-LNZ in its black and green camouflage parked at the side of Salisbury airport runway in mid-1977. It is next to TR-LNY, which by then was being used as a 'spare-bank' to keep the other in the air. This epitomised Jack's operation in the late 1970's: A fine balance between the equally important civilian and military sides of the operation.

Picture from Jack Malloch's private collection. © Greg Malloch

With the upsurge in fighting along all three of Rhodesia's hostile frontiers, the war was putting a heavy strain on the military. In a move to boost its manpower, in January 1977 it was announced that conscription would be increased by three months and men over the age of thirty-eight needed to register for training and service.

As part of this militarisation Jack, at the age of fifty-seven was called up as a reservist to the Rhodesian Air Force. He was given the rank of Flight Lieutenant and was seconded to Number Three (Transport) Squadron. Although the authority and respect he was given far exceeded his lowly 'official' rank.[1] Jack quickly realised that the Air Force, which were limited to a collection of old Second World War-vintage Dakotas, had a critical need for larger transport aircraft. As he now had the CL-44, Jack offered to loan one of his old DC-7s to the Air Force. This arrangement became more or less permanent from early April 1977.

On these military missions the DC-7 was given the Air Force registration number 7230. Interestingly it was also given a South African Defence Force registration number, TLT 907, for exclusively South African military missions. On these assignments Jack would usually fly with George Alexander who was the Commanding Officer of Number Three Squadron.

To begin with much of this flying was shuttling planeloads of Rhodesian soldiers down to Bloemfontein in South Africa to undertake parachute training as Rhodesia focused on building up its airborne assault capability. With these crack paratroops Rhodesia began to make ever larger and more ambitious raids into neighbouring countries to cripple the insurgents' training, and supply facilities. But with this strategy economies of scale started to came into play and the Air Force needed to be able to deploy an ever higher volume of paratroopers. But in the face of modern anti-aircraft weapons, the slow DC-3s were just no longer sufficient.

Jack wondered if the DC-7 could be up for the job. The first challenge was that the DC-7 manufacturer categorically stated that the aircraft was impossible to fly with the side door open which would be a necessity for parachutists. But Jack wasn't too concerned about operating regulations. He had the door removed and took the aircraft for a test flight. It was certainly more challenging to fly, but it wasn't long before he got used to the handling.

Next, he needed some particularly brave soldiers to try jumping out of the DC-7 to see what would happen. There were some terrifying learnings to begin with as Charlie Buchan recalls, "With the DC-3 we jumped using a roof cable, but with the DC-7 the parachutes flipped round the edge of the wing and caught the tail piece, so we moved the cable from the roof to the floor. The first time we

1 'War in the Air. Rhodesian Air Force 1935 - 1980' by Dudley Cowderoy and Roy C. Nesbit. Published by Galago publishing. ISBN 0-947020-13-6.

A sequence of pictures taken from a tracking aircraft monitoring Jack's DC-7 parachute trials. By the position of the floor line this was the last successful trial in June 1977.

Pictures from Jack Malloch's private collection. © RhAF Photographic Section, New Sarum.

used the floor cable we got the full blast of the engines up our arses as we came out. We then ran the cable down to the corner of the doorway with a longer static line so that the parachute opened well beneath the tail."[2]

This was reiterated by one of the Parachute Jumping Instructors who later recalled, "The door was huge compared with the Dak. Drop speed for the Dak was ninety-five knots but the DC-7 would run in at about one hundred and fifteen knots. When we jumped we really felt the blast. Exit position had to be good or you would finish up turning in the slipstream which would cause twisting of the rigging lines during the parachute deployment. This meant wasted time kicking out the twists on the way down, and you had little enough time anyway from the operational drop height of just five hundred feet."[3]

Once these issues had been resolved a training exercise involving a planeload of sixty SAS commandos was organised. After ten run-ins dropping six men at a time the door dispatchers were well versed in how to work within the cargo-configured interior and confirmed they were ready for combat. Jack now just needed an actual operation to test the concept under real battlefield conditions.

Then, suddenly the war became very personal for Jack and the Malloch family.

In June 1977 Blythe's eldest son Dave Kruger was killed along with three other young soldiers when their vehicle hit a landmine in the Binga area. He had been serving with 3 Independent Company of the Rhodesian Regiment. It was the second child that Blythe and Ted had lost so tragically. Then in early August urban terrorism hit Salisbury when a bomb exploded in Woolworth's department store. There were almost one hundred casualties, mostly women and children. With the death of his nephew and the blast in the heart of Salisbury's shopping centre, Jack realised that they were all now on the frontline. Although he was never one for revenge, after this Jack took a much darker view of the war and the need to not just defend themselves, but to start really fighting back.

Although the British government had made every attempt possible to dissuade him, in September 1977 Qais Zawawi, who was the Omani Minister of State for Foreign Affairs, made an official visit to Rhodesia.[4] During the several

2 'A Pride of Eagles' by Beryl Salt. Published by Covos Day Books. ISBN: 0-620-23759-7.

3 Personal correspondence with Kevin Milligan, August 2009.

4 Secret memo to the British Foreign Secretary from the British Ambassador in Oman dated December 1977.

days that he was in the country he held numerous meetings with the Prime Minister Ian Smith, the Foreign Minister P.K. van der Byl and of course with his business partner Jack Malloch, all of which were remarkably productive. To discredit Qais the British complained directly to the Sultan. He simply brushed the matter aside.

While Jack was building his connections with the Omanis, he was also building strong connections amongst the senior Rhodesian Air Force commanders. With the success of his parachuting experiment, a couple of the military planners asked Jack for his opinion on an ambitious plan they were working on. The challenge was that once communist terrorists had infiltrated into the country they spread death and destruction and had to be hunted down individually. It was a classic 'war of attrition' tactic that was grinding down Rhodesia's military resources. Just to sustain themselves Rhodesia needed to maintain a kill ratio of ten to one, but this was difficult. Rhodesia needed to cut the insurgents off at their source where they were concentrated and vulnerable.

The two largest Zanla training and 'staging' camps in Mozambique were Chimoio, ninety kilometres inside Mozambique and Tembue, which was another one hundred kilometres beyond it. These distances made an attack almost impossible and from the outset the decision-makers at Combined Operations rejected the idea as being far too risky.

But Jack strongly believed in the SAS slogan 'who dares wins' and, along with the planning committee felt that with the right deployment of their air assets and a good dose of courage, a successful raid could be made. The distance and audacity of the plan also meant that neither Zanla nor Frelimo, Mozambique's national army, would seriously expect an attack so far from Rhodesia's border. As a result the enemy forces were concentrated in a very tempting target zone.

Eventually, after numerous persuasive presentations the operational plans for both Chimoio and Tembue were finally approved. Jack's role in this was pivotal and according to one of the planners, "...without Jack's personal interest and participation Operation Dingo could not have been undertaken. He was a key player."[5] This is high praise indeed considering the attack on Chimoio and Tembue would end up being one of the most successful cross-border raids of

5 Personal correspondence with Peter Petter-Bowyer, April 21, 2003.

not just the Rhodesian War, but, of any war.

By late October 1977 intelligence reports estimated that the number of fighters at Chimoio had risen to eleven thousand with another four thousand at Tembue. This was five times the number of CTs (communist terrorists) already operating within Rhodesia. If this army of eager insurgents were all to make it across the border there was a real likelihood that the onslaught would overwhelm the country. Jack started work on the intricate logistics and started stockpiling extra munitions. The bombs, missiles and rockets for the air force were brought up from South Africa in the DC-8. These flights were off-loaded at the bottom of the runway by a small team of trusted senior ground staff and taken directly into New Sarum via the 'bottom gate' far away from prying eyes.[6]

The attack had to be made quickly – and before the start of the summer rains as low cloud or stormy weather would compromise visibility and potentially ground the aircraft. Due to sanctions, Rhodesia didn't have access to satellite imagery of the regional weather patterns. These images were beamed down to the Intelsat receiver in Europe and was then transmitted to a network of official receiver stations. Someone in Salisbury, using his own home-made equipment, was able to access this coded signal and download the images, dramatically enhancing the ability of the planners to predict the weather.[7] How Rhodesia was able to pull off this early hacking back in 1977 is unknown, but desperation certainly led to innovation.

While Jack was taking on this more military role at home the business side was growing from strength to strength. According to Nick Meikle, "…it could be said that by 1977 Malloch and ATA were fast approaching their zenith. It was a slick operation and a key element in the Rhodesian effort to thwart sanctions and remain militarily viable. All of this had been achieved on the back of a quarter of a century of Jack Malloch honing his operational and business skills in some of the hottest places in Africa."[8]

There was a lot of legitimate freight work in the Middle East which was financing Cargoman's operations, and those charters were beginning to reach right

6 Personal correspondence with Ian Hunt, February 6, 2020.

7 Personal correspondence with Peter Petter-Bowyer, April 21, 2003.

8 'Malloch's Spitfire. The Story and Restoration of PK350.' by Nick Meikle, published by Casemate Publishers. ISBN: 978-1-61200-252-1.

back into the UK itself. Cargoman had appointed both Air Intergulf of Sharjah and the UK-based Kingsley Aviation Services as agents and by August 1977 the airline had handled their first thirty-eight ton load of British freight.[9] Most of the meat exports were still being handled through Libreville, although a growing amount of Halal-certified meat was also beginning to go to the Omani market. Although Oman was not so much of an export destination and served more as a safe route for imports.

Having convincing, and as often as possible legitimate paperwork for these cargo flights was very important. According to one of Jack's co-pilots at the time, "Flights to the Middle East involved more intrigue. We would fly across Mozambique with the lights off. We would then make contact with an Air Traffic Controller on 'an Indian Ocean island' who got a fee for filing our flight plan as if we originated from his field. We were then legitimised and could proceed normally."[10] Cargos destined for Rhodesia on Cargoman always had genuine paperwork and matching flight plans from Muscat directly to Johannesburg. According to the flight coordinators, "We would then advise Jan Smuts that the aircraft was diverting to Salisbury due to technical problems."[11] From there the suspiciously empty aircraft would continue to Johannesburg to collect their next load.

Flights on the Libreville route north were given the same care. "We covered everything with one genuine waybill. Our paperwork was open to Libreville and then we got a Libreville waybill from there onwards. Sometimes somebody in the Yemeni Embassy in Mozambique did paperwork for us for our Middle Eastern flights. By the end of 1977 we didn't use Swaziland anymore, as European customs had come to realise that Swaziland did not have a beef exporting industry."[12]

Yet it wasn't long before Cargoman also started to take on a military role. Initially the Omanis simply turned a blind eye to the Rhodesians helping themselves to scraps from their own military stores, but over time the support grew to include both training and hardware, remarkably with the tacit knowledge and

9 Middle East Economic Digest, issue of September 30, 1977.
10 Personal correspondence with Brian Meikle dated March 13, 2008.
11 Personal correspondence with Donald Mackie dated March 28, 2010.
12 Interview with Ian Hunt, Gaborone, Botswana, April 14, 2010.

support of the British forces stationed at the Omani military bases.

One of Jack's managers recalls that, "Not all the Brits were against us and we got lots of Hunter spares out of Muscat, Salathat and Thumrat. The British were there on five-minute stand-by, as they were worried that the Iranians would close the Straits of Hormuz. We brought back a whole tailpiece from there once, and I recall another flight that diverted into Thumrat to collect a pile of Hunter wings. The Air Force guys that we took were on the ground stripping the old Hunters of all the parts we needed. The British pilots were sitting in their cockpits ready to go while we were picking up vital parts right under their noses. Jack personally flew those missions."[13] According to 'War in the Air,' "Some aircraft spares were brought in from Oman, often in the original crates marked with the names of the British suppliers. Four spare engines for the Hunters were found in Oman... Six other Hunter engines were recovered from aircraft abandoned by the RAF on a desert airstrip in Sharjah."[14]

As this relationship with the Omanis grew they started sharing their experiences using helicopters against communist terrorists. It was clear these versatile aircraft were the key to rapid deployment and concentrated firepower during contacts. But Rhodesia just had a dwindling collection of old 1960's vintage Alouette helicopters, all of which were taking on more and more battle-damage. The Rhodesians had been impressed with the performance of the Huey's in Vietnam so, very discretely, Landon started making inquiries as to what might be on the market.

Oman was also a conduit to an increasing amount of business in other parts of the Middle East, particularly Iran, where Jack quickly built up a strong and diverse network of connections. As a result, late one night, one of Affretair's flight coordinators received a call from an unexpected executive jet that was about to land. Jack was immediately raised and "he and P.K. van der Byl (Rhodesia's Minister of Foreign Affairs at the time) came hurtling out to the airport." The delegation was from Tehran and had been involved in providing Rhodesia with oil. Now they wanted to explore other trade opportunities. "It

---

13 Interview with Ian Hunt, Gaborone, Botswana, April 14, 2010 and personal correspondence dated April 15, 2019.

14 'War in the Air. The Rhodesian Air Force 1935 – 1980' by Dudley Cowderoy and Roy C. Nesbit published by Galago (1987). ISBN: 0-947020-13-6.

wasn't long afterwards that P.K. had us deliver six pairs of elephant tusks to them. In return we got the Arbor Acres deal which was a two-year contract to supply the entire Chicken House along with twenty-thousand day old chicks every week."[15]

The 'America connection' added an interesting twist to this Arbor Acres deal, as Ian Hunt recalls, "We did a lot of flights into Iran. There was a weekly flight, and then we also set up an industrial scale chicken battery just outside Tehran. We carried everything for them. I remember because Arbor Acres was a big American-owned company, on the waybills for the consignments it said that it was an offence to obstruct the delivery of the consignment according to US Government laws. That was so ironic as according to their own laws it was an offence to deal with us!"[16]

The Iranians weren't the only visitors Jack started to receive from the Middle East. "I remember Qais Zawawi sweeping in through the office doors in his ornate golden robes. Qaboos was the Sultan of Oman, and along with the King of Morocco, was a strong supporter of Rhodesia so we quite often received delegations from Oman, a few were official, but due to sanctions, mostly they were not. They were all such wonderful people. I remember Qaboos' wife never liked him using the title 'Sultan' as she didn't want to be called a 'Sultana'!"[17]

The British were infuriated with this flagrant disregard of their strict policies and U.N. resolutions against Rhodesia. In an internal British Foreign Office report dated September 27th, 1977 they lamented that, "...there is evidence of growing Omani involvement with Rhodesia. Qais Zawawi is known to be personally involved with a major Rhodesian airline engaged in sanctions breaking activity... At this stage we are prepared to take the charitable view that the Omani Government are simply not aware of the implications of getting involved with Rhodesia. We have informed them of our obligation to report suspected breaches of sanctions to the UN Sanctions Committee, but they have as yet shown no disposition to end this link with Rhodesia. This is presumably due to Zawawi's influence in the matter."

While Jack's attention was being divided between the war and the commercial

15 Personal correspondence with Donald Mackie, March 23, 2010.
16 Interview with Ian Hunt, Gaborone, Botswana, April 14, 2010.
17 Interview with Nori Mann, Thakeham, West Sussex, England. May 8, 2019.

needs of the business, the Rhodesian Special Air Service were having remarkable success in the northern Tete Province of Mozambique. In light of this, Rhodesia's military planners decided to redeploy them into the volatile southern Gaza Province, where, according to US Intelligence, Zanla were being trained by more than a thousand Cuban, Soviet and East German military advisors. This accounted for the area having been given the nickname, 'The Russian Front'. The challenge was getting the special forces into the area. It was exactly the type of mission Jack had been waiting for. He suggested a free-fall HALO drop out of the doorless DC-7.

Once again there were reservations. It would be the biggest free-fall operation that the Rhodesians had attempted and just being able to find the right location for the drop was deemed to be almost impossible. That was Jack's role. He had to find the Landing Zone and drop twenty-four men and their heavy equipment in exactly the right spot deep over enemy territory at the dead of night with no moon. Jack, who had an incredible intuition when it came to flying, knew he could do it. At three o'clock in the morning of October 11th, 1977 the twelve-thousand-foot jump was made. The men landed within a few kilometres of the LZ which was described as "an incredible achievement on the part of the pilot." The undercover SAS teams remained in the Russian Front, effectively harassing the enemy until the end of the war.[18] According to Kevin Milligan who was on most of these dangerous parachute deployments, "all the times I worked with Jack I found him to be a terrific character and a privilege to work with. The more challenging the mission, the more he seemed to enjoy it!"[19]

Sadly, in the middle of all this at the beginning of November 1977 Jack's old Fish Air partner Jamie Marshall died. The funeral was held at the Marandellas cemetery and Jack was a pallbearer, along with Jamie's two sons Chris and Tim.

But Jack did not have much time to dwell on the past. With the success of his first SAS mission the commanders started taking Jack's plans for Operation Dingo more seriously. To inflict the maximum number of casualties the Rhodesians wanted to strike the main training camp when all the recruits were lined up on the parade-ground. But the high-pitched whine of the approaching jets would

---

18 'A Pride of Eagles' by Beryl Salt. Published by Covos Day Books. ISBN: 0-620-23759-7.
19 Personal correspondence with Kevin Milligan, August 2009.

compromise the element of surprise. They needed something to mask the sound. Jack suggested a slight change to the DC-8's incoming flight path, timing it to overfly the camp just a few minutes before the strafing jets were scheduled to hit. Over time the residents in the camp "had become accustomed to the sound of the high-flying aircraft because this had been going on for weeks. All homeward bound Air Trans Africa flights had been specifically routed over the Chimoio base in a deliberate move to lull its inhabitants into accepting the sound as routine."[20]

The eventual attack was launched early on November 23rd, 1977. It involved almost every single Air Force aircraft, and almost every single member of the elite Special Air Service, along with almost one hundred hand-picked Rhodesian Light Infantry soldiers. Soon after midnight the helicopters began to assemble. The coordinated attack was due to start at seven minutes past eight, five minutes after Jack's DC-8, to give time for the soldiers to reform in their tightly packed parade ground standing order. At about quarter past seven the massed armada of helicopters, weighted down with shock-troops and extra ammunition, took off. They crossed the border and headed down into the Mozambican plain via a steep-sided river valley.

According to one of the men, "All the helicopters descended to the low ground, initially over abandoned Portuguese farmlands, for the run to target. With helicopters all around and flying low over exquisite countryside, it was hard to fully comprehend that all hell was about to break loose. Halfway to target I saw the DC-7 cruise past on our port side looking quite splendid against the African background. Almost immediately it turned to commence orbits behind the formation of helicopters."[21]

Meanwhile, "The idea of using one noise to cover another worked perfectly. The Zanla men were taking up their places on the parade ground as the Hunters dropped down to release their golf bombs and the Canberras came in fast and low with their Alpha bombs. The helicopter gunships arrived on the scene just

20 'The Rhodesian Front War. Counter-insurgency and guerrilla war in Rhodesia 1962 – 1980.' by H. Ellert, Published by Mambo Press 1989. ISBN: 978-0869224366.

21 Personal correspondence with Peter Petter-Bowyer dated April 21, 2003.

A rare photograph of Jack's old DC-7 seen in its temporary black and green camouflage parked at the far end of Salisbury airport after a long-range paratroop mission.
Picture provided by Bill Sykes. © RhAF Photographic Section, New Sarum.

as this first wave of attack aircraft had gone through the target."[22] Seconds after the first wave of strikes the Hunters and old Vampire jets followed behind the Canberras attacking with their front-guns, rockets and frantan, devastating buildings as the circling helicopter gunships raked the kill zone.

According to Group Captain Peter Petter-Bowyer, "We did not see the air strikes going in southeast of us but landed to prepare to receive the DC-7 drops. The rotors had not yet stopped turning when I spotted the big aircraft already running in from the east. It was two minutes too early, yet the Admin Base protection troops were already peeling out of the huge cargo door before I had chance to call Squadron Leader George Alexander, who was flying second pilot for Captain Jack Malloch. The DC-7 lumbered past and rolled into a slow starboard turn to re-position for its second drop being the fuel drums and palettes of ammunition. On the ground and out of sight five hundred metres away, the troops were gathering up their parachutes"[23]

Meanwhile the first jets, refueled and rearmed, returned to start taking on the

---

22 'War in the Air. Rhodesian Air Force 1935 – 1980' by Dudley Cowderoy and Roy C. Nesbit. Published by Galago publishing. ISBN 0-947020-13-6.

23 Personal correspondence with Peter Petter-Bowyer dated April 21, 2003.

growing list of targets. At times there were as many as four targets lined up for near-simultaneous attention and the whole area was rocked by continual bomb blasts, cannon and anti-aircraft gunfire. The attack went on for a full eight hours. By the end of it even the Rhodesians themselves could hardly comprehend the extent of their victory. By the Zanla High Command's own admission, for the two Rhodesian soldiers killed in the attack the final kill ratio was one thousand to one, while the ratio of injured was about seven hundred to one. For the loss of just one Vampire jet, the devastating attack established the Rhodesian's reputation of near invincibility on the battlefield. With this success, over the next two and a half years thirty more cross-border raids were made by the Rhodesians as they desperately tried to hold back the swelling tide of invasion.

But Jack's role was not over. Twenty-four hours later, after quick repairs to their battle-damaged aircraft, the Rhodesians struck Tembue, codenamed 'Zulu 2' this time two hundred kilometres into enemy territory. During this phase of the attack soldiers were dropped from Jack's DC-7 and retrieved by the Air Force helicopters. But they were right at the limit of the helicopters' range and several couldn't make it home so had to land wherever they could. One ran out of fuel while trying to cross the expanse of Lake Cahora Bassa and landed on a small remote island. Jack was back in the air an hour before first light the next morning. He dropped sixteen more RLI paratroopers to defend some of the scattered helicopters and dropped drums of fuel down to the helicopter that was stranded in the middle of the Mozambican lake.[24]

Through this action Jack had firmly established his reputation as not just a fearless combat pilot, but also as a remarkable military tactician. He was now firmly entrenched into the military establishment, as Nick Meikle so eloquently describes, "ATA was at the forefront of Rhodesian sanctions-busting activities. Even though it was essentially a civilian airline, it displayed a military efficiency in the performance of a strategic role enacted with sublime tactical flexibility. It was rather like Rhodesia's Strategic Air Transport Command."[25]

For these clandestine missions Jack's ground-crews would repaint the DC-7 in dark olive green and black camouflage. "We painted the DC-7 with ordinary

24 Personal correspondence with Neill Jackson, March 9, 2011.

25 'Malloch's Spitfire. The story and restoration of PK350' by Nick Meikle published by Casemate Publishers. ISBN: 978-1-61200-252-1.

The DC-7's old port-side engine explodes into life as it 'takes' in a billowing cloud of blue smoke at the start of its next military mission.

Picture from Jack Malloch's private collection.
© RhAF Photographic Section, New Sarum.

black-board paint, and it quite unexpectedly turned out to be excellent for anti-strela." As they had to use large industrial brooms as brushes, the efforts were very rudimentary. Yet they always ensured that the first big black patch just behind the cockpit was in the distinctive shape of the local dark brown 'dumpie' beer-bottle.[26]

Not all of Jack's flights in the DC-7 were military and during the late 1970s he was regularly contracted to collect prisoners from Buffalo Range to be transported to trial in Salisbury. He would collect them at six o'clock in the morning to get them to the courts on time. Apparently as the aircraft had no seats and the prisoners were mostly dangerous criminals or captured terrorists they were simply manacled to the floor.[27] No doubt this would have constituted another breach of IATA regulations. An easier cargo that Jack was also commissioned to carry was gold and he undertook weekly runs from Salisbury, Bulawayo

26 Interview with Ian Hunt, Gaborone, Botswana, April 14, 2010.
27 Personal correspondence with Hugh Bomford, August 27, 2001.

and Gwelo to the gold depository at the Cam & Motor mine. Once he was also commissioned to deliver twenty motorcycles and a huge gold throne for Emperor Bokassa in the Central African Republic.

While all this was going on Jack's technicians had been making good progress on the rebuilding of the Spitfire. The engine was the key component. Remarkably, the South African Air Force were still using old World War Two-era Shackleton Bombers for their anti-submarine patrols, and those Shackletons used the same twelve-cylinder Rolls Royce Griffon engines as the Spitfire. This meant that the South Africans had all the expertise and spare parts that Jack needed and agreed to fully refurbish the engine for him free of charge. Apparently, this was in appreciation for 'past favours'.[28]

On December 5th, 1977 Angola threatened to intercept any Rhodesian aircraft that strayed into their airspace. This was a concern for Affretair because their aircraft flew over Angola without permission almost every night. Technically they were not Rhodesian as they were registered in Gabon, but Jack and the crews knew that was a technicality. The flights were at four or five o'clock in the morning when it seemed the Angolan air traffic control were fast asleep. Although it was risky the route was almost two hours shorter and saved a lot of expensive fuel compared to the alternative over South West Africa and out over the Atlantic. Jack discussed the threat with his captains and they all agreed it was unlikely to be anything more than bluster.

Over the next three days three pre-dawn flights were made over Angola and with no response from the Angolans everyone began to relax. On December 19th Jack was captaining a flight in the DC-8 from Salisbury to Libreville. This time he had the Rhodesian Minister of Defence onboard who was going on a hunting trip to Gabon. A few minutes after they had quietly slipped into Angolan airspace, Jack received a crisp, curt radio message from Luanda ATC stating that they entered Angolan airspace and were required to land in Luanda. According to the flight engineer, "We did a smart 180 over Vila Luso and were out of their airspace in less than 10 minutes."[29]

For the next week all flights were routed around Angola. But no-one was happy

28 Person correspondence with Lister Pollard, July 29, 2008 and with Donald Mackie, March 30, 2010.

29 Entry in Henry Kinnear's flying logbook.

with the wasted time and money. The last day of December 1977 was Captain Mike Gibson's birthday. On that day he had a flight to Port Gentil and back in the 'Paddle-steamer' as the CL-44 had been named. After careful thought, Mike let his boss know that he was going to try the Angolan route again. The flight crew assigned to Mike that day were Flight Officer Chris Reichman and Flight Engineer Malcolm Porter.[30]

The trip to Gabon was uneventful, but not so the trip back. Halfway over Angola in the gathering dark of evening the Angolan Air Traffic Controller informed Mike that fighter aircraft had intercepted them and that they must land at Huambo or they would be shot down. With little choice Mike agreed and slowly turned towards the new bearing. Mike and Chris informed the ATA office and tried to see if there were indeed any fighters on their tail. With the high tension neither thought to wake Malcolm who was asleep in the tail.[31]

As they neared their new destination the cloud cover increased. Seeing his opportunity Mike slightly adjusted his course to go straight into one of the cloud banks. A minute into the cover he turned hard south and dropped altitude expecting the impact of air-to-air rockets at any moment. Nothing happened and as soon as they cleared the clouds he dropped right down to the deck to get beneath the radar. It was almost half an hour of high tension before they crossed into the safety of South West African airspace. It was a while before Affretair tested the Angolan route again, and when they did, Jack, who had an extraordinarily sharp instinct for danger, was the first to try it.

The Angolan issue meant that the Oman route became ever more viable. Yet Jack was worried about its direct links back to Rhodesia. Back in early 1977 he had started looking for a neutral secondary market that would be an acceptable 'staging post' for the airline. He was looking for another Libreville that would be able to 'launder' the Rhodesian link.

The Seychelles was the obvious choice and Jack started reestablishing his contacts there. In March 1977 he met with the civil aviation authorities and started negotiating landing rights. Just as they were about to finalise a deal the government was overthrown. Landing rights were denied and Jack was

---

30 Entry in Mike Gibson's flying logbook.

31 Personal correspondence with Mike Gibson dated June 20, and August 20, 2009.

blacklisted as an ally of the previous regime. This left just Mauritius, but they were not prepared to risk their tourism and sugar industries to support Rhodesia. The hope had been that when Bob Denard had installed Ali Soilih in the Comoros in late 1975 that would have created a stable pro-western state. It hadn't turned out that way. In 1977 Soilih was back in power but, seduced by the Russians, he had embraced an anti-western, anti-Rhodesian stance.

Meanwhile Jack was talking to his new Chief Executive, Mr. Finlay about the challenge of finding a suitable 'stepping-stone' for their eastern route. Finlay, who had been appointed by the Government at the beginning of 1977 to represent their interest in the airline was an ex-director of the Reserve Bank and head of the Rhodesian Commercial Organisation, ACCOR. As a result he was very well connected and understood the importance of balancing the country's political imperative, central financial oversight and commercial free-enterprise, all of which Jack appreciated.

As Bob Denard was involved in the business, and knew the area well, they brought him into the discussion. He divulged that he was working with the ex-Comorian president Ahmed Abdallah on a plan to get him back into power. Bob suggested that the Rhodesians support the coup which would ensure the ex-President's favour. It all seemed a bit audacious, but the more Jack thought about it the more it made sense. He brought the idea up with some of his friends at Combined Operations and they were equally intrigued. Under the codename 'Operation Atlantis' Bob started putting his plans together, and this time he had the help of some of the world's most battle-hardened military planners who had an entire national army at their disposal.

One of the first people Denard approached for his command team was his old deputy Jean-Louis Domange. But Jean-Louis turned him down. He explained that he was now fully committed to President Bongo and Affretair, where he had got to understand his role in the business and had gained the respect of the captains and crew. According to Mike Gibson, "We knew Jean-Louis's history of course (being an infamous hijacker), but I actually admired and liked the little former mercenary-turned-station-manager. He was highly intelligent and was actually using a computer for business and flight planning at his office which was almost unheard of until the mid-1980s.[32] Jean-Louis had successfully made the transition to civilian life. He did still have his dark side though; "Jean-Louis was up to all sorts of things. He had a weapon in a suitcase. I remember he invited me to his home and showed it to me. It was a very serious sniper rifle that wasn't meant for hunting anything but humans."[33]

With the war growing in intensity Ian Smith continued to search for an acceptable political solution. In early March 1978 these efforts culminated in the signing of the Internal Constitutional Agreement. This was signed by Smith and the moderates Bishop Abel Muzorewa and the Reverend Ndabaningi Sithole. This agreement determined that there would be majority rule in Rhodesia by the end of 1978 and just three weeks later a multiracial transitional government was established. As majority rule had always been the fundamental requirement of Britain, Smith hoped that this transition to black leadership would compel Britain and the US to help the country defend itself against the communist hordes who were hell-bent on total destruction. Once again Smith, and the country as a whole, would be disappointed.

Meanwhile, after a full year of meticulous planning, in March 1978 Bob Denard launched 'Opération Atlantide.' Under the guise of being on an offshore seismic research vessel Bob and his band of fifty carefully trained mercenaries left Lorient and sailed past the Canary Islands, around the bulge of Africa and down to the Cape of Good Hope. Meanwhile a Johannesburg-based commodities trader by the name of Jeff Stephens was approached by the French who said that President Soilih of the Comoros needed food, particularly meat, to quell growing unrest. To pull this deal together, which appears to have been financed by France, Stephens contacted Jack Malloch and the Rhodesian Cold Storage Commission, "both of whom were delighted to have a market so close."

During the course of April and early May Jack did about ten meat flights into Moroni with Jeff. "We always flew directly over Mozambique with no lights and complete radio silence. We hoped for cloud cover so the vapour trail would not be visible. Departure was normally three o'clock in the morning, arriving at six o'clock with the one hour time difference."[34] In addition to the business

32 Personal correspondence with Mike Gibson dated August 10, 2009.
33 Interview with Ian Hunt, Gaborone, Botswana, April 14, 2010.
34 Personal correspondence with Jeff Stephens, February 9, 2008.

itself, they were useful reconnaissance trips and Jack relayed anything that he thought would be of benefit back to Bob Denard.

Yet Denard and his heavily armed 'seismic researchers' were not the only mercenaries plotting an overthrow. In mid-May 1978 Jack's old friend Mike Hoare met with Gonzangue D'Offay a former Seychellois cabinet minister. During the meeting Mike presented his second, revised coup plan for the take-over of the Seychelles and the restoration of ex-President Mancham. Although Jack appears to have been unaware of it, the plan included the use of his aircraft.[35]

The day after Hoare presented his plans, Denard and his heavily armed specialists executed theirs, landing on the beach of Itsandra on Grand Comore. With this green-light Jack took off from Salisbury in the DC-7. This time it was back in its civilian livery so as not to arouse suspicion, even though it was loaded with battle-ready SAS and Rhodesian Light Infantry soldiers. These commandos were reinforcements just in case Bob had unexpected difficulty in seizing control of the islands. They were not needed. Within four hours the capital Moroni had been secured and Ali Soilih had been captured. The DC-7 landed unopposed and the Rhodesians ended up doing nothing but bartering cigarettes for crayfish.

According to one of Jack's coordinators the coup had been sponsored by the French, South African and Rhodesian governments. They were afraid that the Russians would intercede and overthrow the Comoros, as they had done in the Seychelles, so Jack established a radio back-up for the mercenaries in case there was a counter coup. "Every morning at six a.m. they called us on the Single Side Band radio to say, "Robin Air, All Okay." If you heard nothing you were to phone 'Boss Jack' and reinforcements would have been immediately flown in. The call sign 'Robin Air' was very English so was used to avoid any French association."[36]

"The day after the coup we went in with a full load of supplies including forty-four-gallon drums of petrol for the Mercs. You knew when there was something funny happening when you saw the crew with Jack – George Alexander used to fly with him often on these 'smersh' trips, as well as Mike Gibson and

35 'The Seychelles Affair' by Mike Hoare, published by Corgi Books. ISBN: 0-552-12890-2.
36 Personal correspondence with Donald Mackie, March 28 and 30, 2010.

Colin Miller. All captains in their own right but when on a 'funny' they were sitting in the right-hand seat with the Old Man in the left one."[37] By this stage, Jack's employees were commonly using the term 'smersh' to describe these 'James Bond' type missions. Smersh was the Soviet counterintelligence agency that featured in Ian Fleming's early 007 books. The name was formed from two Russian words which roughly meant 'death to spies.'

Quickly Jeff renegotiated his contract with Bob and the 'Foreign Legion' though much of this trade was hinged on Bob's personal friendship with Jack and on their second flight into Moroni Bob invited Jack and Jeff to stay over. "Bob had actually married a couple and we were invited to the wedding breakfast at a restaurant someways up the volcano. I sat next to a Belgian mercenary who told me in halting English that just two weeks earlier he had been a wanted man and now he was the Minister for Defence!"[38] Such were the fortunes of those soldiers-for-hire in the early 1980s.

The coup in the Comoros was not the only 'Smersh' operation that Jack was doing in partnership with the French. Chad had been losing ground to the Libyan-backed Frolinat rebels and with their capital N'Djamena at risk, the French sent in a Marine infantry brigade and eight Jaguar attack aircraft. A week after Denard had taken over the Comoros the French were ready to attack the rebels in Chad. But they needed to quickly and discretely build up their reserves of jet fuel first. Jack suggested a quick 'wet wing' shuttle. The idea was to fly the DC-8 with full tanks of fuel from Libreville to the French base where the excess fuel could be siphoned off for the Jaguars.

But there were dangers, and Jean-Louis got wind of some possible intrigue. To make sure everything went according to plan he personally went on the flights – and took his suitcase rifle with him. Just before landing he assembled the weapon and, the entire time they were on the ground, he sat in the cargo bay door carefully supervising what was going on with the powerful scoped rifle cradled in his arms. It sent a strong message that Affretair were more than capable of looking after themselves and were not to be messed with.

This added drama mystified some of Jack's crew. As far as they were aware they

37 Interview with Ian Hunt, Gaborone, Botswana, April 14, 2010.
38 Personal correspondence with Jeff Stephens, February 9, 2008.

had flown into the desert base, stayed on the ground for an hour or so with Jean-Louis pointing his gun at everyone, and then flew off again. Although it didn't take the Affretair crew long to find their own little business opportunity in this strange arrangement. "During those trips the pilots and crews did a huge trade in small arms, bringing them back into Rhodesia where there was a real shortage of weapons for personal protection. The guys would buy them for almost nothing and we would bring them back in the aircraft's hold."[39] Over the last two weeks of May 1978 the French were able to rout the rebels and secure the central government. Although two of the Jaguars were shot down, along with the old French DC-4 F-BBDD that Jack had used during the Biafran airlift.[40]

At three o'clock in the morning of May 24th, 1978, with a twenty-ton load of oranges and potatoes the old Paddle-Steamer took off from Salisbury airport heading north for Port Gentil. The crew was Captain Tom Philips, First Officer John Murphy, Flight Engineer Les Martin and the Loadmaster was Malcolm Porter. Jack, who had been talking to the technicians on the VHS radio, heard the distinctive turboprop pass over his house. 'The Old Man' was reputed to never sleep and had both HF and VHF radios at his bedside. "The aircraft would call us every hour on the hour, and this was all recorded in a book. 'Boss Jack' would contact us regularly wanting to know where the aircraft were – He lived every flight, day and night. If you didn't receive a call from the aircraft without fail 'Boss Jack' would phone and ask, 'Where's the aircraft?' – You needed to have a good answer."[41]

By the time they got to Victoria Falls they still had not received approval of their flight plan through Angolan airspace. This was not unusual and on many previous occasions they had crossed Angola without formal permission. According to Malcolm 'Tom Philips was not unduly concerned' but the Angolans were being unpredictable so it was an issue. "There was great debate as to whether they should fly over Angola. Jack was there and said that it was up to the captain. So they went."

But this time things were different. "As the flight progressed the Angolans' increasing interest in the 44 worried the First Officer. Repeated requests were

39 Interview with Ian Hunt, Gaborone, Botswana, April 14, 2010.
40 Personal correspondence with Mike Gibson, August 20, 2009.
41 Personal correspondence with Donald Mackie dated March 28, 2010.

made of him to identify the flight plan authority and when none was forthcoming the controller's tone took on a more sinister note."[42] Suddenly out of the darkness a sleek silver delta-winged fighter jet slid into view, pacing the turbo-prop just to the side of the cockpit. It was one of the new MiG 21s that the Cubans had recently deployed to Angola. Then another fighter came into view on the opposite side of the cockpit. On the radio the fighters were demanding a response, but none of the crew could speak Portuguese. They quickly informed ATA of their situation and Jack immediately contacted the Rhodesian Foreign Ministry representative in Libreville.

One of the jets came so close to the cockpit that Tom and Audi Murphy could see the pilot pointing towards the ground. It was a clear signal they were require to land. Tom was afraid their lack of response would be interpreted as non-compliance, so he gave the MiG pilot a big thumbs-up. He then gently rocked the wings in acknowledgment, following the jet westwards towards Nova Lisboa. Tension was high in the CL-44 and Les and Malcolm started rummaging for anything that could link them back to Rhodesia. "We hid everything possible or burnt it in the lavatory. I took off panels everywhere, in the flight deck and in the main cabin, to secrete anything we had that would link us to Rhodesia. The waybill and the Manifest I burnt."[43]

Meanwhile Jack was thinking about the comparative performance of the aircraft. The MiG 21s were notorious for their limited range and had a significantly higher cruising speed than the CL-44. He advised Tom to fly as slowly as possible to force the fighters to orbit and use up their fuel reserves which might give them a chance to escape. As they approached Nova Lisboa the MiGs disappeared, obviously heading back to refuel. The Angolan Air Traffic Control said that there was a Mozambican passenger aircraft coming into land and they would need to circuit until the LAM aircraft had landed.

As they turned on their first circuit cloud enveloped the CL-44. As none of the crew were looking forward to an extended stay in an Angolan jail, Tom took his chance and accelerated away, heading west into the cover. Once through the cloud he dived down into a canyon and "hopping over treetops and skimming

42 'Interception' recollection written by Malcolm Porter.
43 Personal correspondence with Malcolm Porter, April 8, 2003.

around mountains" slowly worked his way towards the South West African border, all the while listening to the excited chatter of their pursuers over the radio.[44] Once out of Angolan airspace the aircraft flew south-east eventually landing in Windhoek on almost empty fuel-tanks.[45] Recalling the incident many years later Malcolm Porter said, "Thanks to the efforts of Tom Philips, we made good our escape – only to do the same trip a few days later!"[46]

However, Tom wasn't the first to go back into 'MiG Alley.' After a thorough debriefing, and delivering his thanks and appreciation to Omar Bongo, the very next morning Jack flew the DC-8 from Salisbury to Libreville taking exactly the same route as the CL-44 had the day before. The difference was that Jack left on time. There were no further MiG incidents, but the time limit was strictly enforced. If there was any delay it meant taking the long route. There was no negotiation. Both the American CIA and the South Africa BOSS were interested in this incident which confirmed that the Angolans had in fact received enhanced radar equipment and sophisticated fighter jets – and were clearly eager to use them.

At least there was some good news though. Timothy Landon had managed to find eleven Augusta Bell 205 helicopters through a contact in Israel. He offered to not only organise the purchase, but also to provide the Rhodesians with conversion training onto the helicopter type. In July 1978 one of the DC-8 flights from Salisbury to Muscat had a lot more passengers than usual. They were the first batch of Rhodesian Air Force pilots who were going to familiarise themselves on the Hueys. Within a few weeks the Rhodesians were flying missions on the Dhofar plateau in readiness for Rhodesia.

Although Landon had passed the Rhodesians off as being oil rig contractors,

---

44 Over time, due to the strict secrecy within Affretair, the lack of official records and no doubt the fading of memories, the general belief is that there was one 'MiG incident.' Having exhaustively researched this there were in fact two MiG incidents: One with Mike Gibson on December 31st 1977 and the other with Tom Philips on May 24th 1978. Mike is an extremely credible witness, his incident happened on his birthday, he did not see the MiGs and he was flying south in the evening. Tom on the other hand was flying north in the early morning. The MiGs also left an indelible impression on his entire crew who were interacting with the MiG pilots. There is no doubt these where two distinctly different and separate events.

45 Interview with Ian Hunt, Gaborone, Botswana, April 14, 2010 and personal correspondence with Ian Hunt, April 21, 2019.

46 Personal correspondence with Malcolm Porter dated May 15, 2009.

just over a year later the magazine 'New African' broke the story. They claimed that the Rhodesian Air Force pilots spent all their time in Oman with British soldiers on secondment to the Sultan of Oman's army. "The British taught the pilots everything they had learnt in fourteen years of warfare using helicopter gunships against guerillas."[47] Ian Hunt was obviously right when he said that 'not all Brits were against us.' According to Henry Ellert, "After the familiarisation programme the aircraft were carefully dismantled, crated and flown to Salisbury on board the Cargoman DC-8."[48] After significant repairs, early in 1979 the first of the helicopters, locally nicknamed 'the cheetah', entered service – and started to make a significant difference on the battlefield.

Jack was always known for his generosity and as international sanctions and the travel embargo further constrained his fellow Rhodesians, Jack was acutely aware of just how valuable air travel was. If there was space available he would willingly allow employees and friends free passage on his flights in to Europe which they would otherwise be unable to do.

But having passengers on sensitive flights often led to dangerous situations that added a great deal of complexity and tension for the crews. In 1978 at the height of the tension between Rhodesia and Angola and soon after the second MiG incident Affretair took a contract to deliver meat into Luanda. To hide their Rhodesian origin they filed a flight plan supposedly coming from Madagascar.

Cacho Cabral recalls what happened next, "On descent the Angolans made it clear they knew we were coming from Salisbury. We decided to play it clean and not deny it. Since I speak Portuguese I talked to the people on the ground. They were kind and treated us well and allowed us to depart without any problems after we had offloaded the consignment." Fortunately the bewildered family who had hitched a ride on their Rhodesian passports were able to hide in the back of the cargo hold and weren't caught. Although it was a nerve-wracking experience for everyone and Cacho admitted that they "…did not do a second flight into Luanda until after the sanctions issue was resolved."[49]

John Pack, who was a fire officer at Salisbury Airport up until 1978 related

---

47 October 1979 edition of the 'New African' magazine.

48 'The Rhodesian Front War. Counter-insurgency and guerrilla war in Rhodesia 1962 – 1980.' by H. Ellert, Published by Mambo Press 1989. ISBN: 978-0869224366.

49 Personal correspondence with Cacho Cabral, December 18, 2007.

another more dramatic incident; "Jack flew my family and I, along with our car to Schipol Airport via Oman when we left Rhodesia to go back to the United Kingdom. That flight was also a bit 'Alastair Maclean' as we hit a bird and damaged an engine so had to make an emergency landing in Brazzaville. The local security wanted to take me and my family off the aircraft, the pilot informed Jack by radio and apparently Jack said no to our being taken off the aircraft and ordered the pilot and crew to take off without ATC permission. We all had our hearts in our mouths until we had got out of Congo airspace in case we had been pursued."[50]

As soon as Bob Denard and his men had secured the Comoros Jeff Stephens saw the opportunity to turn his short-term contract into a long-term partnership. After a quick negotiation he was appointed to supply the islands with Rhodesian beef and over the next couple of years Affretair did more than one hundred meat flights to the archipelago. According to Jeff, "Jack was closely involved since he already knew Bob. The fact that they knew each other made for easier business with the French Foreign Legion."[51] The Comoros were also valuable for Rhodesia as they needed plausible end-user certificates for their arms shipments. With the internationally renowned mercenary Bob Denard now being the power behind the throne, no-one questioned the increased military expenditure, and the desperately needed hardware began to flow, circumventing South Africa's stranglehold.

But weapons were not the only thing that Jack brought back from the islands.

Early one morning at the beginning of July 1978 one of Bob's men were picking through the night's catch at the fish market on the island of Anjouan and saw a remarkable fish. It was a large stout blue fish with white speckles, measuring just over four foot in length – and it seemed to have short stocky legs. It was a very rare coelacanth, the 'missing link' between aquatic fish and land-based mammals which, according to the fossil record, became extinct about three hundred and fifty million years ago. As soon as Bob heard about it he sent an urgent message to his partner at Affretair.

Once Jack confirmed he was interested in the fish, it was bought, apparently

50 Personal correspondence with John Peck, November 1, 2011.
51 Personal correspondence with Jeff Stephens, November 25, 2009.

for the princely sum of four bottles of liquor. Jack and John Minshull, who was from the Rhodesian Museums Department were then on the next flight to Moroni. With them they had huge cylinders of formalin and whatever else they thought they might need to preserve the extremely valuable specimen. As soon as the thirty-kilogram fish was stabilised in a 75% isopropyl solution it was flown back to Salisbury on the next Affretair flight.

As the Air Trans Africa cold room at Salisbury Airport was being used to stock-pile the latest consignment of weapons the coelacanth was moved to one of the Cold Storage Commission's freezers where a growing throng of the curious, including several groups of schoolchildren, were able to see it.[52] Once in his lab John prepared and mounted the coelacanth in a glass showcase enabling it to be viewed from all four sides. It was a magnificent specimen that became the pride of the Queen Victoria Museum in Salisbury. It was a remarkable scientific feat for a small landlocked country, internationally ostracised and fighting for their lives against all but one of their neighbours.

At the end of July the Rhodesians launched another attack against Zanla's Tembue base in northern Mozambique which had been rebuilt after the devastating attacks of Operation Dingo a year earlier. This attack involved both Jack and his nephew Mike Kruger. Mike was piloting his Alouette III helicopter, attacking targets and deploying ground troops, while Jack was captaining the DC-7, flying in fuel and supplies. The battle had included not just Zanla, but a large contingent of Frelimo soldiers who joined the fray firing a steady barrage of RPG-7 and Strela warheads at whatever aircraft they could see.

Those heat-seeking missiles were particularly dangerous for Jack's big slow DC-7 which was certainly not designed for war. According to Group Captain Peter Petter-Bowyer who was the Admin Base Commander coordinating the attack, "What horrified everyone each time the DC-7 passed two hundred feet above us was the bright flaming of its ringed exhaust system that could not possibly be missed by a Strela in the fast-fading light."[53]

And it wasn't just Mozambique who were pitted against Rhodesia, they were joined by Angola, Botswana, Tanzania and Zambia. Yet within this swathe of

52 Personal correspondence with Paul Sheppard, December 10, 2009.

53 'Winds of Destruction' by P.J.H. Petter-Bowyer, published by 30º South Publishers. ISBN: 0-9584890-3-3.

rabidly anti-Rhodesian 'frontline states' the one little nation that had remained at least moderate was Malawi. However, surrounded by warring states, their economy was vulnerable to the regional unrest. Knowing that they couldn't trade directly with Rhodesia Jack set up a joint venture with Air Malawi to route imports and exports from Blantyre to Libreville, from where they could be delivered into Europe via the DC-8. A couple of Affretair staff from the Commerce Department were relocated to Blantyre to run this operation, including Jon Aird, who was the godson of Jamie Marshall, Jack's old Fish Air partner.[54] Although the volumes on this route were comparatively small, it was a good little profit generator which helped bring in additional income for Jack's Gabon-based business.

As the overall business and the web of sub-businesses continued to develop, so too did Jack's personal reputation; "Jack was a terrific guy in all respects, and I think all the crew would always go the extra mile for him. A really great man who would actually meet you at the bottom of the steps personally after some particular trips. I can't think of any other Airline bosses who would fall into that category."[55] Although it has to be said most airline bosses weren't having their crews chased by Soviet MiGs!

Over the years Jack had moved numerous live animals. There were the regular cattle flights to Angola and planeloads of breeding pigs to Malawi. He flew race-horses to the Durban July, cheetahs to Bongo and a herd of exotic wildlife 'for some Sultan' in the Middle East. In late 1978 he had another challenging 'live' consignment – a huge pack of Irish foxhounds which the Selous Scouts wanted to try out for tracking terrorists. According to the Scout's commanding officer, "I had a vet and he had connections in Ireland so Special Branch gave him a forged passport and off he went to find us some dogs. In the end he got seventy-six, all for free. The Irish donated them to us. Of course, it was Jack Malloch who flew them back for us in the back of his DC-8."[56]

Whether these dogs made much difference of not, every day the war seemed

---

54 Interview with John Fletcher, Johannesburg, South Africa, May 16, 2002, and personal correspondence with Jon Aird dated July 27, 2010.

55 Personal correspondence with Sam Richman dated August 20, 2010.

56 Interview with Lieutenant Colonel Ron Reid-Daly, Simon's Town, South Africa. May 8, 2008.

to get inextricably closer. In mid-August Jack Malloch's nephew Mike Kruger was awarded the Commander's Commendation for bravery while deploying troops into a firefight and then directly engaging the enemy. Just over two weeks later a gang of ZIPRA terrorists armed with a SAM-7 missile shot down an Air Rhodesia Viscount full of holidaymakers. Of the fifty-eight people on board eighteen including the air hostess survived the crash. Five of the passengers decided to go for help, just before the insurgents arrived and murdered every remaining survivor they could find, most of whom were women and children.

Later in a BBC interview Joshua Nkomo, leader of ZIPRA, laughed while taking full credit for the act. This was a savage, bitter war with no quarter and no mercy, which explains why the Rhodesians were so compelled to stand up and defend themselves. It was not a racial war with one group of people trying to dominate the other. It was instead a collective defence against savagery and barbarity dressed up in the guise of fashionable anti-colonial 'liberation'. The fact that there were always more black Rhodesian soldiers who volunteered to join the force compared to white Rhodesians who were conscripted is testament to this little-acknowledged fact.

An interesting point has come to light with regard to this atrocity. During a series of conversations with Eila Bannister, a member of the British political establishment in the 1970s, Eila said that he was meeting with Nkomo in London when the news of the attack broke. Apparently Nkomo was elated, jumping about with excitement saying, "We got him! We got him!" Bannister asked who, and Nkomo replied, "Peter Walls, the head of the Rhodesian armed forces." Apparently Nkomo believed Walls was on the flight and the attack had been orchestrated specifically to eliminate him. In turns out that Walls was indeed supposed to have been on the flight but changed his schedule at the last minute. Mugabe then cleverly used Nkomo's elation to project his rival as a heartless monster.[57]

In addition to developing an alternate source for weapons imports through the Comoros and securing a haul of critical fighter and bomber parts out of the Middle East, Jack had also become very involved in fighting the war itself. He personally participated in cross-border raids and had become a highly

57 Personal correspondence with Eila Bannister, November 25, 2009.

respected military strategist who, from late 1977, was involved in many of the High Command's most audacious plans and proposals. In recognition of this in mid-September Jack was informed that he had earned the Independence Commemorative Decoration 'for rendering valuable service to Rhodesia.' Less than a month later he was recommended to become a Commander of the Order of the Legion of Merit. Although Jack appreciated these awards he was completely distracted by the next big cross-border raid that was being planned.

It was Operation Gatling and it was launched on the morning of October 19th, 1978 with simultaneous attacks against three large ZIPRA terrorist training camps in Zambia. This raid was a reprisal for the downing of the civilian Viscount six weeks earlier. Every single member of the Special Air Service took part, as did Jack's nephew Mike Kruger, several members of Affretair's flying crew, including Captain Chris Dixon who gained international fame as 'Green Leader,' and of course Jack himself who was at the controls of the DC-7 deploying special forces. As two of the three camps were within just twelve miles of the centre of the Zambian capital, the Rhodesians were worried that the Zambian Air Force, who now also had MiGs, would intercede. To make sure this didn't happen 'Green Leader' in a fully loaded Canberra bomber circled the main control tower at Lusaka airport, thus commandeering Zambian air space for the duration of the battle.

By the time Jack got back from his four-hour trip to Lusaka and back, news of the attack was breaking. He quickly changed into his 'civvies' in preparation for the inevitable visitors. As Nori Mann explained, "To illustrate just how much of a hub we had become in the military circles, when the aircraft landed at New Sarum after the Green Leader raid, everyone, including the pilots, came straight to Jack's office. They then played the audio recording of what had happened to everyone who gathered there. There was Norman Walsh who was the Director General of Combined Operations, Peter Walls who was Head of the Armed Forces and Air Vice-Marshal Hugh Slatter amongst others. That was the first time anyone had heard the details of the raid. There was a lot of swearing on the tape though and halfway through Jack apologised to me and said that I did not have to stay. He was such an old-school gentleman."[58]

58 Interview with Nori Mann, Thakeham, West Sussex, England. May 8, 2019.

Jack's secretive and nondescript 'White House' head office building at Salisbury airport, seen under the belly of the old DC-7.
© RhAF Photographic Section, New Sarum.

The final tally for Operation Gatling was fifteen hundred ZIPRA combatants killed and thirteen hundred injured. This, for the loss of one SAS soldier killed and three airmen wounded when a helicopter was hit by cannon fire and downed. Although Rhodesia couldn't afford to lose neither man nor machine, on balance it had been a good day.

In addition to Hugh Slatter and Peter Walls 'always being in the office', other regular visitors to the ATA 'White House' included the Prime Minister Ian Smith. He would "quite often come around as Ian and Jack were good friends. Yet Jack would always call Ian either 'Sir' or 'Mr. Prime Minister'. He had a lot of respect for Ian."[59]

With Jack's growing involvement in the war, he still found time for the Spitfire renovation. The aircraft was taking shape and many of the major components had been pieced back together. Some vital parts were still proving hard to find, especially the massive five-bladed wooden propeller, and of course the 20mm

59 Interview with Nori Mann, Thakeham, West Sussex, England. May 8, 2019.

cannons. Eventually Jack found a company in Germany, who was able to rebuild the propellers. The irony of this was clear to everyone. Apparently this was also done free of charge and the blades were brought back to Salisbury with a load of freight in the back of the Air Gabon Cargo DC-8.[60]

As for the guns, those ended up being actual museum pieces, "The guys from the South African Air Force Museum in South Africa were very helpful. They had a test bed and that was very useful, especially to check the hydraulics. The cannons were also very difficult to find and I think it was the SAAF Museum that finally got them."[61] These guns had become quite an obsession for Jack as secretly he was still very serious about demonstrating the aircraft's ground-attack capabilities. Although he had become very involved in operational flying, he still wanted to actually pull the trigger again.

Meanwhile the ATA Traffic Section and their hard-working loadmasters continued to be challenged by the take-off weight issue. This was compounded by the fact that by the late 1970s it wasn't just the Cold Storage Commission that they had to accommodate. They also had to move regular upfront pre-agreed loads of vegetables for Babliolakis to Europe and live chicks for Arbor Acres to Tehran, neither of which could sustain delays. On the DC-8s it had become common practice to depart four tons over the normal operating limit and most of the captains were now comfortable with the developed procedure. Yet there were still high-adrenalin moments which tested everyone's mettle.

Colin Miller, Horse Sweeney and Mike Gibson were all as relaxed about overweight take-offs as Jack was, although Mike's test was taking-off with an overweight load in the heat of midday, which was far from the norm. It was Chris Nelson's first experience with the fast take-off procedure. He had recently joined the ATA Traffic Office from Air Rhodesia, where even a hundred kilograms over the limit could have resulted in a disciplinary. When he realised the aircraft was four tons over he couldn't believe it and went outside to see if it was possible. Just as the aircraft started to lift there was a distinctive 'whomp' from one of the engines. Expecting an imminent crash Chris rushed into the radio room just in time to hear Mike very calmly call in that he thought he

60 Personal correspondence with Lister Pollard, July 29, 2008.
61 Interview with Nori Mann, Thakeham, West Sussex, England. May 8, 2019.

Jack Malloch receiving the prestigious Commander of the Order of the Legion of Merit award from the acting President of Rhodesia Mr. J. W. Pithey at Government House on December 13th 1978. This was just six weeks after being awarded the Independence Commemorative Decoration (Civil) in November.

Picture from Jack Malloch's private collection. © Greg Malloch.

had had a bird strike, but as all the engines were performing in spec he would be continuing on to Libreville. It was Chris's rite of passage and he quickly realised that Affretair was a very unique operation.[62]

On November 3rd, 1978 Jack was presented with his Independence Commemorative Decoration at Government House in Salisbury. He was the only recipient of this prestigious award. Just six weeks later he was back at Government House again, this time to receive his Commander of the Order of the Legion of Merit award.

Although the 'Green Leader' raid had been a great moral boost for the country, the last few months of 1978 did not go so well and in December Salisbury's main fuel depot was attacked. Driving past the facility a gang of terrorists fired RPG-7 rocket propelled grenades into the massive storage tanks. One explosion set off another and quickly most of the tanks were ablaze. The huge fire raged for over a week, clouding Salisbury in black, oily smoke and twenty-five million gallons of fuel were lost, seriously depleting the country's meagre reserves.

At the end of 1978 Ross Malloch, Jack and Zoe's eldest son, completed his 'O' level exams. With the Rhodesian war in full swing all school-leavers had to do

62 Personal correspondence with Ian Hunt, March 1, 2020.

their military service and in December, Ross duly received his call-up papers. It was something Rhodesian families had got used to. So, at the beginning of 1979 Ross reported for duty to start his basic training in the Rhodesian Army. Knowing that his father had been an associate of David Stirling, the founder of the SAS, and was now very involved in the operations of Rhodesia's 'C' Squadron, Ross volunteered to join the Special Air Service. He was a good shot, loved the bush and was exceptionally fit so did well.

With the war grinding on, casualties up on both sides and petrol rationing being tightened there was not a lot to celebrate as 1978 gave way to 1979. Things were also difficult for P.K. van der Byl's gun-running friend Prince Leka of Albania. Since the death of Franco, the Spanish were increasingly embarrassed by the Prince's gunrunning activities. It is also likely that they were bending to pressure applied by the Albanian government who were worried about Leka's aspirations to try and re-establish the monarchy. When the Spanish authorities raided the Prince's estate in early January and discovered a large cache of arms, they gave him a week to leave the country.[63]

Dave Adams was Rhodesia's representative in Madrid and as soon as he heard about what had happened, he briefed P.K. van der Byl. Dave then phoned John Fletcher and asked if Affretair would be prepared to evacuate the entire Leka household; family, dogs, bodyguards etc., for a fee of one million US dollars. There was always conflict between the commercial and political priorities of the airline. Jack was more interested in the political needs of the country, but they often did not make any money which was frustrating for John. This time the political assignment was going to make them a great deal of money so John quickly agreed to take the offer.

Frantic arrangements were then made to get the Prince and Princess out of Spain before they were arrested. They were flown out on the Affretair DC-8, along with their Thai detachment of bodyguards and with as much luggage as they could carry. But the Prince was worried that the Albanian Government was trying to capture him, and his fears were confirmed when they landed in Libreville to refuel. According to Matthew Sweet, "He ran into difficulty

63 'A Biographical Dictionary of Albanian History' by Robert Elsie published by I. B. Tauris & Co, London. ISBN: 978 1 78076 431 3.

during a stop-off in Gabon, where President Omar Bongo was only persuaded not to extradite him to Albania when Leka's bodyguards threatened to blow up the national airport with a bazooka they happened to have in their luggage."[64]

With the aircraft surrounded by troops and Prince Leka himself brandishing an RPG out of the open door, the tense situation could have ruined Jack's relationship with Bongo. According to John Fletcher while 'everyone was pointing guns at each other' the aircraft was on the ground for four or five hours waiting for the agreed fee to be paid. Eventually, once the payment was received they were able to have the aircraft refueled and cleared for take-off without any further escalation. By early evening they landed in Salisbury, and, after a bit a careful negotiation and gentle coaxing, the entourage nervously left the aircraft and handed over their weapons.

According to Ian Hunt, "I remember going into the engine bay where we used to keep spare engines for servicing and I found the whole room full of rocket-launchers, AK-47s etc. Jack told me to get hold of Inspector Hollingsworth who was the police ballistics expert to make a record of the weapons. There was an incredible amount – he had a small army with him. I remember his own personal collection of guns which was amazing, with some very old and rare handguns. Inspector Hollingsworth was fascinated by them, and I'm sure he would have liked to have kept a few 'samples'. I remember he also had all sorts of insignia and piles of Albanian passports which he was more than happy to give out to anyone who helped him."

The Prince, his Australian wife and their little private army settled in Ruwa just outside Salisbury where they remained until Robert Mugabe won the election in 1980 when they had to flee yet again. "During that time Prince Leka was a frequent visitor to Jack. He was a very tall and charismatic chap. Although obviously quite mad, he was a very useful conduit for a lot of weapons for us."[65]

Those weapons, whether sourced from Prince Leka's connections, the Omanis, Bob in the Comoros or from the South Africans were always brought in by Jack's aircraft. "Whenever they were due to come in I would get an instruction

---

64 'The Man who would be King' by Matthew Sweet, as published in the UK Independent on May 11, 1997.

65 Interview with John Fletcher, Johannesburg, South Africa, May 16, 2002 and interview with Ian Hunt, Gaborone, Botswana, April 14, 2010.

from Jack, to get anyone outside of the small trusted inner-circle off-station. Then the aircraft would come in and park far away from anyone else so we could unload it in secret. I remember the one night I was busy off-loading a smersh delivery and was driving the tractor with palettes of bombs. Jack was looking out of the window of his office and suddenly one of the palettes fell off and broke open onto the tarmac. There was this ominous silence broken only by the loud crunching of the rolling steel bombs on the cement. By the time everyone started breathing again, in his usual understated fashion Jack said, 'You took them off. Now you put them back on.'"[66]

There was little news about Prince Leka's dramatic relocation and the implications of him moving to Rhodesia. The news was dominated instead by the Islamic Revolution in Iran where the growing civil unrest against the Shah had paralysed the country for the last four or five months of 1978. Eventually this forced the Shah into exile on January 16th, 1979. Ayatollah Khomeini was invited back to Iran and in mid-February he officially took power, declaring the country an Islamic Republic. Throughout this turbulent change Jack managed to keep his credibility with his Iranian contacts and kept up with his contractual obligations. As the country quickly shifted to a strongly anti-American stance Jack wondered if there would be opportunities for Affretair as the new government started looking for their own suppliers.

By early 1979 Jack was beginning to struggle with his health issues, and the stress of the endless fighting, both on the battlefront and the sanctions-front was taking its toll. As he got older he also suffered from a stiff back, especially after long flights. Leslie Shaw was a chiropractor in Salisbury who treated him, but the bigger concern was his overall fitness. Dr. Gaskell was the airline doctor so knew of Jack's condition and with each licence renewal that required a medical he was ever more concerned. Jack would hear nothing of it though and insisted that he was fine. Although his heart didn't quite agree.

As Nori Mann recalls, "In those last few years his health wasn't that good. I remember he had a bit of a T.I.A. scare (Transient Ischemic Attack, which is a type of short-term mini stroke). But he said to me that he didn't want to tell Zoe as he did not want to worry her. It meant that he needed to make some changes

66 Interview with Ian Hunt, Gaborone, Botswana April 14, 2010.

though and after the T.I.A. he cut out all alcohol as well as tea and coffee. We tried all sorts of options but the only one that Jack could tolerate was a barley cordial which didn't really help."[67]

In February 1979 a second civilian Air Rhodesian Viscount was shot down just after taking off from Kariba on its way back to Salisbury. This time all fifty-nine passengers and crew were killed. In response, just two weeks later the Rhodesians launched their most daring cross-border raid. Canberra bombers supported by Hunters and Dakotas raided a ZIPRA camp near Luso in Angola. The camp was an incredible two thousand kilometres inside enemy territory where they were protected by Cuban-piloted MiGs and Russian radar installations. The raid was a success and over a thousand enemy soldiers, taken completely by surprise, were killed or wounded. While the raid sent a very powerful message that the Rhodesians could strike back anywhere, Jack was worried that the insurgents had effective shoulder-launched ground-to-air missiles and had already carried out probes not far from the Salisbury airport perimeter. The 'sharp end' was no longer two thousand kilometres away, or even at the far-off rural border-areas. It was pushing right up against the capital city itself.

Another area of concern was that for the first time ever the supply of beef from the Cold Storage Commission was beginning to lag and it was getting difficult to meet the high volume of international orders that were coming in. According to some of Jack's senior staff, up until then "it was the C.S.C. who were funding the operation. But towards the end cash-flow was tight as the national herd had been decimated. This meant our meat volumes were not as high as they had been." Many of Rhodesia's commercial farms had become targets in the war zone which didn't help. Without beef to export, Jack knew it was going to be hard to sustain the flow of critical imports.

To get around this Jack and the Cold Storage Commission started exploring other sources to make up the difference. With some introductions from Jeff Stephens an agreement was soon signed between Tony Hall of the C.S.C., Jack Malloch and Cyril Hurvitz, one of Botswana's great cattle barons. The beef from the Hurvitz Group's vast free-range ranches in the Lobatse area quickly

67 Interview with Nori Mann, Thakeham, West Sussex, England. May 8, 2019.

started subsidising Rhodesia's European orders.

Meanwhile Affretair also started flying prime beef in from Argentina to maintain Gabon's domestic needs. The Argentinians appreciated the business and it wasn't long before Jack was working his way into their circles of power within the military junta. They were anti-communist and had no love of Britain so were more than happy to help the Rhodesians. This new arrangement could have actually added some credence to a letter to the Chairman of the U.N. Sanctions Committee that was sent from the Permanent Representative of Gabon on April 9th, 1979. In it the Gabonese Representative stated, "I should like to reiterate that Gabon does not purchase Rhodesian meat."

In March and April Rhodesia geared up for the national elections. This was a difficult task considering that both Mugabe and Nkomo had decided to boycott and threatened to disrupt the vote, viewing any moderate black person as a sell-out. Fortunately the election, which was held over five days, went off smoothly with little disturbance and no successful attacks. The United African National Council won and at the beginning of June 1979 Abel Muzorewa became the next Prime Minister of 'Zimbabwe-Rhodesia' as the country had been renamed. On the 26th Parliament opened under a new black majority government. To celebrate the occasion there was a nine-Hunter fly-past. This was remarkable considering that the country had purchased twelve of these aircraft in 1962 and were still able to fly nine after seventeen years of service, fourteen years of sanctions, and ten years of almost continual warfare. Earlier that very day these same aircraft had been flying in support of 'Operation Carpet' which was an SAS raid in the heart of the Zambian capital Lusaka. They simply refueled and got airborne again for the fly-past. Such had life, so interwoven with war, become.

South Africa was pleased with this new black government. They saw in Muzorewa the opportunity to build an alliance with a moderate black neighbour-state who could become an effective buffer between them and the more radical Afro-Marxist states to the north. Quickly they reinstated almost unlimited military support and the military planners in Salisbury readily took anything they could get, even integrating the South Africans into their next cross-border raid. This ended up being a joint attack against the Gaza Province of Mozambique. Designated as Operation Uric by the Zimbabwe-Rhodesians and as Operation

Bootlace by the South Africans, the aim of the operation was to sever key transport bridges in the province and destroy a major staging point for the Zanla insurgents.

In July while the plans for Uric were being finalised Jack and George flew eight parachute missions, the closest being just twenty minutes flying time from the airport. With this escalation, the war in the Sahel was also flaring up and the Libyans were advancing into northern Chad again. To contain this invasion the French asked Jack to help with a few more of his 'wet wings' flights to keep their Jaguars in action. The first flight was on the 14th and they took a French Air Force sergeant with them from Libreville to N'Djamena to help with the liaison and translations. Apparently Jack did not charge for this service and told the French it was in appreciation for all they had done for him during the Biafra airlift almost ten years earlier.[68] Although his more commercially minded partners didn't always agree with him this was typical of Jack who would make sure he repaid his debts.

On August 10th, during a raid into Botswana, a Rhodesian Alouette III helicopter shot down a Defender aircraft of the Botswana Defence Force. This was claimed to be the first time that a helicopter had shot down a fixed-wing aircraft. This was an issue for Affretair, as Ian Hunt explains, "We always tried not to antagonise Botswana because we were buying meat from them to make up our required quantities."[69] Fortunately the incident did not interrupt their trade.

The British on the other hand were actively trying to be antagonistic, especially in Oman. Over time they had come to realise that the Omanis didn't care about their sanctions against Rhodesia and did not appreciate any diplomatic pressure to comply. This revealed the depth of support that Jack had managed to build within the Omani political leadership, which, it seems, in just a few short years, had reached the 'Bongo' level. To get around this Britain started putting pressure instead on Shell and BP. Their strategy was to try and cut off Cargoman's fuel supply.

In late October, discussing the fall-out of such a fuel restriction, the Embassy concluded that, "the Omanis would find some way of making the companies

68 Personal correspondence with Henry Kinnear, January 19, 2004.
69 Interview with Ian Hunt, Gaborone, Botswana, April 14, 2010.

suffer. As you know, senior Omanis have taken the line that Oman is a sovereign country and will act as she sees fit. More recently Qais Zawawi, the Minister of State for Foreign Affairs and one of the inner-circle of Oman, closely connected with Cargoman activities, has dropped a pretty strong hint to Shell and BP that they should think very carefully about their wider interests in Oman. ...My view is therefore that, in the event of the companies taking the action envisaged, their interests could be very effectively damaged and that it is certainly on the cards that the Omanis might wish to make them suffer, and in some respects they may welcome an excuse to do so."[70]

The Rhodesians launched Operation Uric on September 1st and the battle lasted almost a full week. It was one of the largest external operations of the war and it significantly changed the dimension of the conflict. With the Zimbabwe-Rhodesian and South African armies on one side and Zanla and the Mozambican army and police on the other, Uric internationalised the Rhodesian War. The deep incursion inflicted a high number of FRELIMO casualties and significant infrastructure damage which dramatically impacted the Mozambican economy. Although the Zimbabwe-Rhodesian negotiators at Lancaster House did not realise it at the time, Mozambique could not sustain this degree of punishment and Samora Machel insisted that Mugabe either negotiate a settlement or vacate Mozambique.

In total Jack flew three DC-7 missions in support of Uric, starting the day before launch when he flew twenty-five South African 'Recce' special forces (designated as 'D Squadron SAS' to disguise their origin) to their staging post at Buffalo Range near the eastern border. By the time the operation was wrapping up Jack was already into the detailed planning of his next daring mission. This time it was Operation Cheese and the plan was to down the longest road and rail bridge in Africa. It was located in northern Zambia and was being used to transport military supplies down from Tanzania. This 'Tan-Zam' rail link was also crucial to the Zambian economy as the only other option was the southern trade route through Rhodesia, and that would only be made available if Zambia stopped providing sanctuary to Nkomo's insurgents. It was hoped this attack would force Kaunda and Nkomo to the negotiating table.

70 Confidential memo from H. J. Tunnell at the British Embassy in Oman to A. Burgess at the Rhodesia Department in London dated October 10, 1979.

The logistics for this audacious attack were tricky though as the rail bridge was almost eight hundred kilometres north of Salisbury, well beyond helicopter range. This Chambeshi Bridge had been identified as a strategic target since 1976, but it was considered too far away and too complex to be achievable. But desperate times called for desperate measures.

While there was no way of getting the team of saboteurs out of the target area, a HALO drop from the DC-7 was the ideal way of getting them in. In early September while the battles of Uric were still raging Jack did a couple of night reconnaissance flights over the bridge to find a suitable drop zone. Once he confirmed the DZ the training for the jump began. The first team of four men were due to be dropped on the night of September 12th, just two days after the start of the Lancaster House talks. Kevin Milligan takes up the story, "As the owner of the DC-7, Jack could make sure he was on all the important missions with it. He thrived on it. He had been on the crew for the training jumps and we were in very good hands. Jack, a well-built man, oozing a quiet confidence, was a legend in his own right and had carried out many daring exploits in his time. Nothing phased him and the men found him considerate and amusing."[71] Unfortunately by the time they got over the target zone after midnight it was obliterated by heavy haze and they were forced to abort the mission. As they needed a clear full moon they had to wait almost a full month for the next suitable opportunity.

Operation Cheese wasn't the only thing not going according to plan. At Lancaster House the inexperience and naivety of Muzorewa and his team of negotiators was beginning to show and they were not able to hold their position, especially against the clever and manipulative Robert Mugabe. They also didn't realise that the British were not as trustworthy as they seemed. Ian Smith tried to warn them from the sidelines, but, buoyed by the overwhelming, and multiracial, support they had received in the last election the new government wanted to prove their own capabilities. Unfortunately, even with their best intentions, they achieved the exact opposite.

By then though most people were numbed by the fatigue of war and could

71 'Operation Cheese. Destruction of Chambeshi Bridges, Zambia.' by Kevin Milligan published on November 15, 2017 in High Above & Far Beyond, the history of the Rhodesian Airforce No. 1 Parachute Training School.

hardly pay attention to the intricacies of the long drawn-out discussions. They knew the horrors of post-Independent Africa and the inevitable purges that would come with it, but everyone was desperate for hope and change. Some saw the writing on the wall and began to plan their departure. Still, for Jack it was a fight to the death, and he kept completely focused on winning the war and keeping his two trade routes open.

On September 27th Jack's nephew Mike Kruger was called upon to evacuate an operational casualty. It was a hazardous operation requiring the casevac to be done right in the midst of an ongoing firefight. As Mike managed it successfully with no regard for his own safety he was awarded the Bronze Cross of Rhodesia. A week later with the full moon on October 3rd, 1979 Jack again flew the four-man SAS 'freefall' team back to the Chambeshi bridge.

According to Kevin, "I was very aware that the DC-7 must have sounded very noisy at eight thousand feet. We were already pushing our luck. I frantically peered out for any sign of the river and the crucial bend, but to my great disappointment, again, nothing. With a very heavy heart I told George to abort. I was so angry and frustrated, but had a final look out of the door. It was like something out of a movie. At just the right time and the right angle, I saw the moon glinting on the river bend that I was looking for, just as it was on the reconnaissance photo. There was little time for the normal flat turn corrections on run-in as I called to George "Come left, come left, harder – steady" then "Go! Go! Go!" and off they went. Straight into the storm. Full flap and undercarriage down to slow the aircraft."[72] It was one thirty in the morning on October 4th.

Paul French, who was leading the initial recce team remembers, because of his heavy kit, just flopping into the slipstream, the brief smell of the engines and then the silence of the free fall. As he turned to face the box of canoes and equipment he could clearly see the reflection of the moon and the dark shapes of the other men. He followed them down to 'pull height' and opened the parachute at two thousand feet as he wanted to be close to the box. Strangely the box was never found and the team, with their reduced kit had to improvise. When considering Jack Paul recalled that "Jack Malloch wasn't young anymore. He was slightly overweight and seemed slow to move, but he exuded a calm confidence born

72 Personal correspondence with Kevin Milligan, March 23 and December 19, 2009.

The Mk. XXII Spitfire being carefully re-assembled in the 'north corner' of the Air Trans Africa hanger in late 1979.

of experience, risk-taking and success. He was a motivated man who appeared to be accustomed to getting his own way."[73]

It is telling that, according to Paul, much of Jack's conversation with the commandos wasn't about the mission, but was instead on how the renovation work on the Spitfire was going. And it was going well. The main parts had been reassembled and with the wings and undercarriage in place it was at last looking like a Spitfire again. By the last months of 1979 the attention was on completing the overhaul of the pneumatic system and completing the cockpit fittings in readiness of the installation of the engine. Although they still couldn't find an original Mk. XXII cockpit canopy…[74]

Five nights later, a South African C-130 Hercules dropped the full twelve-man team of SAS commandos and all their equipment over the Chambeshi DZ.

73 'The Operation that went right' by Paul French.
74 'Malloch's Spitfire. The Story and Restoration of PK350' by Nick Meikle. Casemate Publishers. ISBN: 978-1-61200-252-1.

According to Kevin, "Someone in high places had obviously pulled strings and it was in South Africa's interests too to have Kaunda reined in." At two o'clock in the morning of October 12th the bridge was successfully severed and all sixteen commandos were able to hijack a couple of trucks and drive their way to a designated pick-up spot where the helicopters could reach them.

In mid-November as a sign of good faith Muzorewa's delegation at Lancaster House agreed to cease all cross-border raids. Although the military commanders honoured the agreement they knew it was a disaster. As expected, it allowed both ZANLA and ZIPRA an opportunity to regroup and mass their political commissars and intimidators in readiness of the coming election.

As the Lancaster House talks drew to a close, things began to move very quickly on the political front. Four days after Jack received his CLM award the country became a British colony again, officially reverting back to its pre-UDI name of Southern Rhodesia. Four days after that on December 15th, 1979 the Lancaster House talks were finalized. The agreement was formally signed by all parties on the 21st.

A full cease-fire came into effect a week later in preparation for the general election, and the Commonwealth Monitoring Force arrived to 'supervise the ceasefire arrangements and the transfer of power in Zimbabwe-Rhodesia.' This 'transfer of power' was sadly an inevitability as Britain, who crafted the agreement, had ensured that eighty per cent of the seats in the election could only be awarded to black candidates. This ensured that any multi-racial party could never hold enough seats to influence the future political direction of the country. This was ironic considering that it was Britain who were imposing a purely racial allocation policy on a society that had already become fully multi-racial.

According to the terms of the agreement to contest the election all parties had to; comply with the pre-independence arrangements; abide by the cease-fire agreement; campaign peacefully and without intimidation and renounce the use of force for political ends. To achieve this, all ZANLA and ZIPRA forces were to gather in sixteen 'Assembly Points' to ensure they did not interfere with the campaigning or get involved in voter intimidation.

Of course, with just over fifteen hundred people in the Monitoring Force this was impossible to enforce and Mugabe and Nkomo knew it. They also knew that no matter how grievous the breaches of their supporters, Britain would not forfeit the entire agreement which they had been battling for fifteen years to get. For the 'Patriotic Front' it was really a free rein as the Rhodesian forces, seen by Britain as the enemy, were seriously restricted and closely watched.

According to New Zealand's monitors as detailed in their 'Operation Midford' report, "There were many breaches in the ceasefire as all three sides attempted to gain a position of strength, and large numbers of hard-core guerrillas remained outside the camps and continued to intimidate the electorate. The elections were said to be about giving the black population a free and fair vote, however, many, many black Rhodesians wanted to vote for Ian Smith but were barred from such a vote under the terms of the Lancaster House Agreement. This left a two-horse race, and as Mugabe and Nkomo jostled for power, it became commonplace for hand-grenades to be thrown into the interior of each other's beer halls."

Along with the Commonwealth Monitoring Force the world's news media also flooded into Rhodesia, each trying to find a unique newsworthy story from within the closed, war-torn little country. Remarkably the Daily Express chose to tell the story of "Captain Jack – Hero without a medal." In their editorial they said, "Captain Jack Malloch was the doyen of the Rhodesian sanctions busters, the link man of the intricate spider's web of commercial cross-deals which somehow kept Rhodesia alive for 14 years of economic isolation. Many believe that without Jack Malloch, Rhodesia would not have survived. Until now, Malloch, cloaked his usual life in silence. A small airline venture was the beginning of a career that was to turn him into perhaps the most notorious adventurer in the rugged world of African aviation."[75]

In the middle of all this pre-election drama Jack needed to renew his medical examination for his Gabonese, Omani and Zimbabwe-Rhodesian airline transport pilot's licences. Having been described at the time as "rather overweight and somewhat florid of complexion" Jack knew that Dr. Gaskell was unlikely to pass him again. He patiently waited until the doctor was away and booked an appointment to see a young recently graduated doctor by the name of Robert d'Hotman at New Sarum Air Force base. Jack surmised that the new doctor wouldn't have much knowledge of his deeper conditions so he would have a

75 'Captain Jack – Hero without a medal' article in the February 13, 1980 edition of the Daily Express.

better chance of passing. He was wrong.

Jack's eyesight wasn't as good as it used to be and his Omani medical certificate noted that he was "required to wear correctional lenses and carry a spare pair whilst flying." This didn't bother him, just as long as he could keep flying. But at the end of the medical examination Doctor d'Hotman informed Jack that he was not fit enough to fly, at least not solo, and that he should be grounded – at least temporarily – until he could pass to the required standard.

As Jack had been so focused on flying the Spitfire again, which obviously had to be flown solo, this verdict was simply not going to happen. According to one of his close friends, he "bristled at the temerity of this medic who was young enough to be his grandson. In his well-known forthright manner, he instructed Robert to renew the licence and stop messing him around. Eventually Robert succumbed to the pressure and Jack carried on flying."[76]

Back at Combined Operations Headquarters the senior Rhodesian military planners realised that they had all been duped and that the Lancaster House agreement was just a guise for the solution that Britain had always wanted (though would not have to live with). Considering their desperate situation, they brought Jack into their top-secret discussions. Their greatest fear was that Robert Mugabe, who was seen to be much more radical and anti-white than Nkomo, would, one way or the other, grab power.

If this worst-case scenario were to happen, which considering the level of nationwide intimidation, seemed ever more likely, they came up with a bold and desperate counterplan. It was codenamed Operation Quartz and was built around a couple of possible 'what-if' outcomes of the election. The two main concerns were firstly that Mugabe won, and secondly that he lost but launched a coup to snatch power. The basic idea was that Mugabe would be assassinated with as many of his military leaders as possible to 'severe the head of the snake'. This part of the plan was appropriately codenamed Operation Hectic. Then a simultaneous attack would be launched against Mugabe's ZANLA combatants in the Assembly Points, again, with the aim of killing as many as possible to stifle their ability to regroup afterwards. The Rhodesian forces had proven their excellence at launching devastating blows against concentrated fixed targets and

76 Personal correspondence with Group Captain John Mussell, April 18, 2009.

the assembly points had, at least theoretically, drawn the guerrillas out of the rural communities. The challenge this time was that there were eleven targets to attack, all at the same time, instead of the usual two or three.

South Africa, who were also extremely nervous about Mugabe seizing the country, were brought into the plan and agreed to provide South African Air Force Puma helicopters and C-130 Hercules along with their elite Recce units. The scale of this operation was ambitious and required very discrete warehousing and redistribution of the required stockpile of arms and ammunition to ensure that the Monitoring Force didn't get wind of what was being planned. Air Trans Africa was the ideal facility.

The Special Air Service barracks, known as Kabrit was also at the airport, just down the runway from ATA. It was obviously of particular interest to the British who deployed a contingent of the Monitoring Force there to ensure the special forces were complying with the terms of the ceasefire. To get around this the SAS commanders started to use Jack's boardroom for their operational planning meetings. So, while the Selous Scouts and Special Air Service were quietly deployed and the recently acquired Rhodesian T-55 tanks were carefully positioned, the weapons were brought into Jack's premises.

This was done under the usual cover of a normal freight business. The arms and ammunition were brought in loaded on the same Cold Storage Commission trucks that had always been seen shuttling in and out of the hanger. The only difference was that this time the trucks were driven by disguised CIO operatives. Eventually the ATA freight shed was full of countless boxes of ammunition and pallets stacked high with brand new AK-47s and RPD machine guns. According to Ian Hunt, "I was there supervising the off-loading and storage before it was flown south to Waterkloof to come back after dark in a SAAF Hercules to be dropped to the guys who had made their way in civvies out to the various Assembly Points."[77]

The fear was that the Commonwealth Monitoring Force would somehow discover the growing arms cache inside ATA and security was heightened. "Fortunately the Monitoring Force didn't check up on us throughout that period. Only once we saw a British army officer walking across the tarmac towards

77 Personal correspondence with Ian Hunt dated January 28, 2020.

our hanger so one of the chaps and I quickly went out to meet him before he reached us. We just told him we were purely a cargo outfit and he wandered off and we never saw anyone else again."[78]

With all these preparations for all-out war, there were still remarkable business opportunities to be had. Affretair was trying to become the national freight carrier and with the monitoring force traffic Jack was able to get the ground handling for all the extra aircraft that were coming into Salisbury. According to one of Jack's staff, "at that time we were making more money through ground handling than through our own flying. I remember people saying for all the effort of flying and maintaining our own aircraft, we should have just become a ground handling agent and would have made easier money," although that certainly wasn't in Jack's nature.

Finally, with everything in place the general election was held from February 27th to 29th 1980. It went smoothly and the turnout was good, with many people, especially those in the rural areas, voting for the first time in their lives. Counting of the ballots took a while, but with the success of the election itself all the monitoring force personnel were pulled back to a large tented camp at New Sarum from where the RAF started flying them back home. Meanwhile, with their weapons in hand the SAS, Selous Scouts and South African Recces took up their ambush positions. The aircraft were dispersed and armed, artillery was positioned, and the tanks were ready for their first urban engagements. Everyone was on edge waiting for the results and the broadcast of the codeword 'Quartz' which was to signal the start of the attack.

The election results were announced at nine o'clock in the morning on March 4th.

As everyone feared Robert Mugabe had won. Of the eighty black seats in the hundred-member House of Assembly, Mugabe's Zimbabwe African National Union (ZANU) won fifty-seven seats. It was confirmed that Mugabe would assume power as the country's next Prime Minister.

The general population was stunned. The rural population quickly started changing their allegiance to avoid the inevitable reprisals, and the special forces braced for their attack command.

It never came.

---

78 Interview with Ian Hunt, Gaborone, Botswana, April 14, 2010.

Jack was sitting in his office tuned into the radio waiting for the order. As the minutes ticked away his whole world started unraveling as reality started to kick in.

Nori Mann was in the office with him. "I remember that day that the election result was announced and it was official that Mugabe was going to take over. Jack was devastated. He was sitting at his desk and he just had his head down in his hands. I felt that if I went to console him he would burst into tears. I couldn't even pour him a drink, and the horrible barley water wasn't going to help, so I just sat their quietly. It was terrible. Jack knew that his country and everything that he had been fighting for had been lost."[79]

General Walls aborted the mission at the very last minute. Apparently, he went to the Highlands Presbyterian Church on Enterprise Road in Salisbury and sat there for a few hours trying to decide what to do. His great fear was that when the South Africans moved their flying column up into the country from Messina, under the pretext of securing the escape route for white civilians, the Russians and Cubans would counter-attack. Nkomo had assured Walls that his ZAPU and ZIPRA troops in Zambia and Angola would stop this from happening. But Walls didn't trust Nkomo and the whole thing was poised to trigger a major international war.

In the end Walls decided to pull the plug.

It was all over.

The country and the cause were both lost forever.

79 Interview with Nori Mann, Thakeham, West Sussex, England. May 8 2019.

CHAPTER 13

Zimbabwe, Iran-Contra and the Mk. XXII Spitfire: 1980 to 1982

A painting of Jack flying the renovated Mk. XXII Spitfire JMM by the artist Andre du Plessis.

Reproduced with permission. © Andre du Plessis.

For all Jack knew he was going to be declared an enemy of the state and rounded up with anyone else who had actively supported the old regime. His first priority was to get rid of the remaining weapons that were still being held on the Affretair premises that would have implicated them in the 'Quartz Plot'. The only weapon he retained was the loaded 9mm pistol that he had always kept in the bottom drawer of his office desk. His justification for it was that "I have made some enemies around the world and that is why I need to have this handy!"[1]

A day after the election result was announced Mugabe issued a statement to the stunned nation. Rather unexpectedly he called for peace and reconciliation, saying that, "We are beginning a completely new chapter with the hope that there will not be any victimisation of anybody for political reasons." He went on to pledge not to impose any sweeping nationalisation of private property which, although still very skeptical, Jack was relieved to hear. It was enough to calm the panicking population and allowed for, at least, the beginning of a peaceful transition.

But Jack and many of the military leaders who had been primed and ready to launch Operation Quartz couldn't understand why their most daring plan to finally, and decisively win the war had been withheld. In mid-March they went to find solace with their leader Ian Smith, "My old Spitfire colleague, Jack Malloch, our sanctions-buster supreme, dropped in with a few of his SAS friends… They had come to tell me that their whole unit believed they had been betrayed by their leaders. They said they would still follow me, and they were ready to stand and fight if need be."[2] It was too late though. The opportunity had passed and the inevitable had to be faced. The men decided to wait and see what was going to happen.

Needing a diversion Jack focused his attention on the first flight of the Spitfire which was scheduled for Saturday 29th March. In February 1980 the refurbished engine and the massive eleven-foot five-bladed propeller was fitted and a series of ground-run engine tests were made to adjust the carburettor. During one of them a coolant pipe burst. "Jack Malloch was a spectator on the day, wearing his familiar trademark white floppy hat, keeping an eye on things. He was clearly shocked and tried to stop Dave Hann who had raced forward to re-secure the pipes to save precious glycol fluid. Jack was sure Dave would burn himself but fortunately he didn't. Even though a few days were lost, Jack was able to acquire a replacement supply of glycol. In mid-February they had finally

1 Interview with Ian Hunt, Gaborone, Botswana, April 14, 2010 and personal correspondence with Ian, February 16, 2020.

2 'The Great Betrayal' by Ian Smith. Published by Blake Publishing, London, English. ISBN: 1-85782-1769.

managed to find a brand-new Spitfire canopy which was the last critical piece of the puzzle and, along with the four fully functioning 20mm Hispano Suiza cannons, the last phase of the remarkable aircraft assembly was completed. Although the Rhodesian War was now officially over, the guns were carefully zeroed and harmonised to a range of six hundred feet.[3]

In an interview with the Daily Express, when talking about the refurbishment of the Spitfire and the prospect of flying the aircraft again, Jack was quoted as saying that "It'll be the last great adventure."[4] Prophetic words indeed.

Meanwhile the country was feeling the strain of its massive transformation. March 12th was Ian Smith's last day in office. It was less than ten days after the announcement that Mugabe had won the election. By the middle of the month the last members of the Commonwealth Monitoring Force had left the country. Everyone was afraid of just exactly what would come behind them to fill the power vacuum. This dread was accentuated every time soldiers in unfamiliar uniforms were seen on the streets.

The final task that needed to be done before the Spitfire could make its first flight was to paint it in its final colour scheme, but there were two decisions that needed to be made before that could be finalised. The first was whether it should be returned to its original Southern Rhodesian silver finish as it has been in the 1950s, or if it should be painted in camouflage. Although Jack was involved in this discussion no decision was made and in the end it was left to Dave Hann who elected to go with camouflage "in consideration of the current state of Rhodesia, where all military aircraft were finished in camouflage." In the end he opted for the 'European Temperate Day Fighter' scheme which was very similar to how the aircraft had been finished when she initially came off the production line.

The second decision was what numbers, call signs and lettering should be used on the fuselage. There was a misconception that it was Jack's decision to have his initials on the side of the aircraft, but this was not in keeping with his humility and his desire to keep out of the spotlight. Again, according to Dave, "…we waited for guidance…but as nobody was prepared to commit to a call

---

3 'Malloch's Spitfire. The Story and Restoration of PK350' by Nick Meikle. Casemate Publishers. ISBN: 978-1-61200-252-1.

4 Jack Malloch, as quoted in the February 13, 1982 edition of the Daily Express.

Resplendent in its new livery the Spitfire about to taxi out at the beginning of its first flight on the morning of March 29th 1980.
Picture provided by Robert de Maine. © Robert de Maine.

sign, I used JMM (John McVicar Malloch). Once the decision was taken, the apprentices then marked out the signs and masked off the area for painting. When Jack first saw the semi-finished aircraft there was an apprehensive look on his face – I waited for the order to remove the personal touch and would have done so quite willingly but somehow this artwork was accepted. The application of roundel and fin-flashes along with the various warning and instruction signs followed. In a matter of some forty-eight hours, a bare finished aircraft had taken on the look of the majesty of the skies that she really was."[5]

On Friday 28th several hours were spent doing retraction tests and general inspections in readiness of the first flight which had been confirmed for first thing in the morning of Saturday 29th. Jack knew Zoe would be there and thought there might be 'half a dozen' or so others. Yet by half past seven that morning more than two hundred people had gathered to witness the first flight. The First Lady Janet Smith was there with most of the past and present Air Force Commanders, including two Air Marshals, an Air Vice-Marshal, three Group Captains and a Squadron Leader. Within the crowd there were also eleven ex-Spitfire pilots.

5 'Malloch's Spitfire. The Story and Restoration of PK350' by Nick Meikle. Casemate Publishers. ISBN: 978-1-61200-252-1.

A little apprehensive about his unexpected audience, Jack, wearing his original war-time leather flying helmet, squeezed himself into the cockpit and worked through his pre-flight checks with Bob Dodds who knelt on the wing next to him. "Don't do anything spectacular" Bob, who was always skeptical of the aircraft's airworthiness, advised. Jack nodded in acknowledgement. Bob stepped away, the chocks were pulled out from under the wheels and Jack taxied out. He was given clearance and at quarter to eight he took off from Runway 06.

John Fairey, a British national who had volunteered to the Rhodesian Air Force and who had owned his own Spitfire Mk. VIII, set up a portable radio link so he could relay messages between Jack and his engineers. It was just as well, as within the first few moments of being in the air Jack started having trouble. According to John, "...the worst of which was the unserviceability of the Heywood compressor. This affected a number of the Spitfire's controls which were operated by compressed air, including the brakes and the flaps."[6] This resulted in the vintage aircraft suffering a loss of pneumatic pressure which, in turn, caused trouble with the rudder trim.

Although it didn't take long for Jack to get used to the handling of the aircraft as he later said, "When I did the taxying tests I was totally unprepared for its power and responsiveness. It was the first five minutes that bothered me – it took time, but the old feeling soon came rushing back. After that I really enjoyed myself."[7] After thirty-five minutes and a couple of low-level passes just above the heads of the waving crowd, Jack made a perfect flapless landing and brought the aircraft back to the hanger.

There, according to Nick Meikle, "it was time to savour the delight of this incredible achievement. So, the bubbly was poured and as bottles of Cold Duck sparkling wine were handed around, the significance of the achievement began to sink in for Jack Malloch and his engineers. The congratulations flowed and the inevitable questions had to be asked. "Has this been worth all the money, effort and pain?" one of the journalists asked. Jack's reply was simply and unequivocal: "Oh yes, it's been worth every bit of it, every bit of it."

Once the technical issues had been sorted out, during his second flight Jack did a

6 Personal correspondence with John Fairey, June 29, 1998.

7 Interview with Jack Malloch as published in the Sunday Mail on March 30, 1980.

Jack standing on the wing of PK350 cerebrating the success of his first flight in the restored Mk. XXII Spitfire.
© *The Herald / Paddy Grey.*

barrel-roll. From then onwards there was no going back. He immersed himself in the joy of flying the iconic little fighter and took every opportunity to do so. In the run-up to the official hand-over of the country international air traffic increased at Salisbury airport, and when Jack heard that Aeroflot were going to be bringing in a delegation he couldn't help but 'buzz' them as the passengers were disembarking.

According to the Herald newspaper which reported on the incident the next day, "It was all part of the bizarre scene at the airport as white Rhodesian officials, many in uniform, lined the terminal apron gaping glumly at the Russians as they stepped onto the country's soil for the first time. But still most of them cheered in delight as Captain Malloch buzzed the Russians. But a journalist from the Soviet Party newspaper Pravda was not so sure it was funny. Another was said to have paled when he overheard colleagues remarking that the former Rhodesian Prime Minister, Mr. Ian Smith had been a Spitfire pilot during the war." Considering the politics of this, Nick Meikle noted, "We cannot know for sure, but one senses that Jack was only too happy to have achieved his lifetime dream of rebuilding the Spitfire before the country became Zimbabwe…"[8]

This happened on April 18th when Robert Mugabe officially assumed power at a ceremony attended by Prince Charles. In a last-ditch effort to throw the country into chaos and justify an invasion, the South African Special Forces, with the help of a group of relocated Selous Scouts planned to wipe out Mugabe's motorcade on its way to the hand-over ceremony. The plan was to replace the

8 'Malloch's Spitfire. The Story and Restoration of PK350' by Nick Meikle. Casemate Publishers. ISBN: 978-1-61200-252-1.

On April 15th 1980, just three days before Zimbabwe's formal 'Independence,' in what many considered to be a political statement, Jack buzzed the first Soviet Aeroflot airliner to land at Salisbury airport.

© *The Herald.*

large traffic light control boxes that lined the route with powerful roadside explosive devices that would kill everyone including Robert Mugabe, Lord Soames, Lord Carrington and Prince Charles.[9]

At the last minute 'Mac' McGuinness, who had been head of the Selous Scouts clandestine 'Z' Desk, heard about the plot and reported it to the Central Intelligence Organisation. Special Branch raided the safe house that was being used to coordinate the attack. Although the saboteurs had also been tipped-off and had disappeared, the motorcade, and likely the country itself, was saved.

The public remained unaware of any of this intrigue and with much pomp and ceremony the Union Jack was lowered for the last time from Government House in Salisbury. Prince Charles and Lord Soames then headed back to the airport

9 'Assignment Selous Scouts. Inside story of a Rhodesian Special Branch Officer' by Jim Parker. Published by Galago Publishing. ISBN: 1-919854-14-2.

to get out of the country as quickly as possible. Although Soames did ask Jack to give them an unofficial flyby as they were embarking. Jack, who had long since lost his loyalty to the British political establishment, was more than happy to oblige, using the opportunity to do further aileron trim tests.

The depth of this sense of betrayal felt by Rhodesians is hard to over-estimate. Describing this one of Jack's crew recalled, "I remember one night flying south past Paris with an ex-World War Two captain who wanted to take the aircraft and fly it into the Houses of Parliament in London. He was serious and would have done it if I had agreed. Such was the feeling of some of the pilots who had fought for Britain during World War Two."[10] Hannes Wessels very succinctly explains the reason for this deep sense of alienation, "To the best of my knowledge history offers no record of a nation more isolated, ostracised and bereft of allies and no soldiers who fought against greater odds with fewer men or resources as paltry, than those of what was known as Rhodesia."[11] The lesson that Britain should have considered in their dealings with Rhodesia is that even moderate, peace-loving people can be pushed to extreme actions if pushed long enough and hard enough.

Although, on the positive side, with the lifting of sanctions a lot of business opportunities started opening up and to capitalise on this Jack decided, for the first time ever, to openly brand the airline. Having learnt from the Sunday Times exposé back in the early 1970s Jack realised that Affretair, though a bit infamous, was at least well-known in international aviation circles. He decided to rebrand the Harare-based business, which had been known as Air Trans Africa, to Affretair. This was a new and relatively unknown name in Zimbabwe and signified a whole new – and legitimate – rebirth for the business.

One of Affretair's first clients were the United Nations themselves. This was ironic considering that they had spent the last fifteen years trying to destroy Affretair and obviously knew full well that it was the same operation with the same owners. The first contract they gave Jack, which lasted through to the end of 1980, was to fly supplies into Uganda for the U.N. peacekeepers who had been based there since Idi Amin had fled into exile.

10 Personal correspondence with Chris Higginson, November 17, 2007.

11 'A handful of hard men' by Hannes Wessels published by Casemate Publishers, ISBN: 978-1-61200-345-0.

With the growth of this new business Jack was mindful not to neglect his old clients who had supported him over the last decade. The South African military were one of the most important and most loyal of these old supporters. Their need was to have beer delivered to their forces in Katima Mulilo in South West Africa's Caprivi Strip. The gang of 'old hands,' Mike Gibson, Cacho Cabral, Alan Tailor and Ian Hunt were on those flights and relate the drama, "At the time we were changing the livery to Affretair and the DC-7 was just in its pure white undercoat. The closest South African Breweries depot was Salisbury, so we loaded there. As they were already at war with Angola, we went into northern Namibia very low, just above tree-top level with all the herds of wildlife scattering beneath us. When we landed we were greeted by an armoured car and a whole lot of heavily armed troops ready to kill the lot of us. Because the aircraft was pure white they thought we were a U.N. contingent. But when they realised we were just bringing in their beer you'd never seen a faster change of attitude and an aircraft unloaded so quickly!"[12]

Although Mugabe made every effort to assure the white community that they would be welcome to stay in the new Zimbabwe, it was clear that as a revolutionary leader he would be strongly opposed to South Africa. With this rapid shift in political allegiance the South Africans did not want to lose Malloch as well. In early May 1980 the South African Defence Force formally proposed that Jack relocate the airline to Johannesburg. There they promised to set him up to continue, and indeed grow his operation. As Jack was in possession of a South African passport[13] they considered him a national asset worth 'bringing back home.'

While some of Jack's senior managers were keen on the idea Jack himself was hesitant and no longer fully trusted the South Africans. According to John Fletcher, "When Jack did 'funnies' for the South Africans he did them at normal commercial rates even though there was a heavy risk. The South Africans would have paid him ten times the commercial rate. The 'Lieutenant General' was Jack's contact – those guys loved him."[14]

---

12 Interview with Ian Hunt, Gaborone, Botswana, April 14, 2010.

13 Personal correspondence with George de Kulczycki an ex-Rhodesian Immigration Officer seconded to ATA, dated June 8, 2008.

14 Interview with John Fletcher, Johannesburg, South Africa, May 16, 2002.

And it wasn't only the South Africans who were courting Jack. Timothy Landon and the Zawawi Brothers in Oman proposed basing the operation out of Muscat and merging it into the international trading empire they were busy building. Meanwhile Jack's old friend Sir Michael Bishop, who had recently gained a fifty percent stake in British Midland suggested that Jack move to the UK and establish a cargo operation for Midland.

With most people still being in a numb state of political disorientation, the Rhodesian military started to be disassembled as the new Zimbabwe Defence Force began to grow up out of the victor's ranks. Towards the end of May Ian Smith and Jack Malloch attended the final dining-in night for the Special Air Service. Amongst other reasons, Jack was invited because he had flown more SAS paradrops over enemy territory than any other pilot. Interestingly, these had all been done in Jack's privately owned and foreign registered aircraft. It was now a full five weeks since 'independence' and most of the battle-hardened special forces had come to terms with the reality of their situation. The regiment was disbanded a week later and more than half of them left the country as quickly as possible thereafter.

One evening a few days after the SAS function Jack called in to visit Ian Smith at home and, according to the ex-Prime Minister, they "...covered a lot of ground, from the Spitfire to world politics. He had received attractive offers to take his services to other parts of the world, but he was too dedicated to Rhodesia to desert the ship."[15]

Plus of course Jack didn't want to lose the Spitfire which was now technically the property of the Zimbabwe government. Jack loved the aircraft and it had renewed his whole joy of flying. Although it wasn't exactly easy for him, as Nori Mann recalled, "I worried a lot about Jack flying the Spitfire. When he had flown Spitfires in 1944 he was about half the size, and in 1980 he really had trouble fitting into the tiny cockpit. I remember helping Jack commit his pre-flight checks to memory because he literally didn't have the space to hold the checklist card. Sometimes, after he would get back from flying it, his face would be very red. It worried me, but he loved flying that aeroplane."[16]

---

15 'The Great Betrayal' by Ian Smith. Published by Blake Publishing, London, English. ISBN: 1 85782 1769.

16 Interview with Nori Mann, Thakeham, West Sussex, England. May 8, 2019.

The second, and larger, Coelacanth that Jack brought back from the Comoros in late May 1980 on display at the South African Institute of Aquatic Biodiversity in Makhanda (formerly Grahamstown).

Picture provided by Janet Carr. © Janet Carr.

In the middle of all this political and business uncertainty, in late May, while on a flight to the Comoros, Jack was offered another prehistoric Coelacanth. This time it was a bigger one and a half metre long specimen that had been caught just off the main island of Grand Comoro. Appreciating its value Jack immediately bought the fish and organised to have it carefully frozen until he could find a buyer. But with Zimbabwe in a state of transition turmoil no-one was prepared to invest in the fish. Jack put out feelers in South Africa and in the end it was bought by Margaret Smith of the LJB Smith Institute.

Once the Institute had the fish it was decided that they would display it in the South African Institute for Aquatic Biodiversity in Grahamstown. As very few people had seen inside a coelacanth it was decided that the left side of the deep-sea fish would be dissected to show the internal organs. Once the dissection was done the specimen was preserved in a 60% propanol / formalin mix and displayed in a large glass case, where it can still be seen to this day. As for the removed flesh, it was cubed and served to the Institute's board for lunch. They did not like it.

Although the political relationship between the new Zimbabwean government and the Comoros had changed, Jack were still very involved and, by all accounts was fully maintaining his partnership with Denard. According to a commentator at the time, "Abdallah had made Denard Commander of the six-hundred-strong Presidential Guard, effectively elevating him to vice-president. Denard then got South African money to develop Hayaya Airport and persuaded the South Africans that the tourism potential was theirs for the taking. They realised they would be able to use Hayaya Airport as a dispatch and receipt point for their own arms and ammunition trade, so pumped over three hundred million Rand into the project. Jack and Bob were in cahoots in the operation and got money from a variety of sources including Rhodesia, South Africa and Oman to bring the airport up to standard."[17] While this is an interesting claim, and there was certainly a close working relationship between Jack and Bob, there is little evidence that Jack made much money from this. He was not driven by the accumulation of personal wealth and was very much against any form of kickbacks or corruption which he felt had so stifled the development of Africa.

As 1980 progressed the peace seemed to be holding. Although he was still skeptical Jack had to admit that the transition to Zimbabwe had been less traumatic than he had anticipated. Once again, he focused on converting the business into a legitimate cargo airline, but first he had to dispel the rumours of the past. In an interview in the Sunday Mail he adamantly stated, "We operated entirely legally. The meat run was one thing, bringing in arms quite another. One slip would have compromised the whole operation. I made it quite plain from the start – no arms. Not that I ever recall actually being asked to bring any in." As Jack's operations had been so secretive most people took his comments at face value.

With both DC-8s re-branded with the new Affretair livery the business settled down into legitimacy, mainly plying the route to and from Amsterdam through Libreville. But the business out of Oman rapidly dried up. No-one wanted to be involved with the new regime in Zimbabwe, especially after their own war against the communists. Landon nor the Zawawi brothers were prepared to be in partnership with the Mugabe government who were beginning to talk about nationalising 'strategically important' industries, of which Affretair was high on the list.

---

17 Personal correspondence with Ian Dixon dated May 7, 1999.

According to Jed Aird who was posted to the Muscat office, "It was very quiet businesswise and I felt the Omani government would never accept the Mugabe regime. But it seemed that Captain Jack wanted to keep the Oman business open as an option to maybe relocate to if Zimbabwe went the way many feared it might. The 'powers that be' there allowed the office to stay open as a personal favour to him."[18]

After the high pace and high adrenalin of the late 1970s many of Jack's 'old hands' found it hard to adapt to the new business environment and didn't feel the same patriotic commitment to what they were doing. According to Nori Mann "After the government changed the whole business was different. It became terribly legal and terribly boring." She resigned and left later that year along with Colin Miller, John Hodges, Chris Higginson and numerous others. Jack replaced them with willing ex-Rhodesian Air Force pilots such as his nephew Mike Kruger who was looking to make the transition to commercial flying. Jack was also feeling the change of pace, but with the new government now digging into every part of the business, his old clientele, who were all anti-communist, were keeping their distance and finding other options for their 'funnies.'

In mid-August 1980 Jack's Gabonese commercial pilot's licence came up for renewal. He knew he would not be able to beat down the doctor again, so simply ignored the requirement and just kept flying, albeit a bit less frequently. According to Mike Gibson, "In the cockpit he was laid-back, easygoing and let his co-pilots do all the work apart from take-off and landing which he always enjoyed as he didn't get much practice, especially in those later years when the Spitfire became his only flying priority."[19] To ensure that he could legally fly the Spitfire Jack got a student pilot's licence as the medical requirements for a Private Pilot's Licence were not so strict. This most basic certification was sufficient, although it meant that his daughter was now technically more qualified to fly than he was.[20] No further commercial flights were recorded in Jack's logbook after his commercial licences expired, and there were only a few more sporadic Spitfire flights logged. The last of those was on November 7th, 1980. Yet we know he continued to fly the aircraft after that date, and quite

18 Personal correspondence with Jed Aird, August 12, 2010.
19 Personal correspondence with Mike Gibson, August 9, 2009.
20 Personal correspondence with Alyson Dawson, March 10, 2020.

regularly too.

Then, after eight months of transition, things started to get exciting again. In mid-September, Iraq invaded Iran and the Middle East erupted in a major conventional war. Iran had been struggling under a United States trade and arms embargo since the hostage crisis of November 1979. As a result, they were having trouble keeping their American-supplied weapons systems going. Although their air force was strong, they were losing ground to the Iraqi army and needed to find a new source of weapons, and they needed to find it fast.

Through the trauma of the Islamic Revolution Jack had retained his contacts in Iran and continued to do business with them. With the pressure of the war the Iranian military were looking for any opportunity they could find to get around the embargo. A high-level recommendation was made, and they surreptitiously contacted Jack. Looking back on this Ian Hunt recalled, "I remember Jack saying that he had been offered a contract to fly 'air conditioning equipment,' which was his way of saying weapons, from China to Iran. Unfortunately though Jack couldn't get overflying rights from Vietnam and it just became too complicated to make the flight."[21] No matter how hard he tried Jack just couldn't get the Far East to work for him.

Although he was not able to take this first contract, the Iranians were impressed with Jack's honesty, the quality of his advice and the fact that he was obviously extremely well connected in the shady world of international arms dealing. They kept talking and it wasn't long before he was offered a much more valuable contract. Meanwhile his relationship with his new Marxist partners from the Mugabe government was souring, as they were beginning to dig into the business, question his loyalty and interrogate his motives. Although he had committed himself to trying to make Zimbabwe work, he did not like the interference, and particularly did not like the implication that he was now some sort of economic saboteur, or worse, a neo-colonial double-agent.

Gun-running, even for the anti-American Iranians, clearly was not the sort of work that Jack wanted his new government monitors to know about. Very discretely Jack resurrected Afro-Continental. He was the sole proprietor of the business and, using his Israeli secret service contacts, he re-registered the

21 Interview with Ian Hunt, Gaborone, Botswana. April 14, 2010.

Celebrating Alyson's wedding on Saturday January 31st 1981 (from left to right) Jack Malloch, his daughter Alyson, former Rhodesian Prime Minister Ian Smith (in his 237 Squadron tie), Zoe Malloch, the groom Jamie Dawson and former First Lady Janet Smith.

Picture from Jack Malloch's private collection. © Greg Malloch.

business in Israel. Who else was involved in this 'side operation' is not clear but it seems likely that Jean-Louis in Libreville, who also had no love for the new Zimbabwean regime, was at least aware of it.

Although the bigger issue in Jack's life at that stage was the wedding of his daughter Alyson. She was married to James Dawson in Salisbury on Saturday January 31st, 1981. Jamie had been the very first student pilot that Alyson had trained after qualifying as an instructor. Two weeks after the wedding the young couple emigrated to Canada where Jamie had been offered an internship.

Soon after the wedding Jack's Zimbabwe commercial pilot's licence came up for renewal. Once again, he knew he would not be able to pass the medical so ignored the requirement so letting it lapse as well. According to John Fletcher Jack was aware that he had a problem with his heart, and there wasn't a lot he could do about it.[22] His commercial flying days were over and the last Affretair flight that Jack captained was in July 1981.

Although much of Affretair's business was now legitimate and 'above-the-board' Jack's old friends in the CIA still had a need for his 'specialist skills.' This time it was to help with their 'Operation Cyclone,' the clandestine arming of the Afghan mujahideen who were resisting the Soviet forces that had invaded Afghanistan at the end of 1979 and, as usual, discretion was of paramount importance.

Reagan was strongly opposed to the Soviets and dramatically increased the financing of this operation when he assumed the presidency. But getting the weapons into Afghanistan was the challenge and they needed to use an elaborate network of middlemen to obscure America's involvement. Initially the CIA purchased old British Army Lee Enfield rifles from the Indian Army which they smuggled across the Pakistani border, but ammunition was a problem so they decided to send in AK-47s that could use captured Russian supplies.

Jack's role in this was to fly the weapons from Eastern Europe to his contacts in Oman, from where they could be shipped to Pakistan. Oman had long been involved in the arms trade and the logistics were easily arranged. As Jack was hardly flying anymore, he was unable to Captain all of these 'smersh' flights. For the balance he carefully picked crews that he knew he could trust to undertake these dangerous assignments.

It is not known how many of these 'Operation Cyclone' flights Affretair was involved in, but there is record of several, including one that almost ended in disaster.

'Horse' Sweeney did a couple of the flights between Warsaw and Muscat in March 1981. On his second flight it was just getting dark as they were passing over Bahrain and they were beginning to think about starting their decent when a message came through from Flight Control. The traffic controller informed the crew that they had been denied permission to land at Muscat as their point of departure was from behind the Iron Curtain.

Captain Sweeney had no options. He couldn't land anywhere else with a cargo-hold full of weapons that he didn't even have paperwork for. He radioed the airline operations office and insisted that they land at Muscat. He went as

22 Interview with John Fletcher, Johannesburg, South Africa. May 16, 2002.

far as to say that if they found the runway blocked by the time they got there he would simply do a belly landing and hope for the best. Jack quickly started making calls to Landon and Omar Zawawi. Half an hour later he confirmed that they had permission to land, although Horse didn't hear back from the Omani traffic controllers.

As they landed and came to a halt at the designated hanger the aircraft was surrounded by heavily armed soldiers and no-one was allowed off the aircraft. About an hour later a security officer arrived who stated that they had really 'set the cat among the pigeons.' He was able to escort the crew to their hotel while the aircraft was unloaded. The next day they returned to Warsaw where they met with their East German contact to pick up the next load.[23]

In addition to these CIA-funded flights in late March and early April 1981 Jack found himself back into the 'money flight' business. The ex-Cargoman DC-8, which was still registered in Oman, did a series of flights bringing in the new Zimbabwean currency. Although they were dubbed 'COIN' flights, the aircraft was stuffed with millions of dollars' worth of mostly brand-new banknotes, all apparently minted in Germany.[24] When Jack saw the piles of money filling the cargo hold he felt a pang of post-traumatic stress.

Meanwhile the deal that he had come to with the Iranians was for a regular delivery of Israeli weapons flown in from Tel Aviv to Tehran. Understandably the secrecy of this arrangement was paramount. No-one wanted to ever be implicated in it, especially the Israelis and the Americans. It is, no doubt, for this reason that Jack was the linchpin in setting it all up. According to Gustavo Marón, an Argentinian researcher who exposed this operation, "The links and connections between Jack and the American, Israeli and Iranian Intelligence agencies is very robust and explains the role played by Afro Continental during this covert weapons delivery in 1981."[25]

As Affretair had been infiltrated by government spies Jack could not use his own aircraft and needed to keep this operation strictly 'off the books'. To get around this he approached his friends within the Argentinian military who he had got to know through their beef-supply arrangement in the late 1970s. To undertake

23 Interview between Captain James Sweeney and Nigel Hart, September 16, 2014.
24 Entries in Henry Kinnear's flying logbook.
25 Personal correspondence with Gustavo Marón. September 26, 2014.

The Argentinian CL-44 LV-JTN that Jack chartered for the Iranian arms deal in 1981. This picture was taken at Schiphol airport in April 1974 seven years prior to its downing over Soviet territory.

Picture provided by Jo Beeck. © Jo Beeck.

the sensitive flights Jack leased a CL-44 from Transporte Aereo Rioplatense, which was operated by high-ranking Argentine Air Force officers. Hiding this sub-lease deep in the paperwork Jack then set up a complex routing via Cyprus to obscure the Israeli involvement. The operation was fronted by a Scotsman, Stuart Allan McCafferty and a Swiss arms dealer by the name of Andreas Jenni.

With all the pieces in place the flights, between Larnaca and Tehran started in about April or May 1981 with the bulk of the initial cargo not actually being Israeli weapons, but US-made tank spare parts and ammunition. These were actually the very first flights of the now infamous Iran-Contra Affair, and, knowing Jack's connections within the CIA, it is not surprising that he was involved. According to the New York Times, "Reagan campaign officials made a deal with the Iranian Government of Ayatollah Khomeini in the fall of 1980 and… soon after taking office in 1981, the Reagan Administration secretly and abruptly changed United States policy." This allowed secret Israeli arms sales and shipments to Iran to begin later that year.[26]

26 'US said to have allowed Israel to sell arms to Iran' article in the New York Times by Seymour Hersh published on December 8, 1991.

The number of flights made vary depending on the sources, but according to Gustavo Marón, who, having discovered Jack's involvement, I believe is the most credible, forty round trips had been undertaken by mid-July 1981. On these flights the CL-44 purposely made no reference to its real owner or its Argentinian civil registration, LV-JTN. Instead, to obscure its origin, the aircraft flew to Tehran with the flight code KY223 and, for the return leg, as KY224.[27]

Few people knew about these flights and the deep cover seemed to be working, although in early July the flights had come to the notice of the Soviets who asked Israel to explain what they were transporting to Tehran. The Israelis simply ignored the request[28] and there is no evidence that Jack Malloch was even informed about this inquiry.

The Russians were not ones to ignore though, and on July 18th disaster struck. Having made another delivery, the CL-44 was heading back to Cyprus. It appears the crew made a minor navigation error while flying northwest along the Turkish-Azerbaijanian border. They had, unknowingly, drifted some twenty kilometres into Soviet territory.

According to Philippe Domogala this was not a navigation error. He claims that the aircraft had in fact been ambushed by the Soviets who intentionally lured it into Azerbaijanian airspace. He believes that the Russians waited for the aircraft to approach the Iran / Turkish border and they hijacked the VOR frequencies. By using a very powerful transmitter they were able to slightly shift the aircraft's instruments. The crew, who were most likely on autopilot at the time, did not notice the slight turn so were unaware that they were being intentionally pulled into a kill zone.

The Turkish air traffic controllers in Ankara, however, noticed the aircraft drifting toward the restricted border area. They tried to alert the CL-44 but the VHF frequency was jammed and they could not get through to the aircraft.[29] As soon as the CL-44 crossed the border the local Soviet Air Defence (known as the PVO) scrambled four Sukhoi SU-15 supersonic fighter jets (known by

27 Personal correspondence with Gustavo Marón. September 26, 2014.

28 'Profits of War: Inside the secret US-Israeli arms network' by Ari Ben-Menashe. Published by Trine Day. ISBN: 9781634240505.

29 'Famous Aircraft No. 2: Canadair CL44 of Transporte Aero Rioplatense, LV-JTN' article in The Controller, the Journal of Air Traffic Control, by Philippe Domogala.

the NATO codename 'Flagon-E') to intercept the intruder.

It appears the interception was remarkably badly handled with inconsistent procedures, bad communication and incorrect signals to the cargo aircraft which heightened the tension and the likelihood of error and escalation. For a moment the bewildered Argentinian aircraft followed the fighters but, unaware that there was another one on their tail they tried to return to their correct course. Seeing the aircraft turn away the pilot of the trailing Flagon, Captain Valentin Kulyapin, radioed base and said that the enemy aircraft was escaping. At that point he was ordered to 'shoot it down.'

Kulyapin did not have time to open fire. Seconds after the transmission, surprised by the aircraft's manoeuvres, he accidentally flew into the back of the slower cargo plane. The PVO officer ejected while the CL-44, with its right stabiliser cut, spiraled out of control. Stuart McCafferty, Captain Hector Cordero and the other two Argentinian flight crew were killed in the ensuing crash.

Although the Argentinians were outraged, as soon as the aircraft disappeared into the USSR a major cover-up was launched. The Soviets wanted to hide the fact that they had downed an unarmed civilian aircraft and they didn't want their long chain of errors, violations and miscommunications to come to light. The British definitely did not want to get caught up in the diplomatic issue it was causing between the Soviets, Iran, Iraq and Israel. They quickly buried McCafferty and his illegal transportation of weapons, obscuring any British involvement.

Four days later, unable to keep the lid on the incident, the Soviet news agency Tass issued a statement saying that, "An unidentified plane had entered Soviet airspace, failed to identify itself, made a series of dangerous manoeuvres and had finally collided with a Russian plane, then disintegrated and burned up." It was an odd, highly edited admission, but the delay had given time for Jack and the Americans, who had covered their tracks exceptionally well, to quietly slip away before anyone could implicate them.

That is, until almost a full thirty years later when Marón finally got to the bottom of the whole thing. "The name of Afro Continental did not appear in any document or historic reference until I declassified the secret files of the Argentinian Ministry of Foreign Affairs. In a secret encrypted message, the

Argentinian Embassy in Tehran reported the CL-44 flown from Cyprus to Tehran via Turkey was in fact operated by Afro Continental, with no reference to its real owner Transporte Aereo Rioplatense."[30] From there, under the guise of being an Israeli company Jack's involvement came to light. You have to wonder how many other clandestine operations Jack was involved with for either the CIA, or more likely the French Secret Service that have not come to light as yet. There are certainly more than we currently know.

While the downing of the CL-44 was a huge diplomatic issue for the Argentinians they did not blame Jack. In-fact it wasn't going to be long before they were to call on him again as they started to gear up for their long-anticipated invasion of the Falklands.

And they weren't the only ones who were wanting Jack's help. For well over a year Mike Hoare had been working on his plans to overthrow the government in the Seychelles and right from the start he had included Jack in the plot. By mid-September 1981 it was time to actually tell Jack. After a first-hand reconnaissance of the islands Mike flew to Salisbury to meet with him. They had known each other for more than twenty years and Mike had a great deal of respect for the Rhodesian, going on the record to say, "In matters of aviation there was no man like Jack Malloch. He was the most fearless aviator I had ever met."[31] But, as much as Jack wanted to help his old friend, he had a much bigger, and more immediate problem on his hands.

After less than eighteen months in power Mugabe's government now, as a matter of priority, wanted to nationalise Affretair and were putting Jack, who they viewed as an enemy, under serious pressure to hand over the business. Jack explained to Mike that if the government spies who had flooded the operation got wind of the coup-plot they would all be arrested and Mike and his mercenaries wouldn't make it off the tarmac when they arrived in Mahé. But he did put Mike in touch with a local arms supplier and a number of ex-SAS men who were having trouble adjusting to civilian life.

Although Jack was being extra careful the pressure from the government only got worse. A few weeks later when Mike returned to Harare to 'talk arms and

30 Personal correspondence with Gustavo Marón. September 26, 2014.

31 'The Seychelles Affair' by Mike Hoare, published by Transworld Publishers. ISBN: 0-552-12890-2.

aircraft' it appeared that the government were forcibly taking over the company. Although Jack was still positive and promised to help Mike in any way he could, the situation was becoming dire.

Jack realised that there was no place for him or his loyal employees in the new Zimbabwe. If they were going to survive the airline had to be relocated. He regretted having given Mugabe the benefit of the doubt and very discretely contacted his friends in the South African military to see if their offer was still on the table. They were delighted. With the help of Garry Marshall, who was still the liaison with the South Africans, Jack started to formulate his plans for their escape.

Again, this called for the utmost secrecy, but that was something Jack had become a master at. He firmly believed that a secret was no longer a secret if anyone else knew about it. So he never told anyone the full story, and would just give them a small piece of the puzzle which they needed to fulfil their part of the plan. This way no-one could ever see the full picture. The Iran 'air conditioner' flights were one thing, but a relocation of the business and the uplifting of aircraft, employees and their families was quite another. Although it made Jack very uncomfortable, he had no choice and had to bring at least his remaining trusted 'inner circle' into the plan.

Mike Hoare was not so tight with his secrecy and Jack started to hear whisperings in the ex-military circles about the planned coup in the Seychelles. With spies everywhere he was very concerned and in early November informed Mike that he could not be involved. He said he was under surveillance and warned Mike that he was hearing rumours which could alert the authorities. With less than two weeks to go before D-Day there was little Mike could do other than stick to the plan and hope for the best.

Later, during Mike Hoare's trial several mercenaries confirmed Jack's involvement. One said "He was heavily involved in the plot, but pulled out mysteriously about a week or ten days before the operation. I never really found out his reasons." Another echoed this sentiment, stating, "I knew Captain Malloch from Rhodesia and there is no way he pulled out because he got cold feet."[32]

32 'Air Ace link with coup plot' article by Ray Joseph and David Forret in the May 30, 1982 edition of the Sunday Times.

On the evening of Thursday November 20th Jack had a pleasant reprieve. At an event hosted by the Zimbabwe Division of the Royal Aeronautical Society two trophies were presented. Jack was awarded the Pat Judson trophy for 'meritorious service to aviation,' and the Rolls-Royce Trophy was presented to his engineers for their 'technical achievements in aeronautics' for their work restoring the Spitfire. The trophies were presented by Rolls-Royce's Director of Engineering who had flown out especially for the presentation. According to Nick Meikle, "Both of these awards were fully deserved. Jack Malloch had served his adopted country loyally and with great distinction, while his engineers had provided the best possible pool of skills with which to rebuild the Spitfire."[33]

Just five days later, on November 25th, 1981, Mike Hoare, Jerry Puren and his band of 'Frothblower' mercenaries landed in Mahé to launch their coup. But they had been compromised and were ambushed. Just as Jack feared they didn't make it off the tarmac. In the confusion of battle they were eventually able to hijack an Air India 707 and made their escape back to Durban. The South Africans, who did not want to have anything to do with the failed coup, put Mike and his men on trial and sentenced them to jail. Jack was very concerned about his friends but was relieved that he had got out just in time.

Jack's war with the government continued into the New Year, and in early February he was hit with another disaster. Sometime during the lunchbreak on Friday the 6th the CL-44, which was parked just outside the hanger, caught fire. According to Jack's son Greg, who had recently started working as an apprentice at Affretair, "The fire started in the tail and within five minutes had spread throughout the entire fuselage. The smoke was unbelievable. You couldn't see a metre in front of yourself. It took hours to get it under control and by then the aircraft was totally destroyed."[34]

Alan Addison who was a flight engineer on the 44 recalled, "No-one seems to know what happened. It will remain a mystery. The plane was known as 'the Pig' by the ground crew, but I loved that aeroplane. Although I think we got the runt of the litter. There was always something to do whenever you stopped so the ground engineers hated it. Although the more you flew it the better it behaved.

---

33 'Malloch's Spitfire. The Story and Restoration of PK350' by Nick Meikle. Casemate Publishers. ISBN: 978-1-61200-252-1.

34 Personal correspondence with Greg Malloch, February 17, 2020.

A perfectly composed portrait of Jack Malloch passing on his passion for flying to a young child of the next generation.

Picture from Jack Malloch's private collection. © Greg Malloch.

If it came in for a major overhaul, then it would give endless trouble. The fire happened while the aircraft was being serviced. One of the crew were blamed and were accused of having left a smouldering cigarette on the mattress at the back."[35] There was an inquiry, but the cause of the blaze was never determined and no-one was implicated in the incident. But the rumours persisted and even the government-controlled Herald newspaper hinted at the intrigue with their headline, 'Mystery fire guts plane'.

Facing pressure from all sides Jack found consolation in flying the Spitfire. At the controls he felt he could, at least momentarily get away from all the drama, politics and accusations. But not everyone had the same confidence in the little aeroplane. One evening Mike Brough was in the hanger with Bob Dodds admiring the Spitfire. Mike was fascinated with the aircraft having watched Spitfires dueling over his house in the south-east of England during the Battle of Britain.

35 Interview with Alan Addison, Johannesburg, South Africa, March 2002.

Bob was less enthusiastic and sombrely said to Mike, "Mark my words, one of these days Jack is going to die in this aircraft." This was a sentiment shared by Colin Miller, who, in early 1982 was back in Harare on holiday and called in to see Jack. After a couple of reminiscent Scotches, he said "Please Jack, stop flying that aeroplane." The Old Man replied, "My dear Colin I don't take leave and you cannot understand the pleasure it gives me to fly that plane."[36]

A documentary film called 'Pursuit of a Dream' was also being made detailing the renovation. For the final scenes Jack had been asked to do a series of flights for close-up aerial footage. They were fun formation flights with a camera-configured Vampire and really showed off the beauty and majesty of the iconic fighter, so Jack was happy to do them. He also felt that with the impending relocation to South Africa these were likely to be the last flights he would make in the aircraft, so he relished every opportunity he got to fly it.

By mid-March 1982 Jack was almost completely hamstrung in the business with every decision he made being questioned and nit-picked. Yet his old friends were still coming to him for help. Via his CIO confidant Rick May, Jack was approached by the Argentine military who wanted to charter one of the DC-8s to deliver a very important consignment from Cape Town to Buenos Aires. The cargo was 'Exocet air conditioners' and apparently the deal had the approval of the South African Minister of Foreign Affairs himself. Jack was not entirely sure how to organise this. He had wanted to wait until the airline had relocated to South Africa, but the Argentinians were in a hurry and needed the delivery immediately. He couldn't risk Mugabe finding out about it and didn't want to subcontract the flight considering the disaster of LV-JTN just nine months earlier. He decided not to tell anyone else about the contract and continued to mull over it.

At the end of February two Spitfire sorties were flown for the documentary film, but unfortunately there was a problem with the camera and no footage of the flights could be salvaged. Another flight had to be arranged to reshoot the required scenes. Bill Sykes who was overseeing the production wanted the footage to match the scenes they had already taken so specifically wanted a backdrop of cumulus clouds. After weeks of cloudless skies on Thursday 24th

36 Interview with John Fletcher, Johannesburg, South Africa. May 16, 2002.

March the weather report predicted 'isolated thunderstorms to the north of the watershed in the Salisbury area.' It was just what Bill had been waiting for and he quickly organised another filming flight for the next day.

But, surprisingly, Jack was not very keen to fly. It seemed as if he was having another premonition.

His first excuse was that he had an important meeting with the Ministry of Transport in the morning. As tropical storms tended to build up throughout the day Bill said a mid-afternoon take-off would be perfect. Jack then said he had a meeting with the ad agency, Barker McCormac later in the afternoon to discuss new logo options for Affretair. Bill said the flight would be less than an hour so they would be back in time for it. Finally, he admitted he just felt he was getting too old for it, and he knew his blood pressure was through the roof with all the stress the government were putting him under. But after a bit more discussion he agreed to do one last flight. Deep down he knew he would probably need it to unwind after the meeting with the ministry.

As anticipated that meeting, whose main agenda item was the timetable for nationalising Affretair, was in Jack's own words 'difficult'. He just needed to hold off the impatient Minister a little bit longer so they could make the relocation. The trigger for the move was when both DC-8s were going to be on the ground in Johannesburg at the same time, and that was just a matter of days away. With the CL-44 lost and the old DC-7 little more than a flying museum piece there were no other assets to speak of. Although there are rumours that the South Africans had agreed to provide Jack with a pair of new extended DC-8-63s. As Jack knew that his old DC-8s had been financed by government revenues, it would have been against his character to 'steal' them.

The one asset he was sorry to lose was, of course, the Spitfire. Back in 1976 Jack had agreed to the government retaining ownership of the aircraft, and as he always honoured his agreements, the plane had to remain. Although not everyone knew the degree to which Jack took his honour. When, at about lunchtime on March 26th, the Spitfire was pushed out onto the hard-stand in preparation for the afternoon filming flight, one of Jack's senior ground crew actually wondered if the Boss was going to 'make a run in it.' This sentiment was shared by Mike Kruger when he saw Jack flying off later in the day. All this reflects just how close the anticipated escape and the heightened anticipation around that plan was. According to Alan Addision, "I believe the relocation of the business to South Africa was planned for March 28th, just two days after Jack's death."[37]

After trying to relax and refocus over lunch, Jack did a quick flight briefing with Bill Sykes and Neville Weir who would be flying the Vampire. He then got into his flying overalls. "I'll meet you at the presentation" he assured John Fletcher. He then walked outside and climbed into the Spitfire. It was just after three o'clock in the afternoon. Jack knew this was going to be his last flight, so he intentionally savoured each moment, committing as much as he could to memory.

According to Neville, "It was a beautiful summer's afternoon, light winds, a few billowing cumulus clouds, with a cloud base around seven thousand feet. We taxied out together, and, with the wide runway, lined up as a pair. Jack rolled first and shot off into the distance with his far superior acceleration. For me it was the most wonderful experience to see the Spitfire in flight, against the blue sky, flashing past clouds, and at such close quarters… After half an hour or so it came to the point that the Vampire had to return to base due to fuel considerations. We told Jack that we had finished the reel and had to return. He levelled his wings and remained on a steady course. I asked Salisbury Main for a course to steer to base, which was roughly one hundred and eighty degrees to the direction we were heading. Twenty seconds later Jack started a right turn. At that moment we were flying next to a very large cloud – an isolated, towering cumulonimbus. There was sufficient room to do the one eighty right turn. After about one hundred and fifty degrees of turn Jack rolled his wings level, started a gentle descent and flew straight into the side of the cumulus. We followed."[38]

After about fifteen seconds of swirling blackness, heavy hailing and bone-jarring turbulence the two aircraft had a momentary reprieve as they crossed through the vaulted eye of the thunderstorm. Jack knew it had been a mistake to cut through the storm. This towering dark green monster was much bigger and more powerful than anything he had ever encountered before.

As they reached the opposite storm wall Jack braced himself for the impact. In

37 Interview with Alan Addision, Johannesburg, South Africa, March 2002.

38 'Malloch's Spitfire. The Story and Restoration of PK350' by Nick Meikle. Casemate Publishers. ISBN: 978-1-61200-252-1.

Jack being plugged into the cockpit of his renovated MkXXII Spitfire in early 1982.
© *The Herald/Paddy Gray.*

a second he was back into the grey, then the hail and turbulence hit, enveloping Jack in blackness. The noise was overwhelming. The extreme jarring made it impossible to get any read from the spinning dials. Battling to keep any sort of control Jack knew he was being plunged down towards the ground but had no idea of his angle or just exactly where the ground was.

Suddenly the visibility cleared and he roared out of the base of the storm. Although the battered Spitfire was still being pummelled with hail he could see ahead. It was dark.

It was the ground. He was heading straight for it.

He wrenched the control lever back as hard as he could, quickly glanced at his settling instruments. Adjusting the rudder, he brought the wings level and pulled the stick harder, pressing it into his stomach, fighting for every inch of lift he could get.

The rising ground was coming up fast.

A few trees flashed past, then he was over what looked like a scraggly maize-field. 'Thank God it's a mealie-patch' Jack thought to himself, knowing that most of the Goromonzi area he was flying over was covered in rocky granite hills which wouldn't have made for a good crash-landing option.

Jack knew he wasn't going to be able to pull-up in time but hoped he could at least get level. The mealies were a dark green blur filling his view. It seemed as if everything in Jack's life and all the events in his past were becoming concentrated into this swirling moment of high-tension.

He heard the sound of the propeller chopping into the tall crops. There was a sudden hard vibration and then he smashed through a loud barrier of sound into complete blackness.

In that enveloping blackness Jack still felt that he was flying forward. It was as if he had become unrestrained. He wondered if his tight harness had come undone.

Then his thoughts drifted to Zoe and their children, Alyson, Ross and Greg. He had a wonderful family and he felt so proud of them.

Up ahead there was a point of light which he aimed for. His thoughts drifted to his father Vic, and then, as the point of light started getting brighter, he thought about his sister Ruth.

She had died as a result of the tragic roadside fire back in 1937. Such a long time ago.

Yes… It would be good to see them both again too…

CHAPTER 14

The Aftermath: 1982

The impact crater on the edge of a maize field where Jack and his Spitfire finally came to rest on the evening of March 26th 1982. What appears to be a groove from the tail-wheel leads into the crater.

Picture provided by Chuck Osborne. © Chuck Osborne.

When Jack's Spitfire hit the ground it was completely shattered. There was very little fuel left in the aircraft and it was raining heavily so there wasn't a fire-ball. But with the high speed of the aircraft and the extreme impact it exploded into thousands of pieces that were scattered across the darkened, sodden mealie-field.

To give an indication of the severity of the crash, according to the recovery crew the largest piece of wreckage, apart from the undercarriage legs, was a section of the main spar that was just over a metre long. The debris-field spread out

The crash site (in the bottom right corner of this aerial photograph) as it was when Quinton Marais found it on Saturday March 27th 1982. Apart from a scattering of small bits of debris the aircraft had completely disintegrated as a result of the high-speed impact. © *AFZ Photographic Section, New Sarum.*

in a cone-shape from the impact-crater stretching almost right up to the local farmer's little collection of mud-huts in a distant grove of zebrawood msasa trees. The furthest piece of wreckage was found about four hundred metres from the point of impact. It was a two square foot piece of laminated main spar.[1]

As soon as Bill Sykes radioed Salisbury tower that Jack was missing and had likely crashed Chuck Osborne, who was in charge of the Air Force Recovery Section was tasked with leading a team to find him. Due to the lateness of the day they were deployed at first light the next morning. A helicopter positioned Chuck on top of a large granite kopje in the area of Jack's last known position and the search was coordinated with helicopters and fixed wing aircraft from there.

At about midday, having climbed up the high domed hill a young boy arrived at the command helicopter and pointed out the crash site in the valley below.

1 Personal correspondence from Chuck Osborne to Peter Arnold and Bill Musgrave dated December 2002.

A second chopper was vectored in and confirmed the site. That second Air Force helicopter was piloted by Quinton Marais who later recalled, "My memory of the crash site was – no wonder we couldn't find it – we were looking for a Spitfire but this looked like a geological feature or bomb hole with flattened maize, rocky outcrops and short overgrazed grass, and not an aircraft in any way. It was hard to find a major part to confirm it was the Spitfire. And not a sign of life. I remember landing on sloping ground in the Tribal Trust Land not far from a hut and the way the woman by the hut was staring at us the news was obviously bad. …It was a sad affair and a very negative memory."[2] From what Quinton and the other crew saw at the crater they immediately confirmed that Jack had not survived the crash and the search was called off.

Meanwhile everyone at Affretair was devastated. While they hoped he had managed to land safely, everyone knew that it is extremely unlikely. Jean-Louis was on holiday at the time and as soon as he heard the news he immediately raced back to Libreville. He emptied the bank accounts, cleared out the office and deleted as many compromising files and records that he could. While his actions looked extremely suspicious, Jean-Louis was terrified that the Zimbabwe government representatives would arrive at any minute to seize everything. The last thing he needed, for his own safety and that of many of the 'old hands', was for compromising details of their 'side' operations, such as the Iranian contract, the move plan and the negotiations with Argentina coming to light.

Another thing that went missing in those first few days after the crash was the painted brick that Jack used to prop open his office door. Very few people gave the odd, gaudy door-stop a second thought. But the bright paint was reputed to hide the fact that it was actually a bar of pure gold. According to one of the people who related this rumour, "Back sometime between 1980 and 1982 Jack told my mother that if she could pick up the gold bar she could have it. Although she tried desperately to do so, she could not get it even a millimetre off the floor."[3]

Early on the morning of Sunday March twenty-eighth, in two Air Force regiment trucks, Chuck and his recovery team headed north-east out of Salisbury on the

2 Personal correspondence with Quinton Marais dated January 17th and February 2nd 2008.
3 Personal correspondence with Linda McLean dated 13th and 15th March 2008.

Shamva road. After about an hour they turned right into the Chikwaka communal land and found their way to the crash site near the banks of the Nyagui River. This required 'bundu bashing' on the rough tracks that meandered through grassy savannah woodlands. Although the trucks drove considerably further, the site was about sixty kilometres north-east of the airport.

According to Chuck, "We were asked by the Board of Inquiry to locate the guns to give an accurate angle of attack, but after much fruitless digging in the soft, wet ground, the Board told us to stop. At about two p.m. the Board released the wreckage, they instructed us to collect everything, throw it into the crater and fill it in. This was done, except for the engine, which was now a V8 as the front four cylinders had gone AWOL. That was loaded onto the recovery vehicle for further investigation.

There was a lot of dirt thrown by the prop to one side of the crater, which to me showed that it was under power, and this was confirmed the next day when the engined was stripped down.

The final conclusion was the Spitfire had hit the ground with a nose-down angle of about sixteen degrees, with wings level. It was impossible to determine from the instruments what happened, as they were spread far and wide. But I have the feeling that Jack was in complete control because the wings were level. Having spoken to the farmer at the site, I think Jack was trying to get out from under the cloud and heavy rain but ran out of airspace due to the rising ground."[4]

The hardest task for Chuck and his crew was the gristly business of gathering Jack's remains. This disturbing experience would haunt them for the rest of their lives.

With the crash site having been found and it being clear that Jack had not survived the crash news of the tragedy quickly spread. On Saturday evening the Ministry of Defence issued an official statement confirming the loss of both Jack and the Spitfire. The next morning the Sunday Mail headlined their front page with the announcement. The entire country was in shock.

For the next week the bulk of the local Herald and Chronicle newspapers were made up of pages and pages of tiny, black lined condolence notices in their obituary sections.

4 Personal correspondence with Chuck Osborne, dated 15th July 2003.

The Sunday Mail

SECOND EDITION

BOYS' SCHOOLWEAR DEPARTMENT NOW IN STOCK SCHOOL BLAZERS

George Smith

Price 12c

SALISBURY, MARCH 28 1982

ZIMBABWE'S NATIONAL NEWSPAPER

Jack Malloch dies in Spitfire crash

Sunday Mail Reporter

Thousands of people from all walks of life who had been influenced by Jack and who admired him for all he stood for, made their solemn, respectful statements. Most simply said farewell, while many stated briefly how Jack had helped them, all in a myriad of different ways. It was significant how many of the notices were international, from organisations and countries that no-one would have associated Jack with. Yet his influence had spread much further than most people realised.

Jack's funeral was held on Friday April 2nd 1982 at the Garden of Rest Chapel in Salisbury's Warren Hills cemetery. Jack's friend the Reverend Frank Mussell conducted the ceremony. Zoe, Alyson, Ross and Greg, along with the many members of their extended family attended the funeral. They were joined by many hundreds of his friends, employees, business acquaintances and his military and Air Force comrades, all of whom were united in mourning his loss. In his address Reverend Mussell said, "The tragic death of Captain Jack Malloch has brought into bold relief the kind of man that he was, and the many remarkable things he has done in his lifetime. The story of his more dangerous missions during his life will, of course, never be made known. When Jack was on one occasion urged to write his memoirs he smiled and said, 'I've done nothing of note.' He died as he lived, maintaining the high spirit of adventure that never waned all through his many years of aviation." Looking back at this moment Jack's old friend Jerry Puren aptly commented, "Having died in his refurbished Spitfire, it reminded me of a Viking funeral."

One of the more fitting epitaphs written about Jack was penned by Ken Flower the head of Rhodesia's Central Intelligence Organisation. Of Jack he wrote, "A vital aspect of our dealings with the rest of the world in the sanctions game was the air link established by the legendary Jack Malloch. There was no job too small, too remote or too difficult that Malloch would not lend himself to in whatever aircraft could be found... Many of Malloch's exploits must remain shrouded in mystery. But the CIO was aware that he spent much time carrying out dangerous and almost impossible tasks: landing on disused airfields elsewhere in Africa without aids of any sort amidst one shoot-affair after another; carrying arms and ammunition, food and contraband; and evacuating starving or wounded refugees while evading fighter aircraft in foul weather. He would go back time and again to areas where natural or man-made dangers convinced those who needed his assistance that only he could provide it."[5]

Jack Malloch was the last true aviation legend of his generation and his passing was indeed the end of an era.

At the same time that Jack was being laid to rest Argentina launched their invasion of the Falkland Islands. They knew it was a gamble, compounded by the loss of Jack Malloch himself. As John Fletcher later recalled, "Very soon after Jack died we got a call from an Argentinian in Buenos Aries wanting to charter the DC8 to fly a consignment from Cape Town to Buenos Aires. Before the charter was made the Falklands War broke out and the deal fell through. Later it came out that the Argentinians were trying to use us to import Exocets via the South African arms dealers."[6] If Jack had not been killed in the accident it is likely that he would have found a way of making the initial delivery that he had been working on. Considering that Argentina went to war with just five Exocet anti-ship missiles, one more delivery could well have swung the balance of power in their favour.

As noted by Dan Remenyi who visited Bob Nisbet shortly after Jack's death, "The crash had demoralised everyone in Affretair. The shock was palpable and the atmosphere was grim."[7]

And there were more knocks to come.

Just two weeks after Jack's funeral the Zimbabwe Air Force was decimated in a sabotage attack at Thornhill. Half of the country's Air Force aircraft were

5 'Serving Secretly' by Ken Flower published by Galago. ISBN: 0-947020-27-6.
6 Interview with John Fletcher, Johannesburg, South Africa, May 16 2002.
7 'Captain Jack Malloch. The life and times of a Rhodesian Entrepreneur' by Dan Remenyi, published by ACPIL U.K. ISBN: 978-1-910309-19-3.

destroyed, including the Hunters and Hawks. Following this event many of the remaining white Air Force personnel were arrested and tortured. The commonly held belief was that the action was coordinated to purge the Air Force, and the armed forces generally, of their ex-Rhodesian elements.

After simmering unrest between Mugabe's ZANLA and Nkomo's ZIPRA forces which had resulted in uprisings in both 1980 and 1981, an official inquiry concluded that ZIPRA was preparing for war. Whether this was true or not, Mugabe, who had managed to neutralise the ex-Rhodesians, decided that he needed to crush ZIPRA and ensure that the rebellious Matabele didn't challenge him again. In January 1983 the North Korean-trained Fifth Brigade were unleashed. In a prolonged and savage assault thousands of civilians were murdered and maimed in, what became known as, the Gukurahundi genocide.

The country, once so full of potential and hope, spiralled into dictatorship and darkness.

Yet there were still many unanswered questions surrounding the life, and death of Jack Malloch.

The official report and conclusions of the Board of Inquiry have never been released so there is no official ruling on what caused the crash. The only brief paragraph that I have been able to attribute to the report itself dryly stated: "Unable to turn back there was no alternative but to fly into the cloud ahead. Heavy rain was encountered, followed by hail which lasted approximately a minute ... Captain Malloch, in an aircraft much less sophisticated in instrumentation and unpressurised, would have experienced far greater difficulties in the hailstorm. While in the storm the Spitfire crashed, killing the pilot instantly."[8]

No doubt this secrecy has perpetuated the rumours and conspiracy theories that have come to surround the tragedy, although through the many interviews and discussions that have taken place in piecing together this story I believe certain conclusions can be drawn. The main causes that would have been considered by the Board were pilot error, pilot incapacitation, mechanical failure of the aircraft and of course the weather at the time of the accident.

8 Part of a statement issued through the Ministry of Defence by the Board of Inquiry set up to investigate the crash of Spitfire PK350, as quoted in the Sunday Mail edition of June 12 1982.

Putting pilot error aside for a moment, we do know that Jack did have heart trouble and was under massive stress. This was work-related due to the government trying to wrestle his business away from him. It is for this reason that many people felt that Jack probably suffered a major heart attack in the storm and could well have been dead before he hit the ground. I think this is very unlikely as the aircraft appeared to be under control with wings level which would have not been the case if Jack had suffered some type of serious medical issue. It is possible that he might have suffered some type of angina or Transient Ischemic attack triggered by the stress of the storm, but if he did (and there is no evidence to suggest this) Jack was able to maintain control of the aircraft, so it cannot be attributed as the cause of the crash.

Considering the damage that the storm did to the Vampire, some sort of mechanical failure of the Spitfire is also a popular theory. But again, if any critical damage had been done to the aircraft it was only superficial as it was still under control when it hit the ground. Although I do think there is a possibility that some of the more important instruments such as the altimeter and the gyroscope could have been jammed or rendered ineffective in the extreme turbulence. This may have confused Jack as to what his real angle and speed of decent were just before he emerged out of the cloud base. While not the cause of the crash itself, wildly spinning dials could well have been a contributing factor to 'pilot error'.

Although the weather was extreme it also cannot be given exclusive blame for the crash, again due to the fact that the aircraft appeared to be in control when it came out of the storm. But it certainly was a major contributing factor, especially the violent turbulence and the phenomenally strong down-draft which propelled the little fighter so rapidly towards the ground. According to weather experts, along with strong updrafts in powerful thunderstorms you can also get incredibly strong downdrafts with winds of up to a couple of hundred kilometres per hour straight down in a very confined space. This corroborates Bill Sykes' experience of extreme downdrafts in the storm.

There are two other theories that have been rumoured, but which the Board of Inquiry is unlikely to have considered. They are that Jack was sabotaged and killed by the government, or he intentionally chose to commit suicide.

Both of these theories originate from the fact that the relationship between Jack and the Mugabe government had soured to the breaking point. The new government was fully aware of just how much Jack had contributed to the survival of the Rhodesian regime so would have always viewed him as an enemy. While they were certainly not above assassinating their enemies there is no evidence that this was the case with Jack.

If the Mugabe government had wanted to get rid of Jack (which I am sure they were thinking about, and perhaps were even plotting) they would have simply nationalised the airline and forcibly taken it from him. If he had complained or caused trouble they would have then imprisoned him. They had no need to orchestrate a complex 'crash' to get what they wanted, especially on a day when numerous variables (such as the weather) were completely out of their control.

This leaves the question of suicide. This theory stems from that moment when Jack inexplicably turned and flew straight into the thunderstorm instead of continuing to fly around it. While this was a questionable decision, we are not able to know what compelled Jack to turn at that particular moment. He could have been unaware of just how big the storm cloud was, he could have been worried that the Vampire was about to run out of fuel and couldn't sustain a longer meander, perhaps he thought he saw a way through... We just don't know.

Either way I don't think 'ending it all' was ever on his mind. Such defeatism was just not Jack Malloch and would have been completely out of character. Jack also had a great deal to live for. His family for one, as they were his biggest single motivator and joy in life and no amount of work pressure would have superseded that. Plus he was right on the cusp of relocating the entire operation to South Africa, where it was likely that he would be getting new aircraft. He was about to trade his difficult working environment for a much better, more rewarding one.

This was definitely not the hopeless situation that drives someone to suicide.

Considering all of the above, and having discussed this with literally hundreds of people who were involved at the time, I am confident that Jack's death was a very untimely accident. The primary cause was the severity of the hailstorm and the extremely powerful downdrafts that propelled his aircraft towards the ground. By the time he regained visibility and was able to orientate himself, Jack was too close to the ground to be able to pull up. Traveling at a 'turbulence' speed of about two hundred and forty knots he struck the ground hard and fast.

Why Jack flew into the storm we will never know. The consequences of that terrible split-second decision impacted hundreds of people, some for the rest of their lives. Mike Gibson, speaking for all of Jack's employees summed up the enormity of this seismic event, "I am still undecided about what might have happened on that last and fateful – for all of us – day. It definitely changed the direction of my own life and my future."[9]

While we may never know what happened in that pivotal moment, we do know what he left us.

In the modern high-paced 'World of Woke', where we wrestle with the cancel-culture, phone-fixated 'How-dare-you-ists', bipolar-partisans and pan-demics, it is worth considering the role-model example that Jack Malloch was.

Jack was famous as an extraordinary, fearless aviator who loved the adventure of flight. He was also a strong patriot who did his duty for his country in any way that he could. He was an inspiring leader who would always lead by example and he respected everyone, treating them all as equals, no matter what their race or religion. All this at a time when racism was not just the norm, but in some places was legislated. He cared about the innocent victims of oppression and the victims of war, but unlike the rest of us he actually put himself in harm's way to help them. He was a man of principle who believe in honesty, reliability and the honour of his hand-shake.

Above all he was a committed family man who loved his wife and children and who did everything he could to ensure that they had a happy, nurturing home.

Would we not all be a bit better off today if we were able to live by Jack's example?

Jack Malloch.

A true legend of the African skies.

9 Personal correspondence with Mike Gibson, August 9 2009.

Soon after Jack's untimely death the rebranded DC-8 is seen in the Affretair hanger proudly bearing the name, 'Capt. Jack Malloch.'

Picture provided by Greg Malloch. © Greg Malloch.

People consulted

Al J. Venter, author and publisher.

Alan Addison, Flight Engineer, Affretair.

Alan Clements, DC-8 Captain, Air Trans Africa and Affretair.

Alex Forsyth, Flight Engineer, Air Trans Africa.

Alyson Dawson, Jack Malloch's daughter.

Benjamin Davies, son of Rodney Davies, Rhodesian Central Intelligence Organisation.

Beth Lawson, Jack Malloch's sister.

Bill Musgrave, 237 (Rhodesia) Squadron Spitfire pilot.

Blythe Kruger, Jack Malloch's sister.

Cacho Cabral, Chief Loadmaster ATA, Affretair, Air Gabon Cargo and Cargoman.

Chris Halse, son of Rhodesian Air Services and Air Trans Africa Captain Clive Halse.

Chris Higginson, DC-8 Captain, Affretair.

Chris Marshall, son of Jamie Marshall, Jack's Fish Air partner.

Chris Knaggs, Loadmaster, Affretair.

Chuck Osborne, Rhodesian Air Force Recovery Section.

Colin Miller, DC-8 Captain, Air Trans Africa, Affretair and Cargoman.

Dan Remenyi, author.

David Barbour, Rhodesian Auxiliary Air Force Spitfire pilot.

Dennis Rawson, Malloch family friend.

Derek van der Syde, Rhodesian Ministry of Foreign Affairs.

Dicky Bradshaw, Rhodesian Air Force Spitfire pilot, Group Captain Rhodesian Air Force.

Donald Mackie, Flight Coordinator, Air Trans Africa.

Eddie Blackwell, early Fish Air passenger.

Eddie Cross, Cold Storage Commission Executive, Zimbabwean Member of Parliament and founding member of the Movement for Democratic Change.

Eila Bannister, British journalist and political commentator.

Geoff Cartwright, Malloch family friend and early Fish Air passenger.

George de Kulczycki, Rhodesian Immigration Officer

Greg Malloch, Jack Malloch's son and Ground / Flight Engineer, Affretair.

Gustavo Marón, Argentinian historian and investigative journalist.

Guy Geddes, one of Jack Malloch's very first holiday charter passengers.

Henry Kinnear, Flight Engineer, Rhodesian Air Services and Air Trans Africa.

Hugh Bisset, Malloch family friend.

Hugh Bomford, Malloch family friend.

Ian Dixon, Malloch family friend and Hunting Clan Station Manager.

Ian Hunt, Traffic Manager, Affretair.

The Hon. Ian Douglas Smith, Prime Minister of Rhodesia and 237 (Rhodesia) Squadron Spitfire pilot.

Jan Breytenback, Colonel in the South African Defence Force and Commander of 44 Parachute Brigade.

Jean-Louis Domange, Second-In-Command of Bob Denard's Four Commando and Affretair's Libreville Station Manager.

Jeff Stephens, International trader.

Jerry Puren, Commander of the Katanga Air Force and Five Commando senior officer.

Jim Torond, Permanent Secretary for the Rhodesian Ministry of Transport and Power.

Jim Townsend, Chief Engineer, Air Trans Africa.

John Aldridge, DC-7 Captain, Air Trans Africa.

John Fairey, Rhodesian Air Force Spitfire restoration consultant.

John Fletcher, Commercial Manager, Affretair.

John Mussell, Group Captain, Rhodesian Air Force.

John Peck, Fire Office, Salisbury International Airport.

Jon Aird, Traffic / Commercial Dept, Affretair.

Judy Chapman.

Kate Woolard, wife of one of Jack Malloch's captains and recruiter for Alastair Wicks.

Kevin Milligan, Rhodesian Air Force Parachute Jumping Instructor.

Linda McLean, Malloch family friend.

Lister Pollard, Ground Engineer, Air Trans Africa.

Lyn Aldridge, Air Hostess, Rhodesian Air Services and Air Trans Africa.

Malcolm Porter, Loadmaster, Air Trans Africa.

Maureen Kinnear, Air Trans Africa.

Michael Draper, author.

Michele Becchi, Italian WWII military historian.

Mike Brough, Rhodesian Customs Officer.

Mike Daly, aircraft engineer, Field's.

Mike Gibson, DC-4, DC-7 and DC-8 Captain, Air Trans Africa and Affretair.

Mike Kruger, Jack's Malloch's nephew, Rhodesian Air Force helicopter pilot and owner of MK Airlines.

Nick Meikle, author.

Nigel Hart, British author and historian.

Nigel Rittey, early Fish Air passenger.

Nori Mann, Personal Assistant and Executive Secretary to Jack Malloch, Air Trans Africa.

Paul French, Rhodesian Special Air Service (SAS).

Paul Pearson, 237 (Rhodesia) Squadron Spitfire pilot and DC-3 Captain Rhodesian Air Services.

Paul Sheppard, Cold Storage Commission Executive.

Peter Nilson, Malloch family friend.

Peter Petter-Bowyer, Group Captain, Rhodesian Air Force and Director of Operations at Rhodesia's Combined Operations Headquarters.

Peter Stiff, author and publisher.

Quinton Marais, Rhodesian Air Force helicopter pilot.

Reg Smith, international insurance specialist.

Rob Lister, Radio Section, Air Trans Africa.

Rodney Simmonds, Rhodesian Ministry of Foreign Affairs.

Ron Reid-Daly, Rhodesian Army Lieutenant Colonel and founder of the Selous Scounts.

Ronnie Small, Flight Engineer, Air Trans Africa.

Sam Richman, DC-8 Captain, Affretair.

Stefano Merli, Italian author and WWII military historian.

Steve Rowley, Loadmaster, Air Trans Africa.

Ted Kruger, Jack Malloch's brother-in-law and Air Rhodesia B720 Captain.

William (Bill) Sykes, Group Captain, Rhodesian Air Force

Books and papers referenced

A Biographical Dictionary of Albanian History by Robert Elsie published by I. B. Tauris & Co, London. ISBN: 978 1 78076 431 3.

A handful of hard men by Hannes Wessels published by Casemate Publishers, ISBN: 978-1-61200-345-0.

A Pride of Eagles by Beryl Salt, published by Covos Day Books. ISBN: 0-620-23759-7.'Personal

Affaires Africaines by Pierre Péan, published by Fayard (1983). ISBN: 2-213-01324-1.

Apartheid South Africa and African States: From Pariah to Middle Power, 1962 to 1994 by Roger Pfister. Published by I.B. Tauris (2005). ISBN: 9781850436256.

Assignment Selous Scouts. Inside story of a Rhodesian Special Branch Officer by Jim Parker. Published by Galago Publishing. ISBN: 1-919854-14-2.

Banana Sunday – Datelines from Africa' by Christopher Munnion, published by William Waterman Publications. ISBN 1-874959-22-6.

Britain and the Yemen Civil War, 1962 – 1965: Ministers, Mercenaries and Mandarins: Foreign Policy and the limits of covert action' by Clive Jones. Published by Sussex Academic Press 2004. ISBN: 1-903900-23-9.

Captain Jack Malloch. The life and times of a Rhodesian Entrepreneur by Dan Remenyi, published by ACPIL U.K. ISBN: 978-1-910309-19-3.

Cleared for Takeoff: The Ultimate Book of Flight by Rowland White, Published by Chronicle Books (2016). ISBN: 1452135509.

Colours in the Sky: The story of Autair International Airways and Court Line Aviation' by Graham M Simons, published by GMS Enterprises. ISBN 9781904514701.

Famous Aircraft No. 2: Canadair CL44 of Transporte Aero Rioplatense, LV-JTN, article in The Controller, the Journal of Air Traffic Control, by Philippe Domogala.

Ghosts of Sao Tomé by Steve Cook, Flight Journal, December 1999.

How I named Paradise Island by Flash Seaton.

Legacy of Ashes. The History of the CIA by Tim Weiner. Published by Anchor Books. ISBN: 978-0-307-38900-8.

Les générations condamnées. Déliquescence d'une société pré-capitaliste (Democratic Republic of Congo. Generations condemned. Failure of a pre-capitalist society), by Jean Kanyarwunga published by Publibook, Paris, 2006.

Life of the White Sultan shrouded in controversy by Brett Popplewell published by the Globe & Mail on July 14th 2007.

L'Union newspaper, Libreville, Gabon.

Malloch's Spitfire. The Story and Restoration of PK350.' by Nick Meikle, published by Casemate Publishers. ISBN: 978-1-61200-252-1.

Mercenary by Mike Hoare, published by Corgi Books. ISBN: 552-07935-9.

Mercenary Commander by Colonel Jerry Puren as told to Brian Pottinger. Published by Galago Publishing. ISBN 0-947020-21-7.

Neo-colonialism: France's legacy to Africa by Mahmoud Yahya published by Emwai Centre for Political and Economic Research (1994). ISBN: 9783247808.

Oman: Oil entrepreneur extraordinaire by D. Patrick Maley published by United Press International on October 1st 1994.

Oman: The True-Life Drama and Intrigue of an Arab State by John Beasant, published by Mainstream Publishing (Edinburgh) Ltd. ISBN: 1-84018-607-0.

Operation Cheese. Destruction of Chambeshi Bridges, Zambia by Kevin Milligan published in High Above & Far Beyond, the history of the Rhodesian Airforce No. 1 Parachute Training School.

Profits of War: Inside the secret US-Israeli arms network by Ari Ben-Menashe. Published by Trine Day. ISBN: 9781634240505.

Recollections of the History of the Southern Rhodesian Auxiliary Air Force by D. M. Barbour, May 1995.

Rhodesia and Independence by Kenneth Young, published by Eyre & Spottiswoode, London.

Rhodesian Air Force Operations by Preller Geldenhuys. Published by Peysoft Publishing. ISBN: 9780994115409.

São Tomé and the Biafran War (1967–1970) by Gerhard Seibert, published in the International Journal of African Historical Studies Vol. 51, No. 2 (2018).

Serving Secretly by Ken Flower published by Galago. ISBN: 0-947020-27-6.

Shadows, Airlift and Airwar in Biafra and Nigeria 1967 – 1970 by Michael Draper. Published by Hikoko Publications. IBSN 1-902109-63-5.

Special Orders for Ferry Pilots' appendix 'D' to Southern Rhodesian Air Force Commanding Officer No. 2/51.

Spit Epic article written by Group Captain J. P. Moss.

The Daily Express newspaper (UK).

The Evening Standard newspaper (UK).

The Great Betrayal. Ian Smith. The memoirs of Africa's most controversial leader.' By Ian Smith. Published by Blake Publishing Ltd, England. ISBN: 1-85782-1769.

The Inception of Fish Air, recollections of Jamie Marshall.

The Man who would be King by Matthew Sweet, as published in the UK Independent on May 11th 1997.

The New Mercenaries by Anthony Mockler, published by Corgi Books. ISBN 0-552-12558-X.

The New York Times.

The Rhodesian Front War. Counter-insurgency and guerrilla war in Rhodesia 1962 – 1980.' by H. Ellert, Published by Mambo Press 1989. ISBN: 978-0869224366.

The Rhodesian War: A Military History by Paul L. Moorcraft and Peter McLaughlin published by Stackpole Books. ISBN 978-0-8117-0725-1 (pbk).

The Rhodesian Herald newspaper.

The SAS Savage Wars of Peace by Anthony Kemp published by Penguin Books. ISNB 13579108642.

The Seychelles Affair by Mike Hoare. Published by Bantam Press. ISBN 0-552-12890-2.

The Sunday Mail (Rhodesia).

The War History of Southern Rhodesia, Vol. 2. by J.F. MacDonald. Published by Books of Rhodesia Publishing Co. ISBN 0-86920-140-9.

Unpopular Sovereignty: Rhodesian Independence and African Decolonisation' by Luise White, published by the University of Chicago Press, ISBN-13: 978-0-226-23519-6.

War Dog – Fighting Other People's Wars by Al J. Venter. Published by Casemate Philadelphia. ISBN 1-932033-09-2.

War in the Air. Rhodesian Air Force 1935 – 1980 by Dudley Cowderoy and Roy C. Nesbit. Published by Galago Publishing. ISBN 0-947020-13-6.

War PLC: The Rise of the New Corporate Mercenary by Stephen Armstrong, published by Faber & Faber. ISBN-10: 057-124-1255.

Welensky's 4000 Days' by Sir Roy Welensky P.C. K.C.M.G., published by Collins Books, St James Place, London.

Winds of Destruction. The autobiography of a Rhodesian combat pilot by P.J.H. Petter-Bowyer. Published by 30º South Publishers. ISBN: 0-9584890-3-3.